MY SiDEWALKS ON

SCOTT FORESMAN

READIN[illegible]ET

Teacher's Guide

Level C
Volume 2

Editorial Offices: Glenview, Illinois • Parsippany, New Jersey • New York, New York
Sales Offices: Boston, Massachusetts • Duluth, Georgia • Glenview, Illinois
Coppell, Texas • Sacramento, California • Mesa, Arizona

ISBN: 0-328-24791-X

4 5 6 7 8 9 10 V064 15 14 13 12 11 10 09 08 07
CC1

MY SIDEWALKS ON

SCOTT FORESMAN

READING STREET

Intensive Reading Intervention

A Safe Place to Learn

MY SIDEWALKS ON
SCOTT FORESMAN
READING STREET
Intensive Reading Intervention

What can you do when a core reading program with small group instruction isn't enough for your struggling students? You can give them someplace safe where they can learn. Someplace where you can focus your instruction on their specific needs. Someplace where your students feel comfortable and confident as they accelerate and progress to on-level reading. Someplace like *My Sidewalks.*

My Sidewalks is a research-based, intensive reading intervention program that follows the Response to Intervention model. It works side-by-side with *Scott Foresman Reading Street* or any core reading program. It is designed to provide the most effective intervention for students who are struggling to read, with special consideration for English Language Learners. With daily instruction written specifically for Tier III students, you can help struggling readers steadily take steps to become proficient and confident readers.

3-TIER MODEL

TIER I
Core Program

TIER II
Core Plus
Strategic Intervention

TIER III
Intensive
Intervention ← *My Sidewalks*

Three Steps Toward Creating a Safe Place to Learn

1 SUSTAINED INSTRUCTION

My Sidewalks contains lesson plans for 30 full weeks. Every day, for 30–45 minutes, you can put your struggling readers—monolingual and English Language Learners—on solid footing. With instruction that is systematic and explicit, *My Sidewalks* helps you create a learning environment that is both consistent and predictable so your students can sustain progress every day. Your students will make strides with:

- Increased time on task
- Explicit teacher modeling
- Multiple response opportunities
- Tasks broken down into smaller steps

2 INTENSIVE LANGUAGE AND CONCEPT DEVELOPMENT

Research shows that a child's vocabulary entering first grade is a strong predictor of comprehension at eleventh grade. This is a critical area where Tier III students are deficient. *My Sidewalks* helps build a foundation for future comprehension success with daily, intensive language and concept development:

- Unit themes organized around science and social studies concepts
- Five to seven new vocabulary words tied directly to the week's theme
- Four weekly selections that build on the unit concept
- Concepts that connect from week to week

3 CRITICAL COMPREHENSION SKILLS

Along with daily vocabulary instruction, *My Sidewalks* provides explicit and systematic instruction on the comprehension skills and strategies researchers have identified as being the most critical for developing reading success:

- Drawing Conclusions
- Compare/Contrast
- Sequence
- Main Idea and Supporting Details

MY SIDEWALKS ON
SCOTT FORESMAN
READING STREET
Intensive Reading Intervention

Components

Student Readers

My Sidewalks takes high-interest reading selections and puts them in an engaging magazine format. Every week, your Tier III students read four different selections that work together to develop a science or social studies concept. Week in and week out, these fiction and nonfiction selections help your students get a better understanding of the overall unit theme (the same themes and concepts found in *Scott Foresman Reading Street!*). *30 lessons, organized into 6 units. (5 units at Level A)*

Teacher's Guides

My Sidewalks keeps your intervention instruction running smoothly. The Teacher's Guides contain everything you need for Tier III instruction. Complete lesson plans focus on high priority skills and provide daily routines with suggested time frames to help you keep your instruction focused and on time.

2 Volumes per level

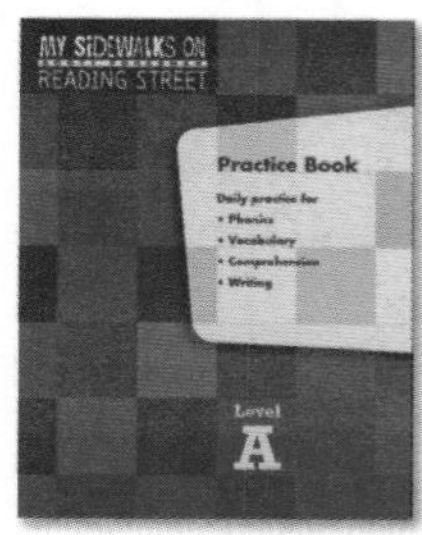

Practice Books

Finally, a practice book written specifically for Tier III students. These consumable workbooks/blackline masters give your students additional practice in phonics, comprehension, vocabulary, and writing. Books are available for each level and have multiple practice selections for every lesson. Plus, each page contains a Home Activity to strengthen the school-home connection. *A Teacher's Manual with answer key is also available.*

Benchmark Readers

What's working for your students? Which students need more targeted instruction? Accurately assess your Tier III students' progress with these unit readers. Each 8-page book contains examples of all the skills targeted in the unit so you can find out instantly whether a student is ready to transition out of *My Sidewalks* or still needs additional intervention.

Alphabet Cards

Help your Tier III students practice letter names and sounds with these colorful cards. *(Level A)*

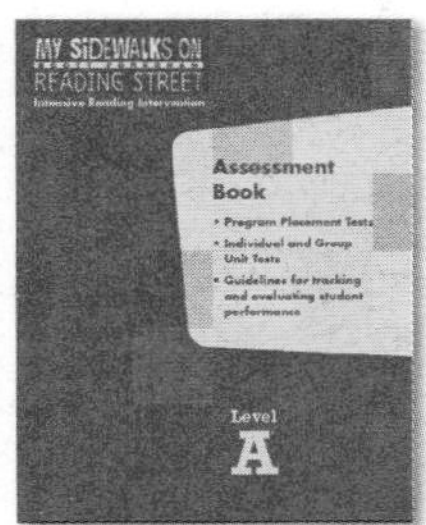

Assessment Book
All your assessment needs, all in one book. Along with assessment instruction, you'll find progress-monitoring forms, placement tests, unit assessments in individual and group formats, and guidelines for students to exit *My Sidewalks*.

Finger Tracing Cards
Hands-on Tracing Cards allow students to connect sounds to letters while they learn their letter shapes. *(Level A)*

Manipulative Letter Tiles
Sturdy, plastic, manipulative tiles are easy for little fingers to practice word building. *(Levels A–B)*

AudioText CD
Recordings of the Student Readers read at a fluent pace give Tier III students complete access to every selection.

Sing with Me Big Book
Large, illustrated Big Books develop oral vocabulary and build background. Pages inspire small group discussions using vocabulary words and include songs that demonstrate the words in context. *(Levels A–B)*

Sing with Me Audio CD
Song recordings accompany each Sing with Me Big Book. *(Levels A–B)*

Sound-Spelling Cards
Colorful cards with instructional routines introduce each sound-spelling in the intervention lesson. *(Levels A–C)*

Sound-Spelling Wall Charts
Large-size formats of the Sound-Spelling Cards are ideal for use in small-group instruction. *(Levels A–C)*

Tested Vocabulary Cards
Flash cards build important vocabulary knowledge and provide additional practice.

Welcome to *My Sidewalks*
This handy guide shows you how to provide effective instruction, manage your time, and help students catch up.

Write-On/Wipe-Off Cards
These cards have a write-on/wipe-off surface and writing lines for practicing letter forms, letter-sounds, spelling, and writing.

Level	Grade
A	1
B	2
C	3
D	4
E	5

MY SIDEWALKS ON SCOTT FORESMAN READING STREET

Intensive Reading Intervention

Authors

My Sidewalks was created by the leading researchers in the area of reading intervention instruction. Their work has helped struggling readers and is the basis for the 3-Tier model of instruction.

"Research shows that for students to make significant progress, they need systematic and intensive instruction that is tailored to their current instructional level."

Sharon Vaughn

Connie Juel, Ph.D.
Professor of Education
School of Education
Stanford University

Jeanne R. Paratore, Ed.D.
Associate Professor of Education
Department of Literacy and Language Development
Boston University

Deborah Simmons, Ph.D.
Professor
College of Education and Human Development
Texas A&M University

Sharon Vaughn, Ph.D.
H.E. Hartfelder/Southland Corporation Regents Professor
University of Texas

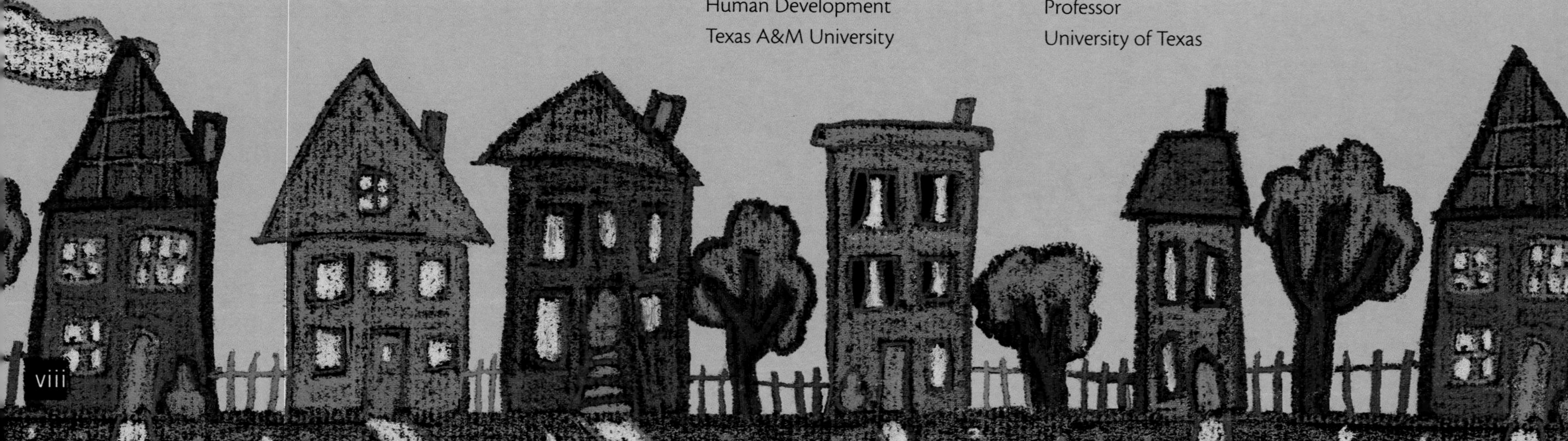

Contents

Unit Skills and Concepts

Unit 4 One of a Kind

Unit 5 Cultures

Unit 6 Freedom

Resources

Distinctions Between Levels

Understanding the Levels of *My Sidewalks*

The goal of the *My Sidewalks* program is to enable struggling readers to succeed with the reading material used in their regular classrooms. To achieve this, *My Sidewalks* focuses on accelerating students' acquisition of priority skills. Each level of *My Sidewalks* is designed to provide a year and a half of reading growth. Consequently there is an overlap of skills between one *My Sidewalks* level and the next.

These pages describe the skills students should have to successfully begin each level of *My Sidewalks* and what they will learn in that level. Use the Placement Tests to help you determine the correct level at which to enter each student.

To begin this level a child should know:	**In this level**, the instructional focus is on:
Early Reading Intervention (Grade K)	
	• Phonological and phonemic awareness • Letter names and sounds • Blending regular short-vowel words • Sentence reading
Level A (Grade 1)	
• Some phonological awareness	• Phonemic awareness • Letter names • Consonants: Individual letter-sounds, blends, and digraphs • Vowels: Short, long (CVCe), and *r*-controlled • Blending words and fluent word reading • High-frequency words • Oral vocabulary and concept development • Building fluency (40–60 WCPM) • Passage reading and retelling

To begin this level a student should know:	**In this level**, the instructional focus is on:
Level B (Grade 2)	
• Letter names • Individual consonant letter-sounds • Some basic high-frequency words • And be able to read Benchmark Reader A2 with accuracy and comprehension	• Phonemic awareness • Letter names and sounds • Blending words and fluent word reading • High-frequency words • Oral vocabulary and concept development • Building fluency (70–90 WCPM) • Passage reading and retelling
Level C (Grade 3)	
• Consonants: Individual letter-sounds, blends, and digraphs • Vowels: Short and long (CVCe) and be able to distinguish between them • A wider range of high-frequency words • And be able to read Benchmark Reader B2 with accuracy and comprehension	• Blending words and fluent word reading • Decoding multisyllabic words, including words with one or more affixes • Phonics: Vowels • Concept vocabulary • Building fluency (100–120 WCPM) • Passage reading and summarizing
Level D (Grade 4)	
• Consonants: Individual letter-sounds, blends, and digraphs • Vowels: Short and long (CVCe) and be able to distinguish between them • How to decode regular VC/CV words with short and long (CVCe) vowels • Many high-frequency words • And be able to read Benchmark Reader C1 with accuracy and comprehension	• Decoding multisyllabic words, including words with one or more affixes • Phonics: Less frequent vowel patterns, such as vowel diphthongs • Concept vocabulary • Building fluency (110–130 WCPM) • Passage reading and summarizing
Level E (Grade 5)	
• Consonants: Individual letter-sounds, blends, and digraphs • Vowels: Short and long (CVCe) and be able to distinguish between them • How to decode regular VC/CV words with short and long (CVCe) vowels • Many high-frequency words • And be able to read Benchmark Reader D1 with accuracy and comprehension	• Decoding multisyllabic words, including words with one or more affixes • Phonics: Less frequent vowel patterns, such as vowel diphthongs • Concept vocabulary • Building fluency (120–140 WCPM) • Passage reading and summarizing

Differentiating Instruction

The charts on these pages show instruction during a week in *My Sidewalks*. The charts can also be used as guides for **reteaching** or **accelerating** through parts of the lessons. In addition, the ***If... then...*** directions will help you identify how to customize instruction for your students.

Reteaching To meet the needs of the lowest performing readers, it may be necessary to modify the pacing and intensity of instruction. Activities shown in gray boxes on the charts may be repeated for these students.

Accelerating A child who shows mastery of skills following initial instruction may be ready for instruction at a faster pace with fewer repetitions. Activities shown in green boxes might be omitted for these students.

Levels A–B

	PHONEMIC AWARENESS	PHONICS	HIGH-FREQUENCY WORDS	CONCEPTS/ ORAL VOCABULARY	PASSAGE READING	FLUENCY	WRITING
Day 1	Phonemic Awareness	Blending Strategy	High-Frequency Words	Concepts/ Oral Vocabulary	Read a Passage	Reread for Fluency	
Day 2	Phonemic Awareness	Blending Strategy	High-Frequency Words		Read a Passage	Reread for Fluency	Write
Day 3	Phonemic Awareness	Blending Strategy	High-Frequency Words	Concepts/ Oral Vocabulary	Read a Passage	Reread for Fluency	
Day 4		Fluent Word Reading		Concepts/ Oral Vocabulary	Read Together	Reread for Fluency	Write
Day 5		Assess Word Reading	Assess Word/ Sentence Reading	Check Oral Vocabulary	Assess Passage Reading/ Reread		Write

Reteach   Omit for acceleration

If... a child is struggling with word reading,
then... reteach Word Work activities and include More Practice extensions.

If... a child lacks oral language,
then... elicit extended language from the child, provide ample opportunities for the child to respond when building concepts, and expand the structured picture walks before reading each selection.

If... a child's reading is so slow that it hinders comprehension,
then... provide additional models of fluent reading, give more corrective feedback during fluency practice, and include More Practice extensions when rereading for fluency.

If... an English learner struggles with sounds,
then... repeat appropriate practice activities.

Levels C–E

	VOCABULARY	COMPREHENSION	PASSAGE READING	PHONICS	FLUENCY	WRITING
Day 1	Vocabulary		Read a Passage	Blending Strategy (Level C)	Reread for Fluency	Write (Levels D–E)
Day 2	Vocabulary	Comprehension Skill	Read a Passage	Phonics	Reread for Fluency	Write (Levels D–E)
Day 3	Vocabulary	Comprehension Skill Assess (Levels D–E)	Read a Passage	Phonics	Reread for Fluency	Write
Day 4	Vocabulary	Comprehension Skill/Strategy Assess (Levels D–E)	Read Together (Level C) Read a Passage (Levels D–E)	Phonics Review (Level C)	Reread for Fluency	Write
Day 5	Vocabulary	Assess Comprehension	Read Together (Levels D–E) Reread (Level C)	Assess Sentence Reading (Level C)	Assess Fluency	Write

If... a student is struggling with word reading,
then... reteach Vocabulary and Phonics activities and include More Practice extensions.

If... a student lacks oral language,
then... elicit extended language from the student, provide ample opportunities for the student to respond when building concepts, and expand the After Reading discussion for each selection.

If... a student's reading is so disfluent that it hinders comprehension,
then... provide additional models of fluent reading, give more corrective feedback during fluency practice, and include More Practice extensions for fluency.

If... a student lacks comprehension and is unable to retell or summarize,
then... reteach comprehension skills and strategies, provide additional modeling of retelling and summarizing, and give more corrective feedback during practice.

If... an English learner lacks English vocabulary for known concepts,
then... say the unknown English word, have the student repeat it, and ask questions that will allow the student to use the word in a meaningful context.

Meeting ELL Needs

My Sidewalks was developed to provide intensive reading intervention for Tier III students struggling to read and write. The program has been designed to reflect current research on literacy instruction for English language learners (ELLs)—not as additional notes, but integral to all elements of instruction. From its original conception, instruction to meet the needs of both native English speakers and English learners (who have some basic English conversational skills) has been integrated into the curriculum, teaching practices, and learning activities. Since English language learners acquire literacy skills in much the same way as their English-speaking peers, both will benefit from the same good instructional practices.

Research Says **"ELLs at risk for reading problems profit considerably in their literacy skills from systematic and explicit interventions that address the core reading skills of beginning reading: phonemic awareness, phonics, fluency, vocabulary, and comprehension. . . . Our work with ELLs suggests that postponing interventions to wait for language to become more proficient is not necessary, and supporting literacy acquisition in the language of instruction provided by the school for students at risk is beneficial."** Vaughn, S., Linan-Thompson, S., *et al.* 2005. "Interventions for 1st Grade English Language Learners with Reading Difficulties." *Perspectives*, 31 (2), p. 31–35.

English language learners need . . .	*My Sidewalks* provides . . .
Phonemic Awareness	
• to develop familiarity with the sounds of English • to practice identifying, segmenting, and blending sounds in English words • to learn the sounds of English within words, in isolation and in meaningful contexts	• explicit and systematic modeling of sounds in words • scaffolded instruction that evokes active responses by children • ample practice identifying, counting, segmenting, blending, adding, and deleting sounds in words • clear lessons that tie phonemic awareness to phonics
Phonics	
• to learn the letters and letter-sound correspondences of English • to master identifying, segmenting, and blending the variety of sounds that letters represent in English words • to understand how to complete phonics activities • to use the phonics they learn—seeing, saying, reading, and writing words—with growing proficiency • to learn the sounds and spellings of written English words in meaningful contexts	• explicit phonics instruction with regular practice • routines for practicing the core English phonics elements • clear, step-by-step blending strategies understandable to students learning English as they learn to read • active learning—hearing, speaking, reading, and writing—that ties phonics to decodable text (Levels A–C) and to decoding of multisyllabic words in text (Levels D–E) • practice decoding and reading words related to concepts explored in oral language and texts

English language learners need . . .	*My Sidewalks* provides . . .
Vocabulary	
• to develop oral vocabulary in English, including words already familiar to English-speaking children • to learn functional English vocabulary, including high-frequency words • to encounter new words in meaningful oral and written contexts • to hear, see, and use new words repeatedly • to learn academic English vocabulary	• multiple exposures to each vocabulary word • a routine for learning high-frequency words (at Levels A and B) • a routine for learning oral vocabulary (at Levels A and B) • a focus on words related to science and social studies concepts • multiple opportunities to practice using and producing oral and written vocabulary, including academic English • development of deep meaning for key concepts and words
Comprehension	
• to continually improve their comprehension of oral English • to read comprehensible texts and develop abilities to interpret more complex written language • to use their prior knowledge in order to comprehend texts • to acquire understanding of sentence structures and text organizations of academic English • to learn about cultural concepts embodied in the readings	• an emphasis on oral language and concept development, to improve students' English proficiency and comprehension • an abundance of comprehensible reading materials focused on science and social studies concepts • modeling, instruction, and practice of priority comprehension skills and reading strategies, including prereading routines • explicit instructional routines that model new skills, build on students' prior knowledge, use visual elements to clarify ideas, and incorporate ample practice and review • exposure to the structures of English, text organization, and cultural concepts of the readings and lessons
Fluency	
• to hear models of fluent reading of instructional-level texts • to practice and improve their fluent reading • corrective feedback on their reading	• teacher modeling to familiarize students with expressive, meaningful reading of instructional-level academic texts • engaging practice opportunities that include choral reading, paired reading, and reading with AudioText, which provide many models for building fluency • instruction in reading rate, accuracy, expression, and intonation • repeated readings and corrective feedback, to help students see words in context and pronounce them • progress monitoring and assessments to aid in fluency growth
Writing	
• to develop their English proficiency by writing as well as reading • to write about ideas related to reading topics • to practice communicating their ideas in English through manageable, interesting writing activities	• opportunities to respond to literature about themes • scaffolded writing instruction including sentence frames for young children, manageable writing prompts for all students, and self-checking activities • feedback for writers from teacher and fellow students

Unit 4

Skills Overview

Why These Skills? *My Sidewalks* focuses on the priority skills students need in order to succeed at learning to read. **Priority skills** are the critical elements of early reading—phonemic awareness, phonics, fluency, vocabulary, and text comprehension. Scientifically based research has shown that these skills are the foundations of early reading and must be taught in a systematic sequence.

		WEEK 1 5–30 **Being Unique**	WEEK 2 31–56 **From Top to Bottom**
Phonics	**Blending Strategy**	Diphthongs *oi, oy;* Prefixes *un-, re-* REVIEW Reading Longer Words with Affixes	Sound of *oo* in *moon;* Silent Consonants *mb, kn, gn* REVIEW Diphthongs
	Spelling	Words with Diphthongs *oi, oy*	Words with Sound of *oo* in *moon*
Vocabulary	**Concept**	**What are talents?**	**When is nature a challenge?**
	Vocabulary	*audience, famous, instrument, perform, talent, unique*	*depth, height, peak, position, scale, summit*
Comprehension	**Skill**	Sequence	Compare/Contrast
	Strategies	Preview, Ask Questions, Use Story Structure, Summarize	Preview, Ask Questions, Use Story Structure, Summarize
	Writing	Response to Literature	Response to Literature
Fluency		Reread for Fluency Practice	Reread for Fluency Practice

WEEK 3	WEEK 4	WEEK 5
57–82 **Hobbies**	83–108 **Being the First**	109–134 **People and Animals**
Vowel Patterns *ew, ue;* Silent Consonants *st, wr* REVIEW Silent Consonants	Sound of *oo* in *foot, u* in *put;* Suffixes *-ness, -less* REVIEW Compounds with *oo* in *foot*	Short *e: ea;* Prefixes *mis-, dis-* REVIEW Vowel Sound of *ew, ue, oo*
Words with Vowel Patterns *ew, ue*	Words with Sound of *oo* in *foot, u* in *put*	Words with Short *e: ea*
What are some unique hobbies?	**Why do people want to be the first to do something?**	**How do people and animals adjust to each other?**
collection, delight, interest, rare, special, unusual	*adventure, attempt, distance, impossible, remarkable, waterfall*	*adjust, adult, communicate, mimic, opportunity, realize*
Draw Conclusions	Compare/Contrast	Main Idea
Preview, Ask Questions, Use Story Structure, Summarize	Preview, Ask Questions, Use Story Structure, Summarize	Preview, Ask Questions, Use Story Structure, Summarize
Response to Literature	Response to Literature	Response to Literature
Reread for Fluency Practice	Reread for Fluency Practice	Reread for Fluency Practice

Unit 5

Skills Overview

Why These Skills? *My Sidewalks* focuses on the priority skills students need in order to succeed at learning to read. **Priority skills** are the critical elements of early reading—phonemic awareness, phonics, fluency, vocabulary, and text comprehension. Scientifically based research has shown that these skills are the foundations of early reading and must be taught in a systematic sequence.

		WEEK 1	WEEK 2
		5–30 **Dressing Up**	31–56 **Our World**
Phonics	Blending Strategy	Vowel Sound in *ball: a, al; ph*/f/, *dge*/j/ REVIEW Consonants *c*/s/, *g*/j/, *dge*/j/	Vowel Sound in *ball: au, aw;* Suffixes *-er, -or* REVIEW Endings *-s, -es, -ed, -ing* and Suffixes *-er, -or*
	Spelling	Words with Vowel Sound in *ball*	Words with Vowel Sound in *ball: au, aw*
Vocabulary	Concept	**What do our clothes tell about us?**	**How are communities and families similar around the world?**
	Vocabulary	*clothing, custom, decade, ordinary, style, tradition*	*country, culture, language, popular, similar, transfer*
Comprehension	Skill	Compare/Contrast	Draw Conclusions
	Strategies	Preview, Ask Questions, Use Story Structure, Summarize	Preview, Ask Questions, Use Story Structure, Summarize
	Writing	Response to Literature	Response to Literature
Fluency		Reread for Fluency Practice	Reread for Fluency Practice

WEEK 3	WEEK 4	WEEK 5
57–82 **Coming to America**	83–108 **Let's Eat!**	109–134 **Other Times, Other Places**
Vowel Sound in *ball: augh, ough;* Prefixes *over-, under-, out-* REVIEW Vowel Sound in *ball*	Long *i: ind, ild;* Long *o: ost, old;* Suffixes *-y, -ish* REVIEW Compound Words	Syllables VCCCV REVIEW Read Longer Words: Syllable Patterns
Words with Vowel Sound in *ball: augh, ough*	Words with Long *i,* Long *o*	Words with Syllables VCCCV
What changes when people move from one culture to another?	**What is ethnic food?**	**How do we experience the past today?**
address, apartment, immigrant, journey, museum, photograph	*delicious, dinnertime, ethnic, mixture, recipe, restaurant*	*compare, hardship, improve, opposite, settle, surround*
Sequence	Draw Conclusions	Main Idea
Preview, Ask Questions, Use Story Structure, Summarize	Preview, Ask Questions, Use Story Structure, Summarize	Preview, Ask Questions, Use Story Structure, Summarize
Response to Literature	Response to Literature	Response to Literature
Reread for Fluency Practice	Reread for Fluency Practice	Reread for Fluency Practice

Unit 6

Skills Overview

Why These Skills? *My Sidewalks* focuses on the priority skills students need in order to succeed at learning to read. **Priority skills** are the critical elements of early reading—phonemic awareness, phonics, fluency, vocabulary, and text comprehension. Scientifically based research has shown that these skills are the foundations of early reading and must be taught in a systematic sequence.

		WEEK 1 5–30 **American Symbols**	WEEK 2 31–56 **Animal Freedom**
Phonics	**Blending Strategy**	Suffixes *-hood, -ment;* Prefixes *pre-, mid-, post-* REVIEW Read Longer Words: Suffixes and Prefixes	Syllables V/V as in *piano* REVIEW Read Longer Words: Syllables VCCCV
	Spelling	Words with Suffixes *-hood, -ment*	Words with Syllables V/V
Vocabulary	**Concept**	**What are some important American symbols or monuments?**	**What can we do to help animals?**
	Vocabulary	*enormous, liberty, monument, president, sculptor, symbol*	*adopt, capture, comfort, exercise, provide, struggle*
Comprehension	**Skill**	Main Idea	Sequence
	Strategies	Preview, Ask Questions, Use Story Structure, Summarize	Preview, Ask Questions, Use Story Structure, Summarize
	Writing	Response to Literature	Response to Literature
Fluency		Reread for Fluency Practice	Reread for Fluency Practice

WEEK 3	WEEK 4	WEEK 5
57–82 **Expressing Yourself**	83–108 **It's the Law!**	109–134 **Poetry**
Common Syllables; Multisyllabic Word Practice REVIEW Syllable Pattern V/V	Blending Multisyllabic Words REVIEW Read Longer Words: Suffixes and Prefixes	Related Words REVIEW Read Longer Words: Common Syllables
Words with Common Syllables	Multisyllabic Words	Related Words
How can we express ourselves?	**Why do we have laws?**	**What is a poem?**
amuse, create, display, express, inspire, theater	*annoy, cooperate, disturb, intention, pollution, require*	*compose, delicate, emotion, poetry, recite, rhythm*
Compare/Contrast	Main Idea	Draw Conclusions
Preview, Ask Questions, Use Story Structure, Summarize	Preview, Ask Questions, Use Story Structure, Summarize	Preview, Ask Questions, Use Story Structure, Summarize
Response to Literature	Response to Literature	Response to Literature
Reread for Fluency Practice	Reread for Fluency Practice	Reread for Fluency Practice

Unit 4

Concept Development

to Foster Reading Comprehension

Theme Question: What does it mean to be unique?

Concept: One of a Kind

	Week 1	Week 2	Week 3	Week 4	Week 5
EXPAND THE CONCEPT	Lesson Focus **What are talents?**	Lesson Focus **When is nature a challenge?**	Lesson Focus **What are some unique hobbies?**	Lesson Focus **Why do people want to be the first to do something?**	Lesson Focus **How do people and animals adjust to each other?**
DEVELOP LANGUAGE	Vocabulary audience famous instrument perform talent unique Background Reading **"Let's Explore Talents"**	Vocabulary depth height peak position scale summit Background Reading **"Let's Explore Mountains"**	Vocabulary collection delight interest rare special unusual Background Reading **"Let's Explore Hobbies"**	Vocabulary adventure attempt distance impossible remarkable waterfall Background Reading **"Let's Explore Famous Firsts"**	Vocabulary adjust adult communicate mimic opportunity realize Background Reading **"Let's Explore Having a New Pet"**
READ THE LITERATURE	Biography **"Very Young, Very Talented"** Realistic Fiction **"The Talent Show"** Expository Nonfiction **"Weird and Wacky Talents"** Activities **"4 You 2 Do"**	Expository Nonfiction **"Go Climb a Mountain"** Realistic Fiction **"Get Over It!"** Expository Nonfiction **"Free Diving"** Activities **"4 You 2 Do"**	Narrative Nonfiction **"Glass Bottle Buildings"** Realistic Fiction **"What Are You Looking For?"** How-to Article **"Hobby Hunting"** Activities **"4 You 2 Do"**	Narrative Nonfiction **"Over Niagara Falls"** Realistic Fiction **"A Smoothie Sensation"** Expository Nonfiction **"Guinness Book of World Records"** Activities **"4 You 2 Do"**	Narrative Nonfiction **"Making Friends with Gorillas"** Narrative Nonfiction **"A Chimp's New Home"** Expository Nonfiction **"Helping Each Other"** Activities **"4 You 2 Do"**
TEACH CONTENT	Time for Social Studies • Self-Esteem • Freedom of Expression	Time for Science • Geology/Landforms • Physical Challenges • Life in the Ocean	Time for Science • Recycling • Living Things: Insects	Time for Social Studies • Geography • Initiating Change • Freedom of Expression	Time for Science • Taking Care of Pets • Instincts • Living Things: Animals

Unit 4 develops the same concepts and content-area knowledge as in Scott Foresman's *Reading Street*, Grade 3, Unit 4.

Concept Development

to Foster Reading Comprehension

Theme Question: What happens when two ways of life come together?

Concept: Cultures

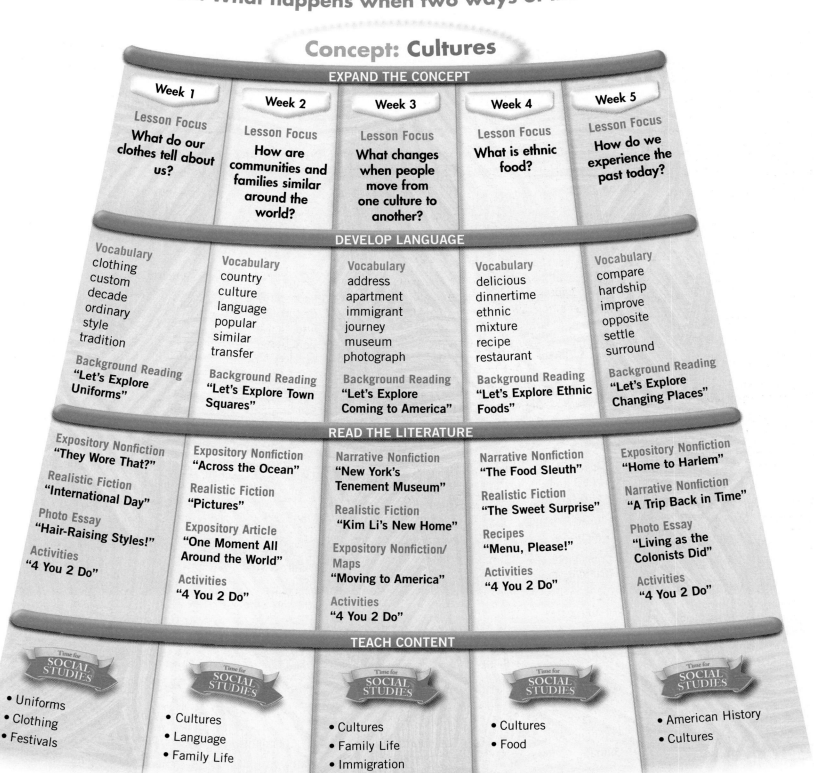

	Week 1	Week 2	Week 3	Week 4	Week 5
EXPAND THE CONCEPT	Lesson Focus **What do our clothes tell about us?**	Lesson Focus **How are communities and families similar around the world?**	Lesson Focus **What changes when people move from one culture to another?**	Lesson Focus **What is ethnic food?**	Lesson Focus **How do we experience the past today?**
DEVELOP LANGUAGE	Vocabulary clothing custom decade ordinary style tradition Background Reading **"Let's Explore Uniforms"**	Vocabulary country culture language popular similar transfer Background Reading **"Let's Explore Town Squares"**	Vocabulary address apartment immigrant journey museum photograph Background Reading **"Let's Explore Coming to America"**	Vocabulary delicious dinnertime ethnic mixture recipe restaurant Background Reading **"Let's Explore Ethnic Foods"**	Vocabulary compare hardship improve opposite settle surround Background Reading **"Let's Explore Changing Places"**
READ THE LITERATURE	Expository Nonfiction **"They Wore That?"** Realistic Fiction **"International Day"** Photo Essay **"Hair-Raising Styles!"** Activities **"4 You 2 Do"**	Expository Nonfiction **"Across the Ocean"** Realistic Fiction **"Pictures"** Expository Article **"One Moment All Around the World"** Activities **"4 You 2 Do"**	Narrative Nonfiction **"New York's Tenement Museum"** Realistic Fiction **"Kim Li's New Home"** Expository Nonfiction/ Maps **"Moving to America"** Activities **"4 You 2 Do"**	Narrative Nonfiction **"The Food Sleuth"** Realistic Fiction **"The Sweet Surprise"** Recipes **"Menu, Please!"** Activities **"4 You 2 Do"**	Expository Nonfiction **"Home to Harlem"** Narrative Nonfiction **"A Trip Back in Time"** Photo Essay **"Living as the Colonists Did"** Activities **"4 You 2 Do"**
TEACH CONTENT	Time for Social Studies • Uniforms • Clothing • Festivals	Time for Social Studies • Cultures • Language • Family Life	Time for Social Studies • Cultures • Family Life • Immigration	Time for Social Studies • Cultures • Food	Time for Social Studies • American History • Cultures

Unit 5 develops the same concepts and content-area knowledge as in Scott Foresman's *Reading Street*, Grade 3, Unit 5.

Concept Development

to Foster Reading Comprehension

Theme Question: What does it mean to be free?

Concept: Freedom

	Week 1	Week 2	Week 3	Week 4	Week 5
EXPAND THE CONCEPT	Lesson Focus **What are some important American symbols or monuments?**	Lesson Focus **What can we do to help animals?**	Lesson Focus **How can we express ourselves?**	Lesson Focus **Why do we have laws?**	Lesson Focus **What is a poem?**
DEVELOP LANGUAGE	Vocabulary enormous liberty monument president sculptor symbol Background Reading **"Let's Explore Symbols of Freedom"**	Vocabulary adopt capture comfort exercise provide struggle Background Reading **"Let's Explore A Farm Sanctuary"**	Vocabulary amuse create display express inspire theater Background Reading **"Let's Explore Expressing Yourself"**	Vocabulary annoy cooperate disturb intention pollution require Background Reading **"Let's Explore The Bill of Rights"**	Vocabulary compose delicate emotion poetry recite rhythm Background Reading **"Let's Explore Poetry"**
READ THE LITERATURE	Expository Nonfiction **"She Stands for Freedom"** Expository Nonfiction **"The Men on the Mountain"** Expository Nonfiction **"Stars and Stripes"** Activities **"4 You 2 Do"**	Narrative Nonfiction **"Lost and Found"** Realistic Fiction **"Critters in the Corn Patch"** Expository Nonfiction **"Running Free"** Activities **"4 You 2 Do"**	Expository Nonfiction **"Not a Typical Theater"** Realistic Fiction **"What Makes an Artist?"** How-to Article **"Puppet Magic"** Activities **"4 You 2 Do"**	Expository Nonfiction **"Sound Off"** Biography **"Mr. Civil Rights"** Expository Nonfiction **"Silly State Laws"** Activities **"4 You 2 Do"**	Expository Nonfiction **"Bringing Words to Life"** Realistic Fiction **"Amy the Shy"** How-to Article **"Be a Poet"** Activities **"4 You 2 Do"**
TEACH CONTENT	Time for Social Studies • History • Cultures: Symbols • Government History	Time for Social Studies • Freedom: Animals • Humane Society • Animal Rights	Time for Social Studies • Freedom of Expression • Theater • Art	Time for Science • Environmental Laws	Time for Social Studies • History • Freedom of Expression

Unit 6 develops the same concepts and content-area knowledge as in Scott Foresman's *Reading Street*, Grade 3, Unit 6.

Unit 4 Week 1 *Being Unique*

What are talents?

Objectives *This week students will ...*

Vocabulary
- build concepts and vocabulary: *audience, famous, instrument, perform, talent, unique*

Phonics
- blend and read words with diphthongs *oi*, *oy* and prefixes *un-*, *re-*
- apply knowledge of letter-sounds and word structure to decode unknown words when reading

Text Comprehension
- read connected text
- use sequence to improve comprehension
- write in response to literature

Fluency
- practice fluency with oral rereading

Word Work *This week's phonics focus is ...*

Diphthongs *oi, oy*   Prefixes *un-, re-*

Concept Words *Tested Vocabulary*

The week's vocabulary is related to the concept of being unique. The first appearance of each word in the Student Reader is noted below.

audience a group of people gathered to hear or see something (p. 10)

famous very well known (p. 11)

instrument a device for producing musical sounds (p. 24)

perform to act, play, sing, or do tricks in public (p. 18)

talent a special natural ability (p. 9)

unique very unusual, rare; being the only one of its kind (p. 9)

Student Reader Unit 4 *This week students will read the following selections.*

8	**Talents**	Expository Nonfiction
10	**Very Young, Very Talented**	Biography
18	**The Talent Show**	Realistic Fiction
26	**Weird and Wacky Talents**	Expository Nonfiction
30	**4 You 2 Do**	Activity Page

Daily Lesson Plan

	ACTIVITIES	MATERIALS
Day 1	**Build Concepts** Weekly Concept: Being Unique Vocabulary: *audience, famous, instrument, perform, talent, unique* **Word Work** Phonics: Diphthongs *oi* and *oy* **Read a Passage** "Talents," pp. 8–9 Comprehension: Use Strategies Reread for Fluency	Student Reader: Unit 4 Routine Cards 1, 3, 5, 6, 7 Tested Vocabulary Cards Sound-Spelling Card 26 Student White Boards AudioText Practice Book, p. 75, Diphthongs *oi, oy*
Day 2	**Reread for Fluency** **Word Work** Phonics: Prefixes *un-*, *re-* Vocabulary **Comprehension** Sequence **Read a Passage** "Very Young, Very Talented," pp. 10–17	Student Reader: Unit 4 AudioText Routine Cards 1, 2, 3, 4, 5, 7, 8 Tested Vocabulary Cards Student White Boards Graphic Organizer 5 Practice Book, p. 76, Prefixes *un-, re-*
Day 3	**Reread for Fluency** **Word Work** Phonics: Diphthongs *oi, oy;* Prefixes *un-*, *re-* Vocabulary **Read a Passage** "The Talent Show," pp. 18–25 Comprehension: Sequence **Write** Response to Literature	Student Reader: Unit 4 AudioText Routine Cards 1, 3, 4, 5, 7 Student journals Practice Book, pp. 75–77, Diphthongs *oi, oy;* Prefixes *un-, re-;* Sequence
Day 4	**Reread for Fluency** **Word Work** Phonics: Spiral Review Vocabulary **Read a Passage** "Weird and Wacky Talents," pp. 26–29 Comprehension: Sequence; Listening **Write** Response to Literature	Student Reader: Unit 4 AudioText Routine Cards 3, 4, 5 Student White Boards Practice Book, pp. 77–78, Sequence; Vocabulary
Day 5	**Assessment Options** Fluency, Comprehension Sentence Reading Passage Reading **Build Concepts** Vocabulary **Read to Connect** **Write** Response to Literature: "4 You 2 Do," p. 30	Student Reader: Unit 4 Reproducible p. 217 Sentence Reading Chart, p. 222 Student White Boards Fluency Progress Chart, p. 215 Routine Card 6 Practice Book, pp. 78–79, Vocabulary; Writing

See pp. xvi–xvii for how *My Sidewalks* integrates instructional practices for ELL.
See pp. 251–254 for Phonemic Awareness Activities.

ACTIVITY 1

Build Concepts

Vocabulary

10–15 minutes

	To Do	To Say
Develop word meaning.	See Routine Card 6.* Discuss pp. 7–8.	Read Words 2 the Wise on p. 7. Have students turn to p. 8. **Look at the pictures. What do you notice?** (a girl drawing, a boy on a skateboard, a boy hanging on bars) **Can you use the words *talent* and *unique* to describe any of these pictures?** (Example: *The artist has a unique talent.*)
Scaffold instruction.	Create a concept web.	In the center of a web, write *Being Unique.* **This week's concept is *being unique. Unique* means "very unusual, rare, or one of a kind."** Provide examples to demonstrate meaning. **A person who can juggle suitcases has a unique talent. Every snowflake is unique, with a pattern that is different from all other snowflakes.** Add the other vocabulary words. Discuss the meaning of each word as it relates to being unique, using the glossary as needed. (See p. 2 in this Teacher's Guide for definitions.)

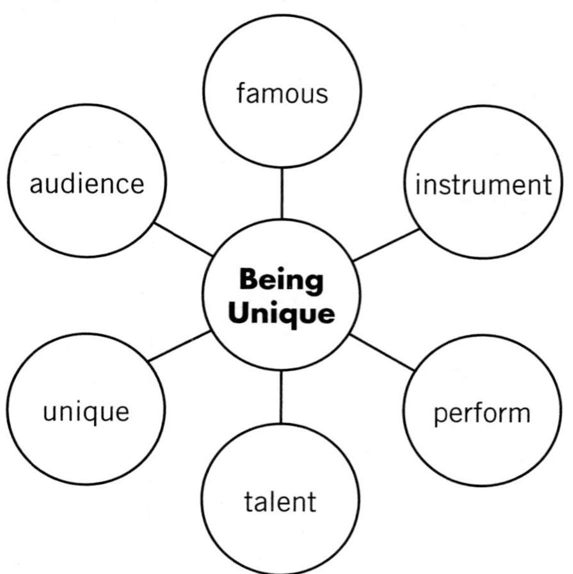

	To Do	To Say
Model the multisyllabic word strategy.	Display each word. Say it as you display it. Think aloud.	Use the Tested Vocabulary Cards. Follow this routine for each word: • **Look for Meaningful Parts** Remind students to look for meaningful parts. **As you say each word, ask yourself: Do I see any parts I know?** • **Chunk Words with No Recognizable Parts** Model how to chunk the word *instrument* to read it. • **Model I see a chunk at the beginning of the word: *in.* I see a part in the middle: *stru.* I see a part at the end of the word: *ment.* I say each chunk slowly: *in stru ment.* I say the chunks fast to make a whole word: *instrument.* Is it a real word? Yes, I know the word *instrument.*** • Have students practice reading each word.
Preview.	Read p. 6 with students.	**Do you see any of the words we just learned on this page?** Together with students, read the sentences on p. 6 describing each selection. Talk about how the concept words might be used in the selections.
MORE PRACTICE	Deepen understanding of *unique.*	Have students demonstrate understanding by answering questions. **Which one is *unique,* a toy you buy at a store or a toy you make from things you find at home? Why? If a drawing is *unique,* are there many drawings like it or is it unusual? What makes a person *unique?***

*Routine Cards can be found at the back of this Teacher's Guide.

ACTIVITY 2 Word Work

Blending Strategy Diphthongs *oi, oy*

5–10 minutes

	To Do	To Say
Use the blending routine.	Write *now* and *brown*.	**1 Connect** You already can read words like these. What are the words? What is the vowel sound in *now*? (/ou/) in *brown*? (/ou/) What two letters make the sound? *(ow)* Now you will learn another sound that is spelled with two letters.
Scaffold instruction.	Display Sound-Spelling Card 26.	**2 Use Sound-Spelling Card** This is oil. You put oil in a car, and you cook with oil. What sound do you hear at the beginning of *oil?* (/oi/) Say it with me: /oi/. The two letters *oi* both contribute to the sound /oi/.
	Distribute white boards.	**3 Listen and Write** Write the letters *oi* for /oi/. As you write, say the sound to yourself: /oi/. Now say the sound aloud.
	Write *coin.*	**4 Model** The two letters *oi* stand for /oi/. This is how I blend this word: /k/ /oi/ /n/, *coin.* Now you try: /k/ /oi/ /n/, *coin.* The letters *oi* stand for a diphthong, /oi/. In a diphthong each vowel contributes to the sound heard.
	Write *toy.*	Repeat with *toy.* Point out that the sound /oi/ can be spelled with *oi* or *oy.* c oi n → → → t oy → →
CORRECTIVE FEEDBACK	Write each practice word. Monitor student practice.	**5 Group Practice** Let's try the same thing with these words. Support students as they blend progressively more difficult words. Give feedback, using the *if . . . then* statements on Routine Card 1. join boy joy coin voice point choice noise enjoy joyful annoy rejoice cowboy noisily **6 Individual Practice** Have each student blend several words from the row best matched to his or her ability. boil soy* Roy soil* moist* spoil broil toys poison boiling royal pointed destroy spoiling
	Check understanding of practice words.	*Students need to make sense of words that they segment and blend. If needed, help students with meanings. *Soy* is a bean that is used to make soy sauce. *Soil* is dirt. You plant flowers in soil. *Moist* means a little wet. I clean the chalkboard with a moist rag.
MORE PRACTICE	Distribute white boards. Model building and spelling words.	**Build Words** Write *boy.* Can you blend this word? (/b/ /oi/) Have students write words on white boards. Write *boy.* Now change the *b* in *boy* to *t.* What is the new word? *(toy)* • Change the *t* in *toy* to *s.* What is the new word? *(soy)* • Change the *s* in *soy* to *j.* What is the new word? *(joy)* • Now add *en* to the beginning of *joy.* What is the new word? *(enjoy)* • Add *ing* to the end of *enjoy.* What is the new word? *(enjoying)*

Routine

ACTIVITY 3 Read a Passage

Build Background "Talents," pp. 8–9

	To Do	To Say (10 minutes)
Develop language and concepts.	See Routine Cards 3 and 7. Ask questions and elaborate on answers.	**Before Reading** Read the title aloud. Do a structured picture walk with students. p. 8 **What do you see?** (a boy hanging from a bar, a boy on a skateboard, a child drawing) **Yes, one boy may be great on bars and the other on a skateboard. Perhaps they have real talent for these activities. A talent is a natural ability. What abilities, or talents, would you need to do well on bars or a skateboard?** (balance, speed) **This girl may be a wonderful artist. She may be very talented. Perhaps she is a child prodigy. A child prodigy is someone who shows amazing talent from an early age. A three-year-old who can play the piano or do complex math would be a child prodigy.**
Scaffold instruction.	Key concepts: *ability, gymnast, artist, practice, prodigy, talent, talented*	p. 9 **What is this child doing?** (a back bend) **She is a gymnast. A gymnast is someone who can balance on a beam, do handsprings, back flips, and so on. You need to be strong and flexible to be a gymnast. You also have to practice a lot. Let's read to find out what unique talents some people have. As you read, ask yourself: What is this mainly about? What am I learning?**
Guide compre-hension.	Read pp. 8–9 aloud.	**During Reading** Read the article as students follow along. Then read it a second time, having students join in. If necessary, stop at the end of each paragraph to check comprehension. Ask questions to promote discussion and develop the concept. • **What examples of talents are given in the article?** • **What does the author say you can do to find out what your unique talent is?** • **What words on the concept web could help you describe the people pictured in this article?**
	Use vocabulary to develop the concept.	**After Reading** **What did you learn about *talents?* What makes each person *unique?* How can you develop your *talent?***

Reread for Fluency "Talents," p. 9

	To Do	To Say (5–10 minutes)
CORRECTIVE FEEDBACK	Monitor oral reading.	**Read p. 9 aloud. Read it three or four times so your reading gets better each time.** Give feedback on students' oral reading and use of the blending strategy. See Routine Cards 1 and 5.
MORE PRACTICE		Instead of rereading just p. 9, have students reread the entire selection three or four times. You may want to have students read along with the AudioText.

Homework Practice Book, p. 75, Phonics: Diphthongs *oi, oy*

ACTIVITY 1 Reread for Fluency

Paired Reading "Talents," p. 9

	To Do	To Say 5–10 minutes
CORRECTIVE FEEDBACK	Pair students. Monitor paired reading.	Students read aloud p. 9, switching readers for each paragraph. Have partners reread; now the other partner begins. For optimal fluency, students should reread three or four times. Give feedback, using Routine Card 5.
MORE PRACTICE		Instead of rereading just p. 9, have students reread the entire selection three or four times. You may want to have students read along with the AudioText.

ACTIVITY 2 Word Work

Blending Strategy Prefixes *un-*, *re-*

To Do | To Say — 5–10 minutes — Routine

Use the blending routine.

Write *slowly* and *careful*.

1 Connect You studied words like these already. What do you know about reading them? (They both contain suffixes that are separate syllables from the base word.) Today we will learn about adding prefixes *un-* and *re-* to the beginning of words. Each prefix has a specific meaning:

un- "not" or "do the opposite of" *re-* "again" or "back"

Scaffold instruction.

Write *unfair*.

2 Model Point to *unfair.* This is a two-syllable word formed from the base word *fair* and the prefix *un-.* You can cover the prefix, read the base word, and then blend the prefix and base word to read the whole word. What is the word? *(unfair)* What does it mean? ("not fair") Let's blend this word together: *un fair, unfair.*

un fair

Write *unfold, refill,* and *repay.*

Repeat with *unfold* ("to do the opposite of fold"), *refill* ("to fill something again"), and *repay* ("to pay someone back").

Distribute white boards.

3 Listen and Write Have students write on white boards. Write the word *fair.* Write *un* in front of it. As you write, say the new word to yourself: *unfair.* Now say the word aloud. Do the same with *refill.*

CORRECTIVE FEEDBACK

Write each practice word. Monitor student practice.

4 Group Practice Let's try the same thing with these words. Support students as they blend progressively more difficult words. Give feedback, using the *if . . . then* statements on Routine Card 1.

unfed	retell	unkind	reread	unpack	unlike
reprint	replay	reopen	uneven	unclear	
unafraid	reinvent	unlikely	unusual	unwanted	refinish

5 Individual Practice Have each student blend several words from the row best matched to his or her ability.

untie	unlock	unmade	rename	repay	
rethink	unplug	rematch	refreeze	restart	redo
unhappy	relocate	unfriendly	unlucky	rediscover	reappear

For more practice, see next page.

MORE PRACTICE

Model spelling words with prefixes.	**Spell and Write** You can spell words with prefixes by thinking about the prefix and the base word. What prefix and base word make up *replay?* (*re-* and *play*) Start with the sounds in the base word: /plā/. What letters spell *play?* Write *play.* Now add the prefix *re-.* Now spell *replay.* Repeat with *unlike, unroll, uncover, rebuild, reread, refill.*

Vocabulary

	To Do	To Say (5 minutes)
Review vocabulary.	Display the concept web from Day 1.	Review the concept web. See Routine Card 2 for the multisyllabic word routine. The words *audience, famous, perform, talent,* and *unique* will be in the selection you are reading today. Remind students that *unique* means "one of a kind."
	Deepen word understanding of *famous* and *talent.*	A *famous* person is someone who is very well known. Name some famous people you know. Why are they famous? (Answers may include musical, sports, or acting ability; wealth or political power; beauty; crime; and so on.) A person can be *famous* because of his or her *talent,* or natural ability. Which people that you mentioned are famous for their *talent?* (Encourage discussion of different examples, asking, *Is this a talent? Why or why not?* For example, musicians, actors, and sports figures are often famous for their talent, but criminals are not.)
Lead cumulative review.		Use the Tested Vocabulary Cards to review concept words from previous weeks.

ACTIVITY 3 Comprehension

Sequence

	To Do	To Say (5 minutes)
Scaffold instruction.	Introduce sequence.	Today you will read about some real people who were young and talented. When you read about a person's life, it's important to keep track of the sequence, or order, of events, because it may help you understand the person. Pay attention to words that tell you how old a person was when something happened.
	Model the skill.	For example, if I read that at *three years old* this person was already playing the piano, and *at age five* he was writing music, I need to pay attention to the sequence to help me understand how quickly this person developed his talent.
	Distribute Graphic Organizer 5.	As you read "Very Young, Very Talented," look for words that help you track the sequence of events in each child's life. Add these sequence words to your graphic organizer. See Routine Card 8.

ACTIVITY 4 Read a Passage

Reading "Very Young, Very Talented," pp. 10–17

5–10 minutes

	To Do	To Say
Develop language and concepts.	See Routine Cards 3 and 7.	**Before Reading** Have students recall what they learned about child prodigies. Read the title. Introduce proper nouns, if necessary. Do a structured picture walk with students.
Scaffold instruction.	Ask questions and elaborate on answers.	pp. 10–12 **The selection is about young people who are talented. What talents do these people have?** (singing, making music) **This is Judy Garland. She sang, danced, and performed in movies. Yo-Yo Ma is a famous cello player. The cello is a string instrument played with a bow. It is related to the violin. Can you tell from the picture how big a cello is?** (It's much bigger than a violin.)
	Key concepts: *artist, athlete, audience, cello, famous, instrument, musician, perform, talent*	pp. 13–14 **What talents do these people have?** (making music) **These are two musicians. What is this young woman doing?** (playing piano) **Yes, she is performing for an audience. This boy is Mozart, one of the most famous musicians of all time. He played and wrote music for the piano and violin.**
		pp. 15–17 **What talents do these people have?** (golf, soccer, art) **These two athletes compete in golf and soccer. Pablo Picasso is one of the great artists of modern times. Here is one of his paintings. How would you describe it?** (fun, weird, colorful)
Guide compre-hension.	Use Routine Card 4.	**During Reading** **Read the pages in a whisper. Raise your hand if you need help with a word. As you read, ask yourself: What am I learning about people who showed talent early in life? What is this mainly about?**
	Monitor independent reading.	pp. 10–13 **What did you learn about young people who are talented? Tell me about one of the people you read about.** (Example: Tori Amos could play the piano by ear and started music school at age six.)
		pp. 14–17 **What did you learn about famous child prodigies? Tell me about one of the people described on these pages. Use some sequence words.** (Example: Freddy Adu moved to the U.S. when he was eight and joined a professional soccer team in 2003 when he was fourteen.)
	Model using context for word meaning.	Read aloud the paragraph with *unusual* on p. 13. Explain how the final sentence provides clues to the meaning of *unusual.*
Model summarizing.	Think aloud.	**After Reading** **What did you learn about young people with talent? What was the selection mainly about?** Model how to summarize. **The selection is about people who have a unique talent that developed when they were very young.**
MORE PRACTICE	Have students reread p. 14.	**Reread** As they read, have students note the sequence in which things happen. Point out the phrase *when he was five years old,* which tells when Mozart began to write music. Draw attention to the word *today,* which indicates that his music is still popular. Students can add these sequence words to their graphic organizers.
	Homework	Practice Book, p. 76, Phonics: Prefixes *un-, re-*

3

ACTIVITY 1 Reread for Fluency

Oral Reading "Very Young, Very Talented," pp. 10–12

	To Do	To Say
		5–10 minutes
CORRECTIVE FEEDBACK	Monitor oral reading.	**Read pp. 10–12 aloud. Read them three or four times so your reading gets better each time.** Give feedback on students' oral reading and use of the blending strategy. Use Routine Cards 1 and 5.
MORE PRACTICE		Have students reread pp. 10–17 three or four times. You may want to have students read along with the AudioText.

ACTIVITY 2 Word Work

Fluent Word Reading Diphthongs *oi, oy;* Prefixes *un-, re-*

	To Do	To Say
		5–10 minutes
Review phonics.	Review the homework.	Ask students to share answers from Practice Book, pp. 75–76.
Use word-reading routine.	Write *rethink.*	Routine **1 Connect** **You can read this word because you know that a word that begins with *re-* is often a two-syllable word formed from a base word and the prefix *re-*. What is the base word?** *(think)* **What is the word?** *(rethink)*
	Write *uncover, oyster,* and *broiler.*	**2 Model** **When you come to a new word, look for meaningful parts. If you don't recognize any meaningful parts, then look for chunks you can read. Look at all the letters in the chunk and think about the vowel sound. Say the parts of the word to yourself, and then read the word.** Model reading *uncover, oyster,* and *broiler* in this way. **When you come to a new word, what are you going to do?**
Scaffold instruction.	Write each practice word.	**3 Group Practice** **Let's read these words. Look for meaningful parts and chunks, think about the vowel sound in each chunk, and say the parts to yourself. We will read words with the sound /oi/ and with prefixes *un-* and *re-*. When I point to the word, let's read it together.** Allow 2–3 seconds previewing time for each word. Support students as they blend progressively more difficult words. foil refill toy noise rerun unjust unseen uneasy employ rebuilding replayed loyal pointing
CORRECTIVE FEEDBACK	**MONITOR PROGRESS**	***If . . .*** students have difficulty previewing and reading whole words, ***then . . .*** have them use sound-by-sound blending. ***If . . .*** students can't read words fluently at a rate of 1–2 seconds per word, ***then . . .*** continue practicing the list.
MORE PRACTICE	Model reading words in sentences.	**When I read a sentence, I read each word without stopping between the words. If I come to a word I don't know, I blend it. Then I read the sentence again.** Model reading this sentence, stopping to blend *reopen: The store will reopen in half an hour.*
	Write practice sentences.	Have each student read the sentence best matched to his or her ability. **Unplug that noisy toy!** **The boys enjoyed the unusual play.** **We dug in the soil and uncovered an old coin.**

Vocabulary

5 minutes

	To Do	To Say
Review vocabulary.	Display the concept web from Day 1.	Review the concept web. **The words *audience, instrument, perform, talent,* and *unique* will be in the selection you read today.** Review the meanings of the words.

ACTIVITY 3 Read a Passage

Reading "The Talent Show," pp. 18–25

10–15 minutes

	To Do	To Say
Scaffold instruction.	Review sequence.	Remind students that clue words can help them follow the sequence. **Look for phrases such as *all morning, at lunch,* and *after school.* As you read "The Talent Show," look for the sequence of events.**
	Use Routine Cards 3 and 7.	**Before Reading** Read the title. Do a structured picture walk.
Develop language and concepts.	Ask questions and elaborate on answers.	pp. 18–21 **Where are these children?** (in a classroom and the cafeteria) **What can you tell about them?** (They're having fun. One boy is performing.)
	Key concepts: *audience, guitar, instrument, perform*	pp. 22–25 **What do you think the children are doing in the picture on p. 24?** (pretending to be cowboys and cowgirls) **They are performing in front of an audience. What instrument is this?** (a guitar)
Guide compre-hension.	Use Routine Card 4.	**During Reading** **Read the pages in a whisper. Raise your hand if you need help with a word. As you read, ask yourself: Who are the characters? What happens first, next, and last?**
	Monitor independent reading.	pp. 18–21 **What is the first important thing that happens in the story?** (Miss Tilden announces the talent show.) **How does Peter feel about the show?** (He is nervous and worried.)
		pp. 22–23 **What happens later when they meet at Peter's home?** (They plan to perform together at the talent show. They decide to pretend to be cowboys.)
		pp. 24–25 **What happens at the end?** (The group performs, with Peter playing a guitar. The audience claps and Peter is not afraid anymore.)
	Monitor comprehension.	**After Reading** Discuss the What Do You Think? question.
	Guide retelling.	Have one student retell the story using sequence words while the others assist. Prompt students by asking: **Who are the characters? What happens first? next? How does the story end?** See Monitoring Retelling on p. 216.
MORE PRACTICE	Have students reread p. 24.	**Reread** As they read, tell students to draw their own pictures to show what the children looked like in their performance.

ACTIVITY 4 Write

Response to Literature

5 minutes

	To Do	To Say
Prompt journal writing.		**Take out your journals. Tell what you would do if you were going to perform in a talent show. Write about what you would do and why.**

Homework Practice Book, p. 77, Sequence

4

ACTIVITY 1

Reread for Fluency

Paired Reading "The Talent Show," p. 21

	To Do	To Say	5–10 minutes
CORRECTIVE FEEDBACK	Pair students. Monitor paired reading.	Students read aloud p. 21, switching readers for each paragraph. Have partners reread; now the other partner begins. For optimal fluency, students should reread three or four times. You may want to have students read along with the AudioText. Give feedback, using Routine Card 5.	
MORE PRACTICE	**READERS' THEATER**	Students can use the dialogue as a script for a Readers' Theater. Have them rehearse, with one student being the narrator and the others the friends.	

ACTIVITY 2

Word Work

Spiral Review Reading Longer Words

To Do | To Say | *5 minutes*

Review reading words with affixes and endings.

To Do: Write *unfriendly.*

To Say: **Look at this word. You can read this word because you know how to read words with prefixes, suffixes, and endings. Cover the prefix and suffix. What is the base word?** *(friend)* Uncover the prefix. **What is the prefix?** *(un-)* Uncover the suffix. **What is the suffix?** *(-ly)* **Now read the word parts from left to right:** ***un friend ly.*** **What is the word?** *(unfriendly)*

To read a word such as ***unfriendly,*** **I figure out its parts, read them from left to right, and blend the parts to read the whole word.**

Scaffold instruction.

CORRECTIVE FEEDBACK

To Do: Write practice words. Monitor student work.

To Say: **Decode Longer Words** Have individuals read the following words. If students make an error, provide help blending the parts of the words as needed. Have students repeat the blending with you. To check meaning, call on individuals to use the words in sentences.

joy	**joyful**	**joyfully**	**want**	**wanted**	**unwanted**
tell	**retell**	**retelling**	**expect**	**expected**	**unexpected**
start	**restart**	**restarted**	**care**	**careful**	**carefully**

Vocabulary

To Do | To Say | *5–10 minutes*

Extend word knowledge.

To Do: Write on the board or a transparency: *It was the group's turn to perform.*

To Say: Use the word *perform* to extend word knowledge. **Remember we read this word earlier this week. We learned that it means to act, sing, or play music in public. Today I want to talk about other words that are related to** ***perform.*** **We can use this word to read other words.**

Can you think of other words that contain the word ***perform*****?** *(performs, performing, performed, performance, performer)* Write words as students name them and add any they don't mention. Point out that *-er* is a suffix that means "one who," so *performer* means "one who performs." A *performance* is a show.

MORE PRACTICE

To Do: Deepen word understanding.

To Say: Have students use *perform* and *instrument* in a sentence. (For example, *I will perform a song on my instrument.*) Share sentences. Ask, **What are some examples of instruments?** (piano, guitar, cello, violin, and so on)

ACTIVITY 3 Read a Passage

Read Together "Weird and Wacky Talents," pp. 26–29

10–15 minutes

	To Do	To Say
Scaffold instruction.	Review sequence (homework).	Ask volunteers to read the passage and share answers from Practice Book p. 77. Remind students of the importance of following the sequence. **When you read, the sequence of events is important. Often clue words tell the order in which things happen. Look for these words. You might also try to picture in your mind the events as they happen.**
Develop language and concepts.	See Routine Cards 3 and 4.	**Before Reading** **This article is about unique talents. What talents do you see in the pictures?** (blowing big bubbles, playing spoons, juggling, and making faces) **Why do you think these talents are considered unique?** (Only a few people can do these things.) **Let's read to find out more about these unique talents.**
Model fluent reading.	Read pp. 26–29 aloud. Model prosody.	**Reading** **Listen to my voice as I read this article.** Read the article with expression as students follow along. Read it a second time, having students point to each word. **Now read the article aloud with me. Try to make your voice sound like mine as we read.** Reread the article several times with students.
Monitor compre-hension.	Monitor listening comprehension.	**After Reading** Prompt discussion to monitor comprehension. Listen as students answer questions. **What does the author say is necessary to make giant bubbles?** (You have to use two or three pieces of gum and blow slowly.) **How can people use spoons as an instrument?** (They hold two spoons together and tap them on their legs.) **Which of these talents do you think would be hardest to learn? Which would you most enjoy watching?** (Answers will vary.) **Summarize** Have one student describe the wacky talents mentioned in the article while the others assist.
MORE PRACTICE	Have students reread p. 28.	**Reread** As they read, tell students to look for information about juggling. After reading, they can tell a partner what they learned about juggling.

ACTIVITY 4 Write

Response to Literature

5 minutes

	To Do	To Say
Prompt narrative writing.	Writing elements: organization	**Write a story about someone who blew a giant bubble with gum. Tell about each step the person took to make the giant bubble. Be sure to use words like *first* and *next* that help tell the order.**

Homework Practice Book, p. 78, Vocabulary

5

ACTIVITY 1 Assessment Options

Sentence Reading

	To Do	To Say 5 minutes
Assess sentence reading.	Use reproducible p. 217.	Have each student read the sentences. Record scores on the Sentence Reading Chart, p. 222. While you work with one student, others can complete the Write Sentences activity below. **Joy was unhappy when she lost the coins. We enjoyed watching the rerun on TV. The boy spoke with an unfriendly voice.**
CORRECTIVE FEEDBACK	**MONITOR PROGRESS**	***If . . .*** students have trouble reading words with *oi, oy* /oi/ or prefixes, ***then . . .*** reteach the blending strategy lessons on pp. 5 and 7. ***If . . .*** students misread a word in the sentence, ***then . . .*** correct the error and have them reread the word and then the sentence.
Practice sentence writing.	Provide white boards.	**Write Sentences** Have students copy the sentences from reproducible p. 217 on white boards. Have them confirm spellings by comparing the words they wrote to the words in the sentences.

Passage Reading

	To Do	To Say 5–10 minutes
Assess fluency and compre-hension.	Determine which students to assess this week.	Choose from these options: monitoring fluency (see pp. 214–215) and/or monitoring retelling (see p. 216). Have students reread "The Talent Show." Be sure each student is assessed every other week.
		If you have time, assess every student.

ACTIVITY 2 Build Concepts

Vocabulary

	To Do	To Say 5–10 minutes
Review concept and vocabulary.	Review the homework. Display the concept web you began on Day 1.	Ask students to go over answers and share their writing from Practice Book, p. 78. **This week's question is *What are talents?* How do this week's words relate to the question?** (Have students answer the question, using some of the vocabulary they learned this week.) Ask students to add more words to the concept web. Have students explain how each word relates to being unique. Monitor students' understanding of vocabulary as they discuss the web. See Routine Card 6.
MORE PRACTICE		Students can write sentences using three of the vocabulary words.

ACTIVITY 3 Read to Connect

Reread "Talents," pp. 8–9

10 minutes

	To Do	To Say
Monitor comprehension.	Have students reread "Talents" silently.	**As you read, think about what the article says about talent.** After rereading, ask: • **What kinds of talents are described?** (running, skateboarding, singing, making toys, writing stories) • **When do people discover what their talents are?** (Some people show a talent quite young, but others don't discover their talents until they are older.) **We also read "Very Young, Very Talented." Find that selection. What talents are described?** Record students' ideas. **We also read "The Talent Show." What did the children in that story decide to do at the talent show?** Record students' ideas.
Make connections.	Have students make connections across texts.	**What can you say in general about talents?** (Sample answers: People have many different talents. Some people discover their talents when they are very young.)

Write

Response to Literature "4 You 2 Do," p. 30

5–10 minutes

	To Do	To Say
Guide response activities.	Discuss the directions. Tell students to choose one activity to complete. Monitor handwriting. See pp. 227–229.	**Word Play** Have students complete the list on their own and then meet with a partner to share word lists. **Making Connections** Discuss the question in a group or in pairs. **On Paper** Brainstorm a list of instruments with the group before students write. Have them write on their own. Students can use Practice Book p. 79 to structure their written response, or you can send the Practice Book page home for them to complete later. (Descriptions of the instrument should include details and a reason why it is a favorite.)
MORE PRACTICE		If you have more time, direct students to complete all the activities.

Homework Practice Book, p. 79, Writing

Unit 4 Week 2 *From Top to Bottom*

When is nature a challenge?

Objectives *This week students will ...*

Vocabulary
- build concepts and vocabulary: *depth, height, peak, position, scale, summit*

Phonics
- blend and read words with the sound of *oo* in *moon* and silent consonants *mb, kn, gn*
- apply knowledge of letter-sounds and word structure to decode unknown words when reading

Text Comprehension
- read connected text
- use compare and contrast to improve comprehension
- write in response to literature

Fluency
- practice fluency with oral rereading

Word Work *This week's phonics focus is ...*

Sound of *oo* in *moon* Silent Consonants *mb, kn, gn*

Concept Words *Tested Vocabulary*

The week's vocabulary is related to the concept of challenges.
The first appearance of each word in the Student Reader is noted below.

depth	the distance from top to bottom (p. 47)
height	how tall or high someone or something is (p. 36)
peak	the pointed top of a mountain or hill (p. 36)
position	the way a person's body is placed (p. 51)
scale	to climb (p. 40)
summit	the highest point; top (p. 40)

Student Reader Unit 4 *This week students will read the following selections.*

Daily Lesson Plan

	ACTIVITIES	MATERIALS
Day 1	**Build Concepts** Weekly Concept: From Top to Bottom Vocabulary: *depth, height, peak, position, scale, summit* **Word Work** Phonics: Sound of *oo* in *moon* **Read a Passage** "Mountains," pp. 34–37 Comprehension: Use Strategies Reread for Fluency	Student Reader: Unit 4 Routine Cards 1, 3, 5, 6, 7 Tested Vocabulary Cards Sound-Spelling Card 37 Student White Boards AudioText Practice Book, p. 80, Vowels *oo* in *moon*
Day 2	**Reread for Fluency** **Word Work** Phonics: Silent Consonants *mb, kn, gn* Vocabulary **Comprehension** Compare and Contrast **Read a Passage** "Go Climb a Mountain," pp. 38–45	Student Reader: Unit 4 AudioText Routine Cards 1, 2, 3, 4, 5, 7, 8 Tested Vocabulary Cards Sound-Spelling Cards 19, 20 Student White Boards Graphic Organizer 3 or 4 Practice Book, p. 81, Silent Consonants *mb, kn, gn*
Day 3	**Reread for Fluency** **Word Work** Phonics: Sound of *oo* in *moon;* Silent Consonants *mb, kn, gn* Vocabulary **Read a Passage** "Get Over It!" pp. 46–53 Comprehension: Compare and Contrast **Write** Response to Literature	Student Reader: Unit 4 AudioText Routine Cards 1, 3, 4, 5, 7, 8 Student journals Practice Book, pp. 80–82, Vowels *oo* in *moon;* Silent Consonants *mb, kn, gn;* Compare and Contrast
Day 4	**Reread for Fluency** **Word Work** Phonics: Spiral Review Vocabulary **Read a Passage** "Free Diving," pp. 54–55 Comprehension: Compare and Contrast; Listening **Write** Response to Literature	Student Reader: Unit 4 AudioText Routine Cards 3, 4, 5 Student White Boards Practice Book, pp. 82–83, Compare and Contrast; Vocabulary
Day 5	**Assessment Options** Fluency, Comprehension Sentence Reading Passage Reading **Build Concepts** Vocabulary **Read to Connect** **Write** Response to Literature: "4 You 2 Do," p. 56	Student Reader: Unit 4 Reproducible p. 217 Sentence Reading Chart, p. 222 Student White Boards Fluency Progress Chart, p. 215 Practice Book, pp. 83–84, Vocabulary; Writing

See pp. xvi–xvii for how *My Sidewalks* integrates instructional practices for ELL.
See pp. 251–254 for Phonemic Awareness Activities.

ACTIVITY 1 Build Concepts

Vocabulary

	To Do	To Say 10–15 minutes
Develop word meaning.	See Routine Card 6. Discuss pp. 33–35.	Read Words 2 the Wise on p. 33. Have students turn to p. 34–35. **Look at the picture. What do you see?** (mountains) **Can you use the word *height* to describe a mountain?** (Example: *A mountain has a great height.*) **Which of these things has great height, a doghouse or a high-rise building?**
Scaffold instruction.	Create a concept web.	In the center of a web, write *Challenges*. **This week's concept is *challenges*. *Challenges* are things that are hard to do or that take skill.** Provide examples to demonstrate meaning. **Running a long race, climbing a mountain, and acting bravely when afraid are all challenges.** Add the other vocabulary words. Discuss the meaning of each word as it relates to the concept of challenges, using the glossary as needed. (See p. 16 in this Teacher's Guide for definitions.)
Model the multisyllabic word strategy.	Display each word. Say it as you display it. Think aloud.	Use the Tested Vocabulary Cards. Follow this routine for the multisyllabic words: • **Look for Meaningful Parts** Remind students to look for meaningful parts. **As you say each word, ask yourself: Do I see any parts I know?** • **Chunk Words with No Recognizable Parts** Model how to chunk the word *summit* to read it. • **Model I see a chunk at the beginning of the word: *sum.* I see a part at the end of the word: *mit.* I say each chunk slowly: *sum mit.* I say the chunks fast to make a whole word: *summit.* Is it a real word? Yes, I know the word *summit.*** • Have students practice reading each word.
Preview.	Read p. 32 with students.	**Do you see any of the words we just learned on this page?** Together with students, read the sentences on p. 32 describing each selection. Talk about how the concept words might be used in the selections.
MORE PRACTICE	Deepen understanding of *scale.*	Have students demonstrate understanding by answering questions. **If you *scale* a wall, do you climb over it or crawl under it? What could you use to help you *scale* a wall? What kinds of things should a mountain climber use to *scale* a mountain? Explain.**

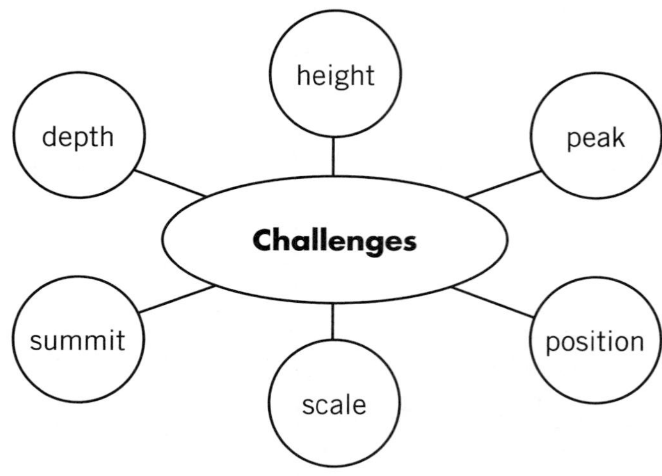

ACTIVITY 2

Word Work

Blending Strategy Vowels *oo* in *moon*

5–10 minutes

Routine

	To Do	To Say
Use the blending routine.	Write *keep* and *feed.*	**1 Connect** You already can read words like these. What are the words? What is the vowel sound in *keep?* (/ē/) in *feed?* (/ē/) What two letters make the sound? *(ee)* Now you will learn a sound that is spelled with two *o*'s together.
Scaffold instruction.	Display Sound-Spelling Card 37.	**2 Use Sound-Spelling Card** This is a moon. What sound do you hear in the middle of *moon?* (/ü/) Say it with me: /ü/. The letter pair *oo* often stands for the vowel sound in *moon.*
	Distribute white boards.	**3 Listen and Write** Write the letters *oo* for /ü/. As you write, say the sound to yourself: /ü/. Now say the sound aloud.
	Write *boot.*	**4 Model** The two letters *oo* stand for /ü/. This is how I blend this word: /b/ /ü/ /t/, *boot.* Now you try: /b/ /ü/ /t/, *boot.* The letters *oo* stand for the sound /ü/ as in the word *moon.* b oo t → → → ——→
CORRECTIVE FEEDBACK	Write each practice word. Monitor student practice.	**5 Group Practice** Let's try the same thing with these words. Support students as they blend progressively more difficult words. Give feedback, using the *if . . . then* statements on Routine Card 1. zoo loop cool mood pool scoop boost* droop pooch stool igloo blooming smoother loosely spoonful moonlight
		6 Individual Practice Have each student blend several words from the row best matched to his or her ability. moo noon zoom fool soon shoot booth proof smooth choose coolest scooter shampoo toothbrush kangaroo
	Check understanding of practice words.	*Students need to make sense of words that they segment and blend. If needed, help students with meanings. A *boost* is something that helps. Dancing can be a *boost* to your feelings. It can help you feel happy.
MORE PRACTICE	Distribute white boards. Model building and spelling words.	**Build Words** Write *food.* Can you blend this word? (/f/ /ü/ /d/) Have students write words on white boards. Write *food.* Now change the *d* in *food* to *l.* What is the new word? *(fool)* • Change the *f* in *fool* to *p.* What is the new word? *(pool)* • Change the *p* in *pool* to *t.* What is the new word? *(tool)* • Change the *t* in *tool* to *f.* What is the new word? *(fool)* • Add *ing* to the end of *fool.* What is the new word? *(fooling)*

ACTIVITY 3 Read a Passage

Build Background "Mountains," pp. 34–37

10 minutes

	To Do	To Say
Develop language and concepts.	See Routine Cards 3 and 7. Ask questions and elaborate on answers.	**Before Reading** Read the title aloud. Introduce the proper nouns. Do a structured picture walk with students. p. 35 **What do you see?** (mountains, mountain range) **Yes, the picture shows some mountains that are in North America. North America is the continent we live on. A continent is a large area of land on the Earth. Can you name any other continents?** p. 36 **What is the person in this picture called?** (a mountain climber) p. 37 Call students' attention to the chart and read the title and column headings aloud. **This chart lists the names of all the continents and a mountain found on each continent. Can you find the height of Mount McKinley? All these mountains have great heights. Which is the lowest mountain peak on the chart? On what continent is Mount Elbrus located?** **Let's read to find out what else makes mountains important in our lives. As you read, ask yourself: What is this mainly about? What am I learning?**
Scaffold instruction.	Key concepts: *continent, great heights, peak*	
Guide comprehension.	Read pp. 34–37 aloud.	**During Reading** Read the selection as students follow along. Then read it a second time, having students join in. If necessary, stop at the end of each paragraph to check comprehension. Ask questions to promote discussion and develop the concept. • **In what ways are mountains important in our lives?** • **What does the author say about mountains and oceans?** • **What words on the concept web could help you explain what you learned about mountains in this selection?**
	Use vocabulary to develop the concept.	**After Reading** **What did you learn about the *heights* of mountains in the Himalayas? What mountain has the highest *peak* on Earth? Would you ever want to climb the mountain with the highest *peak?* Why or why not?**

Reread for Fluency "Mountains," p. 36

5–10 minutes

	To Do	To Say
CORRECTIVE FEEDBACK	Monitor oral reading.	**Read p. 36 aloud. Read it three or four times so your reading gets better each time.** Give feedback on students' oral reading and use of the blending strategy. See Routine Cards 1 and 5.
MORE PRACTICE		Instead of rereading just p. 36, have students reread the entire selection three or four times. You may want to have students read along with the AudioText.

Homework Practice Book, p. 80, Phonics: Sound of *oo* as in *moon*

ACTIVITY 1 Reread for Fluency

Paired Reading "Mountains," p. 35

	To Do	To Say 5–10 minutes
CORRECTIVE FEEDBACK	Pair students. Monitor paired reading.	Students read aloud p. 35, switching readers for each sentence. Have partners reread; now the other partner begins. For optimal fluency, students should reread three or four times. Give feedback, using Routine Card 5.
MORE PRACTICE		Instead of just p. 35, have students reread the entire selection three or four times. You may want to have students read along with the AudioText.

ACTIVITY 2 Word Work

Blending Strategy Silent Consonants *mb, kn, gn*

	To Do	To Say 5–10 minutes
Use the blending routine.	Write *ham* and *nap.*	Routine **1 Connect** **You already can read words like these. What are the words? What is the sound at the end of *ham?*** (/m/) **What letter makes this sound?** *(m)* **What sound do you hear at the beginning of *nap*?** (/n/) **What letter makes this sound?** *(n)* **Today you will learn other ways to spell the sounds /m/ and /n/.**
Scaffold instruction.	Display Sound-Spelling Card 20.	**2 Use Sound-Spelling Card** **This is a nurse. What sound do you hear at the beginning of *nurse?*** (/n/) **Say it with me: /n/. The letters *kn* and *gn* can also stand for /n/.**
	Distribute white boards.	**3 Listen and Write** **Write the letters *kn* for /n/. As you write, say the sound to yourself: /n/. Now say the sound aloud.** Do the same with *gn*/n/.
	Write *knob.* Write *gnat.*	**4 Model** **The letters *kn* stand for /n/ in *knob.* This is how I blend this word: /n/ /o/ /b/, *knob.* Now let's blend this word together: /n/ /o/ /b/, *knob.*** Repeat with *gnat.* Point out that the letters *gn* can also stand for /n/. kn o b gn a t
	Write *dumb.*	Display Sound-Spelling Card 19 for *-mb.* Repeat Steps 2, 3, and 4, using the word *dumb.* **The letters *mb* stand for /m/ in *dumb.* This is how I blend this word: /d/ /u/ /m/, *dumb.*** d u mb
CORRECTIVE FEEDBACK	Write each practice word. Monitor student practice.	**5 Group Practice** **Let's try the same thing with these words.** Support students as they blend progressively more difficult words. Point out that the letter *i* stands for the long *i* sound in the words *sign* and *climb.* Give feedback, using the ***if . . . then*** statements on Routine Card 1. numb knees sign knot jamb* know climb gnash* thumb plumber climbed knowing signed knitted knuckle

For more practice, see next page.

Continued Blending Strategy

To Do	To Say
	6 Individual Practice Have each student blend several words from the row best matched to his or her ability.
	knife gnome* limb lamb knock knit
	knight kneel gnarl* dumber dumbest
	plumb* knapsack kneecap climbing thumbtack knothole
Check understanding of practice words.	*If needed, help students with meanings. A *jamb* is a piece that forms the side of a door or window. To *gnash* your teeth is to grind them together. A *gnome* is a story character like a dwarf. A *gnarl* is a hard lump on a tree. *Plumb* means straight up and down.

MORE PRACTICE

To Do	To Say
Model building and spelling words.	**Build Words** Write *knit.* Can you blend this word? (/n/ /i/ /t/) Have students write words on white boards. Write *knit.* Now change the *i* to *o.* What is the new word? *(knot)* Change the *t* to *b.* What is the new word? *(knob)* Repeat with *numb, dumb, crumb,* and *thumb.*

Vocabulary

5 minutes

Review vocabulary.

Lead cumulative review.

To Do	To Say
Display the concept web from Day 1.	Review the concept web. See Routine Card 2 for the multisyllabic word routine. The words *peak, scale,* and *summit* will be in the selection you are reading today. Remind students that *peak* means "the highest point at the top of a mountain."
Deepen word understanding of *summit.*	The *summit* is the top of a mountain. Things at the bottom of a mountain look small from the summit. This is because they are so far away. Imagine you are looking down from the summit of a mountain. What might you see? (tops of trees, roofs of houses, road, cars, lake, and so on)
	Use the Tested Vocabulary Cards to review concept words from previous weeks.

ACTIVITY 3 Comprehension

Compare and Contrast

5 minutes

Scaffold instruction.

To Do	To Say
Introduce compare and contrast.	Today you will read about how climbers prepare to scale a mountain. And you will read about mountain climbers who have reached the summit of Earth's highest mountain, Mount Everest. When you read about these climbers, compare and contrast them. Think about how they are alike and how they are different. Look for clue words such as *too, both, but,* and *also.* Keep track of likenesses and differences to understand what it takes to climb the highest mountains.
Model the skill.	For example, if I read that climbers must stay calm, then I know this is one way the climbers were alike. If I read that two men climbed Mount Everest and later a woman climbed it, then I know this is one way the climbers were different.
Distribute Graphic Organizer 3 or 4.	Pay attention as you read "Go Climb a Mountain" to ways successful mountain climbers are alike. (strong, prepared, experienced, determined) Notice how those who climbed Mount Everest are different from each other. (disabled person, different ages, climbed different number of times) Add these likenesses and differences to your graphic organizer. See Routine Card 8.

ACTIVITY 4 Read a Passage

Reading "Go Climb a Mountain," pp. 38–45

10–15 minutes

	To Do	To Say
Develop language and concepts.	See Routine Cards 3 and 7. Ask questions and elaborate on answers.	**Before Reading** Have students recall what they learned about mountains. Read the title. Introduce the proper nouns. Do a structured picture walk.
		pp. 38–39 **Look at the picture on p. 38. What things is the climber using to help scale the mountain?** (a rope, a harness, special shoes) **The equipment mountain climbers use for a climb is called gear. It's important to be prepared for climbing with the right gear.**
Scaffold instruction.	Key concepts: *climbing wall, gear, oxygen, peak, prepared, summit, supplies*	pp. 40–41 **Why would water and oxygen be important supplies for mountain climbers?** (Climbers need lots of water and may have trouble breathing up high.) **What special gear is the climber on p. 41 using?** (ice axe, boots for ice) **What do climbers need to know in order to prepare for this kind of climbing?** (weather conditions)
		pp. 42–43 **The men pictured on p. 42 were the first humans to reach the summit of Mount Everest, the highest mountain peak in the world. How can you tell that they were prepared for the climb?** (They seem to have the necessary gear and supplies.) **Why do you think the author of this selection calls these men "Peak Performers"?** (They climbed Everest, the highest peak, which required top skills.)
		p. 45 **What is the child on p. 45 doing?** (climbing a wall in a gym) **Practicing on a climbing wall can help someone prepare to climb a mountain.**
Guide compre-hension.	Use Routine Card 4.	**During Reading Read the pages in a whisper. Raise your hand if you need help with a word. As you read, ask yourself: What am I learning about mountain climbing? What is this mainly about?**
	Monitor independent reading.	pp. 38–41 **What did you learn about the dangers of climbing high peaks? Tell me three dangers you read about.** (getting dizzy, having trouble breathing, stormy weather)
		pp. 42–45 **What did you learn about a climbing wall? Tell me how climbing a wall and climbing a mountain are alike and different.** (Alike: need gear for both, need skills for both; Different: wall indoors/mountain outdoors, no bugs on wall/bugs on mountain, no bad weather on wall/bad weather on mountain, no falling rocks on wall/mountains are rocky)
	Model using context for word meaning.	Point out the word *disability* on p. 44. Explain how the phrase "knees were hurt in a car accident" provides clues to the meaning of *disability.*
Model summarizing.	Think aloud.	**After Reading What did you learn about mountain climbing? What was the selection mainly about?** Model how to summarize. **The selection gives details about mountain climbing skills and dangers and tells about successful mountain climbers. It is mainly about how those who want to climb a mountain should prepare and practice to do so.**
MORE PRACTICE	Have students reread p. 42.	**Reread** As they read, have students note how Edmund Hillary and Tenzig Norgay were alike. Have them identify three ways. (Both were strong. Both had climbed before. Both were determined to reach Mount Everest's summit.)
	Homework	Practice Book, p. 81, Phonics: *mb, kn, gn*

3

ACTIVITY 1 Reread for Fluency

Oral Reading "Go Climb a Mountain," pp. 38–39

	To Do	To Say *5–10 minutes*
CORRECTIVE FEEDBACK	Monitor oral reading.	**Read pp. 38–39 aloud. Read them three or four times so your reading gets better each time.** Give feedback on students' oral reading and use of the blending strategy. Use Routine Cards 1 and 5.
MORE PRACTICE		Have students reread additional pages of the selection three or four times. You may want to have students read along with the AudioText.

ACTIVITY 2 Word Work

Fluent Word Reading Vowels *oo* in *moon;* Silent consonants *mb, kn, gn*

	To Do	To Say *5–10 minutes*
Review phonics.	Review the homework.	Ask students to share answers from Practice Book, pp. 80–81.
Use word-reading routine.	Write *lamb.*	**1 Connect** **You can read this word because you know that when the letters *mb* appear together in a word, the *b* is usually silent. Can you blend this word?** (/l/ /a/ /m/) **What is the word?** *(lamb)*
	Write *know, gnome,* and *room.*	**2 Model** **When you come to a new word, look for meaningful pairs of letters. Think about two consonants together in which one letter is silent. Think about two of the same vowels together and the sound they make. Say the parts of the word to yourself, and then read the word.** Model reading *know, gnome,* and *room* in this way. **When you come to a new word, what are you going to do?**
Scaffold instruction.	Write each practice word.	**3 Group Practice** **Let's read these words. Look for meaningful pairs of letters. Think about consonant pairs with a silent letter and a vowel pair with the same two letters. Say the parts of a word to yourself. We will read words with the vowel sound /ü/ and words with silent consonants. When I point to the word, let's read it together.** Allow 2–3 seconds previewing time for each word. Support students as they blend progressively more difficult words. **hoot knot gnat sign crumb soon** **climbed choosing dumber knocking moonbeam knotted**
CORRECTIVE FEEDBACK	**MONITOR PROGRESS**	***If . . .*** students have difficulty previewing and reading whole words, ***then . . .*** have them use sound-by-sound blending. ***If . . .*** students can't read words fluently at a rate of 1–2 seconds per word, ***then . . .*** continue practicing the list.
MORE PRACTICE	Model reading words in sentences.	**When I read a sentence, I read each word without stopping between the words. If I come to a word I don't know, I blend it. Then I read the sentence again.** Model reading this sentence, stopping to blend *gnome: I read a tale about a gnome named Tiny.*
	Write practice sentences.	Have each student read the sentence best matched to his or her ability. **Boohoo, a gnat just bit my thumb!** **Take food in your knapsack for the climb.** **My pooch knocked the knife and spoon off the tray.**

Routine

Vocabulary

	To Do	To Say 5 minutes
Review vocabulary.	Display the concept web from Day 1.	Review the concept web. **The words *depth, height,* and *position* will be in the selection you are reading today.** Review the meanings of the words.

ACTIVITY 3 Read a Passage

Reading "Get Over It!" pp. 46–53

	To Do	To Say 10–15 minutes
Scaffold instruction.	Review compare and contrast.	Remind students that they can compare and contrast things in a story. **Notice how Charlie and Lisa are alike and different as you read "Get Over It!"**
	Use Routine Cards 3 and 7.	**Before Reading** Read the title. Do a structured picture walk.
Develop language and concepts.	Ask questions and elaborate on answers.	pp. 46–50 **Where are the children?** (at a swimming pool) **What do you think they will do there?** (swim and dive) **How might Charlie feel about using the diving board?** (He looks frightened.) **Some people are afraid of heights. Sometimes they can overcome their fear.**
	Key concepts: *fear of heights, overcoming a fear*	pp. 51–53 **What makes you think that Charlie might have overcome his fear of heights?** (He jumped into the pool and seems happy.)
Guide compre-hension.	Use Routine Card 4.	**During Reading** **Read the pages in a whisper. Raise your hand if you need help with a word. As you read, ask yourself: Who are the characters? What happens first, next, and last?**
	Monitor independent reading.	pp. 46–48 **What is the first important thing that happens in the story?** (Charlie can't dive off the high board.) **Why can't he dive?** (He feels nervous and sick.)
		pp. 49–50 **What happens the next day?** (Charlie is nervous at the pool.) **What does Lisa tell Charlie?** (that he has a fear of heights) **Why does Charlie believe this is true?** (He realizes he has never liked high things.)
		pp. 51–53 **What happens at the end?** (Charlie jumps off the high board and overcomes his fear of heights.)
	Monitor comprehension. Guide retelling.	**After Reading** Discuss the What Do You Think? question. Have one student retell the story while the others assist. Prompt students by asking: **Who are the characters? What happens first? next? How does the story end?** See Monitoring Retelling on p. 216.
MORE PRACTICE	Have students reread p. 52.	**Reread** Remind students that *position* means the way a body is arranged. After they read, have students draw a picture of Charlie in a diving position.

ACTIVITY 4 Write

Response to Literature

	To Do	To Say 5 minutes
Prompt journal writing.		**Take out your journals. Imagine you are afraid to go to the top floor of a tall building. Write about what you would do to overcome this fear of heights.**

Homework Practice Book, p. 82, Compare and Contrast

4

ACTIVITY 1 Reread for Fluency

Paired Reading "Get Over It!" pp. 50–51

	To Do	To Say	*5–10 minutes*
CORRECTIVE FEEDBACK	Pair students. Monitor paired reading.	Have partners read aloud pp. 50–51, switching readers for each paragraph. For optimal fluency, students should reread three or four times. Give feedback, using Routine Card 5.	
MORE PRACTICE	**READERS' THEATER**	Students can use the dialogue as a script for a Readers' Theater. Have them rehearse, with one student being the narrator and the others the friends.	

ACTIVITY 2 Word Work

Spiral Review Diphthongs *ou, ow, oi, oy*

5 minutes

	To Do	To Say
Review blending words with *ou, ow, oi, oy.*	Write *brown* and *count.*	**You can read these words because you know *ow* and *ou* can stand for the sound /ou/. What sound can *ow* stand for?** (/ou/) **What is the word?** *(brown)* **What sound can *ou* stand for?** (/ou/) **What is the word?** *(count)* Remind students that *ow* can also stand for the long *o* sound, as in *throw.* **When you read a word with *ow,* try both sounds, /ō/ and /ou/, and see which pronunciation of the word makes sense in the sentence.**
Scaffold instruction.	Write *broil* and *enjoy.*	**You can read these words because you know *oi* and *oy* stand for the sound /oi/. What sound does *oi* stand for?** (/oi/) **What is the word?** *(broil)* **What sound does *oy* stand for?** (/oi/) **What is the word?** *(enjoy)*
	Distribute white boards.	**Sort Words** Write *broil* and *brown* as labels for two rows. Have students copy the chart. **Let's sort words by vowel sounds. When I say a word, tell me where to write it: *moist, grouch, round, joyful, coins, bounce, spoiled, poison, scout, clown.***
CORRECTIVE FEEDBACK	Monitor student work.	Write each word in the appropriate row. If students make an error, say the word, emphasize the vowel sound and have students repeat after you. Have students read the completed lists and write the words in their own charts.

broil	moist	joyful	coins	spoiled	poison
brown	grouch	round	bounce	scout	clown

Vocabulary

5–10 minutes

	To Do	To Say
Extend word knowledge.	Write on the board or a transparency: *Would you like to scale a high mountain?*	Use the word *scale* to extend word knowledge. **Remember we read this word earlier this week. We learned that it means to climb up or over something. In this sentence, *scale* describes an action. Today I want to talk about other meanings for *scale.*** **Can you think of other meanings for *scale?*** (something for weighing objects, a thin flake that covers a fish) Provide meanings students don't mention. Write and read aloud sentences to illustrate. **The vet set my cat on a *scale.* A cod is a fish with green *scales.* In both sentences, scale (scales) names a thing, not an action.**
MORE PRACTICE	Deepen word understanding.	Remind students that *depth* means how deep something is from top to bottom. Have students arrange the following bodies of water according to depth, from shallowest to deepest: ocean, stream, swimming pool. (stream, swimming pool, ocean)

ACTIVITY 3 Read a Passage

Read Together "Free Diving," pp. 54–55

10–15 minutes

	To Do	To Say
Scaffold instruction.	Review compare and contrast (homework).	Ask volunteers to read the passage and share answers from Practice Book p. 82. Remind students of the importance of comparing and contrasting. **Sometimes when you read a selection, recognizing how things are alike and different can help you understand what you are reading. Often there are clue words, such as *but, like,* or *not like,* when things are compared. Look for words such as these in the selection we will read today. They may help you understand what is being explained.**
Develop language and concepts.	See Routine Cards 3 and 4.	**Before Reading** **This selection is about a kind of diving called *free diving*. Where do you think the divers in these pictures are diving?** (in an ocean, in deep water) **Why do you think divers like to dive into the depth of an ocean?** (to get a close-up look at fish and other sea animals) **Let's read to find out what divers do to prepare for free diving.**
Model fluent reading.	Read pp. 54–55 aloud. Model prosody.	**Reading** **Listen to my voice as I read this selection.** Read the selection with expression as students follow along. Read it a second time, having students point to each word. **Now read the selection aloud with me. Try to make your voice sound like mine as we read.** Reread the selection several times with students.
Monitor comprehension	Monitor listening comprehension.	**After Reading** Prompt discussion to monitor comprehension. Listen as students answer questions. **What are some things free divers can see in the depth of an ocean?** (schools of fish, sharks, coral) **How are free divers and ocean mammals different?** (Free divers have to learn how to dive and hold their breath underwater. Ocean mammals already know how to dive and hold their breath underwater.) **Would you like to be a free diver? Why or why not?** (Some students might say no because preparing for it would be too hard. Other students might say yes because they would like to see the ocean the way a whale sees it.) **Summarize** Have one student summarize how divers prepare for free diving while other students assist.
	Have students reread p. 54.	**Reread** As they read, tell students to look for information about how divers breathe during free diving. After reading, they can tell a partner what they learned about free diving.

ACTIVITY 4 Write

Response to Literature

5 minutes

	To Do	To Say
Prompt descriptive writing.	Writing elements: support	**Tell how a free diver and a dolphin are alike and different. Use some words that compare or contrast.**

Homework Practice Book, p. 83, Vocabulary

5

ACTIVITY 1 Assessment Options

Sentence Reading

	To Do	To Say 5 minutes
Assess sentence reading.	Use reproducible p. 217.	Have each student read the sentences. Record scores on the Sentence Reading Chart, p. 222. While you work with one student, others can complete the Write Sentences activity below. **Did you know a lamb came to school today?** **The tiny gnome sat on a tree limb in the moonlight.** **The knight's pet owl, Hoot, likes to sit on his knee.**
CORRECTIVE FEEDBACK	**MONITOR PROGRESS**	***If . . .*** students have trouble reading words with *oo* /ü/ or silent consonants, ***then . . .*** reteach the blending strategy lessons on pp. 19 and 21. ***If . . .*** students misread a word in the sentence, ***then . . .*** correct the error and have them reread the word and then the sentence.
Practice sentence writing.	Provide white boards.	**Write Sentences** Have students copy the sentences from reproducible p. 217 on white boards. Have them confirm spellings by comparing the words they wrote to the words in the sentences.

Passage Reading

	To Do	To Say 5–10 minutes
Assess fluency and compre-hension.	Determine which students to assess this week.	Choose from these options: monitoring fluency (see pp. 214–215) and/or monitoring retelling (see p. 216). Have students reread "Get Over It!" Be sure each student is assessed every other week.
		If you have time, assess every student.

ACTIVITY 2 Build Concepts

Vocabulary

	To Do	To Say 5–10 minutes
Review concept and vocabulary.	Review the homework. Display the concept web you began on Day 1.	Ask students to go over answers and share their writing from Practice Book, p. 83. **This week's question is *When is nature a challenge?* How do this week's words relate to the question?** (Have students answer the question, using some of the vocabulary they learned this week.) Ask students to add more words to the concept web. Have students explain how each word relates to a challenge in nature. Monitor students' understanding of vocabulary as they discuss the web.
MORE PRACTICE		Students can extend the web by adding more related words.

ACTIVITY 3 Read to Connect

Reread "Mountains," pp. 34–37

	To Do	To Say 10 minutes
Monitor compre-hension.	Have students reread "Mountains" silently.	**As you read, think about what the article says about mountains.** After rereading, ask: • **Where are there mountains with great heights?** (on each continent) • **Why is Mount Everest an important mountain?** (It has the highest peak on our planet.) **We also read "Go Climb a Mountain." Find that selection. What information does it give about the challenges of mountain climbing?** Record students' ideas. **We also read "Get Over It!" What did Charlie learn about meeting challenges in that story?** Record students' ideas.
Make connections.	Have students make connections across texts.	**What can you say in general about challenges?** (Sample answers: Meeting challenges is not easy. You have to overcome fears. You have to prepare and practice to meet nature's challenges.)

ACTIVITY 4 Write

Response to Literature "4 You 2 Do," p. 56

	To Do	To Say 5–10 minutes
Guide response activities.	Discuss the directions. Tell students to choose one activity to complete.	**Word Play** Have students complete the list on their own and then meet with a partner to share word lists. **Making Connections** Have students discuss the question in small groups or in pairs. (Answers should include two examples and words such as *also* and *but* that compare and contrast.) **On Paper** Help students decide which person they would interview, a mountain climber or a free diver. Have them write on their own. Students can use Practice Book p. 84 to structure their written response, or you can send the Practice Book page home for them to complete later. (Students should ask thoughtful questions that cannot be answered with just *yes* or *no.*)
MORE PRACTICE	Monitor handwriting. See pp. 227–229.	If you have more time, direct students to complete all the activities.
	Homework	Practice Book, p. 84, Writing

Unit 4 Week 3 *Hobbies*

What are some unique hobbies?

Objectives *This week students will ...*

Vocabulary
- build concepts and vocabulary: *collection, delight, interest, rare, special, unusual*

Phonics
- blend and read words with vowel patterns *ew* and *ue* and silent consonants *st, wr*
- apply knowledge of letter-sounds and word structure to decode unknown words when reading

Text Comprehension
- read connected text
- draw conclusions to improve comprehension
- write in response to literature

Fluency
- practice fluency with oral rereading

Word Work *This week's phonics focus is ...*

Vowel Patterns *ew, ue*   Silent Consonants *st, wr*

Concept Words *Tested Vocabulary*

The week's vocabulary is related to the concept of hobbies.
The first appearance of each word in the Student Reader is noted below.

collection a group of similar things gathered from many places and belonging together (p. 60)

delight great pleasure; joy (p. 63)

interest a feeling of wanting to know, see, do, own, or take part in something (p. 60)

rare not often seen or found; unusual (p. 64)

special unusual or different in a particular way (p. 61)

unusual not in common use; rare (p. 72)

Student Reader Unit 4 *This week students will read the following selections.*

60	**Hobbies**	Narrative Nonfiction
62	**Glass Bottle Buildings**	Narrative Nonfiction
70	**What Are You Looking For?**	Realistic Fiction
78	**Hobby Hunting**	How-to Article
82	**4 You 2 Do**	Activity Page

Daily Lesson Plan

	ACTIVITIES	MATERIALS
Day 1	**Build Concepts** Weekly Concept: Hobbies Vocabulary: *collection, delight, interest, rare, special, unusual* **Word Work** Phonics: Vowel Patterns *ew* and *ue* **Read a Passage** "Hobbies," pp. 60–61 Comprehension: Use Strategies Reread for Fluency	Student Reader: Unit 4 Routine Cards 1, 3, 5, 6, 7 Tested Vocabulary Cards Sound-Spelling Card 37 Student White Boards AudioText Practice Book, p. 85, Vowel Patterns *ew, ue*
Day 2	**Reread for Fluency** **Word Work** Phonics: Silent Consonants *st, wr* Vocabulary **Comprehension** Draw Conclusions **Read a Passage** "Glass Bottle Buildings," pp. 62–69	Student Reader: Unit 4 AudioText Routine Cards 1, 2, 3, 4, 5, 7, 8 Tested Vocabulary Cards Sound-Spelling Cards 30, 31 Student White Boards Graphic Organizer 2 Practice Book, p. 86, Silent Consonants *st, wr*
Day 3	**Reread for Fluency** **Word Work** Phonics: Vowel Patterns *ew, ue;* Silent Consonants *st, wr* Vocabulary **Read a Passage** "What Are You Looking For?" pp. 70–77 Comprehension: Draw Conclusions **Write** Response to Literature	Student Reader: Unit 4 AudioText Routine Cards 3, 4, 5, 7 Student journals Practice Book, pp. 85–87, Vowel Patterns *ew, ue;* Silent Consonants *st, wr;* Draw Conclusions
Day 4	**Reread for Fluency** **Word Work** Phonics: Spiral Review Vocabulary **Read a Passage** "Hobby Hunting," pp. 78–81 Comprehension: Draw Conclusions; Listening **Write** Response to Literature	Student Reader: Unit 4 AudioText Routine Cards 3, 4, 5 Student White Boards Practice Book, pp. 87–88, Draw Conclusions; Vocabulary
Day 5	**Assessment Options** Fluency, Comprehension Sentence Reading Mid-Unit Passage Reading **Build Concepts** Vocabulary **Read to Connect** **Write** Response to Literature: "4 You 2 Do," p. 82	Student Reader: Unit 4 Reproducible p. 217 Sentence Reading Chart, p. 222 Student White Boards Assessment Book p. 81 Fluency Progress Chart, p. 215 Routine Card 6 Practice Book, pp. 88–89, Vocabulary; Writing

See pp. xvi–xvii for how *My Sidewalks* integrates instructional practices for ELL.
See pp. 251–254 for Phonemic Awareness Activities.

ACTIVITY 1 Build Concepts

Vocabulary

10–15 minutes

	To Do	To Say
Develop word meaning.	See Routine Card 6. Discuss pp. 59–61.	Read Words 2 the Wise on p. 59. Have students turn to pp. 60–61. **Look at the pictures. What groups of objects do you notice?** (dolls, stamps, shells) **Can you use the word *collection* to describe any of these pictures?** (Example: *The man and boy are looking at a stamp collection.*)
Scaffold instruction.	Create a concept web.	In the center of a web, write *Hobbies.* **This week's concept is *hobbies.* Enjoying a collection of objects can be a hobby. A *collection* is a group of similar things gathered together.** Provide examples to demonstrate meaning. **A collection of toy cars might include a fire engine. My cousin found a hawk's feather to add to her collection of feathers.** Add the other vocabulary words. Discuss the meaning of each word as it relates to the concept of hobbies, using the glossary as needed. (See p. 30 in this Teacher's Guide for definitions.)
Model the multisyllabic word strategy.	Display each word. Say it as you display it. Think aloud.	Use the Tested Vocabulary Cards. Follow this routine for each word: • **Look for Meaningful Parts** **Do you recognize any parts of this word? What do these parts mean? Use the parts to read the word.** • **Model** **I see *un-* at the beginning of *unusual.* I know that *un-* can mean "not." I also recognize the word *usual.* I know *usual* means "common" or "ordinary." So I think *unusual* means "not common or ordinary."** • **Chunk Words with No Recognizable Parts** Model how to chunk the word *interest* to read it. **I see a chunk at the beginning of the word: *in.* I see a part in the middle: *ter.* I see a part at the end: *est.* I say each chunk slowly: *in ter est.* I say the chunks fast to make a whole word: *interest.* Is it a real word? Yes, I know the word *interest.*** • Have students practice reading each word.
Preview.	Read p. 58 with students.	**Do you see any of the words we just learned on this page?** Together with students, read the sentences on p. 58 describing each selection. Talk about how the concept words might be used in the selections.
MORE PRACTICE	Deepen understanding of *special.*	Have students demonstrate understanding by answering questions. **Which kind of greeting card is *special,* one someone makes for you or one someone buys. Why? If a photo is *special,* would you keep it or throw it away? What holiday is *special* to you?**

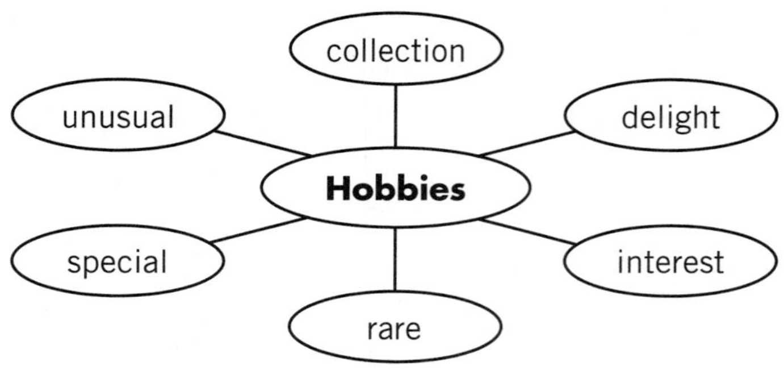

ACTIVITY 2 Word Work

Blending Strategy Vowel Patterns *ew, ue*

5–10 minutes

Use the blending routine.

Scaffold instruction.

To Do	To Say
Write *join* and *spoil*.	**1 Connect** You already can read words like these. What are the words? What is the vowel sound in *join?* (/oi/) in *spoil?* (/oi/) What two letters make the sound? (*oi*) Today you will learn another vowel sound that is spelled with two letters.
Display Sound-Spelling Card 37.	**2 Use Sound-Spelling Card** This is a moon. What sound do you hear in the middle of *moon?* (/ü/) Say it with me: /ü/. The letter pair *oo* often stands for the vowel sound in *moon.* Now you will learn other letter pairs that can spell the /ü/ sound: *ew* and *ue.*
Distribute white boards.	**3 Listen and Write** Write the letters *ew* for /ü/. As you write, say the sound to yourself: /ü/. Now say the sound aloud.
Write *new.*	**4 Model** The two letters *ew* stand for /ü/. This is how I blend this word: /n/ /ü/, *new.* Now you try: /n/ /ü/, *new.* The letters *ew* stand for the sound /ü/.
Write *blue.*	Repeat with *blue.* Point out that the sound /ü/ can be spelled *ew* or *ue.*

Routine

n e w   b l u e

CORRECTIVE FEEDBACK

Write each practice word. Monitor student practice.

5 Group Practice Let's try the same thing with these words. Support students as they blend progressively more difficult words. Give feedback, using the *if . . . then* statements on Routine Card 1.

dew*	Sue	pews*	news	glue	
	knew	clue	brew*	threw	drew
rescue	pursue	avenue	bluebird	untrue	

6 Individual Practice Have each student blend several words from the row best matched to his or her ability.

few	new	cue	due	grew	
stew	flew	clues		true	shrewd*
statue	continue	renewal	dewdrop	blueberry	

Check understanding of practice words.

*Students need to make sense of words that they segment and blend. If needed, help students with meanings. *Dew* is small drops of water that form on things, such as lawns, during the night. *Pews* are benches in a church. *Brew* means "to make something to drink, such as tea or coffee, by boiling." *Shrewd* means "clever."

MORE PRACTICE

Distribute white boards. Model building and spelling words.

Build Words Write *dew.* Can you blend this word? (/d/ /ü/) Have students write words on white boards. Write *dew.* Now change the *d* in *dew* to *dr.* What is the new word? *(drew)*

- Change the *dr* in *drew* to *cr.* What is the new word? *(crew)*
- Change the *cr* in *crew* to *ch.* What is the new word? *(chew)*
- Add *s* to the end of *chew.* What is the new word? *(chews)*
- Now change the *s* at the end of *chews* to *ing.* What is the new word? *(chewing)*

ACTIVITY 3

Read a Passage

Build Background "Hobbies," pp. 60–61

10 minutes

	To Do	To Say
Develop language and concepts.	See Routine Cards 3 and 7. Ask questions and elaborate on answers.	**Before Reading** Read the title aloud. Do a structured picture walk with students. p. 60 **What is the girl's hobby?** (collecting dolls) **Yes, the picture shows her doll collection. Dolls are special to her. What kind of collection is special to the boy?** (stamp collection)
Scaffold instruction.	Key concepts: *collection, special, interest*	p. 61 **What does this girl have an interest in?** (seashells) **What is the young man's hobby?** (dancing) **Yes, he seems to have an interest in dancing.** **Let's read to get some ideas for things you could collect or things you could do. As you read, ask yourself: What is this mainly about? What am I learning?**
Guide compre-hension.	Read pp. 60–61 aloud.	**During Reading** Read the selection as students follow along. Then read it a second time, having students join in. If necessary, stop at the end of each paragraph to check comprehension. Ask questions to promote discussion and develop the concept. • **What ideas for collections are given in the selection?** • **What questions does the author suggest you ask yourself?** • **What should the answers to these questions help you do?**
	Use vocabulary to develop the concept.	**After Reading** **Why might someone decide to start a *collection* of things? What are some things people have an *interest* in collecting? If you are looking for a hobby, what *special* things might you collect?**

Reread for Fluency "Hobbies," p. 60

5–10 minutes

	To Do	To Say
CORRECTIVE FEEDBACK	Monitor oral reading.	**Read p. 60 aloud. Read it three or four times so your reading gets better each time.** Give feedback on students' oral reading and use of the blending strategy. See Routine Cards 1 and 5.
MORE PRACTICE		Instead of rereading just p. 60, have students reread the entire selection three or four times. You may want to have students read along with the AudioText.

Homework Practice Book, p. 85, Phonics: Vowel Patterns *ew, ue*

ACTIVITY 1 Reread for Fluency

Paired Reading "Hobbies," p. 61

	To Do	To Say 5–10 minutes
CORRECTIVE FEEDBACK	Pair students. Monitor paired reading.	Students read aloud p. 61, switching readers for each sentence. Have partners reread; now the other partner begins. For optimal fluency, students should reread three or four times. Give feedback, using Routine Card 5.
MORE PRACTICE		Instead of rereading just p. 61, have students reread the entire selection three or four times. You may want to have students read along with the AudioText.

ACTIVITY 2 Word Work

Blending Strategy Silent Consonants *st, wr*

	To Do	To Say 5–10 minutes
Use the blending routine. **Scaffold instruction.**	Write *lamb.*	Routine **1 Connect** You studied words like this already. What is this word? *(lamb)* What is the sound at the end of lamb? (/m/) What two letters make this sound? *(mb)* The *b* is silent. Today we will learn other words with silent letters.
	Display Sound-Spelling Card 31.	**2 Use Sound-Spelling Card** This is a submarine. What sound do you hear at the beginning of *submarine?* (/s/) Say it with me: /s/. In *submarine,* the letter *s* stands for the sound /s/. The letters *st* can also stand for /s/.
	Distribute white boards.	**3 Listen and Write** Write the letters *st* for /s/. As you write, say the sound to yourself: /s/. Now say the sound aloud.
	Write *castle.*	**4 Model** The letters *st* stand for /s/ in *castle.* This is how I blend this word: /k/ /a/ /s/, /ə/ /l/, *castle.* Now let's blend this word together: /k/ /a/ /s/, /ə/ /l/, *castle.* When the letters *st* appear together in the middle of a word, the *t* is often silent. c a s t l e
	Display Sound-Spelling Card 30. Write *write.*	Repeat Steps 2, 3, and 4, using the word *write.* The letters *wr* stand for /r/ in *write.* This is how I blend this word: /r/ /ī/ /t/, *write.* w r i t e
CORRECTIVE FEEDBACK	Write each practice word. Monitor student practice.	**5 Group Practice** Let's try the same thing with these words. Support students as they blend progressively more difficult words. Give feedback, using the *if . . . then* statements on Routine Card 1. wreck listen fasten wrap thistle* wrench wrist wrinkle wrestle **6 Individual Practice** Have each student blend several words from the row best matched to his or her ability. wrote wren* bustle* fasten wring whistle wreath bristles* glisten* *If needed, help students with meanings. A *thistle* is a kind of wild plant. A *wren* is a kind of bird. To *bustle* means to be in a hurry. *Bristles* are the hairs of a paintbrush. To *glisten* is to sparkle.

For practice, see next page.

MORE PRACTICE

Model building and spelling words with *wr*.	**Spell and Write** Write *wrap*. Once you know that *wrap* is spelled with *wr*, you can spell words related to *wrap*. Write *wrap*. Now write these words: *wraps, wrapped, wrapping, unwrap, rewrap, rewrapped.*

Vocabulary

5 minutes

	To Do	To Say
Review vocabulary.	Display the concept web from Day 1.	Review the concept web. See Routine Card 2 for the multisyllabic word routine. The words *collection, delight, rare,* and *special* will be in the selection you are reading today. Remind students that *special* means "unusual or different in a particular way."
	Deepen understanding of *rare*.	A *rare* object is an uncommon object. It may be one of a kind or hard to find. A coin from a pirate ship is *rare*. What kind of stamp might be *rare*? (Answers may include one from long ago or one from a faraway country.) Why are objects from long ago *rare*? (Answers may include that many objects from long ago have been lost, thrown away, or damaged.)
Lead cumulative review.		Use the Tested Vocabulary Cards to review concept words from previous weeks.

ACTIVITY 3 Comprehension

Draw Conclusions

5 minutes

	To Do	To Say
Scaffold instruction.	Introduce draw conclusions.	Today you will read about two people, Bob and Dora Cain, and their hobby. You will learn some facts and details. When you read an article, it's important to think about the facts and details and decide something about them, or draw conclusions. You should use the information in the article and what you know to draw conclusions.
	Model the skill.	For example, I can use these facts and details to draw a conclusion about Bob and Dora: They had an idea of things they wanted to collect. They made a plan. They spent three years making a collection. I can draw the conclusion that Bob and Dora were serious about their hobby.
	Distribute Graphic Organizer 2.	As you read "Glass Bottle Buildings," look for facts and details that can help you draw conclusions about Bob and Dora. How would you describe their personalities? Do others enjoy their glass bottle buildings? Add your conclusions to your graphic organizer along with the facts and details that helped you draw the conclusions. See Routine Card 8.

ACTIVITY 4 Read a Passage

Reading "Glass Bottle Buildings," pp. 62–69

10–15 minutes

	To Do	To Say
Develop language and concepts. **Scaffold instruction.**	See Routine Cards 3 and 7. Ask questions and elaborate on answers. Key concepts: *collection, rare, special.*	**Before Reading** Have students recall what they learned about hobbies. Read the title. Introduce proper nouns, if necessary. Do a structured picture walk with students. pp. 62–63 **What things did Bob and Dora collect as their hobby?** (glass bottles) **Why would people have to be careful with a glass bottle collection?** (The bottles could break.) pp. 64–65 **What is special about the buildings in these pictures?** (They're made of glass bottles.) **What can you tell from the pictures about the size of Bob and Dora's bottle collection?** (They had a huge number of bottles in their collection!) **Do you think this kind of collection is common or rare?** (It is rare. Few people collect bottles to build things.) pp. 66–67 **The picture on page 66 shows a wishing well. What is special about the bottles in the wishing well?** (They're different colors.) **How are the bottles arranged?** (in a design)
Guide comprehension.	Use Routine Card 4.	**During Reading** **Read the pages in a whisper. Raise your hand if you need help with a word. As you read, ask yourself: What am I learning about Bob and Dora's hobby? What is this mainly about?**
	Monitor independent reading.	pp. 62–65 **What was unusual about Bob and Dora's hobby of collecting bottles?** (They had thousands of bottles in their collection. Bob and Dora made buildings to show their collection.)
	Model using context for word meaning.	Read aloud the paragraph with *wreck* on page 63. Explain how the sentence "Sometimes the bottles would break" provides clues to the meaning of *wreck*. pp. 66–69 **What conclusion can you draw about Bob and Dora's personalities? Tell me the facts and details you used to draw your conclusion.** (Bob and Dora were friendly and proud of their buildings. Facts and details include they liked visitors, Bob gave tours of the buildings, they liked sharing their collection.)
Model summarizing.	Think aloud.	**After Reading** **What did you learn about Bob and Dora's hobby? What was the article mainly about?** Model how to summarize. **The article told facts and details about Bob and Dora's collection of glass bottles. It was mainly about the buildings they built with the glass bottles.**
MORE PRACTICE	Have students reread p. 66.	**Reread** After reading, ask students what made visiting the glass bottle buildings enjoyable. (Bob and Dora's friendliness, tours, and music)
	Homework	Practice Book, p. 86, Phonics: Silent Consonants *st, wr*

3

ACTIVITY 1 Reread for Fluency

Oral Reading "Glass Bottle Buildings," pp. 64–65

5–10 minutes

	To Do	To Say
CORRECTIVE FEEDBACK	Monitor oral reading.	Students read aloud pp. 64–65, switching readers for each sentence. Have partners reread; now the other partner begins. For optimal fluency, students should reread three or four times. Give feedback, using Routine Card 5.
MORE PRACTICE		Instead of rereading just pp. 64–65, have students reread the entire selection three or four times. You may want to have students read along with the AudioText.

ACTIVITY 2 Word Work

Fluent Word Reading Vowel Patterns *ew, ue;* Silent Consonants *st, wr*

5–10 minutes

	To Do	To Say
Review phonics.	Review the homework.	Ask students to share answers from Practice Book, pp. 85–86.
Use word-reading routine.	Write *wren.*	Routine **1 Connect** **You can read this word because you know when the consonants *wr* are together, the *w* is silent. What sound do the letters *wr* stand for?** (/r/) **What is the word?** *(wren)*
	Write *nestle, drew,* and *fuel.*	**2 Model** **When you come to a new word, look at all the letters and think about the consonant and vowel sounds. Say the sounds in the word to yourself and then read the word.** Model reading *nestle, drew,* and *fuel* in this way. **When you come to a new word, what are you going to do?**
Scaffold instruction.	Write each practice word.	**3 Group Practice** **Let's read these words. Look at the letters, think about the consonant and vowel sounds, and say the sounds to yourself. We will read words with *wr* or *st* and words with the vowel sound /ü/. When I point to the word, let's read it together.** Allow 2–3 seconds previewing time for each word. Support students as they blend progressively more difficult words. **castle wrong chew hasten wrap true** **jewel unglued unwritten overdue newspaper**
CORRECTIVE FEEDBACK	**MONITOR PROGRESS**	***If . . .*** students have difficulty previewing and reading whole words, ***then . . .*** have them use sound-by-sound blending. ***If . . .*** students can't read words fluently at a rate of 1–2 seconds per word, ***then . . .*** continue practicing the list.
MORE PRACTICE	Model reading words in sentences.	**When I read a sentence, I read each word without stopping between the words. If I come to a word I don't know, I blend it. Then I read the sentence again.** Model reading this sentence, stopping to blend *wrench: Dad has a wrench in his toolbox.*
	Write practice sentences.	Have each student read the sentence best matched to his or her ability. **Listen to the clues I wrote.** **His new blue shirt is wrinkled.** **The dewdrops on Sue's van glistened in the sun.**

Vocabulary

	To Do	To Say 5 minutes
Review vocabulary.	Display the concept web from Day 1.	Review the concept web. **The words *collection, delight, interest, special,* and *unusual* will be in the story you read today.** Review the meanings of the words.

ACTIVITY 3 Read a Passage

Reading "What Are You Looking For?" pp. 70–77

	To Do	To Say 10–15 minutes
Scaffold instruction.	Review draw conclusions.	Remind students that they can use facts and details to draw conclusions about what they read. **Look for facts and details as you read "What Are You Looking For?"**
Develop language and concepts.	Use Routine Cards 3 and 7.	**Before Reading** Read the title. Introduce proper nouns, if necessary. Do a structured picture walk.
	Ask questions and elaborate on answers.	pp. 70–73 **Can you guess the girl's hobby?** (collecting jewelry) **Can you guess the boy's hobby?** (collecting insects)
	Key concepts: *collection, delight, interest, special, unusual*	pp. 74–75 **Look at the special necklace on p. 75. What is unusual about this necklace?** (It has a stone shaped like a beetle.) **Why might this necklace interest the boy?** (He has an insect collection.) pp. 76–77 **What do you think the children are looking at?** (a special insect)
Guide compre-hension.	Use Routine Card 4.	**During Reading Read the pages in a whisper. Raise your hand if you need help with a word. As you read, ask yourself: Who are the characters? What happens first, next, and last?**
	Monitor independent reading.	pp. 70–71 **Whom does Kevin meet at the beginning of the story?** (Tina) pp. 72–74 **When Tina comes back the next day, how does Kevin act?** (uninterested) **What changes how he feels?** (He learns she knows about insects.) pp. 75–77 **What happens at the end that surprises Kevin?** (Tina shows him a stone shaped like a dung beetle. Then they find a real dung beetle.)
	Monitor comprehension.	**After Reading** Discuss the What Do You Think? question. Help students draw a conclusion. (Tina is a new friend. She knows about insects. Now Kevin values friends.)
	Guide retelling.	Have a student retell the story while others assist. Ask: **Who are the characters? What happens first? next? last?** See Monitoring Retelling on p. 216.
MORE PRACTICE	Have students reread p. 75.	**Reread** Have students name the special insect Kevin was looking for.

ACTIVITY 4 Write

Response to Literature

	To Do	To Say 5 minutes
Prompt journal writing.		**Take out your journals. Use facts and details from the story to tell what you think about Kevin's personality. Tell what you think he is like.**

Homework Practice Book, p. 87, Draw Conclusions

4

ACTIVITY 1 Reread for Fluency

Paired Reading "What Are You Looking For?" p. 74

5–10 minutes

	To Do	To Say
CORRECTIVE FEEDBACK	Pair students. Monitor paired reading.	Students read aloud p. 74, switching readers for each paragraph. Have partners reread; now the other partner begins. For optimal fluency, students should reread three or four times. You may want to have students read along with the AudioText. Give feedback, using Routine Card 5.
MORE PRACTICE	**READERS' THEATER**	Students can use the dialogue as a script for a Readers' Theater. Have them rehearse, with one student being the narrator, Kevin, and others as Kevin's dad and Tina.

ACTIVITY 2 Word Work

Spiral Review Silent Consonants *mb, kn, gn, st, wr*

5 minutes

	To Do	To Say
Review blending words with *mb, kn, gn, st,* and *wr.*	Write *limb, knee, gnat, castle,* and *wreck.*	**Look at these words. You can read these words because you know how to read words with silent consonants. Look at all the letters, think about the consonant sounds, say the sounds to yourself, and read the word.** Review the spelling patterns with students as they read the words: **If the letters *mb* are together, *b* is silent. If the letters *kn* are together, *k* is silent. If the letters *gn* are together, *g* is silent. If the letters *st* are together in the middle of the word, usually *t* is silent. If the letters *wr* are together, *w* is silent.**
Scaffold instruction. **CORRECTIVE FEEDBACK**	Distribute white boards. Monitor student work.	**Build Words** Write *mb, kn, gn, st,* and *wr* as headings on a five-column chart. Have students copy the chart. Below each heading, write several words with those letters omitted. For example, for *thumb*, write thu___. Have students add the missing letters to each word. Ask students to read the completed words. If students make an error, review the spelling pattern, model reading the word correctly, and have students repeat after you.

mb	*kn*	*gn*	*st*	*wr*
thu___	___it	___ome	bu___le	___ap
la___	___ot	___ash	whi___le	___ite
cli___	___ife	___at	thi___le	___eath

Vocabulary

5–10 minutes

	To Do	To Say
Extend word knowledge.	Write on the board or a transparency: *The woman has a coin collection.*	Use the word *collection* to extend word knowledge. **We learned that *collection* means a group of similar things gathered together. What base word do you see in *collection?*** *(collect)* Circle *collect.* **We can use *collect* to read other words.** **What other words contain the word *collect?*** *(collects, collecting, collected, collector)* **Write these words and discuss their meanings. Point out that *-or* is a suffix meaning "one who," so *collector* means "one who collects."**
MORE PRACTICE	Deepen word understanding.	**Some children have an *interest* in doing a sport. Name sports children have an *interest* in.** (baseball, soccer, skiing, and so on)

ACTIVITY 3 Read a Passage

Read Together "Hobby Hunting," pp. 78–81

	To Do	To Say *10–15 minutes*
Scaffold instruction.	Review draw conclusions (homework).	Ask volunteers to read the passage and share answers from Practice Book, p. 87. Remind students of the importance of drawing conclusions. **When you read, it's often important to draw conclusions. Think about facts and details to make decisions about the information.**
Develop language and concepts.	See Routine Cards 3 and 4.	**Before Reading** **This selection suggests things you could collect or do as a hobby. What examples of hobbies do you see in the pictures on pp. 78–79?** (collecting cars, collecting seashells, making origami objects, reading, playing soccer) **Let's read to find out more about choosing a hobby.**
Model fluent reading.	Read pp. 78–81 aloud. Model prosody.	**Reading** **Listen as I read the selection. Notice how I read the questions and lists of ideas.** Read the selection with appropriate intonation for questions. Pause briefly after each question and after each item in the lists. **I stopped briefly to think about each question and idea.** Read the selection a second time, having students point to each word. **Now read the selection aloud with me. Try to read as if you are speaking and thinking about the ideas.** Reread the selection several times with students.
Monitor compre-hension.	Monitor listening comprehension.	**After Reading** Prompt discussion to monitor comprehension. Listen as students answer questions. • **What objects listed in question 2 might you like to collect? What are some other objects you might collect?** • **What activities listed in question 3 would you like to do as a hobby? What are some other activities you would add to the list?** • **Are there subjects or topics in question 4 that interest you? Which ones? Is there another topic that interests you?** **Summarize** Have one student summarize how to choose a hobby. Encourage other students to assist.
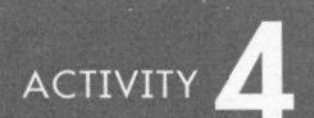 **MORE PRACTICE**	Have students reread p. 80.	**Reread** Tell students to think about Karina's interests as they read. After reading, invite students to suggest what Karina might choose as a hobby.

ACTIVITY 4 Write

Response to Literature

	To Do	To Say *5 minutes*
Prompt personal narrative.	Writing elements: focus	**Look back at the questions. Think about your answers. What are your interests? Tell a story about a hobby you could do. Be sure all your sentences are about this hobby and the steps you take to do it.**

Homework Practice Book, p. 88, Vocabulary

5

ACTIVITY 1

Assessment Options

Sentence Reading

	To Do	To Say 5 minutes
Assess sentence reading.	Use reproducible p. 217.	Have each student read the sentences. Record scores on the Sentence Reading Chart, p. 222. While you work with one student, others can complete the Write Sentences activity below. **Both the bluebird and the wren flew away.** **I knew the book about castles was overdue.** **Andrew will fasten a red bow to the wreath.**
CORRECTIVE FEEDBACK	**MONITOR PROGRESS**	***If . . .*** students have trouble reading words with *ew, ue* for /ü/ or silent consonants *st, wr,* ***then . . .*** reteach the blending strategy lessons on pp. 33 and 35. ***If . . .*** students misread a word in the sentence, ***then . . .*** correct the error and have them reread the word and then the sentence.
Practice sentence writing.	Provide white boards.	**Write Sentences** Have students copy the sentences from reproducible p. 217 on white boards. Have them confirm spellings by comparing the words they wrote to the words in the sentences.

Mid-Unit Passage Reading

	To Do	To Say 5–10 minutes
Assess fluency and compre-hension.	Determine which students to assess. Use Assessment Book, p. 81.	Choose from these options: monitoring fluency (see pp. 214–215) and/or monitoring retelling (see p. 216). Have students read the Unit 4 Mid-Unit Fluency Passage in the Assessment Book. Be sure each student is assessed every other week.
		If you have time, assess every student.

ACTIVITY 2

Build Concepts

Vocabulary

	To Do	To Say 5–10 minutes
Review concept and vocabulary.	Review the homework. Display the concept web you began on Day 1.	Ask students to go over answers and share their writing from Practice Book, p. 88. **This week's question is *What are some unique hobbies?* How do this week's words relate to the question?** Have students answer the question, using some of the vocabulary they learned this week. Ask students to add more words to the concept web. Have students explain how each word relates to hobbies. Monitor students' understanding of vocabulary as they discuss the web. See Routine Card 6.
MORE PRACTICE		Students can write a sentence telling about something that has *delighted* them.

ACTIVITY 3 Read to Connect

Reread "Hobbies," pp. 60–61

10 minutes

	To Do	To Say
Monitor compre-hension.	Have students reread "Hobbies" silently.	**As you read, think about what the selection says about hobbies.** After rereading, ask: • **Why does the selection mention collections?** (Collecting things can be a hobby.) • **What are some things a person could collect?** (stamps, baseball cards, blue things, coins) **We also read "Glass Bottle Buildings." Find that selection. What was unique about Bob and Dora's hobby?** Record students' ideas. **We also read "What Are You Looking For?" What did you learn about the collections of the characters in that story?** Record students' ideas.
Make connections.	Have students make connections across texts.	**What can you say in general about hobbies?** (Sample answers: A hobby can be collecting things or doing activities you like. Some people collect unusual things. You can answer questions about your interests to help you choose a hobby.)

ACTIVITY 4 Write

Response to Literature "4 You 2 Do," p. 82

5–10 minutes

	To Do	To Say
Guide response activities.	Discuss the directions. Tell students to choose one activity to complete. Monitor handwriting. See pp. 227–229.	**Word Play** Have students unscramble the words on their own and then meet with a partner to compare answers. **Making Connections** Have students discuss and answer the question in small groups. (They all had a hobby that they really enjoyed.) **On Paper** Before students write, brainstorm a list of hobbies, inviting students to include their hobbies as well as other hobbies. Have students write on their own. Students can use Practice Book, p. 89, to help prepare their written response, or you can send the Practice Book page home for them to complete later.
MORE PRACTICE		If you have more time, direct students to complete all the activities.

Homework Practice Book, p. 89, Writing

Unit 4 Week 4 *Being the First*

Why do people want to be the first to do something?

Objectives *This week students will ...*

Vocabulary

- build concepts and vocabulary: *adventure, attempt, distance, impossible, remarkable, waterfall*

Phonics

- blend and read words with sound *oo* in *foot, u* in *put* and suffixes *-ness, -less*
- apply knowledge of letter-sounds and word structure to decode unknown words when reading

Text Comprehension

- read connected text
- use compare/contrast to improve comprehension
- write in response to literature

Fluency

- practice fluency with oral rereading

Word Work *This week's phonics focus is ...*

Sound of *oo* in *foot, u* in *put*   suffixes *-ness, -less*

Concept Words *Tested Vocabulary*

The week's vocabulary is related to the concept of being the first.
The first appearance of each word in the Student Reader is noted below.

adventure	an unusual or exciting experience (p. 86)
attempt	a try; effort (p. 97)
distance	the amount of space between things (p. 98)
impossible	not able to happen (p. 95)
remarkable	worth noticing because it is unusual (p. 89)
waterfall	a stream of water that falls from a high place to a lower place (p. 88)

Student Reader Unit 4 *This week students will read the following selections.*

86	**Famous Firsts**	Narrative Nonfiction
88	**Over Niagara Falls**	Narrative Nonfiction
96	**A Smoothie Sensation**	Realistic Fiction
104	**Guinness Book of World Records**	Expository Nonfiction
108	**4 You 2 Do**	Activity Page

Daily Lesson Plan

	ACTIVITIES	MATERIALS
Day 1	**Build Concepts** Weekly Concept: Being the First Vocabulary: *adventure, attempt, distance, impossible, remarkable, waterfall* **Word Work** Phonics: Vowels *oo* in *foot*, *u* in *put* **Read a Passage** "Famous Firsts," pp. 86–87 Comprehension: Use Strategies Reread for Fluency	Student Reader: Unit 4 Routine Cards 1, 3, 5, 6, 7 Tested Vocabulary Cards Sound-Spelling Card 38 Student White Boards AudioText Practice Book, p. 90, Vowels *oo* in *foot*, *u* in *put*
Day 2	**Reread for Fluency** **Word Work** Phonics: Suffixes *-ness, -less* Vocabulary **Comprehension** Compare and Contrast **Read a Passage** "Over Niagara Falls," pp. 88–95	Student Reader: Unit 4 AudioText Routine Cards 1, 2, 3, 4, 5, 7, 8 Tested Vocabulary Cards Student White Boards Graphic Organizer 3 or 4 Practice Book, p. 91, Suffixes *-ness, -less*
Day 3	**Reread for Fluency** **Word Work** Phonics: Vowels *oo* in *foot*, *u* in *put;* Suffixes *-ness, -less* Vocabulary **Read a Passage** "A Smoothie Sensation," pp. 96–103 Comprehension: Compare and Contrast **Write** Response to Literature	Student Reader: Unit 4 AudioText Routine Cards 1, 3, 4, 5, 7 Student journals Practice Book, pp. 90–92, Vowels *oo* in *foot*, *u* in *put;* Suffixes *-ness, -less;* Compare and Contrast
Day 4	**Reread for Fluency** **Word Work** Phonics: Spiral Review Vocabulary **Read a Passage** "Guinness Book of World Records," pp. 104–107 Comprehension: Compare and Contrast; Listening **Write** Response to Literature	Student Reader: Unit 4 AudioText Routine Cards 3, 4, 5 Student White Boards Practice Book, pp. 92–93, Compare and Contrast; Vocabulary
Day 5	**Assessment Options** Fluency, Comprehension Sentence Reading Passage Reading **Build Concepts** Vocabulary **Read to Connect** **Write** Response to Literature: "4 You 2 Do," p. 108	Student Reader: Unit 4 Reproducible p. 218 Sentence Reading Chart, p. 222 Student White Boards Fluency Progress Chart, p. 215 Routine Card 6 Practice Book, pp. 93–94, Vocabulary; Writing

ACTIVITY 1

Build Concepts

Vocabulary

	To Do	To Say
		10–15 minutes
Develop word meaning.	See Routine Card 6. Discuss pp. 85–87.	Read Words 2 to the Wise on p. 85. Have students turn to p. 86. **Look at the picture. What does it show?** (an airplane, a person who will fly in it) **What do you notice about this airplane and the person flying it?** (The airplane is open. The person flying is out in the open.) **Can you use the word *adventure* to describe this picture?** (Example: *It is an adventure to fly into the sky.)*
Scaffold instruction.	Create a concept web.	In the center of a web, write *Being the First.* **This week's concept is *being the first.*** Discuss what it means to be the first. **A first can be something that is made or built for the first time, like the first airplane, the first car, or the first computer. A first also can be a person who did something before anyone else did. For example, a person can be the first to attempt to fly in an airplane.** Have students turn to p. 87. **These people are remarkable because they were the first to do something.** Add the other vocabulary words. Discuss the meaning of each word as it relates to being the first, using the glossary as needed. (See p. 44 in this Teacher's Guide for definitions.) 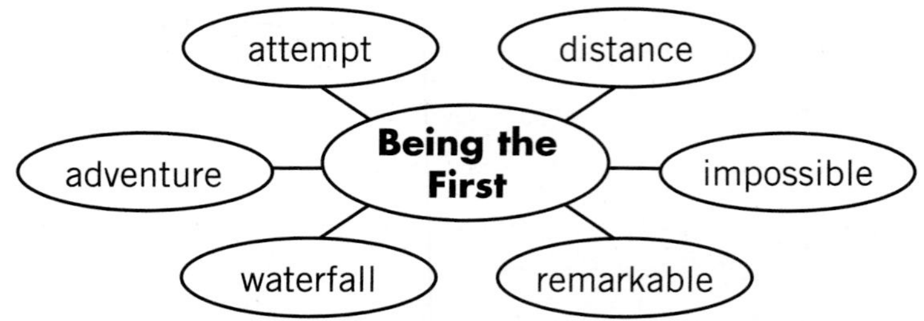
Model the multisyllabic word strategy.	Display each word. Say it as you display it.	Use the Tested Vocabulary Cards. Follow this routine for each word: • **Look for Meaningful Parts** Remind students to look for meaningful parts. **As you say each word, ask yourself: Do I see any parts I know?** • **Chunk Words with No Recognizable Parts** Model how to chunk the word *adventure* to read it.
	Think aloud.	• **Model** **I see a chunk at the beginning of the word: *ad.* I see a part in the middle: *ven.* I see a part at the end of the word: *ture.* I say each chunk slowly: *ad ven ture.* I say the chunks fast to make a whole word: *adventure.* Is it a real word? Yes, I know the word *adventure.*** • Have students practice reading each word.
Preview.	Read p. 84 with students.	**Did you see any of the words we just learned on this page?** Together with students, read the sentences on p. 84 describing each selection. Talk about how the concept words might be used in the selections.
MORE PRACTICE	Deepen understanding of *adventure.*	Have students demonstrate understanding by answering questions. **Which is more of an *adventure,* watching television or going for a hike in the woods? Why? Is it exciting to go on an adventure? Why? What kind of adventure would you like to go on?**

ACTIVITY 2

Word Work

Blending Strategy Vowels *oo* in *foot, u* in *put*

5–10 minutes

Routine

	To Do	To Say
Use the blending routine. **Scaffold instruction.**	Write *moon.*	**1 Connect** You already can read this word. What is the word? What is the vowel sound in *moon?* (/ü/) What two letters make the sound? *(oo)* Now you will learn another sound that is spelled with the letters *oo.*
	Display Sound-Spelling Card 38.	**2 Use Sound-Spelling Card** This is *book.* You can read a *book.* What sound do you hear in the middle of *book?* (/u̇/) Say it with me: /u̇/. The two letters *oo* both contribute to the sound /u̇/.
	Distribute white boards.	**3 Listen and Write** Write the letters *oo* for /u̇/. As you write, say the sound to yourself: /u̇/. Now say the sound aloud.
	Write *foot.*	**4 Model** The two letters *oo* in this word stand for /u̇/. This is how I blend this word: /f/ /u̇/ /t/, *foot.* The letters *oo* stand for the vowel sound.
	Write *put.*	Repeat with *put.* Point out that the sound /u̇/ can be spelled with *oo* or *u.* f oo t → → → p u t → → →
CORRECTIVE FEEDBACK	Write each practice word. Monitor student practice.	**5 Group Practice** Let's try the same thing with these words. Support students as they blend progressively more difficult words. Give feedback, using the *if . . . then* statements on Routine Card 1. look good hood pull full crook* shook brook* notebook wooden pullover* understood **6 Individual Practice** Have each student blend several words from the row best matched to his or her ability. wood bush full stood bulldog pudding footstep pushes armful overlook*
	Check understanding of practice words.	*Students need to make sense of words that they segment and blend. If needed, help students with meanings. A *crook* is someone who steals or does something else dishonest. A *brook* is a small stream. A *pullover* is a sweater you can pull over your head. *Overlook* is a verb that means to be able to look down over something. A window can *overlook* a garden.
MORE PRACTICE	Distribute white boards. Model building and spelling words.	**Build Words** Write *look.* Can you blend this word? (/l/ /u̇/ /k/) Have students write words on white boards. Write *look.* Now change the *l* in *look* to *t.* What is the new word? *(took)* • Change the *t* in *took* to *br.* What is the new word? *(brook)* • Change the *br* in *brook* to *sh.* What is the new word? *(shook)* • Change the *sh* in *shook* to *h.* What is the new word? *(hook)* • Add *ed* to the end of *hook.* What is the new word? *(hooked)*

ACTIVITY 3

Read a Passage

Build Background "Famous Firsts," pp. 86–87

	To Do	To Say *10 minutes*
Develop language and concepts.	See Routine Cards 3 and 7. Ask questions and elaborate on answers.	**Before Reading** Read the title aloud. Do a structured picture walk with students.
Scaffold instruction.	Key concepts: *dreamers, remarkable, impossible, adventure*	p. 86 **What machine do you see?** (an airplane) **How does it look different from airplanes you have seen or been in?** (Answers will vary.) **People travel all over the world in airplanes. How do airplanes make travel easier?** (It takes less time to get to a place.) **Why do you think traveling in an airplane would be a great adventure?** (Accept any reasonable response.) **It was once impossible for people to fly. People had to figure out how to build the first airplane. But first there needed to be dreamers who dreamed of flying as a means of travel.** p. 87 **Which picture shows the first president of the United States?** (top right picture) **Which picture do you think shows the first person to walk on the moon?** (Answers will vary.) **Let's read to find out about some firsts. As you read, ask yourself: What is this mainly about? What am I learning? Why are these people remarkable?**
Guide compre-hension.	Read pp. 86–87 aloud.	**During Reading** Read the selection as students follow along. Read aloud the picture captions. Then read it a second time, having students join in. If necessary, stop at the end of each paragraph to check comprehension. Ask questions to promote discussion and develop the concept. • **What examples of firsts are given in the selection?** • **Why is it important for dreamers to be hard workers too?** • **What words on the concept web could help you describe the people and machine pictured in this selection?**
	Use vocabulary to develop the concept.	**After Reading** **What are some firsts that you learned about? Choose a person from the selection. How did this person make a difference and do something that was once impossible?**

Reread for Fluency "Famous Firsts," p. 87

	To Do	To Say *5–10 minutes*
CORRECTIVE FEEDBACK	Monitor oral reading.	**Read p. 87 aloud. Read it three or four times so your reading gets better each time.** Give feedback on students' oral reading and use of the blending strategy. See Routine Cards 1 and 5.
MORE PRACTICE		Instead of rereading just p. 87, have students reread the entire selection three or four times. You may want to have students read along with the AudioText.

Homework Practice Book, p. 90, Phonics: Vowels *oo* in *foot*, *u* in *put*

ACTIVITY 1 Reread for Fluency

Paired Reading "Famous Firsts," p. 87

	To Do	To Say 5–10 minutes
CORRECTIVE FEEDBACK	Pair students. Monitor paired reading.	Students read aloud p. 87, switching readers for each paragraph. Have partners reread; now the other partner begins. For optimal fluency, students should reread three or four times. Give feedback, using Routine Card 5.
MORE PRACTICE		Instead of rereading just p. 87, have students reread the entire selection three or four times. You may want to have students read along with the AudioText.

ACTIVITY 2 Word Work

Blending Strategy Suffixes *-ness, -less*

	To Do	To Say 5–10 minutes (Routine)
Review blending routine.	Write *unsure* and *replay.*	**1 Connect** You studied words like this already. What do you know about reading them? (They contain prefixes that are separate syllables from the base words.) Today we will learn about adding suffixes *-ness* and *-less* to the ending of words. Each suffix has a specific meaning: *-ness* means "a state, condition, or quality" *-less* means "without" or "free of" or "free from"
Scaffold instruction.	Write *sadness.*	**2 Model** Point to *sadness.* This is a two-syllable word formed from the base word *sad* and the suffix *-ness.* You can cover the suffix, read the base word, and then blend the suffix and base word to read the whole word. What is the word? *(sadness)* What does it mean? ("a sad state") Let's blend this word together: *sad ness, sadness.*
	Write *homeless, careless,* and *happiness.*	Repeat with *homeless* ("without a home"), *careless* ("free from care"), and *happiness* ("a happy condition"). Note that in *happiness*, the base word is *happy.* The *y* in *happy* was changed to *i* before adding the *-ness* suffix. h a p p i n e s s
	Distribute white boards.	**3 Listen and Write** Have students write on white boards. Write the word *sad.* Write *ness* at the end of it. As you write, say the new word to yourself: *sadness.* Now say the word aloud. Do the same with *homeless.*
CORRECTIVE FEEDBACK	Write each practice word. Monitor student practice.	**4 Group Practice** Let's try the same thing with these words. Support students as they blend progressively more difficult words. Give feedback, using the *if . . . then* statements on Routine Card 1. sadness, shyness, homeless, careless fondness, coldness, painless, sightless silliness, happiness, carelessness **5 Individual Practice** Have each student blend several words from the row best matched to his or her ability. hopeless, leafless, softness, dryness tiredness, prettiness, soundless, playfulness friendless, forgiveness, effortless, heaviness

For more practice, see next page.

MORE PRACTICE

Model spelling words with suffixes.

Spell and Write You can spell words with suffixes by thinking about the suffix and the base word. What suffix and base word make up *sadness?* (*sad* and *-ness)* Start with the sounds in the base word: /sad/. What letters spell *sad?* Write *sad.* Now add the suffix *-ness.* Now spell *sadness.* Repeat with *gladness, endless,* and *wetness.*

Vocabulary

To Do	To Say	5 minutes
Review vocabulary. Display the concept web from Day 1.	Review the concept web. See Routine Card 2 for the multisyllabic word routine. The words *adventure, waterfall, remarkable,* and *impossible* will be in the selection you are reading today. Remind students that *waterfall* means "a stream of water that falls from a high place to a lower place."	
Deepen word understanding of *remarkable* and *impossible.*	*Remarkable* means "worth noticing." Think of an airplane. An airplane is a *remarkable* invention because it made it possible for people to fly. *Impossible* means "not able to happen." Before airplanes, it was *impossible* for people to fly. *Remarkable* can also describe people. Someone can have a *remarkable* smile, or a *remarkable* sense of humor. Can you name other things that might be remarkable about a person? (Answers may include skills, character, talents, and so on.) Sometimes people are remarkable because they do things that seem impossible. Look at the picture of the waterfall on pp. 88–89. Why would it be remarkable for a person to go over the falls or to walk on a tightrope over the falls? (Encourage discussion of how dangerous and scary it would be.) Why do you think people try to do these things that seem impossible? (They are brave, daring, and adventurous. They want to be the first.)	
Lead cumulative review.	Use the Tested Vocabulary Cards to review concept words from previous weeks.	

ACTIVITY 3 Comprehension

Compare and Contrast

To Do	To Say	5 minutes
Scaffold instruction. Introduce compare and contrast.	Today you will read about some real people who went over Niagara Falls. When you read about these people, pay attention to how they did it. Think about how these ways are alike and how they are different.	
Model the skill.	When I think about how two or more characters, ideas, or events are alike, I compare. When I think about how characters, ideas, or events are different, I contrast. As I read, I ask myself, "What things are alike? What things are different?"	
Distribute Graphic Organizer 3 or 4.	As you read "Over Niagara Falls," choose two people in the story to compare and contrast. List facts in your graphic organizer to tell how they are alike and how they are different. See Routine Card 8.	

ACTIVITY 4 Read a Passage

Reading "Over Niagara Falls," pp. 88–95

	To Do	To Say 10–15 minutes
Develop language and concepts.	See Routine Cards 3 and 7.	**Before Reading** Remind students that some people are remarkable because they do things that seem impossible. Read the title. Introduce proper nouns, if necessary. Do a structured picture walk with students.
	Ask questions and elaborate on answers.	pp. 88–89 **The selection is about people who went over Niagara Falls. How would you describe this waterfall?** (big, high, huge) **Notice that the water rushes down. The force of the waterfall is strong. Many people thought that it was impossible to survive going over Niagara Falls.**
Scaffold instruction.	Key concepts: *waterfall, remarkable, impossible, adventure, brave, fearless, famous*	pp. 90–91 **Look at the picture on the top left. What does it show?** (a woman standing beside a barrel) **This woman performed a remarkable act with that barrel. It was quite an adventure. Would you describe the woman as brave or fearless? Why?**
		pp. 92–93 **What are the people in these pictures doing?** (walking on a tightrope high over water) Point out that the tightrope is over Niagara Falls. **Do you think people did this just to become famous?**
		pp. 94–95 **This man is inside a rubber ball. He went over Niagara Falls in that ball.** Discuss reasons people might go over the waterfall in these ways. (to have an adventure, to see if they can do it, to become famous) Point out the time line on p. 95. **What does a time line show?** (events in order)
Guide compre-hension.	Use Routine Card 4.	**During Reading** **Read the pages in a whisper. Raise your hand if you need help with a word. As you read, ask yourself: What remarkable adventures did these people have going over the waterfall? How were these people brave and fearless?**
	Monitor independent reading.	pp. 88–91 **What remarkable adventure did Annie Taylor have?** (She went over Niagara Falls in a barrel. She was the first person to do this.)
	Model using context for word meaning.	Read aloud the paragraph with *remarkable* on p. 89. Explain how the other sentences in the paragraph provide clues to the meaning of *remarkable.*
		pp. 92–95 **How were The Great Blondin and Maria Spelterini alike?** (They both crossed Niagara Falls on a tightrope.) **What words would you use to describe all the people you read about?** (brave, fearless, famous) **Some people who tried died. What does this tell you about going over the falls?** (It is a very dangerous thing to do.)
Model summarizing.	Think aloud.	**After Reading** **What did you learn about the adventures people have had with Niagara Falls? What was the selection mainly about?** Model how to summarize. **The selection told details about remarkable ways people have gone over Niagara Falls. People have gone over the falls in a barrel, in a large rubber ball, and without anything. They have also walked over the falls on a tightrope.**
MORE PRACTICE	Have students reread p. 95.	**Reread** As they read, have students compare and contrast what Annie Taylor, Jean Lussier, and Roger Woodward did. Point out that all three went over Niagara Falls and lived, but each person did it in a different way.

Homework Practice Book, p. 91, Phonics: Suffixes *-ness, -less*

3

ACTIVITY 1 Reread for Fluency

Oral Reading "Over Niagara Falls," pp. 90–91

5–10 minutes

	To Do	To Say
CORRECTIVE FEEDBACK	Monitor oral reading.	**Read pp. 90–91 aloud. Read them three or four times so your reading gets better each time.** Give feedback on students' oral reading and use of the blending strategy. Use Routine Cards 1 and 5.
MORE PRACTICE		Instead of rereading just pp. 90–91, have students reread the entire selection three or four times. You may want to have students read along with the AudioText.

ACTIVITY 2 Word Work

Fluent Word Reading Vowels *oo* in *foot, u* in *put;* Suffixes *-ness, -less*

5–10 minutes

	To Do	To Say
Review phonics.	Review the homework.	Ask students to share answers from Practice Book pp. 90–91.
Use word-reading routine.	Write *dryness.*	**1 Connect** **You can read this word because you know that a word ending with *-ness* is often a two-syllable word formed from a base word and the suffix *-ness.* What is the base word?** *(dry)* **What is the word?** *(dryness)*
	Write *careless, wool,* and *pull.*	**2 Model** **When you come to a new word, look for meaningful parts. If you don't recognize any meaningful parts, then look for chunks you can read. Look at all the letters in the chunk and think about the vowel sound. Say the parts of the word to yourself, and then read the word.** Model reading *careless, wool,* and *pull* in this way. **When you come to a new word, what are you going to do?**
Scaffold instruction.	Write each practice word.	**3 Group Practice** **Let's read these words. Look for meaningful parts and chunks, think about the vowel sound in each chunk, and say the parts to yourself. We will read words with the sound *oo* in *foot* and *u* in *put,* and with the suffixes *-ness* and *-less.* When I point to the word, let's read it together.** Allow 2–3 seconds previewing time for each word. Support students as they blend progressively difficult words. **full stood pulled softness leafless newness friendless** **cooking happiness pointless wooden togetherness bulldog**
CORRECTIVE FEEDBACK	**MONITOR PROGRESS**	***If . . .*** students have difficulty previewing and reading whole words, ***then . . .*** have them use sound-by-sound blending. ***If . . .*** students can't read words fluently at a rate of 1–2 seconds per word, ***then . . .*** continue practicing the list.
MORE PRACTICE	Model reading words in sentences.	**When I read a sentence, I read each word without stopping between the words. If I come to a word I don't know, I blend it. Then I read the sentence again.** Model reading this sentence, stopping to blend *cooking: What are you cooking in the pot?*
	Write practice sentences.	Have each student read the sentence best matched to his or her ability. **The wind shook the bush.** **This book is about a fearless bull.** **The careless crook left countless clues.**

Routine

Vocabulary

5 minutes

	To Do	To Say
Review vocabulary.	Display the concept web from Day 1.	Review the concept web. **The words *attempt, distance,* and *impossible* will be in the selection you are reading today.** Review the meanings of the words.

ACTIVITY 3 Read a Passage

Reading "A Smoothie Sensation," pp. 96–103

10–15 minutes

	To Do	To Say
Scaffold instruction.	Review compare and contrast.	Remind students that they can compare and contrast information they read. **As you read "A Smoothie Sensation," pay attention to what Hannah does. Think about the ways she is the same as and different from the other people mentioned in the story. How is what she accomplishes different from the other things she tries to do?**
Develop language and concepts.	Use Routine Cards 3 and 7. Ask questions and elaborate on answers. Key concepts: *attempt, hopeful distance*	**Before Reading** Read the title. Do a structured picture walk. pp. 96–99 **What is the girl in the front of the picture attempting to do?** (stack pennies and later walk a distance with a bottle on her head) **Why are these hard to do?** (Pennies fall. Bottle won't stay on your head.) pp. 100–103 **What do the girls mix in the kiddie pools?** (milk, yogurt, and berries)
Guide comprehension.	Use Routine Card 4. Monitor independent reading.	**During Reading Read the pages in a whisper. Raise your hand if you need help with a word. As you read, ask yourself: What does Hannah do? Why does she do it? How is this the same as or different from what other people have done?** pp. 96–99 **Why does Hannah attempt to do the things she does?** (She wants to break a world record.) **How are her attempts alike so far?** (They haven't gotten her a world record.) pp. 100–103 **How does Hannah become a world-record holder at last?** (She makes the world's biggest smoothie.) **How is this attempt different from other things she tried to do?** (She did something she was good at.)
	Monitor comprehension. Guide retelling.	**After Reading** Discuss the What Do You Think? question. Have one student retell the story while the others assist. Prompt students by asking: **What does Hannah do first, next, and last? How is Hannah like other people in the *World Record Book?*** See Monitoring Retelling on p. 216.
MORE PRACTICE	Have students reread p. 100.	**Reread** As they read, tell students to think about how Hannah comes up with her next idea. How is it different from the other ideas she has come up with?

ACTIVITY 4 Write

Response to Literature

5 minutes

	To Do	To Say
Prompt journal writing.		**Take out your journals. Think about something you are good at. Write about a world record you would like to attempt.**

Homework Practice Book, p. 92, Compare/Contrast

4

ACTIVITY 1

Reread for Fluency

Paired Reading "A Smoothie Sensation," p. 99

	To Do	To Say *5–10 minutes*
CORRECTIVE FEEDBACK	Pair students. Monitor paired reading.	Students read aloud p. 99, switching readers for each paragraph. Have partners reread; now the other partner begins. For optimal fluency, students should reread three or four times. You may want to have students read along with the AudioText. Give feedback, using Routine Card 5.
MORE PRACTICE	**READERS' THEATER**	Students can use the dialogue as a script for a Readers' Theater. Have them rehearse, with one student being the narrator and the others the friends.

ACTIVITY 2

Word Work

Spiral Review Compounds and *oo* in *foot*

	To Do	To Say *5 minutes*
Review compounds and *oo* in *foot*.	Write *foot* and *book*.	**Look at these words. You can read these words because you have studied words that have the vowel sound /ů/ spelled *oo*.**
	Write *footstep* and *bookmark*.	**You can read these words because you have learned that compound words are made up of two words put together. When you say a compound word, you blend the two words together. Each of these compound words has a word with the vowel sound /ů/ spelled *oo*.** Have students identify the words that make up each compound.
Scaffold instruction. **CORRECTIVE FEEDBACK**	Distribute white boards. Monitor student work.	**Build Words** Write the three headings shown below. Distribute word cards with these words: *print, hard, ball, worm, store, case, stool, red.* Students tell where to add the words to make compound words. List the compounds as they name them. If students make an error, help them identify and blend the small words in the compound. Read the word and have students repeat after you. *book___* / bookcase / bookstore / bookworm *foot_____* / footprint / football / footstool *_____wood* / hardwood / redwood

Vocabulary

	To Do	To Say *5–10 minutes*
Extend word knowledge.	Write on the board or a transparency: *We had a picnic by the waterfall.*	Use the word *waterfall* to extend word knowledge. **We learned that *waterfall* means "a stream of water that falls from a high place to a lower place." The word *waterfall* is a compound word. What is a compound word?** (a word made up of two smaller words) **What two smaller words make up *waterfall*?** *(water, fall)* **What other compound words contain the word *fall*?** *(rainfall, snowfall)* **What other compound words contain the word *water*?** *(watercolor, waterproof, watermelon, waterway)* Write words as students name them. Draw a line (/) between the two words that make up each compound. Talk about the meanings of the compound words.
MORE PRACTICE	Deepen word understanding.	Have students use *distance* and *waterfall* in a sentence. (For example, *We walked a great distance to see the waterfall.*) Share sentences.

ACTIVITY 3 Read a Passage

Read Together "Guinness Book of World Records," pp. 104–107

	To Do	To Say *10–15 minutes*
Scaffold instruction.	Review compare and contrast (homework).	Ask volunteers to read the passage and share answers from Practice Book, p. 92. Remind students of the importance of comparing and contrasting. **When you read a selection, think about how characters, ideas, and events are alike and how they are different. Sometimes there are clue words, such as *like*, *in the same way*, *but*, *different*, and *unlike*. Often there are no clue words. As you read, ask yourself: What does this remind me of? How is this like other information I have read? How is it different?**
Develop language and concepts.	See Routine Cards 3 and 4. Display pp. 104–107.	**Before Reading** **This selection is about a famous book. The book tells about people and things that are remarkable and unusual. What do you see in the pictures?** (dog and apple, child looking up at tall man, skateboarder, cookie) **Let's read to find out more about how these things and people are remarkable.**
Model fluent reading.	Read pp. 104–107 aloud. Model prosody.	**During Reading** **Listen to my voice as I read this selection.** Read the selection with expression as students follow along. Read it a second time, having students point to each word. **Now read the selection aloud with me. Try to make your voice sound like mine as we read.** Reread the selection several times with students.
Monitor comprehension.	Monitor listening comprehension.	**After Reading** Prompt discussion to monitor comprehension. Listen as students answer questions. **How are all the people and things in the *Guinness Book of World Records* alike?** (They have all held world records.) **How are the dog and apple alike?** (They are about 5 inches tall.) **Which of these world records surprised you the most?** (Answers will vary.) **Summarize** Have one student describe the world records mentioned in the article while the others assist.
 **MORE PRACTICE**	Have students reread p. 104.	**Reread** As they read, tell students to look for information about what the *Guinness Book of World Records* is. After reading, they can tell a partner what they learned about the book.

ACTIVITY 4 Write

Response to Literature

	To Do	To Say *5 minutes*
Prompt expository writing.	Writing elements: support	**Tell how the record for the tall man and the record for the chocolate chip cookie are alike. Give details to support your statements.**

Homework Practice Book, p. 93, Vocabulary

5

ACTIVITY 1

Assessment Options

Sentence Reading

	To Do	To Say 5 minutes
Assess sentence reading.	Use reproducible p. 218.	Have each student read the sentences. Record scores on the Sentence Reading Chart, p. 222. While you work with one student, others can complete the Write Sentences activity below. **Our walk in the woods seemed endless.** **The happy bulldog jumped up with eagerness.** **Don't be careless when you put away my tools!**
CORRECTIVE FEEDBACK	**MONITOR PROGRESS**	***If . . .*** students have trouble reading words with *oo in foot, u in put,* or suffixes, ***then . . .*** reteach the blending strategy lessons on pp. 47 and 49. ***If . . .*** students misread a word in the sentence, ***then . . .*** correct the error and have them reread the word and then the sentence.
Practice sentence writing.	Provide white boards.	**Write Sentences** Have students copy the sentences from reproducible p. 218 on white boards. Have them confirm spellings by comparing the words they wrote to the words in the sentences.

Passage Reading

	To Do	To Say 5–10 minutes
Assess fluency and compre-hension.	Determine which students to assess this week.	Choose from these options: monitoring fluency (see pp. 214–215) and/or monitoring retelling (see p. 216). Have students read "A Smoothie Sensation." Be sure each student is assessed every other week.
		If you have time, assess every student.

ACTIVITY 2

Build Concepts

Vocabulary

	To Do	To Say 5–10 minutes
Review concept and vocabulary.	Review the homework. Display the concept web you began on Day 1.	Ask students to go over answers and share their writing from Practice Book, p. 93. **This week's question is *Why do people want to be the first to do something?* How do this week's words relate to the question?** Have students answer the question, using some of the vocabulary they learned this week. Ask them to add more words to the vocabulary web. Have students explain how each word relates to wanting to be first. Monitor students' understanding of vocabulary as they discuss the web. Use Routine Card 6.
MORE PRACTICE		Students can write sentences using three of the vocabulary words.

ACTIVITY 3 Read to Connect

Reread "Famous Firsts," pp. 86–87

	To Do	To Say *10 minutes*
Monitor compre-hension.	Have students reread "Famous Firsts" silently.	**As you read, think about what the selection says about being the first.** After rereading, ask: • **What kinds of firsts are described?** (first airplane, first U.S. president, first woman on U.S. Supreme Court, first person on the moon) • **How are people who become firsts role models?** (They show others how to dream and work to make their dreams come true.) **We also read "Over Niagara Falls." Find that selection. What firsts are described?** Record students' ideas. **We also read "A Smoothie Sensation." What was the girl in that story trying to do?** Record students' ideas.
Make connections.	Have students make connections across texts.	**What can you say about people who want to become the first to do something?** (Sample answers: They are dreamers. They are brave. They don't give up. They want to be famous.)

ACTIVITY 4 Write

Response to Literature "4 You 2 Do," p. 108

	To Do	To Say *5–10 minutes*
Guide response activities.	Discuss the directions. Tell students to choose one activity to complete. Monitor handwriting. See pp. 227–229.	**Word Play** Have students work in pairs to create a sign using as many of the week's concept words as possible. (Possible answer: "After many attempts, Lopez crossed an impossible distance in this remarkable adventure.") **Making Connections** Discuss the question in a group or in pairs. (Possible answer: Both break a world record; Hannah is make-believe and a child, while Anne was a real person and an adult.) **On Paper** Brainstorm ideas with the group before students write. For example, students might write about accomplishments in sports or about being the youngest to do something, such as get drafted by a professional sports team or attend medical school. Have them write their own responses. Students can use Practice Book, p. 94, to help prepare their written response, or you can send the Practice Book page home for them to complete later.
MORE PRACTICE		If you have more time, direct students to complete all the activities.

Homework Practice Book, p. 94, Writing

Unit 4 Week 5 *People and Animals*

How do people and animals adjust to each other?

Objectives *This week students will ...*

Vocabulary
- build concepts and vocabulary: *adjust, adult, communicate, mimic, opportunity, realize*

Phonics
- blend and read words with short *e: ea* and prefixes *mis-, dis-*
- apply knowledge of letter-sounds and word structure to decode unknown words when reading

Text Comprehension
- read connected text
- use main idea to improve comprehension
- write in response to literature

Fluency
- practice fluency with oral rereading

Word Work *This week's phonics focus is ...*

Short *e: ea* Prefixes *mis-, dis-*

Concept Words *Tested Vocabulary*

The week's vocabulary is related to the concept of people and animals. The first appearance of each word in the Student Reader is noted below.

adjust	to get used to something new and different (p. 112)
adult	a grown up person or animal (p. 116)
communicate	to give or exchange information or news (p. 112)
mimic	to copy closely; imitate (p. 122)
opportunity	a good chance to do something (p. 122)
realize	to understand well (p. 116)

Student Reader Unit 4 *This week students will read the following selections.*

112	**Having a New Pet**	Expository Nonfiction
116	**Making Friends with Gorillas**	Narrative Nonfiction
124	**A Chimp's New Home**	Narrative Nonfiction
132	**Helping Each Other**	Expository Nonfiction
134	**4 You 2 Do**	Activity Page

Daily Lesson Plan

	ACTIVITIES	MATERIALS
Day 1	**Build Concepts** Weekly Concept: People and Animals Vocabulary: *adjust, adult, communicate, mimic, opportunity, realize* **Word Work** Phonics: Short *e* Spelled *ea* **Read a Passage** "Having a New Pet," pp. 112–115 Comprehension: Use Strategies Reread for Fluency	Student Reader: Unit 4 Routine Cards 1, 3, 5, 6, 7 Tested Vocabulary Cards Sound-Spelling Card 9 Student White Boards AudioText Practice Book, p. 95, Short *e* Spelled *ea*
Day 2	**Reread for Fluency** **Word Work** Phonics: Prefixes *mis-, dis-* Vocabulary **Comprehension** Main Idea **Read a Passage** "Making Friends with Gorillas," pp. 116–123	Student Reader: Unit 4 AudioText Routine Cards 1, 2, 3, 4, 5, 7, 8 Tested Vocabulary Cards Student White Boards Graphic Organizer 1 Practice Book, p. 96, Prefixes *mis-, dis-*
Day 3	**Reread for Fluency** **Word Work** Phonics: Short *e* Spelled *ea;* Prefixes *mis-, dis-* Vocabulary **Read a Passage** "A Chimp's New Home," pp. 124–131 Comprehension: Main Idea **Write** Response to Literature	Student Reader: Unit 4 AudioText Routine Cards 1, 3, 4, 5, 7 Student journals Practice Book, pp. 95–97, Short *e* Spelled *ea;* Prefixes *mis-, dis-*; Main Idea
Day 4	**Reread for Fluency** **Word Work** Phonics: Spiral Review Vocabulary **Read a Passage** "Helping Each Other," pp. 132–133 Comprehension: Main Idea; Listening **Write** Response to Literature	Student Reader: Unit 4 AudioText Routine Cards 3, 4, 5 Student White Boards Practice Book, pp. 97–98, Main Idea; Vocabulary
Day 5	**Assessment Options** Fluency, Comprehension Sentence Reading End-of-Unit Test **Build Concepts** Vocabulary **Read to Connect** **Write** Response to Literature: "4 You 2 Do," p. 134	Student Reader: Unit 4 Reproducible p. 218 Sentence Reading Chart, p. 222 Student White Boards Fluency Progress Chart, p. 215 Routine Card 6 Practice Book, pp. 98–99, Vocabulary; Writing Assessment Book, p. 50

See pp. xvi–xvii for how *My Sidewalks* integrates instructional practices for ELL.
See pp. 251–254 for Phonemic Awareness Activities.

ACTIVITY 1

Build Concepts

Vocabulary

10–15 minutes

	To Do	To Say
Develop word meaning.	See Routine Card 6. Discuss pp. 111–115.	Read Words 2 the Wise on p. 111. Have students look at pp. 112–115. **What do you notice?** (people and animals) **These animals are pets. Can you use the words *communicate* and *adjust* to describe any of these pictures?** (Examples: *When you hug a pet, you communicate love. Pets and people adjust to each other.*)
Scaffold instruction.	Create a concept web.	In the center of a web, write *People and Animals.* **This week's concept is *people and animals.* People and animals all share the planet Earth. Some people have animals for pets. People have to adjust their lives to take care of their pets. What are some things people do to care for their pets?** (Examples: feed them, take them for walks, give them love, play with them) Add the other vocabulary words. Discuss the meaning of each word as it relates to people and animals, using the glossary as needed. (See p. 58 in this Teacher's Guide for definitions.)
Model the multisyllabic word strategy.	Display each word. Say it as you display it. Think aloud.	Use the Tested Vocabulary Cards. Follow this routine for each word: • **Look for Meaningful Parts** Remind students to look for meaningful parts. **As you say each word, ask yourself: Do I see any parts I know?** • **Chunk Words with No Recognizable Parts** Model how to chunk the word *opportunity* to read it. • **Model** **I see a chunk at the beginning of the word: *op.* I see parts in the middle: *por, tu, ni.* I see a part at the end of the word: *ty.* I say each chunk slowly: *op por tu ni ty.* I say the chunks fast to make a whole word: *opportunity.* Is it a real word? Yes, I know the word *opportunity.*** • Have students practice reading each word.
Preview.	Read p. 110 with students.	**Did you see any of the words we just learned on this page?** Together with students, read the sentences on p. 110 describing each selection. Talk about how the concept words might be used in the selections.
MORE PRACTICE	Deepen understanding of *mimic.*	Have students demonstrate understanding by each making a gesture and then calling on a volunteer to mimic that gesture. Have students work in pairs. Students take turns making a gesture or a sound. The other student mimics. **What do you do when you mimic?** (You copy someone else's moves or sounds.)

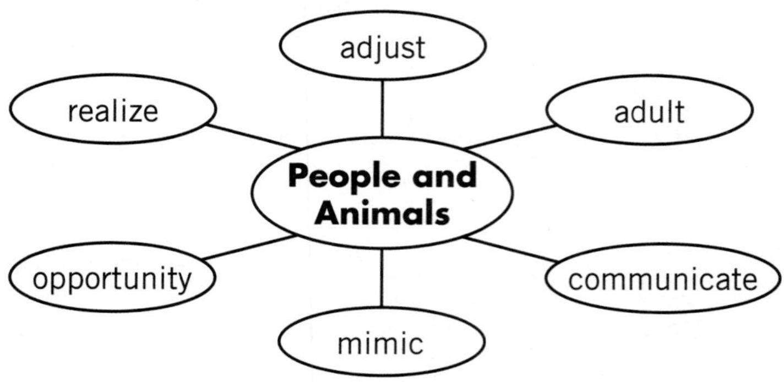

ACTIVITY 2 Word Work

Blending Strategy Short *e* Spelled *ea*

5–10 minutes

Routine

	To Do	To Say
Use the blending routine. **Scaffold instruction.**	Write *boat.*	**1 Connect** You can read this word. What is the word? *(boat)* What is the vowel sound in *boat?* (/ō/) What letters make the sound? *(oa)* You will learn another sound that can be spelled with two letters.
	Display Sound-Spelling Card 9. Write *head.*	**2 Use Sound-Spelling Card** This is *elephant.* What sound do you hear at the beginning of elephant? (/e/) Say it with me: /e/. This sound can be made by the letter *e.* Point to the elephant's head. Write *head* on the board. What sound do you hear in the middle of *head?* (/e/) Say it with me: /e/. The letters *ea* both contribute to the sound /e/. In some words the letters *ea* are pronounced /ē/. The word *read* can be pronounced /red/ or /rēd/. When you read how that word is used in a sentence, you can figure out which pronunciation to use.
	Distribute white boards.	**3 Listen and Write** Write the letters *ea* for /e/. As you write, say the sound to yourself: /e/. Now say the sound aloud. **4 Model** The two letters *ea* in this word stand for /e/. This is how I blend this word: /h/ /e/ /d/, *head.* Now you try: /h/ /e/ /d/, *head.* h ea d
CORRECTIVE FEEDBACK	Write each practice word. Monitor student practice.	**5 Group Practice** Let's try the same thing with these words. Support students as they blend progressively more difficult words. Give feedback, using the *if . . . then* statements on Routine Card 1. deaf head ready bread dread* sweater heavy meant breath thread already meadow* **6 Individual Practice** Have each student blend several words from the row best matched to his or her ability. dead steady* sweat weapon threat feather health weather leather
	Check understanding of practice words.	*Students need to make sense of words that they segment and blend. If needed, help students with meanings. When you *dread* something, you are afraid of it. A *meadow* is a field of grass. *Steady* can mean not changing much. A snowfall can be *steady.* *Steady* can also mean regular. A customer who always shops at the same store is a *steady* customer.
MORE PRACTICE	Distribute white boards. Model building and spelling words.	**Build Words** Write *dead.* Can you blend this word? (/d/ /e/ /d/) Have students write words on white boards. Write *dead.* Now change the *d* in *dead* to *dr.* What is the new word? *(dread)* • Change the *dr* in *dread* to *thr.* What is the new word? *(thread)* • Change the *thr* in *thread* to *spr.* What is the new word? *(spread)* • Change the *spr* in *spread* to *br.* What is the new word? *(bread)* • Add *ginger* to the beginning of *bread.* What is the new word? *(gingerbread)*

ACTIVITY 3

Read a Passage

Build Background "Having a New Pet," pp. 112–115

10 minutes

	To Do	To Say
Develop language and concepts.	See Routine Cards 3 and 7.	**Before Reading** Read the title aloud. Introduce proper nouns, if necessary. Do a structured picture walk with students.
	Ask questions and elaborate on answers.	p. 112–113 **Look at all the pictures. What are these pictures mainly about?** (pets and people) **The boy is brushing his dog. Where is the dog's paw?** (on the boy's leg) **This communicates to the boy that the dog trusts him.**
Scaffold instruction.	Key concepts: *adjust, communicate, realize*	p. 114–115 **Look at the picture on p. 114. What do you realize about the person? What kind of job does this person have? What is she doing?** (The person is a doctor who takes care of pets. She is checking the cat's health.) **Let's read to find out about how people and pets adjust to each other and communicate with each other. As you read, ask yourself: What is this mainly about? What am I learning?**
Guide compre-hension.	Read pp. 112–115 aloud.	**During Reading** Read the selection as students follow along. Then read it a second time, having students join in. If necessary, stop at the end of each paragraph to check comprehension. Ask questions to promote discussion and develop the concept. • **What things do you need to do to take care of a pet?** • **How can families work together to care for a pet?** • **What can people do to keep a pet healthy?** • **What words on the concept web could help you describe the people and things pictured in this selection?**
	Use vocabulary to develop the concept.	**After Reading** **What are some things you learned about people and pets? How do pets *adjust* to people? How do people *adjust* to pets?**

Reread for Fluency "Having a New Pet," p. 112

5–10 minutes

	To Do	To Say
CORRECTIVE FEEDBACK	Monitor oral reading.	**Read p. 112 aloud. Read it three or four times so your reading gets better each time.** Give feedback on students' oral reading and use of the blending strategy. See Routine Cards 1 and 5.
MORE PRACTICE		Instead of rereading just p. 112, have students reread the entire selection three or four times. You may want to have students read along with the AudioText.

Homework Practice Book, p. 95, Phonics: Short *e* Spelled *ea*

ACTIVITY 1 Reread for Fluency

Paired Reading "Having a New Pet," p. 114

	To Do	To Say 5–10 minutes
CORRECTIVE FEEDBACK	Pair students. Monitor paired reading.	Students read aloud p. 114, switching readers for each paragraph. Have partners reread; now the other partner begins. For optimal fluency, students should reread three or four times. Give feedback, using Routine Card 5.
MORE PRACTICE		Instead of rereading just p. 114, have students reread the entire selection three or four times. You may want to have students read along with the AudioText.

ACTIVITY 2 Word Work

Blending Strategy Prefixes *mis-*, *dis-*

	To Do	To Say 5–10 minutes
Use the blending routine.	Write *undo* and *retell.*	Routine **1 Connect** You studied words like these already. What do you know about reading them? (They contain prefixes that are separate syllables from the base word.) Today we will learn about adding the prefixes *mis-* and *dis-* to the beginning of words. Each prefix has a specific meaning: *mis-* means "bad" or "wrong" *dis-* means "not" or "opposite of"
Scaffold instruction.	Write *mislead.*	**2 Model** Point to *mislead.* This is a two-syllable word formed from the prefix *mis-* and the base word *lead.* Let's cover the prefix, read the base word, and then blend the prefix and base word to read the whole word. *(mis lead, mislead)* What is the word? *(mislead)* What does it mean? ("to lead someone the wrong way") dis trust
	Write *distrust, misplace,* and *dishonest.*	Repeat with *distrust* ("not trust"), *misplace* ("to put something in the wrong place"), and *dishonest* ("not honest").
	Distribute white boards.	**3 Listen and Write** Have students write on white boards. Write the word *lead.* Write *mis* at the beginning of it. As you write, say the new word to yourself: *mislead.* Now say the word aloud. Do the same with *distrust.*
CORRECTIVE FEEDBACK	Write each practice word. Monitor student practice.	**4 Group Practice** Let's try the same thing with these words. Support students as they blend progressively more difficult words. Give feedback, using the *if . . . then* statements on Routine Card 1. disband misfit misprint disown dislike disband disobey dismount misspell disappear misbehave mispronounce **5 Individual Practice** Have each student blend several words from the row better matched to his or her ability. mismatch displease mistrust discount misbehave disown misunderstand

For more practice, see next page.

MORE PRACTICE

Model spelling words with prefixes.	**Spell and Write** You can spell words with prefixes by thinking about the prefix and the base word. What prefix and base word make up *misfit?* (*mis-* and *fit*) Start with the sounds in the base word: /fit/. What letters spell *fit?* Write *fit.* Now add the prefix *mis-.* Now spell *misfit.* Repeat with *disarm, disorder, mistook, mismatch, disconnect,* and *misfile.*

Vocabulary

5 minutes

	To Do	To Say
Review vocabulary.	Display the concept web from Day 1.	Review the concept web. See Routine Card 2 for the multisyllabic word routine. The words *adult, communicate, opportunity, mimic,* and *realize* will be in the selection you are reading today. Remind students that *mimic* means "to copy or imitate how someone else acts or talks."
	Deepen word understanding of *communicate* and *opportunity.*	How do people communicate with each other? (talk, write, make gestures) Think of an animal. Tell about a way that it communicates with other animals. Does it communicate with people? How? (Discuss examples, such as the sounds that dogs, birds, cats, and cows make and movements such as tail wagging.) *Opportunity* means "a chance to do something." What do you think you would do if you had an opportunity to go to Africa and observe animals in their habitats? Would you do it? Why or why not?
Lead cumulative review.		Use the Tested Vocabulary Cards to review concept words from previous weeks.

ACTIVITY 3 Comprehension

Main Idea

5 minutes

	To Do	To Say
Scaffold instruction.	Introduce main idea.	Today you will read about a woman who had an opportunity to make friends with gorillas. As you read the selection, think about what the main idea is. The main idea is the most important idea about the topic.
	Model the skill.	A main idea is sometimes stated in a sentence within a paragraph. When the main idea is not stated, you must figure it out on your own and state it in your own words. As you read, ask yourself: What is the story all about? Think about the details or information the author gives that tell about the main idea. These details support the main idea.
	Distribute Graphic Organizer 1.	As you read "Making Friends with Gorillas," look for the main idea of the selection. Look for details that support the main idea. Use Graphic Organizer 1 to write the main idea and the supporting details. See Routine Card 8.

ACTIVITY 4 Read a Passage

Reading "Making Friends with Gorillas," pp. 116–123

	To Do	To Say
		10–15 minutes
Develop language and concepts.	See Routine Cards 3 and 7. Ask questions and elaborate on answers.	**Before Reading** Remind students what they learned about how people and animals communicate. Read the title. Introduce proper nouns, if necessary. Do a structured picture walk with students. pp. 116–118 **The selection is about a woman who studied and became friends with gorillas. Look at the gorillas. What words would you use to describe a gorilla?** (large, strong, powerful) **Would you like an opportunity to study gorillas? Why or why not?**
Scaffold instruction.	Key concepts: *communicate, mimic, observe, opportunity, realize, trust*	pp. 119–123 **Scientists observe animals to learn about them. What are some of the things you observe the gorillas doing?** (eating, resting, communicating) Point to the map on p. 120. **This map shows where gorillas live. They live in countries called the Democratic Republic of Congo, Uganda, and Rwanda. These countries are in Africa. Look at the picture on p. 121. What do you think the gorilla is communicating?** (Stay away!)
Guide compre-hension.	Use Routine Card 4.	**During Reading** **Read the pages in a whisper. Raise your hand if you need help with a word. As you read, ask yourself: What is the main idea? What are the supporting details that give information about the main idea?**
	Monitor independent reading.	pp. 116–119 **Why did Dian need to get close to the gorillas?** (to observe how they act) **What did Dian realize she had to do first?** (She had to watch the gorillas from far away.) **Do you think this was a good way to gain the trust of the gorillas?**
	Model using context for word meaning.	Read aloud the paragraph with *charged* on p. 117. Explain how the phrases "ran toward" and "yelled and screamed" provide clues to the meaning of *charged*.
		pp. 120–123 **What did Dian mimic as she moved closer to the gorillas?** (She mimicked the happy noises they made.) **How did a gorilla act like a friend to her?** (He realized that she felt sad and hugged and patted her.)
Model summarizing.	Think aloud.	**After Reading** **What did you learn about how people and animals adjust to each other? What was the selection mainly about?** Model how to summarize. **The selection told about the things that Dian did to gain the gorillas' trust so that she could get closer to them. In the end, she made friends with them, and the gorillas accepted her.**
MORE PRACTICE	Have students reread p. 119.	**Reread** As they read, have students note the details that support the main idea "making friends with gorillas." Point out that Dian knew she had to gain the gorillas' trust. She watched them as they looked for food and played together. She worked at being a friend to the gorillas.

Homework Practice Book, p. 96, Phonics: Prefixes *mis-, dis-*

3

ACTIVITY 1

Reread for Fluency

Oral Reading "Making Friends with Gorillas," pp. 122–123

5–10 minutes

	To Do	To Say
CORRECTIVE FEEDBACK	Monitor oral reading.	**Read pp. 122–123 aloud. Read them three or four times so your reading gets better each time.** Give feedback on students' oral reading and use of the blending strategy. Use Routine Cards 1 and 5.
MORE PRACTICE		Instead of rereading just pp. 122–123, have students reread the entire selection three or four times. You may want to have students read along with the AudioText.

ACTIVITY 2

Word Work

Fluent Word Reading Short *e* Spelled *ea*; Prefixes *mis-, dis-*

5–10 minutes

	To Do	To Say
Review phonics.	Review the homework.	Ask students to share answers from Practice Book, pp. 95–96.
Use word-reading routine.	Write *dislike.*	Routine **1 Connect** **You can read this word because you know that a word beginning with *dis-* is a word formed from a base word and the prefix *dis-*. What is the base word?** *(like)* **What is the word?** *(dislike)*
	Write *mistake* and *pleasure.*	**2 Model** **When you come to a new word, look for meaningful parts. If you don't recognize any meaningful parts, then look for chunks you can read. Look at all the letters in the chunk and think about the vowel sound. Say the parts of the word to yourself, and then read the word.** Model reading *mistake* and *pleasure* in this way. **When you come to a new word, what are you going to do?**
Scaffold instruction.	Write each practice word.	**3 Group Practice** **Let's read these words. Look for meaningful parts and chunks, think about the vowel sound in each chunk, and say the parts to yourself. We will read words with a short *e* spelled *ea* and with the prefixes *mis-* and *dis-*. When I point to the word, let's read it together.** Allow 2–3 seconds previewing time for each word. Support students as they blend progressively more difficult words. **head bread death misdeed instead pleasant** **discover bedspread weather disrespect disappoint misunderstand**
CORRECTIVE FEEDBACK	**MONITOR PROGRESS**	***If . . .*** students have difficulty previewing and reading whole words, ***then . . .*** have them use sound-by-sound blending. ***If . . .*** students can't read words fluently at a rate of 1–2 seconds per word, ***then . . .*** continue practicing the list.
MORE PRACTICE	Model reading words in sentences. Write practice sentences.	**When I read a sentence, I read each word without stopping between the words. If I come to a word I don't know, I blend it. Then I read the sentence again.** Model reading this sentence, stopping to blend *instead: Would you like to see a movie or read a book instead?* Have each student read the sentence best matched to his or her ability. **I dislike bread.** **We discovered a treasure.** **No one dislikes pleasant weather.**

Vocabulary

	To Do	To Say 5 minutes
Review vocabulary.	Display the concept web from Day 1.	Review the concept web. **The words *adjust, adult,* and *opportunity* will be in the selection you read today.** Review the meanings of the words.

ACTIVITY 3 Read a Passage

Reading "A Chimp's New Home," pp. 124–131

	To Do	To Say 10–15 minutes
Scaffold instruction.	Review main idea.	Remind students that a main idea can be stated or not stated. **As you read "A Chimp's New Home," look for information that tells the main idea. Look for details that support the main idea.**
Develop language and concepts.	Use Routine Cards 3 and 7.	**Before Reading** Read the title. Introduce proper nouns, if needed. Do a structured picture walk.
	Ask questions and elaborate on answers.	pp. 124–127 **Look at the pictures of the adult chimpanzee. How do you think the chimpanzee feels?** (The chimpanzee seems upset or sad.) **What clue tells you that this chimpanzee is not in its natural habitat?** (the toy animals on p. 127)
	Key concepts: *adult, adjust, diet, habitat, health*	pp. 128–131 **The chimpanzees seem to be adjusting to the new environment. What are they doing?** (swinging from a tree, playing with different toys) **Why do you think this is good for the chimps' health?** (They keep busy and active.)
Guide compre-hension.	Use Routine Card 4.	**During Reading** **Read the pages in a whisper. Raise your hand if you need help with a word. As you read, ask yourself: What is this selection all about?**
	Monitor independent reading.	pp. 124–126 **In what ways did Denyse live like a human?** (She ate human foods; she had human "parents"; she did not see other chimps.) pp. 127–131 **How was Denyse's new home at the conservation center different?** (There were many other apes. It was a place for apes, with outdoor habitats and swings and toys.) **Why did it take time for Denyse to adjust to her new home?** (She had to get used to being in a new place and to eating new foods.)
	Monitor comprehension.	**After Reading** Discuss the What Do You Think? question.
	Guide retelling.	Have one student retell the story while the others assist. Prompt students by asking: **Where did Denyse live at the beginning? Why did she move? Where did she move to?** See Monitoring Retelling on p. 216.
MORE PRACTICE	Have students reread p. 129.	**Reread** As they read, tell students to think about things apes need in order to be happy and healthy.

ACTIVITY 4 Write

Response to Literature

	To Do	To Say 5 minutes
Prompt journal writing.		**Take out your journals. Which place do you think is a better place for a chimpanzee to live, in a human home or in the ape home? Write your opinion.**

Homework Practice Book, p. 97, Main Idea

4

ACTIVITY 1

Reread for Fluency

Paired Reading "A Chimp's New Home," pp. 126–127

	To Do	To Say (5–10 minutes)
CORRECTIVE FEEDBACK	Pair students. Monitor paired reading.	Students read aloud pp. 126–127, switching readers for each paragraph. Have partners reread; now the other partner begins. For optimal fluency, students should reread three or four times. You may want to have students read along with the AudioText. Give feedback, using Routine Card 5.
MORE PRACTICE	**READERS' THEATER**	Adapt the story of Denyse and her family by adding dialogue. Let students use it as a Readers' Theater.

ACTIVITY 2

Word Work

Spiral Review Vowel Sound of *ew, ue, oo (moon)*

	To Do	To Say (5 minutes)
Review blending words with *ew, ue, oo.*	Write *moon.*	Look at this word. You can read this word because you know *oo* can stand for /ü/. What is the word? *(moon)*
	Write *knew* and *glue.*	Look at both of these words. The letters *ew* and the letters *ue* both stand for /ü/. What sound does *ew* stand for? (/ü/) What is the word? *(knew)* What sound does *ue* stand for? (/ü/) What is the word? *(glue)* What letters spell the vowel sound in *knew? (ew)* What letters spell the vowel sound in *glue? (ue)*
Scaffold instruction.	Distribute white boards.	**Sort Words** Write *oo, ew,* and *ue* as headings. Have students copy the chart. Let's sort words by vowel spellings. When I say a word, tell me where to write it.
CORRECTIVE FEEDBACK	Monitor student work.	Write each word in the appropriate column and underline the letters that stand for the vowel sound. If students make an error, say and spell the word. Ask students to identify the pattern and repeat the word after you. Have students read the completed lists and write the words on their own charts.

oo	*ew*	*ue*
fool	dew	clue
cool	grew	avenue
soon	threw	blue

Vocabulary

	To Do	To Say (5–10 minutes)
Extend word knowledge.	Write on the board or a transparency: *I realize that the dog needs to go for a walk.*	Use the word *realize* to extend word knowledge. We learned earlier this week that *realize* means "to understand well." Circle the word *real* in *realize.* The word *realize* has the word *real* in it. *Real* means "true, not imaginary." Can you think of other words that have the word *real* in them? *(really, reality, realistic, unreal, unrealistic)* Write these words and discuss their meanings. Point out that *unreal* and *unrealistic* have the prefix *un-*, meaning "not."
MORE PRACTICE	Deepen word understanding.	Have students choose one of the words that contains *real* and use that word in a sentence. (For example, *I had a really good time at the party. The dinosaur in the film looked realistic.*) Share sentences.

ACTIVITY 3 Read a Passage

Read Together "Helping Each Other," pp. 132–133

10–15 minutes

	To Do	To Say
Scaffold instruction.	Review main idea (homework).	Ask volunteers to share their work from Practice Book, p. 97. Remind students of the importance of identifying the main idea and supporting details. **When you read a selection, ask yourself: What is this mainly about? Remember that the main idea can be stated in the selection. If it isn't, the reader must figure it out from information given.**
Develop language and concepts.	See Routine Cards 3 and 4.	**Before Reading** Introduce and pronounce the names of different animals prior to reading the selection. **This selection tells about different pairs of animals that help each other in different ways. Look at the alligator and the bird on p. 132. How do you think these two animals help each other?** (Responses will vary. Example: The bird might be cleaning the alligator's mouth.) **Let's read to find out ways animals help each other out.**
Model fluent reading.	Read pp. 132–133 aloud. Model prosody.	**Reading** **Listen to my voice as I read this selection.** Read the selection with expression as students follow along. Read it a second time, having students point to each word. **Now read the selection aloud with me. Try to make your voice sound like mine as we read.** Reread the selection several times with students.
Monitor compre-hension.	Monitor listening comprehension.	**After Reading** Prompt discussion to monitor comprehension listen as students answer questions. **In which relationships does one animal get food and the other animal get cleaned?** (the grouper and smaller cleaning fish; the crocodile and plover) **Why do the honeyguide bird and the honey badger need each other?** (The bird leads the badger to the beehive and the badger opens the hive.) **Which two animals helping each other surprised you the most?** (Answers will vary.) **Summarize** Have one student name an animal mentioned in the selection. Have another student name the animal that helps it and is helped by it.
	Have students reread p. 133.	**Reread** As they read, tell students to look for information about how swimming above sea anemones helps protect the clownfish. After reading, they can tell a partner what they learned about the animals that help each other.

ACTIVITY 4 Write

Response to Literature

5 minutes

	To Do	To Say
Prompt expository writing.	Writing elements: focus	**Tell about which animals make food that both the honey badgers and the honeyguide birds eat and how these animals get that food.**

Homework Practice Book, p. 98, Vocabulary

5

ACTIVITY 1 Assessment Options

Sentence Reading

	To Do	To Say — 5 minutes
Assess sentence reading.	Use reproducible p. 218.	Have each student read the sentences. Record scores on the Sentence Reading Chart, p. 222. While you work with one student, others can complete the Write Sentences activity below. **Do you dislike this leather bag?** **I already fixed that mistake on the test.** **The baker discounts bread that is a day old.**
CORRECTIVE FEEDBACK	**MONITOR PROGRESS**	***If . . .*** students have trouble reading words with *short e* spelled *ea* or prefixes *mis-* and *dis-*, ***then . . .*** reteach the blending strategy lessons on pp. 61 and 63. ***If . . .*** students misread a word in the sentence, ***then . . .*** correct the error and have them reread the word and then the sentence.
Practice sentence writing.	Provide white boards.	**Write Sentences** Have students copy the sentences from reproducible p. 218 on white boards. Have them confirm spellings by comparing the words they wrote to the words in the sentences.

End-of-Unit Test

	To Do	To Say — 10 minutes
Assess fluency and compre-hension.	Use the Assessment Book, p. 50.	Options for end-of-unit assessment are available in the Assessment Book.

ACTIVITY 2 Build Concepts

Vocabulary

	To Do	To Say — 5–10 minutes
Review concept and vocabulary.	Review the homework. Display the concept web you began on Day 1.	Ask students to go over answers and share their writing from Practice Book, p. 98. **This week's question is *How do people and animals adjust to each other?* How do this week's words relate to the question?** (Have students answer the question, using some of the vocabulary they learned this week.) Ask students to add more words to the vocabulary web. Have students explain how each word relates to people and animals. Monitor students' understanding of vocabulary as they discuss the web. See Routine Card 6.
MORE PRACTICE		Students can write sentences using three of the vocabulary words.

ACTIVITY 3 Read to Connect

Reread "Having a New Pet," p. 112

	To Do	To Say *5 minutes*
Monitor comprehension.	Have students read part of "Having a New Pet" silently.	**As you read, think about what the selection says about caring for a pet.** After rereading, ask: • **What does a pet need to do in a new home?** (adjust) • **What must families do?** (work together and communicate) **We also read "Making Friends with Gorillas." Find that selection. How did Dian make friends with gorillas?** (by observing them and getting them to trust her) **We also read "A Chimp's New Home." What is the main idea of that selection?** (Denyse the chimp adjusts to her new home at the ape conservation center.)
Make connections.	Have students make connections across texts.	**What did you learn about people and animals?** (Sample answers: Some animals live as pets with people. Some people observe animals in their own habitats. Animals have different ways to communicate. People treat pets as family members.)

ACTIVITY 4 Write

Response to Literature "4 You 2 Do," p. 134

	To Do	To Say *5–10 minutes*
Guide response activities.	Discuss the directions. Tell students to choose one activity to complete. Monitor handwriting. See pp. 227–229.	**Word Play** Have students complete the list on their own and then meet with a partner to share word lists. **Making Connections** Discuss the question in a group or in pairs. (Possible responses: Animals have personalities. Every animal is different. People and animals can have special relationships.) **On Paper** Have students write their own responses. Students can use Practice Book, p. 99, to help prepare their written response, or you can send the Practice Book page home for them to complete later. (Possible answer: Both Dian and Denyse had to adjust to a new way of life. They had to learn to communicate and act with the creatures in their new environments.)
MORE PRACTICE		If you have more time, direct students to complete all the activities.

Homework Practice Book, p. 99, Writing

Unit 5 Week 1 *Dressing Up*

What do our clothes tell about us?

Objectives *This week students will ...*

Vocabulary
- build concepts and vocabulary: *clothing, custom, decade, ordinary, style, tradition*

Phonics
- read words with the vowel sound in *ball* and consonant digraphs *ph*/f/ and *dge*/j/
- apply knowledge of letter-sounds and word structure to decode unknown words when reading

Text Comprehension
- read connected text
- compare and contrast to improve comprehension
- write in response to literature

Fluency
- practice fluency with oral rereading

Word Work *This week's phonics focus is ...*

Vowel Sound in *ball: a, al* *ph*/f/, *dge*/j/

Concept Words *Tested Vocabulary*

The week's vocabulary is related to the concept of what clothes tell about us. The first appearance of each word in the Student Reader is noted below.

clothing what people wear; clothes (p. 10)

custom a long-established or accepted way of doing things (p. 13)

decade a period of ten years (p. 12)

ordinary not special; common; everyday (p. 20)

style made in a particular way or form (p. 8)

tradition beliefs, opinions, customs, stories, and so forth, handed down from parents to children (p. 10)

Student Reader Unit 5 *This week students will read the following selections.*

8	**Uniforms**	Expository Nonfiction
12	**They Wore That?**	Expository Nonfiction
20	**International Day**	Realistic Fiction
28	**Hair-Raising Styles!**	Photo Essay
30	**4 You 2 Do**	Activity Page

Daily Lesson Plan

	ACTIVITIES	MATERIALS
Day 1	**Build Concepts** Weekly Concept: Dressing Up Vocabulary: *clothing, custom, decade, ordinary, style, tradition* **Word Work** Phonics: Vowel Sound in *ball: a, al* **Read a Passage** "Uniforms," pp. 8–11 Comprehension: Use Strategies Reread for Fluency	Student Reader: Unit 5 Routine Cards 1, 3, 5, 6, 7 Tested Vocabulary Cards Sound-Spelling Card 4 Student White Boards AudioText Practice Book, p. 100, Vowel Sound in *ball: a, al*
Day 2	**Reread for Fluency** **Word Work** Phonics: Consonants *ph*/f/, *dge*/j/ Vocabulary **Comprehension** Compare and Contrast **Read a Passage** "They Wore That?" pp. 12–19	Student Reader: Unit 5 AudioText Routine Cards 1, 2, 3, 4, 5, 7, 8 Sound-Spelling Cards 12, 17 Student White Boards Tested Vocabulary Cards Graphic Organizer 3 or 4 Practice Book, p. 101, *ph/f/, dge/j/*
Day 3	**Reread for Fluency** **Word Work** Phonics: Vowel Sound in *ball: a, al;* Consonants *ph*/f/, *dge*/j/ Vocabulary **Read a Passage** "International Day," pp. 20–27 Comprehension: Compare and Contrast **Write** Response to Literature	Student Reader: Unit 5 AudioText Routine Cards 1, 3, 4, 5, 7 Student journals Practice Book, pp. 100–102, Vowel Sound in *ball: a, al; ph/f/; dge/j/*; Compare and Contrast
Day 4	**Reread for Fluency** **Word Work** Phonics: Spiral Review Vocabulary **Read a Passage** "Hair-Raising Styles!" pp. 28–29 Comprehension: Compare and Contrast; Listening **Write** Response to Literature	Student Reader: Unit 5 AudioText Routine Cards 3, 4, 5 Student White Boards Practice Book, pp. 102–103, Compare and Contrast; Vocabulary
Day 5	**Assessment Options** Fluency, Comprehension Sentence Reading Passage Reading **Build Concepts** Vocabulary **Read to Connect** **Write** Response to Literature: "4 You 2 Do," p. 30	Student Reader: Unit 5 Reproducible p. 218 Sentence Reading Chart, p. 223 Student White Boards Fluency Progress Chart, p. 215 Routine Card 6 Practice Book, pp. 103–104, Vocabulary; Writing

See pp. xvi–xvii for how *My Sidewalks* integrates instructional practices for ELL.
See pp. 251–254 for Phonemic Awareness Activities.

ACTIVITY 1

Build Concepts

Vocabulary

	To Do	To Say
		10–15 minutes
Develop word meaning.	See Routine Card 6. Discuss pp. 7–11.	Read Words 2 the Wise on p. 7. Have students flip through pages 8–11. **Look at the pictures. What do you notice?** (Possible answer: people in uniforms—a doctor, a firefighter, a police officer, a chef, a pilot, basketball players, a nurse) **Can you use the words *clothing* and *tradition* to describe any of these pictures?** (Example: *The police officer's clothing is a tradition.*)
Scaffold instruction.	Create a concept web.	In the center of a web, write *Dressing Up.* **This week's concept is *dressing up.* We dress up for different occasions and different jobs.** Provide examples to demonstrate meaning. **Firefighters wear special clothes to protect them when they do their jobs. Athletes wear clothes that they can move easily in.** Add the other vocabulary words. Discuss the meaning of each word as it relates to what people wear, using the glossary as needed. (See p. 72 in this Teacher's Guide for definitions.)

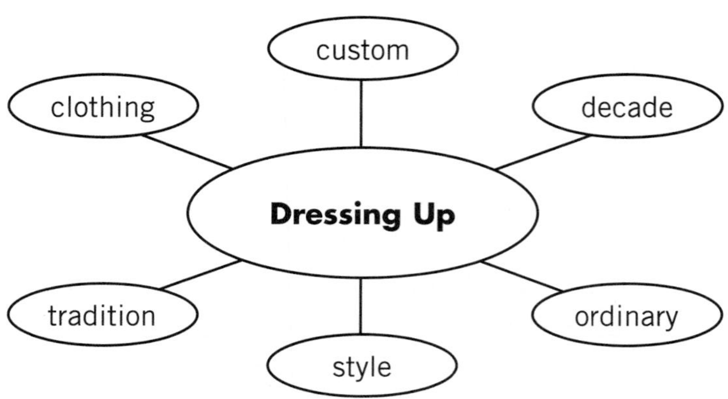

	To Do	To Say
Model the multisyllabic word strategy.	Display each word. Say it as you display it. Think aloud.	Use the Tested Vocabulary Cards. Follow this routine for each word: • **Look for Meaningful Parts** Remind students to look for meaningful parts. **As you say each word, ask yourself: Do I see any parts I know?** • **Model** Point to the word *clothing.* **I ask myself, what does the part *cloth* mean? I know that *clothes* are what people wear and are made of cloth. I know that *-ing* is sometimes added to words. I use the parts to read the word *clothing.* The clothes that people wear are called *clothing.*** • **Chunk Words with No Recognizable Parts** Model how to chunk the word *tradition.* **I see a chunk at the beginning of the word: *tra.* I see a part in the middle: *di.* I see a part at the end of the word: *tion.* I say each chunk slowly: *tra di tion.* I say the chunks fast to make a whole word: *tradition.* Is it a real word? Yes, I know the word *tradition.*** • Have students practice reading each word.
Preview.	Read p. 6 with students.	**Do you see any of the words we just learned on this page?** Together with students, read the sentences on p. 6 describing each selection. Talk about how the concept words might be used in the selections.
MORE PRACTICE	Deepen understanding of *clothing.*	Have students demonstrate understanding by answering questions. **What kind of *clothing* does a firefighter wear to work? What kind of *clothing* do you like to wear to school? What kind of *clothing* do you wear when the weather is very cold? How is a uniform a kind of *clothing?***

ACTIVITY 2 Word Work

Blending Strategy Vowel Sound in *ball: a, al*

5–10 minutes

	To Do	To Say
Use the blending routine.	Write *bath.*	**1 Connect** You already can read words like this. What is the word? *(bath)* What is the vowel sound in *bath?* (/a/) Today we will learn a new sound the letter *a* has when *l* comes after it.
Scaffold instruction.	Display Sound-Spelling Card 4.	**2 Use Sound-Spelling Card** This is an audience. An audience watches something, like a play. What sound do you hear at the beginning of *audience?* (/ȯ/) Say it with me: /ȯ/. This is the same vowel sound you hear in *ball.* When *a* is followed by *l* or *ll,* the *a* usually stands for the sound /ȯ/.
	Distribute white boards.	**3 Listen and Write** Write the letters *al* for /ȯ/. As you write, say the sound to yourself: /ȯ/. Now say the sound aloud.
	Write *call* and *talk.*	**4 Model** When *a* is followed by *l* or *ll,* the *a* often stands for /ȯ/. This is how I blend this word: /k/ /ȯ/ /l/, *call.* Now you try it: /k/ /ȯ/ /l/, *call.* Repeat with *talk.* In some words, the two letters *al* stand for the sound /ȯ/ and the *l* has no sound. c a ll → → → t al k → → →
CORRECTIVE FEEDBACK	Write each practice word. Monitor student practice.	**5 Group Practice** Let's try the same thing with these words. Support students as they blend progressively more difficult words. Give feedback, using the *if . . . then* statements on Routine Card 1. ball mall walk stall stalk* bald* false tallest all-star also already ballpoint **6 Individual Practice** Have each student blend several words from the row best matched to his or her ability. hall wall chalk small salt halt walked almost smallest always although stalling
	Check understanding of practice words.	*Students need to make sense of words that they segment and blend. If needed, help students with meanings. The main stem of a plant is a *stalk. Stalk* can also mean to follow silently and carefully. A cat will *stalk* a mouse. To be *bald* is to have no hair on your head.
MORE PRACTICE	Distribute white boards. Model building and spelling words.	**Build Words** Write *tall.* Can you blend this word? (/t/ /ȯ/ /l/) Have students write words on white boards. Write *tall.* Now change the *t* in *tall* to *w.* What is the new word? *(wall)* • Change the *w* in *wall* to *h.* What is the new word? *(hall)* • Change the *h* in *hall* to *st.* What is the new word? *(stall)* • Now add *in* to the beginning of *stall.* What is the new word? *(install)* • Add *ing* to the end of *install.* What is the new word? *(installing)*

Routine

ACTIVITY 3 Read a Passage

Build Background "Uniforms," pp. 8–11

10 minutes

	To Do	To Say
Develop language and concepts.	See Routine Cards 3 and 7.	**Before Reading** Read the title aloud. Do a structured picture walk with students.
	Ask questions and elaborate on answers.	p. 8 What do you see? (a woman in a white coat) Yes, the white coat may be part of a uniform. A uniform is a special style, or kind, of clothing. Maybe the woman wearing this uniform is a doctor or a nurse.
Scaffold instruction.	Key concepts: *clothing, emergency, firefighter, style, uniform*	p. 9 What is this person's job? (firefighter) He is a firefighter. Firefighters wear special uniforms to protect them. How would you describe the uniform this person is wearing? (a heavy coat, gloves, and a helmet) Firefighters have to move quickly in an emergency.
		p. 10 What do you see on this page? (a police officer, a chef, a pilot) How can you tell what jobs these people have? (I can tell by their uniforms, by what they are wearing, or the objects near them.)
		p. 11 What are the people in the top picture doing? (playing basketball) When people play basketball, they wear a certain kind of uniform. What do basketball players wear? (shorts, shirts with numbers on them, gym shoes) What do you think the person in the bottom picture does? (works as a doctor or nurse) How can you tell? (I can tell by what she is wearing and the things in her pockets.)
		Let's read to find out what special uniforms people wear when they work and play. As you read, ask yourself: What is this mainly about? What am I learning?
Guide compre-hension.	Read pp. 8–11 aloud.	**During Reading** Read the article as students follow along. Then read it a second time, having students join in. If necessary, stop at the end of each paragraph to check comprehension. Ask questions to promote discussion and develop the concept. • What examples of uniforms are given in the article? • What does the author say about why people wear different kinds of uniforms? • What words on the concept web could help you describe the people and uniforms pictured in this article?
	Use vocabulary to develop the concept.	**After Reading** What did you learn about *uniforms?* What can the *style* of a *uniform* tell us about the person who wears it*?* What *uniforms* do you wear*?* Where do you wear them?

Reread for Fluency "Uniforms," p. 11

5–10 minutes

	To Do	To Say
CORRECTIVE FEEDBACK	Monitor oral reading.	Read p. 11 aloud. Read it three or four times so your reading gets better each time. Give feedback on students' oral reading and use of the blending strategy. See Routine Cards 1 and 5.
MORE PRACTICE		Have students reread additional pages of the selection three or four times. You may want to have them read along with the AudioText.
	Homework	Practice Book, p. 100, Phonics: Vowel Sound in *ball: a, al*

ACTIVITY 1 Reread for Fluency

Paired Reading "Uniforms," pp. 8–10

5–10 minutes

	To Do	To Say
CORRECTIVE FEEDBACK	Pair students. Monitor paired reading.	Students read aloud pp. 8–10, switching readers for each paragraph. Have partners reread; now the other partner begins. For optimal fluency, students should reread three or four times. Give feedback, using Routine Card 5.
MORE PRACTICE		Have students reread additional pages of the selection three or four times. You may want to have students read along with the AudioText.

ACTIVITY 2 Word Work

Blending Strategy Consonants *ph*/f/; *dge*/j/

5–10 minutes

Routine

	To Do	To Say
Use the blending routine.	Write *lace* and *page.*	**1 Connect** You can already read words like these. What are the words? What is the second consonant sound in *lace*? (/s/) What two letters make the sound? *(ce)* What is the second consonant sound in *page*? (/j/) What two letters make the sound? *(ge)* Now you will learn about other consonant sounds that are spelled with two or more letters.
Scaffold instruction.	Write *firefighter.* Display Sound-Spelling Cards 12 and 17.	**2 Use Sound-Spelling Card** This is a firefighter. What sound do you hear at the beginning of *firefighter*? (/f/) Say it with me: /f/. The sound for the consonant *f* can also be spelled *ph.* The two letters *p* and *h* spell the consonant sound /f/. Repeat with *dge* using Sound-Spelling Card 17.
	Distribute white boards.	**3 Listen and Write** Write the letters *ph* and *dge.* As you write, say the sounds to yourself: /f/ and /j/. Now say the sounds aloud.
	Write *phone* and *edge.*	**4 Model** The two letters *ph* stand for /f/. This is how I blend this word: /f/ /ō/ /n/, *phone.* Now you try: /f/ /ō/ /n/, *phone.* The letters *ph* stand for the consonant *f.* Repeat with *edge:* /e/ /j/, *edge.* ph o ne e dge
CORRECTIVE FEEDBACK	Write each practice word. Monitor student practice.	**5 Group Practice** Let's try the same thing with these words. Support students as they blend progressively more difficult words. Give feedback, using the *if . . . then* statements on Routine Card 1. phase, ridge, ledge, fudge, dodge phrase, bridge, graph, phonics, pledge telephone, dodging, gopher, trophy, telegraph, nephew **6 Individual Practice** Have each student blend several words from the row best matched to his or her ability. judge, phone, edge, lodge, hedge, wedge bridges, graphic, phony, dodging nephew, triumph, hodgepodge, photograph

For more practice, see next page.

MORE PRACTICE	Model building and spelling words.	**Build Words** Write *graph*. **Can you blend this word?** (/gr/ /a/ /f/) Have students write words on white boards. **Write** ***graph*****. Now add** ***ic*** **to the end of** ***graph*****. What is the new word?** *(graphic)*

Vocabulary

	To Do	To Say *5 minutes*
Review vocabulary.	Display the concept web from Day 1.	Review the concept web. See Routine Card 2 for the multisyllabic word routine. **The words** ***clothing, custom, decade,*** **and** ***style*** **will be in the selection you are reading today.** Remind students that clothing means "the clothes a person wears."
	Deepen word understanding of *custom*, *decade,* and *style.*	**A** ***custom*** **is a long-established or accepted way of doing things. Shaking hands when you meet someone is a custom. What are some other customs?** (taking your hat off when you are inside; applauding after a performance; watching fireworks on the Fourth of July; eating turkey on Thanksgiving) **A** ***decade*** **is a period of ten years. Twenty years would be two** ***decades*****. Clothing** ***styles*** **can change a lot in a** ***decade*****. But clothing styles that are a** ***custom*** **may not change at all. For example, people have been wearing neckties for many, many** ***decades*****. The** ***style*** **of tie may change, but the** ***custom*** **of wearing a tie remains the same.**
Lead cumulative review.		Use the Tested Vocabulary Cards to review concept words from previous weeks.

ACTIVITY 3 Comprehension

Compare and Contrast

	To Do	To Say *10–15 minutes*
Scaffold instruction.	Introduce compare and contrast.	**Today you will read about the style of clothes people have worn in the past. When you read about things that change over a period of time, it is helpful and interesting to compare and contrast one thing with another. When you compare things, you tell how they are alike. When you contrast things, you tell how they are different. Look for clue words or phrases that help you see likenesses and differences, such as** ***like, but, also, the same as, in the same way, in spite of, on the other hand,*** **and** ***however.***
	Model the skill.	**For example, if I read that in the 1950s, unlike today, boys and girls dressed up to go to school, I would see that the word** ***unlike*** **is a clue word that signals a difference.**
	Distribute Graphic Organizer 3 or 4.	**As you read "They Wore That?" look for words that help you compare and contrast the clothes people wore in the past. List some of the likenesses and differences you read about on your graphic organizer. Also add words and phrases to your graphic organizer that signal likenesses and differences you find.** See Routine Card 8.

ACTIVITY 4 Read a Passage

Reading "They Wore That?" pp. 12–19

10–15 minutes

	To Do	To Say
Develop language and concepts.	See Routine Cards 3 and 7.	**Before Reading** Have students recall what they learned about the clothes and uniforms people wear. Read the title. Do a structured picture walk with students.
Scaffold instruction.	Ask questions and elaborate on answers. Key concepts: *clothing, comfortable, decade, formal*	pp. 12–13 **How would you describe the clothes these children are wearing?** (Their clothes look like adult clothes. They look dressed up.) **That's right, they are dressed in a very formal style. Kids didn't start wearing clothes made just for them until around 1850. Can you tell from the pictures why children's clothes today might be easier to wear?** (Today's clothes are more comfortable and easier to move and play in.) pp. 14–17 **How do the clothes these young people are wearing change from one decade to another?** (They get more colorful and fun.) **These pictures show the styles of children's clothing over a period of five decades. How long is seven decades?** (seventy years) pp. 18–19 **These pictures show the style of clothing children wore in the 1990s. How do these styles compare with the ones you saw at the beginning of the article?** (They are more fun, more comfortable, and much less formal. The children are not so dressed up.) **Have you ever worn clothes like these? Do you think your parents wore clothes like these?**
Guide compre-hension.	Use Routine Card 4.	**During Reading** **Read the pages in a whisper. Raise your hand if you need help with a word. As you read, ask yourself: What am I learning about how people dressed in the past? What is this mainly about?**
	Monitor independent reading.	pp. 12–16 **What did you learn about how the clothes young people wore changed over these decades? Compare two clothing styles you read about.** (Example: In the 1960s, girls and boys still dressed up for school. But the clothes they wore at home became more colorful and fun.) pp. 17–19 **What did you learn about the style of clothing young people wore during these decades? Compare and contrast the styles for two decades.** (Example: In the 1980s, kids wanted to wear clothes they saw on TV. In the 1990s, brand-name and designer clothes became popular.)
	Model using context for word meaning.	Read aloud the sentence with *knickers* on p. 14. Point out that this word is defined in context as "pants that came to their knees."
Model summarizing.	Think aloud.	**After Reading** **What did you learn about how the clothes young people wore changed from one decade to the next? What was the selection mainly about?** Model how to summarize. **The selection tells details about the styles of clothing young people wore from one decade to the next. It is mainly about how the styles changed.**
MORE PRACTICE	Have students reread p. 17.	**Reread** As they read, have students note how the clothing young people wore in the 1970s and 1980s was alike and different. Encourage them to identify words or phrases that suggest how the styles changed or stayed the same. Have students add these ideas to their graphic organizers.

Homework Practice Book, p. 101, Phonics: Consonants *ph*/f/, *dge*/j/

3

ACTIVITY 1 Reread for Fluency

Oral Reading "They Wore That?" pp. 12–14

5–10 minutes

	To Do	To Say
CORRECTIVE FEEDBACK	Monitor oral reading.	**Read pp. 12–14 aloud. Read them three or four times so your reading gets better each time.** Give feedback on students' oral reading and use of the blending strategy. Use Routine Cards 1 and 5.
MORE PRACTICE		Have students reread additional pages of the selection three or four times. You may want to have students read along with the AudioText.

ACTIVITY 2 Word Work

Fluent Word Reading Vowel Sound in *ball: a, al* Consonant *ph*/f/, *dge*/j/

5–10 minutes

	To Do	To Say
Review phonics.	Review the homework.	Ask students to share answers from Practice Book, pp. 100–101.
Use word-reading routine.	Write *stall.*	Routine **1 Connect** **You can read this word because you know that when *a* is followed by *l* or *ll,* the *a* usually stands for /ò/. What is the word?** *(stall)*
	Write *judged, phoning,* and *trophies.*	**2 Model** **When you come to a new word, look for meaningful parts. If you don't recognize any meaningful parts, then look for chunks you can read. Look at all the letters in the chunk and think about the vowel sound. Say the parts of the word to yourself, and then read the word.** Model reading *judged, phoning,* and *trophies* in this way. **When you come to a new word, what are you going to do?**
	Write each practice word.	**3 Group Practice** **Let's read these words. Look for meaningful parts and chunks, think about the vowel sound in each chunk, and say the parts to yourself. We will read words with the vowel sound in *ball* and the consonant sounds /j/ spelled *dge* and /f/ spelled *ph.* When I point to the word, let's read it together.** Allow 2–3 seconds previewing time for each word. Support students as they blend progressively more difficult words. **phase edge fall badge malt talk** **almost tallest graph ballroom trophy telephone**
CORRECTIVE FEEDBACK	**MONITOR PROGRESS**	***If . . .*** students have difficulty previewing and reading whole words, ***then . . .*** have them use sound-by-sound blending. ***If . . .*** students can't read words fluently at a rate of 1–2 seconds per word, ***then . . .*** continue practicing the list.
MORE PRACTICE	Model reading words in sentences.	**When I read a sentence, I read each word without stopping between the words. If I come to a word I don't know, I blend it. Then I read the sentence again.** Model reading this sentence, stopping to blend *photograph: I took a photograph of trees.* Have each student read the sentence best matched to his or her ability.
	Write practice sentences.	**Call me on your phone.** **I took a photo of the bridge.** **I always win a trophy for my special fudge.**

Vocabulary

	To Do	To Say 5 minutes
Review vocabulary.	Display the concept web from Day 1.	Review the concept web. **The words *clothing, ordinary,* and *tradition* will be in the selection you are reading today.** Review meanings of the words.

ACTIVITY 3 Read a Passage

Reading "International Day," pp. 20–27

	To Do	To Say 10–15 minutes
Scaffold instruction.	Review compare and contrast.	Remind students that when they compare and contrast things, they tell how they are alike and different. Clue words can tell how things are alike and different. **Look for words such as *not, the same,* and *different.* As you read "International Day," look for likenesses and differences.**
Develop language and concepts.	See Routine Cards 3 and 7.	**Before Reading** Read the title. Introduce proper nouns, if necessary. Do a structured picture walk.
	Ask questions and elaborate on answers.	pp. 20–24 **How are most children dressed?** (in native clothing) **What kinds of food are on the table?** (foods from different countries) **Why are there many different flags?** (They are from different countries.) **What do you think International Day is?** (a day honoring different countries and cultures) Point out the word *nation* in *international.*
	Key concepts: *photograph, international, native, countries*	pp. 25–27 **What do you think is happening in this story?** (The girl is photographing children wearing clothing from their native countries.)
Guide compre-hension.	Use Routine Card 4.	**During Reading** **Read the pages in a whisper. Raise your hand if you need help with a word. As you read, ask yourself: How are things being described? How are they alike and different?**
	Monitor independent reading.	pp. 20–27 **What is the first important thing that happens in the story?** (Ms. Menacho asks Fay to take photos for International Day.) **How does Fay feel?** (nervous and worried) **What happens later when Fay and Ms. Menacho get to the gym?** (Fay takes pictures of children wearing native clothes.) **What happens at the end?** (Fay is proud of the pictures.)
	Monitor comprehension.	**After Reading** Discuss the What Do You Think? question.
	Guide retelling.	Have one student retell the story while the others assist. Prompt students by asking: **Who are the main characters? What do they do in the story? How does the story end?** See Monitoring Retelling on p. 216.
	Have students reread pp. 23–24.	**Reread** As they read, tell students to list words and phrases that tell how the costumes of the two countries are alike and different.

ACTIVITY 4 Write

Response to Literature

	To Do	To Say 5 minutes
Prompt journal writing.		**Take out your journals. What would you do if you were going to take part in an International Day? Write what you would do and why.**

Homework Practice Book, p. 102, Compare and Contrast

4

ACTIVITY 1

Reread for Fluency

Paired Reading "International Day," pp. 24–25

5–10 minutes

	To Do	To Say
CORRECTIVE FEEDBACK	Pair students. Monitor paired reading.	Students read aloud pp. 24–25, switching readers for each paragraph. Have partners reread; now the other partner begins. For optimal fluency, students should reread three or four times. You may want to have students read along with the AudioText. Give feedback, using Routine Card 5.
MORE PRACTICE	**READERS' THEATER**	Students can use the dialogue as a script for a Readers' Theater. Have them rehearse, with one student being the narrator and the others, Fay and Ms. Menacho.

ACTIVITY 2

Word Work

Spiral Review Consonants *c/s/, g/j/, dge/j/*

5 minutes

	To Do	To Say
Review blending: *c/s/, g/j/,* and *dge/j/*.	Write *race, cage,* and *badge.*	You can read this word because you know the sound the letter *c* stands for when *e* comes after it. What sound does *c* stand for? (/s/) What is the word? *(race)* You can read this word because you know the sound the letter *g* can stand for when *e* comes after it. What sound does *g* stand for? (/j/) What is the word? *(cage)* You can read this word because you know the sound the letters *dge* can stand for. What sound does *dge* stand for? (/j/) What is the word? *(badge)* Point out that *dge* always comes after a short vowel sound.
Scaffold instruction. **CORRECTIVE FEEDBACK**	Distribute white boards. Monitor student work.	**Build Words** Write *ce, ge,* and *dge* as headings on a three-column chart. Have students copy the chart on their white boards. Below each heading write several words with those letters omitted. For example, for *trace,* write *tra___*. Have students add the missing letters to each word and copy the words on their white boards. Ask students to read the completed words. If students make an error, model the target sound and have them use sound-by-sound blending.

ce	*ge*	*dge*
tra___	sta___	fu___
twi___	pa___s	gru___
___nter	___ntle	ri___s

Vocabulary

5–10 minutes

	To Do	To Say
Extend word knowledge.	Write on the board or a transparency: *Each native costume was a different style.*	Use the word *style* to extend word knowledge. We learned that *style* means "made in a particular way." We can use *style* to read other words. Can you think of words that contain the word *style? (styles, styling, styled, stylish, restyle)* Write words as students name them and add any they don't mention. Talk about the meanings of the words. Point out that *re-* is a prefix that means "to do again," so *restyle* means "to style again." *Stylish* means "having style."
MORE PRACTICE	Deepen word understanding.	Have students use *tradition* and *clothing* in the same sentence. (For example, Wearing native *clothing* is a *tradition.)* Share sentences. Ask, What are some examples of native *clothing?* (sari, burka, kimono)

ACTIVITY 3 Read a Passage

Read Together "Hair-Raising Styles!" pp. 28–29

	To Do	To Say *10–15 minutes*
Scaffold instruction.	Review compare and contrast (homework).	Ask volunteers to read the passage and share answers from Practice Book, p. 102. Remind students of the importance of recognizing how things are alike and different. **When you read, seeing how things are alike and different can help you understand what you are reading and makes your reading more interesting. Often there are clue words or phrases that signal how things are alike or different. Look for these words and phrases. It may also help to review the pictures and illustrations as you read.**
Develop language and concepts.	See Routine Cards 3 and 4.	**Before Reading** **This article is about hairstyles through the decades. What styles do you see in the pictures on p. 28?** (bobbed hair, pony tail, and beehive) **Why do you think the beehive and pony tail have the names they do?** (They look like the things they are named after.) **Let's read to find out more about these hairstyles.**
Model fluent reading.	Read pp. 28–29 aloud. Model prosody.	**During Reading** **Listen to my voice as I read this article.** Read the article with expression as students follow along. Read it a second time, having students point to each word. **Now read the article aloud with me. Try to make your voice sound like mine as we read.** Reread the selection several times with students.
Monitor comprehension.	Monitor listening comprehension.	**After Reading** Prompt discussion to monitor comprehension. Listen as students answer questions. **Which hairstyles have changed? Which have stayed the same over several decades?** (The beehive is no longer popular, and men seldom wear wigs today. Women still wear pony tails, and crew cuts are still worn by some men.) **How have men's hairstyles changed?** (Hundreds of years ago men wore long wigs. From the 1930s on, a short hairstyle called a crew cut became popular. Some boys wore mohawks in the 1980s.) **Which of these hairstyles do you like best? How do you like to style your hair?** (Answers will vary.) **Summarize** Have one student describe the hairstyles mentioned in the article while the others assist.
MORE PRACTICE	Have students reread p. 29.	**Reread** As they read, tell students to look for information about hairstyles. After reading, they can tell a partner what they learned about hairstyles.

ACTIVITY 4 Write

Response to Literature

	To Do	To Say *5 minutes*
Prompt descriptive writing.	Writing elements: support, organization, conventions.	**Compare and contrast two popular hairstyles from the past. Try to use some clue words or phrases and describing words. Be sure to check your spelling.**

Homework Practice Book, p. 103, Vocabulary

5

ACTIVITY 1 Assessment Options

Sentence Reading

5 minutes

	To Do	To Say
Assess sentence reading.	Use reproducible p. 218.	Have each student read the sentences. Record scores on the Sentence Reading Chart, p. 223. While you work with one student, others can complete the Write Sentences activity below. **My brother is too small to reach the ledge.** **We walked along the ridge of the hill.** **The photos of the bridge were beautiful.**
CORRECTIVE FEEDBACK	**MONITOR PROGRESS**	***If . . .*** students have trouble reading words with *al, ph,* or *dge,* ***then . . .*** reteach the blending strategy lessons on pp. 75 and 77. ***If . . .*** students misread a word in the sentence, ***then . . .*** correct the error and have them reread the word and then the sentence.
Practice sentence writing.	Provide white boards.	**Write Sentences** Have students copy the sentences from reproducible p. 218 on white boards. Have them confirm spellings by comparing the words they wrote to the words in the sentences.

Passage Reading

5–10 minutes

	To Do	To Say
Check fluency.	Determine which students to assess this week.	Choose from these options: monitoring fluency (see pp. 214–215) and/or monitoring retelling (see p. 216). Have students reread "International Day." Be sure each student is assessed every other week.
		If you have time, assess every student.

ACTIVITY 2 Build Concepts

Vocabulary

5–10 minutes

	To Do	To Say
Review concept and vocabulary.	Review homework. Display the concept web you began on Day 1.	Ask students to go over answers and share their writing from Practice Book, p. 103. **This week's question is *What do our clothes tell about us?* How do this week's words relate to the question?** (Have students answer the question, using some of the vocabulary they learned this week.) Ask students to add more words to the concept web. Have students explain how each word relates to dressing up. Monitor students' understanding of vocabulary as they discuss the web. See Routine Card 6.
MORE PRACTICE		Pairs of students can make up ads using two or more vocabulary words.

ACTIVITY 3 Read to Connect

Reread "Uniforms," pp. 8–11

10 minutes

	To Do	To Say
Monitor compre-hension.	Have students reread "Uniforms" silently.	**As you read, think about what the article says about uniforms.** After rereading, ask: • **What kinds of uniforms are described?** (pilot, doctor, nurse, chef, firefighter, police officer, basketball player) • **Why do people wear certain uniforms for work or play?** (People wear uniforms for certain jobs. They tell us what kinds of jobs the people have. Some uniforms protect workers. Some uniforms are worn because it is a tradition.) **We also read "They Wore That?" Find that article. How have the styles of clothing changed over the decades?** Record students' ideas. **We also read "International Day." What did the children in that story do to share traditions and customs about their native countries?** Record students' ideas.
Make connections.	Have students make connections across texts.	**What can you say in general about the clothes people wear?** (Sample answers: People wear many different styles of clothing. Some styles of clothing are worn for jobs. Other styles are worn for play. Some styles of clothing are traditional. Clothing styles can change from one decade to the next.)

ACTIVITY 4 Write

Response to Literature "4 You 2 Do," p. 30

5–10 minutes

	To Do	To Say
Guide response activities.	Discuss the directions. Tell students to choose one activity to complete. Monitor handwriting. See pp. 227–229.	**Word Play** Have students list new words on their own and then meet with a partner to share their words. **Making Connections** Discuss the question in a group or in pairs. (Answers will vary.) **On Paper** Brainstorm a list of reasons why kids don't wear clothing from their native countries every day. Have students write on their own. They can use Practice Book, p. 104, to structure their written responses, or you can send the Practice Book page home for them to complete later.
MORE PRACTICE		If you have more time, direct students to complete all the activities.

Homework Practice Book, p. 104, Writing

Unit 5 Week 2 *Our World*

How are communities and families similar around the world?

Objectives *This week students will ...*

Vocabulary
- build concepts and vocabulary: *country, culture, language, popular, similar, transfer*

Phonics
- blend and read words with the vowel sound in *ball: au, aw* and suffixes *-er, -or*
- apply knowledge of letter-sounds and word structure to decode unknown words when reading

Text Comprehension
- read connected text
- draw conclusions to improve comprehension
- write in response to literature

Fluency
- practice fluency with oral rereading

Word Work *This week's phonics focus is ...*

Vowel Sound in *ball*: *au, aw*   Suffixes *-er*, *-or*

Concept Words *Tested Vocabulary*

The week's vocabulary is related to how communities and families around the world are similar. The first appearance of each word in the Student Reader is noted below.

country the land of a group of people with the same government (p. 34)

culture the beliefs, arts, and tools of a country or people (p. 46)

language the speech of one nation or other large group of people (p. 36)

popular liked by most people (p. 36)

similar alike in some way (p. 36)

transfer a change in job or school location (p. 44)

Student Reader Unit 5 *This week students will read the following selections.*

34	**Town Squares**	Expository Nonfiction
36	**Across the Ocean**	Expository Nonfiction
44	**Pictures**	Realistic Fiction
52	**One Moment All Around the World**	Expository Article
56	**4 You 2 Do**	Activity Page

Daily Lesson Plan

	ACTIVITIES	MATERIALS
Day 1	**Build Concepts** Weekly Concept: Our World Vocabulary: *country, culture, language, popular, similar, transfer* **Word Work** Phonics: Vowel Sound in *ball: au, aw* **Read a Passage** "Town Squares," pp. 34–35 Comprehension: Use Strategies Reread for Fluency	Student Reader: Unit 5 Routine Cards 1, 3, 5, 6, 7 Tested Vocabulary Cards Sound-Spelling Card 4 Student White Boards AudioText Practice Book, p. 105, Vowel Sound in *ball: au, aw*
Day 2	**Reread for Fluency** **Word Work** Phonics: Suffixes *-er, -or* Vocabulary **Comprehension** Draw Conclusions **Read a Passage** "Across the Ocean," pp. 36–43	Student Reader: Unit 5 AudioText Routine Cards 1, 2, 3, 4, 5, 7, 8 Tested Vocabulary Cards Student White Boards Graphic Organizer 2 Practice Book, p. 106, Suffixes *-er, -or*
Day 3	**Reread for Fluency** **Word Work** Phonics: Vowel Sound in *ball: au, aw;* Suffixes *-er, -or* Vocabulary **Read a Passage** "Pictures," pp. 44–51 Comprehension: Draw Conclusions **Write** Response to Literature	Student Reader: Unit 5 AudioText Routine Cards 5, 7 Student journals Practice Book, pp. 105–107, Vowel Sound in *ball: au, aw;* Suffixes *-er, -or;* Draw Conclusions
Day 4	**Reread for Fluency** **Word Work** Phonics: Spiral Review Vocabulary **Read a Passage** "One Moment All Around the World," pp. 52–55 Comprehension: Draw Conclusions; Listening **Write** Response to Literature	Student Reader: Unit 5 AudioText Routine Cards 3, 4, 5 Student White Boards Practice Book, pp. 107–108, Draw Conclusions; Vocabulary
Day 5	**Assessment Options** Fluency, Comprehension Sentence Reading Passage Reading **Build Concepts** Vocabulary **Read to Connect** **Write** Response to Literature: "4 You 2 Do," p. 56	Student Reader: Unit 5 Reproducible p. 219 Sentence Reading Chart, p. 223 Student White Boards Fluency Progress Chart, p. 215 Routine Card 6 Practice Book, pp. 108–109, Vocabulary; Writing

See pp. xvi–xvii for how *My Sidewalks* integrates instructional practices for ELL.
See pp. 251–254 for Phonemic Awareness Activities.

ACTIVITY 1

Build Concepts

Vocabulary

10–15 minutes

	To Do	To Say
Develop word meaning.	See Routine Card 6. Discuss pp. 33–35.	Read Words 2 the Wise on p. 33. Have students turn to p. 34. **What do you notice?** (Large open areas where people are enjoying themselves in cities around the world.) **Can you use the words *country* and *similar* to describe any of these pictures?** (Example: *Town squares in different countries are similar.*)
Scaffold instruction.	Create a concept web.	In the center of a web, write *Our World.* **This week's concept is *our world. Our world* means "all the countries and cultures around the world."** Provide examples to demonstrate meaning. **There are many different countries in our world. Our world is made up of many cultures and people.** Add the other vocabulary words. Discuss the meaning of each word as it relates to our world, using the glossary as needed. (See p. 86 in this Teacher's Guide for definitions.) 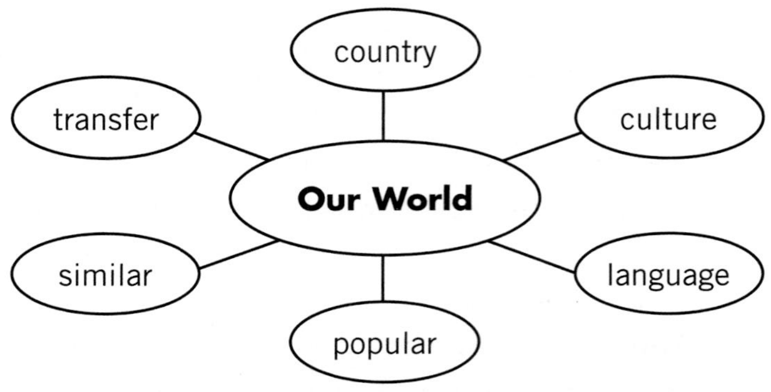
Model the multisyllabic word strategy.	Display each word. Say it as you display it.	Use the Tested Vocabulary Cards. Follow this routine for each word: • **Look for Meaningful Parts** Remind students to look for meaningful parts. **As you say each word, ask yourself: Do I see any parts I know?** • **Chunk Words with No Recognizable Parts** Model how to chunk the word *popular* to read it.
	Think aloud.	• **Model** **I look for word chunks that have at least one vowel. I see a chunk at the beginning of the word: *pop.* I see a part in the middle: *u.* I see a part at the end of the word: *lar.* I say each chunk slowly: *pop u lar.* I say the chunks fast to make a whole word: *popular.* Is it a real word? Yes, I know the word *popular.*** • Have students practice reading each word.
Preview.	Read p. 32 with students.	**Do you see any of the words we just learned on this page?** Together with students, read the sentences on p. 32 describing each selection. Talk about how the concept words might be used in the selections.
MORE PRACTICE	Deepen understanding of *culture.*	Have students demonstrate understanding by answering questions. **What are some clothes from different *cultures?* From which *culture* does pizza come? Is there just one *culture* or many different *cultures* around the world? What are some *cultural* traditions in your family?**

ACTIVITY 2 Word Work

Blending Strategy Vowel Sound in *ball: au, aw*

5–10 minutes

	To Do	To Say
Use the blending routine. **Scaffold instruction.**	Write *saw.*	**1 Connect** What is the vowel sound in *saw?* (/ò/) What two letters make the sound in this word? *(aw)* Today we will study two different spellings that stand for the sound /ò/.
	Display Sound-Spelling Card 4.	**2 Use Sound-Spelling Card** This is an audience. An audience is a group of people who gather to hear or see something. What sound do you hear at the beginning of *audience?* (/ò/) Say it with me: /ò/. The letters *au* and *aw* both stand for the sound /ò/.
	Distribute white boards.	**3 Listen and Write** Write the letters *au* for /ò/. As you write, say the sound to yourself: /ò/. Now say the sound aloud.
	Write *haul* and *raw.*	**4 Model** The two letters *au* stand for /ò/. This is how I blend this word: /h/ /ò/ /l/. Now you try: /h/ /ò/ /l/, *haul.* The letters *au* stand for the vowel sound /ò/. Repeat with *raw.* Point out that the sound /ò/ can be spelled with *au* or *aw.* h a u l r a w
CORRECTIVE FEEDBACK	Write each practice word. Monitor student practice.	**5 Group Practice** Let's try the same thing with these words. Support students as they blend progressively more difficult words. Give feedback, using the *if . . . then* statements on Routine Card 1. vault* maul* law saw pause cause* drawn straw auto because awful sawdust
		6 Individual Practice Have each student blend several words from the row that is best matched to his or her ability. raw fault* paw awe* sauce launch fawn lawn seesaw laundry lawful awkward
	Check understanding of practice words.	*Students need to make sense of words that they segment and blend. If needed, help students with meanings. *A vault* is a place to store things that are valuable. *Maul* means to injure badly using claws or teeth. To *cause* is to make something happen. A strong wind can *cause* branches to fall from trees. *Fault* is blame for something that happened. *Awe* is great wonder and respect.
MORE PRACTICE	Distribute white boards. Model building and spelling words.	**Build Words** Write *paw.* Can you blend this word? (/p/ /ò/) Have students write words on white boards. Write *paw.* Now change the *p* in *paw* to *s.* What is the new word? *(saw)* • Change the *s* in *saw* to *r.* What is the new word? *(raw)* • Change the *r* in *raw* to *l.* What is the new word? *(law)* • Now add *ful* to the end of *law.* What is the new word? *(lawful)* • Add *un* to the beginning of *lawful.* What is the new word? *(unlawful)*

Routine

ACTIVITY 3

Read a Passage

Build Background "Town Squares," pp. 34–35

10 minutes

	To Do	To Say
Develop language and concepts.	See Routine Cards 3 and 7. Ask questions and elaborate on answers.	**Before Reading** Read the title aloud. Introduce proper nouns, if necessary. Do a structured picture walk with students. p. 34 **What do you see?** (a fountain, statues, buildings, and people) **Yes, the statues and fountain may be in a town in this country or some other country. The fountain seems to be in the center of a large public square. The people seem to be enjoying themselves. What do you think the people are doing?** (enjoying the fountain and talking to one another) **Yes, it looks like some of the people are enjoying the fountain area and the beautiful day. In some places where there are fountains or public squares, people sell goods they make or have feasts for all the townspeople to enjoy.**
Scaffold instruction.	Key concepts: *country, feasts, goods, public, town square*	p. 35 **What is happening in these pictures?** (Children are playing around a statue. People are walking by temples and statues.) **Yes, one of the statues looks like a mermaid. A mermaid is a make-believe creature that lives in the sea. It is half human and half fish. These other statues and temples look like they are in a part of the world called Asia.** **Let's read to find out where these pictures were taken and what the people are doing. As you read, ask yourself: What is this mainly about? What am I learning?**
Guide comprehension.	Read pp. 34–35 aloud.	**During Reading** Read the selection as students follow along. Then read it a second time, having students join in. If necessary, stop at the end of each paragraph to check comprehension. Ask questions to promote discussion and develop the concept. • **What is a town square, and why do people gather in them?** • **How are town squares around the world alike and different?** • **What words on the vocabulary web could help you describe the town squares pictured in this selection?**
	Use vocabulary to develop the concept.	**After Reading** **What did you learn about *town squares?* How are town squares *similar?* In what *countries* do you think town squares are *popular?* Have you ever gone to a *town square?* If so, what was it like and what did you do there?**

Reread for Fluency "Town Squares," p. 34

5–10 minutes

	To Do	To Say
CORRECTIVE FEEDBACK	Monitor oral reading.	**Read p. 34 aloud. Read it three or four times so your reading gets better each time.** Give feedback on students' oral reading and use of the blending strategy. See Routine Cards 1 and 5.
MORE PRACTICE		Have students reread the entire selection three or four times. You may want to have students read along with the AudioText.

Homework Practice Book, p. 105, Phonics: Vowel Sound in *ball: au, aw*

ACTIVITY 1 Reread for Fluency

Paired Reading "Town Squares," p. 34

	To Do	To Say — 5–10 minutes
CORRECTIVE FEEDBACK	Pair students. Monitor paired reading.	Students read aloud p. 34, switching readers for each paragraph. Have partners reread; now the other partner begins. For optimal fluency, students should reread three or four times. Give feedback, using Routine Card 5.
MORE PRACTICE		Have students reread the entire selection three or four times. You may want to have students read along with the AudioText.

ACTIVITY 2 Word Work

Blending Strategy Suffixes *-er, -or*

To Do | To Say — *5–10 minutes* — Routine

Use the blending routine. — Write *fearless* and *jumping.*

1 Connect **You can already read words like these. What do you know about reading them?** (They end with suffixes that are separate syllables from the base word.) **Today we will learn about adding two other suffixes, *-er* and *-or,* to the ends of words. Both suffixes have the same meaning:**

***-er* and *-or* mean "a person or thing that"**

Scaffold instruction. — Write *teacher.*

2 Model Point to *teacher.* **This is a two-syllable word formed from the base word *teach* and the suffix *-er*. You can cover the suffix, read the base word, and then blend the base word and the suffix to read the whole word. What is the word?** *(teacher)* **What does it mean?** ("a person who teaches") **Let's blend this word together: *teach er, teacher.***

Write *painter, actor,* and *sailor.*

Repeat with *painter* ("a person who paints"), *actor* ("a person who acts"), and *sailor* ("a person who sails").

p a i n t e r

Distribute white boards.

3 Listen and Write Have students write on white boards. **Write the word *teach.* Write *er* at the end of it. As you write, say the new word to yourself: *teacher.* Now say the word aloud.** Do the same with *actor.*

CORRECTIVE FEEDBACK — Write each practice word. Monitor student practice.

4 Group Practice **Let's try the same thing with these words.** Support students as they blend progressively more difficult words. Give feedback, using the ***if . . . then*** statements on Routine Card 1.

singer	worker	director	sailor	
visitor	speaker	traveler	conductor	
inspector	toaster	projector	skater	performer

5 Individual Practice Have each student blend several words from the row best matched to his or her ability.

farmer	talker	actor	printer
dreamer	sailor	trainer	teacher
founder	learner	reporter	translator

For more practice, see next page.

MORE PRACTICE

Model spelling words with suffixes.	**Spell and Write** You can spell words with suffixes by thinking about the suffix and the base word. What suffix and base word make up *dreamer?* (*dream* and *-er*) Start with the sounds in the base word: /drēm/. What letters spell *dream?* Write *dream.* Now add the suffix *-er.* Now spell *dreamer.* Repeat with *player, trainer, actor, painter,* and *sailor.*

Vocabulary

5 minutes

	To Do	To Say
Review vocabulary.	Display the concept web from Day 1.	Review the concept web. See Routine Card 2 for the multisyllabic word routine. The words *language, similar, popular,* and *country* will be in the selection you are reading today. Remind students that *similar* means "alike in some way."
	Deepen word understanding of *popular* and *country.*	Something that is *popular* is liked by most people. Name some things that most of your friends like. (Answers may include popular clothing styles, music, television programs, sports, food, and so on.) Some things from one country may become popular in another country. Which things that you mentioned were popular first in one country and then in another? Encourage discussion of different examples, asking: Can you think of some kinds of foods from other countries that have become popular in this country? Can you think of clothing styles that were popular first in one country and then in another?
Lead cumulative review.		Use the Tested Vocabulary Cards to review concept words from previous weeks.

ACTIVITY 3 Comprehension

Draw Conclusions

5 minutes

	To Do	To Say
Scaffold instruction.	Introduce draw conclusions.	Today you will read about the many things and ideas that America and Japan have shared. When you read a selection like this, it is important to draw conclusions because it may help you better figure out what the author is trying to say. To draw a conclusion is to think about facts and details and decide something about them.
	Model the skill.	For example, if I read that two countries shared clothing styles, food, music, and so forth, I might draw the conclusion that the people of the two countries had a lot in common. I might also conclude that the two countries shared many things.
	Distribute Graphic Organizer 2.	As you read "Across the Ocean," look for facts and details that help you draw conclusions about America and Japan. List in your graphic organizer some of the conclusions you draw. Also add facts and details to your graphic organizer that helped you draw your conclusions. See Routine Card 8.

ACTIVITY 4 Read a Passage

Reading "Across the Ocean," pp. 36–43

10–15 minutes

	To Do	To Say
Develop language and concepts.	See Routine Cards 3 and 7.	**Before Reading** Have students recall what they learned about town squares. Read the title. Introduce proper nouns, if necessary. Do a structured picture walk with students.
	Ask questions and elaborate on answers.	pp. 36–37 **This selection is about things Japanese and American people share. Do you know anyone who has traveled to Japan or speaks the Japanese language? What are these people doing?** (singing along, playing baseball, practicing martial arts) **The man is doing karaoke, which is a Japanese word that means "empty band." This is a popular form of entertainment in Japan and now in America. The American game of baseball is very popular in Japan. Martial arts are popular in this country. Which martial arts have you heard about?**
Scaffold instruction.	Key concepts: *country, entertainment, exchange, language, popular, similar, teenagers, traveled*	pp. 38–40 **What are the pictures on these pages mainly about?** (food) **Most of the pictures show Japanese food. Many Japanese dishes are popular in America. What is the girl using to eat her food?** (chopsticks) **Have you ever tried to eat with chopsticks?**
		pp. 41–43 **Do you recognize the monster on this page?** (Godzilla) **Many Americans have seen Godzilla movies. The very first Godzilla movie was made in Japan. What does the picture on p. 42 show?** (a rack of comic books) **Many American bookstores sell Japanese comic books. Japanese and American teenagers are similar in many ways. One way is that they like to read comic books. Teenagers often exchange their books with friends so they can read an entire series.**
Guide comprehension.	Use Routine Card 4.	**During Reading** **Read the pages in a whisper. Raise your hand if you need help with a word. As you read, ask yourself: What am I learning about things America and Japan share? What is this mainly about?**
	Monitor independent reading.	pp. 36–40 **What do people in America like that comes from Japan? What are some things that people in Japan like that come from America?** (Example: Many people in America enjoy karaoke, martial arts, and Japanese food. Baseball, skateboarding, and fast-food restaurants are very popular in Japan.)
		pp. 41–43 **Tell me some things you learned about the movie monster Godzilla?** (Godzilla's name in Japan is Gojira. The name was changed for American movies. It is probably from a story written by an American.) **What are some of the things you read about that you have seen or done?**
Model summarizing.	Think aloud.	**After Reading** **What did you learn about the things that America and Japan have shared? What was the selection mainly about?** Model how to summarize. **The selection told facts and details about food, sports, and entertainment that Japan and America have in common. The selection was mainly about things that the people of these two countries share.**
MORE PRACTICE	Have students reread p. 37.	**Reread** As they read, have students draw some conclusions about the things Americans and Japanese share. Point out that baseball and skateboarding come from America and are very popular in Japan. Karaoke and the martial arts judo and kendo come from Japan and are very popular in America. Suggest that students look for words that they can add to their graphic organizers.

Homework Practice Book, p. 106, Phonics: Suffixes *-er, -or*

3

ACTIVITY 1 Reread for Fluency

Oral Reading "Across the Ocean," pp. 38–40

5–10 minutes

	To Do	To Say
CORRECTIVE FEEDBACK	Monitor oral reading.	**Read pp. 38–40 aloud. Read them three or four times so your reading gets better each time.** Give feedback on students' oral reading and use of the blending strategy. Use Routine Cards 1 and 5.
MORE PRACTICE		Instead of rereading just pp. 38–40, have students reread the entire selection three or four times. You may want to have students read along with the AudioText.

ACTIVITY 2 Word Work

Fluent Word Reading Vowel Sound in *ball: au, aw;* Suffixes *-er, -or*

5–10 minutes

	To Do	To Say
Review phonics.	Review the homework.	Ask students to share answers from Practice Book, pp. 105–106.
Use word-reading routine.	Write *player.*	**1 Connect** **You can read this word because you know that a word ending with *-er* is often a two-syllable word formed from a base word and the suffix *-er.* What is the base word?** *(play)* **What is the word?** *(player)*
	Write *actor, draw,* and *haul.*	**2 Model** **When you come to a new word, look for meaningful parts. If you don't recognize any meaningful parts, then look for chunks you can read. Look at all the letters in the chunk and think about the vowel sound. Say the parts of the word to yourself, and then read the word.** Model reading *actor, draw,* and *haul* in this way. **When you come to a new word, what are you going to do?**
Scaffold instruction.	Write each practice word.	**3 Group Practice** **Let's read these words. Look for meaningful parts and chunks, think about the vowel sound in each chunk, and say the parts to yourself. We will read words with the vowel sound /ò/ and the suffixes *-er* and *-or.* When I point to the word, let's read it together.** Allow 2–3 seconds previewing time for each word. Support students as they blend progressively more difficult words. **paw talker dawn claw haul pause sailor** **lawful drawn fault launch speaker director employer**
CORRECTIVE FEEDBACK	**MONITOR PROGRESS**	***If . . .*** students have difficulty previewing and reading whole words, ***then . . .*** have them use sound-by-sound blending. ***If . . .*** students can't read words fluently at a rate of 1–2 seconds per word, ***then . . .*** continue practicing the list.
MORE PRACTICE	Model reading words in sentences.	**When I read a sentence, I read each word without stopping between the words. If I come to a word I don't know, I blend it. Then I read the sentence again.** Model reading this sentence, stopping to blend *speaker: The speaker talked about Japanese comic books.*
	Write practice sentences.	Have each student read the sentence best matched to his or her ability. **The farmer grows rice.** **The sailor saw many countries.** **There was a fawn standing on the lawn.**

Routine

Vocabulary

	To Do	To Say 5 minutes
Review vocabulary.	Display the concept web from Day 1.	Review the concept web. **The words *country, culture, transfer,* and *language* will be in the selection you read today.** Review the meanings of the words.

ACTIVITY 3 Read a Passage

Reading "Pictures," pp. 44–51

	To Do	To Say 10–15 minutes
Scaffold instruction.	Review draw conclusions.	Remind students that they draw conclusions by thinking about story details and deciding more about them. **Think about what the details tell you about this story.**
	See Routine Card 7.	**Before Reading** Read the title. Do a structured picture walk.
Develop language and concepts.	Key concepts: *culture, country, Hindi, language, sari, transfer, uniform*	pp. 44–49 **This story is about a girl whose father gets a transfer to India. What do you see?** (a girl talking with her parents) **What can you tell about this country?** (The clothes are different.) **Her teacher wears a sari.** pp. 50–51 **Does it look like the girl is adjusting to her new culture?** (yes)
Guide comprehension.	Monitor independent reading.	**During Reading Read the pages in a whisper. Raise your hand if you need help with a word. As you read, ask yourself: What conclusions can I draw?** pp. 44–47 **How does Anna feel about moving to a new country?** (She does not want to move. She is frightened.) **Remember *Mrs.* is a title put in front of a married woman's name. How does Anna feel after her first day of school?** (different) **How does Anna adjust to life in India?** (She learns the language and culture.)
	Model using context for meaning.	Read aloud the paragraph with *transfer* on p. 44. Explain how the phrase "moving to India" in the next sentence provides clues to the meaning of *transfer.* pp. 48–51 **How was Anna feeling about her new home by the end of the story?** (She was happy and enjoying her new life.)
	Monitor comprehension.	**After Reading** Discuss the What Do You Think? question.
	Guide retelling.	Have one student retell the story while the others assist. Prompt students by asking: **Who are the main characters? What do they do in the story? How does the story end?** See Monitoring Retelling on p. 216.
MORE PRACTICE	Have students reread pp. 46–47.	**Reread** As they read, tell students to draw a picture that shows what they think Anna felt like after her first day at school.

ACTIVITY 4 Write

Response to Literature

	To Do	To Say 5 minutes
Prompt journal writing.		**Take out your journals. How would you feel about moving to a different country for a while? Write how you would feel and why.**

Homework Practice Book, p. 107, Draw Conclusions

4

ACTIVITY 1 Reread for Fluency

Paired Reading "Pictures," pp. 49–51

	To Do	To Say *5–10 minutes*
CORRECTIVE FEEDBACK	Pair students. Monitor paired reading.	Students read aloud pp. 49–51, switching readers for each paragraph. Have partners reread; now the other partner begins. For optimal fluency, students should reread three or four times. You may want to have students read along with the AudioText. Give feedback, using Routine Card 5.
MORE PRACTICE	**READERS' THEATER**	Students can use the dialogue as a script for Readers' Theater. Have them rehearse, with students as the narrator and the story characters.

ACTIVITY 2 Word Work

Spiral Review Inflected Endings and Suffixes *-er, -or*

	To Do	To Say *5 minutes*
Review inflected endings.	Write *drawing.*	**Look at this word. You can read this word because you know how to blend the base word and the ending *-ing* together. Blend the sounds in the base word. What is the base word?** *(draw)* **Now blend the two parts. What is the word?** *(drawing)*
	Write *actor.*	**You can read this word because you know how to blend the base word and the *-or* ending. Blend the sounds in the base word. What is the base word?** *(act)* **Blend the base word and the *-or* ending. What is the word?** *(actor)*
Scaffold instruction.	Distribute white boards.	**Build Words** Use a chart to make new words. Write *paint, wash, farm,* and *direct* under the heading *Words.* Have students copy the words and add inflected endings *-s* or *-es, -ing, -ed;* and suffixes *-er* or *-or.* Call on individuals to use the new words in sentences. If students have difficulty using the word form correctly, model several sentences for them. Have them try again, using another word of the same form.
CORRECTIVE FEEDBACK	Monitor student work.	

Words	*-s/-es*	*-ed*	*-ing*	*-er/or*
paint	paints	painted	painting	painter
wash	washes	washed	washing	washer
direct	directs	directed	directing	director

Vocabulary

	To Do	To Say *5–10 minutes*
Extend word knowledge.	Write on the board or a transparency: *Each <u>culture</u> has its own kind of food.*	Use the word *culture* to extend word knowledge. **We learned that *culture* means "the beliefs, arts, and tools of a country or people." Today I want to talk about other words that are related to *culture.* We can use this word to read other words.** **Can you think of other words that contain the word *culture?*** *(cultures, cultured, cultural)* Write these words and discuss their meanings. Point out that adding the suffix *-al* makes *cultural,* which means "about culture." Adding the suffix *-ed* makes *cultured,* which means "having a good education and good manners."
MORE PRACTICE	Deepen word understanding.	Have students use *culture* and *country* in the same sentence. (For example, *Each country has its own culture.*) Share sentences. Ask, **What are some examples of things from different cultures?**

ACTIVITY 3 Read a Passage

Read Together "One Moment All Around the World," pp. 52–55

10–15 minutes

	To Do	To Say
Scaffold instruction.	Review draw conclusions (homework).	Ask volunteers to read the passage and share answers from Practice Book, p. 107. Remind students of the importance of drawing conclusions from the facts and details that they read. **When you read, drawing conclusions is important. As you read, think about the facts and details and decide something about them. Looking at the pictures and illustrations may also help you draw conclusions.**
Develop language and concepts.	See Routine Cards 3 and 4.	**Before Reading** **This selection is about what is happening at a particular moment in different countries around the world. What are the children in these pictures doing?** (A girl is getting on a bus, a boy is eating lunch, a girl and her father are at a zoo, children are playing soccer, a girl is doing homework, and a boy is sleeping.) **Let's read to find out more about what is happening at one moment around the world and why.**
Model fluent reading.	Read pp. 52–55 aloud. Model prosody.	**Reading** **Listen to my voice as I read this selection.** Read the selection with expression as students follow along. Read it a second time, having students point to each word. **Now read the selection aloud with me. Try to make your voice sound like mine as we read.** Reread the selection several times with students.
Monitor comprehension.	Monitor listening comprehension.	**After Reading** Prompt discussion to monitor comprehension. Listen as students answer questions. **What does the author say about time zones?** (At any one moment, it is a different time of day in many countries around the world.) **How do you know what time it is in the countries mentioned in the selection?** (The times are shown on the map and each picture is labeled with the time of day.) **Which time zone is closest to where you live?** (Denver) **What do think is happening in Nairobi, Kenya, when you are just going to school?** (Answers will vary, but children should recognize that it will be evening in Nairobi when it is morning where they live.) **Summarize** Have one student identify the activities described in the selection while the others assist.
MORE PRACTICE	Have students reread pp. 52–53.	**Reread** As they read, tell students to look for information about time zones and how they affect what people do in different countries around the world. After reading, they can tell a partner what they learned.

ACTIVITY 4 Write

Response to Literature

5 minutes

	To Do	To Say
Prompt narrative writing.	Writing elements: focus	**Write a story about someone who visits a time zone on the opposite side of the world. Tell about what the person must do to communicate with family in the United States by phone. Be sure to stay on the topic of communication.**

Homework Practice Book, p. 108, Vocabulary

5

ACTIVITY 1 Assessment Options

Sentence Reading

5 minutes

	To Do	To Say
Assess sentence reading.	Use reproducible p. 219.	Have each student read the sentences. Record scores on the Sentence Reading Chart, p. 223. While you work with one student, others can complete the Write Sentences activity below. **The inventor saw his mistake.** **I can draw a picture of the teacher.** **Several visitors paused outside the house.**
CORRECTIVE FEEDBACK	**MONITOR PROGRESS**	***If . . .*** students have trouble reading words with *au, aw* or suffixes *-er* or *-or*, ***then . . .*** reteach the blending strategy lessons on pp. 89 and 91. ***If . . .*** students misread a word in the sentence, ***then . . .*** correct the error and have them reread the word and then the sentence.
Practice sentence writing.	Provide white boards.	**Write Sentences** Have students copy the sentences from reproducible p. 219 on white boards. Have them confirm spellings by comparing the words they wrote to the words in the sentences.

Passage Reading

5–10 minutes

	To Do	To Say
Assess fluency and comprehension.	Determine which students to assess this week.	Choose from these options: monitor fluency (see pp. 214–215) and/or monitoring retelling (see p. 216). Have students reread "Pictures." Be sure each student is assessed every other week.
		If you have time, assess every student.

ACTIVITY 2 Build Concepts

Vocabulary

5–10 minutes

	To Do	To Say
Review concept and vocabulary.	Review the homework.	Ask students to go over answers and share their writing from Practice Book, p. 108.
	Display the concept web you began on Day 1.	**This week's question is *How are communities and families similar around the world?* How do this week's words relate to the question?** (Have students answer the question, using some of the vocabulary they learned this week.) Ask students to add more words to the vocabulary web. Have students explain how each word relates to the week's question. Monitor students' understanding of vocabulary as they discuss the web. See Routine Card 6.
MORE PRACTICE		Students can extend the web by adding more related words.

ACTIVITY 3 Read to Connect

Reread "Town Squares," pp. 34–35

	To Do	To Say *10 minutes*
Monitor comprehension.	Have students reread "Town Squares" silently.	**As you read, think about what the selection says about town squares.** After rereading, ask: • **What is a town square?** (A town square is an open area that forms the heart of many cities.) • **Why do people go to a town square?** (They go there to meet new friends and to enjoy dances, festivals, and holidays. People can buy, sell, and trade goods there. They can get caught up on town news.)
Make connections.	Have students make connections across texts.	**We also read "Across the Ocean." Find that selection. What are some things that Japan and America have shared?** Record students' ideas. **We also read "Pictures." What did Anna do to help her enjoy and learn about her new country?** Record students' ideas. **What can you say in general about how communities are similar around the world?** (Sample answers: Communities in different countries have different cultures. People enjoy sharing their cultures with others.)

ACTIVITY 4 Write

Response to Literature "4 You 2 Do," p. 56

	To Do	To Say *5–10 minutes*
Guide response activities.	Discuss the directions. Tell students to choose one activity to complete. Monitor handwriting. See pp. 227–229.	**Word Play** Have students work with partners to unscramble the words. Suggest that they use each word in a sentence. **Making Connections** Discuss the question in a group or as a class. **On Paper** Brainstorm with the class a list of things new in American culture that someone in Japan might enjoy. Have students write their letters on their own. Students can use Practice Book, p. 109, to help prepare their written responses, or you can send the Practice Book page home for them to complete later.
MORE PRACTICE		If you have more time, direct students to complete two or more of the activities.

Homework Practice Book, p. 109, Writing

Unit 5 Week 3 *Coming to America*

What changes when people move from one culture to another?

Objectives *This week students will ...*

Vocabulary
- build concepts and vocabulary: *address, apartment, immigrant, journey, museum, photograph*

Phonics
- read words with vowel sound in *ball: augh, ough;* and prefixes *over-, under-, out-*
- apply knowledge of letter-sounds and word structure to decode unknown words when reading

Text Comprehension
- read connected text
- use sequence to improve comprehension
- write in response to literature

Fluency
- practice fluency with oral rereading

Word Work *This week's phonics focus is ...*

Vowel Sound in *ball: augh, ough*   Prefixes *over-, under-, out-*

Concept Words *Tested Vocabulary*

The week's vocabulary is related to people moving from one culture to another. The first appearance of each word in the Student Reader is noted below.

address	the place to which mail is sent (p. 73)
apartment	room or group of rooms to live in (p. 63)
immigrant	someone who comes into a country or region to live there (p. 61)
journey	a long and sometimes difficult trip (p. 60)
museum	a place to display things related to science, art, life in another time or place, or other subjects (p. 63)
photograph	a picture you make with a camera (p. 71)

Student Reader Unit 5 *This week students will read the following selections.*

60	**Coming to America**	Expository Nonfiction
62	**New York's Tenement Museum**	Narrative Nonfiction
70	**Kim Li's New Home**	Realistic Fiction
78	**Moving to America**	Expository Nonfiction/Maps
82	**4 You 2 Do**	Activity Page

Daily Lesson Plan

	ACTIVITIES	MATERIALS
Day 1	**Build Concepts** Weekly Concept: Coming to America Vocabulary: *address, apartment, immigrant, journey, museum, photograph* **Word Work** Phonics: Vowel Sound in *ball: augh, ough* **Read a Passage** "Coming to America," pp. 60–61 Comprehension: Use Strategies Reread for Fluency	Student Reader: Unit 5 Routine Cards 1, 3, 5, 6, 7 Tested Vocabulary Cards Sound-Spelling Card 4 Student White Boards AudioText Practice Book, p. 110, Vowel Sound in *ball: augh, ough*
Day 2	**Reread for Fluency** **Word Work** Phonics: Prefixes *over-, under-, out-,* Vocabulary **Comprehension** Sequence **Read a Passage** "New York's Tenement Museum," pp. 62–69	Student Reader: Unit 5 AudioText Routine Cards 1, 2, 3, 4, 5, 7, 8 Tested Vocabulary Cards Student White Boards Graphic Organizer 5 Practice Book, p. 111, Prefixes *over-, under-, out-*
Day 3	**Reread for Fluency** **Word Work** Phonics: Vowel Sound in *ball: augh, ough;* Prefixes *over-, under-, out-* Vocabulary **Read a Passage** "Kim Li's New Home," pp. 70–77 Comprehension: Sequence **Write** Response to Literature	Student Reader: Unit 5 AudioText Routine Cards 3, 4, 7 Student journals Practice Book, pp. 110–112, Vowel Sound in *ball: augh, ough;* Prefixes *over-, under-, out-;* Sequence
Day 4	**Reread for Fluency** **Word Work** Phonics: Spiral Review Vocabulary **Read a Passage** "Moving to America," pp. 78–81 Comprehension: Sequence; Listening **Write** Response to Literature	Student Reader: Unit 5 AudioText Routine Cards 3, 4, 5 Student White Boards Practice Book, pp. 112–113, Sequence; Vocabulary
Day 5	**Assessment Options** Fluency, Comprehension Sentence Reading Mid-Unit Passage Reading **Build Concepts** Vocabulary **Read to Connect** **Write** Response to Literature: "4 You 2 Do," p. 82	Student Reader: Unit 5 Reproducible p. 219 Sentence Reading Chart, p. 223 Student White Boards Fluency Progress Chart, p. 215 Routine Card 6 Practice Book, pp. 113–114, Vocabulary; Writing Assessment Book, p. 82

See pp. xvi–xvii for how *My Sidewalks* integrates instructional practices for ELL.
See pp. 251–254 for Phonemic Awareness Activities.

ACTIVITY 1 Build Concepts

Vocabulary

10–15 minutes

	To Do	To Say
Develop word meaning.	See Routine Card 6. Discuss pp. 59–61.	Read Words 2 the Wise on p. 59. Have students look over pages 60–61. **Look at the pictures. What do you notice?** (a boy eating; a group of people that looks like an Asian family) **Can you use the words *journey* and *immigrant* to describe any of these pictures?** (Example: *Immigrants journey from other lands to live in America.*)
Scaffold instruction.	Create a concept web.	In the center of a web, write *Coming to America.* **This week's concept is *coming to America. Coming to America* refers to the people who come to this country from other lands.** Provide examples to demonstrate meaning. **The people of America come from many different lands and cultures. People are still coming to America to fulfill their dreams of a better life.** Add the other vocabulary words. Discuss the meaning of each word as it relates to people coming to America, using the glossary as needed. (See p. 100 in this Teacher's Guide for definitions.)

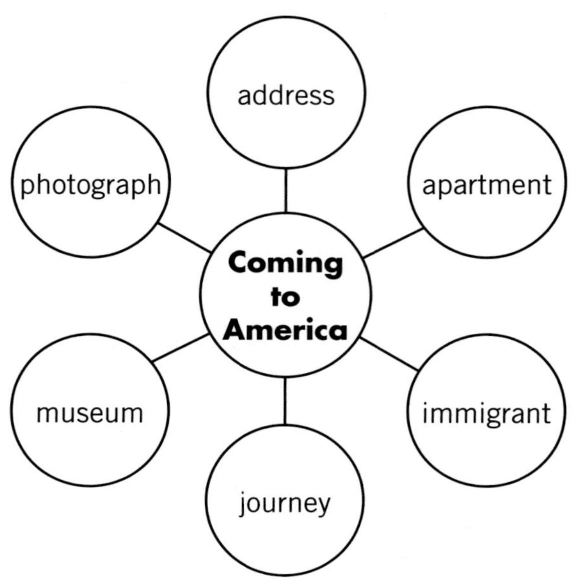

	To Do	To Say
Model the multisyllabic word strategy.	Display each word. Say it as you display it.	Use the Tested Vocabulary Cards. Follow this routine for each word: • **Look for Meaningful Parts** Remind students to look for meaningful parts. **As you say each word, ask yourself: Do I see any parts I know?** • **Chunk Words with No Recognizable Parts** Model how to chunk the word *apartment* to read it.
	Think aloud.	• **Model I see a chunk at the beginning of the word: *a.* I see a chunk in the middle: *part.* I see a chunk at the end of the word: *ment.* I say each chunk slowly: *a part ment.* I say the chunks fast to make a whole word: *apartment.* Is it a real word? Yes, I know the word *apartment.*** • Have students practice reading each word.
Preview.	Read p. 58 with students.	**Do you see any of the words we just learned on this page?** Together with students, read the sentences on p. 58 describing each selection. Talk about how the concept words might be used in the selections.
MORE PRACTICE	Deepen understanding of *immigrant.*	Have students demonstrate understanding by answering questions. **Someone who moves from one country to live in another country is an *immigrant.* An early group of *immigrants* came to America from England on the *Mayflower.***

ACTIVITY 2 Word Work

Blending Strategy Vowel Vowel Sound in *ball: augh, ough*

5–10 minutes

	To Do	To Say
Use the blending routine.	Write *walk, saw,* and *haul.*	Routine **1 Connect** You can already read words like these. What are the words? *(walk, saw, haul)* What is the vowel sound in *walk?* (/ò/) in *saw?* (/ò/) in *haul?* (/ò/) What letter combinations stand for this sound? *(al, aw, au)* Now you will learn some other letter combinations that can stand for this vowel sound.
Scaffold instruction.	Display Sound-Spelling Card 4.	**2 Use Sound-Spelling Card** This is a picture of an audience. An audience watches or listens to something, such as a play. What vowel sound do you hear at the beginning of *audience?* (/ò/) Say it with me: /ò/. The two letters *au* both contribute to make the /ò/ sound you hear in *ball.* When the letters *au* and *ou* are followed by *gh,* all four letters stand for the vowel sound in *ball,* /ò/, and the letters *gh* are silent.
	Distribute white boards.	**3 Listen and Write** Write the letters *augh* and *ough* for the vowel sound /ò/. As you write, say the sound to yourself: /ò/. Now say the sound aloud.
	Write *taught.*	**4 Model** The letters *augh* and *ough* usually have the vowel sound /ò/ as in *ball.* This is how I blend this word: /t/ /ò/ /t/, *taught.* Now you try: /t/ /ò/ /t/, *taught.* t a u g h t
	Write *brought.*	Repeat with *brought.* Point out that the vowel sound /ò/ can be spelled *augh* or *ough.*
CORRECTIVE FEEDBACK	Write each practice word. Monitor student practice.	**5 Group Practice** Let's try the same thing with these words. Support students as they blend progressively more difficult words. Give feedback, using the *if . . . then* statements on Routine Card 1. ought caught taught sought* thought retaught brought daughter naughty **6 Individual Practice** Have each student blend several words from the row matched to his or her ability. bought caught ought fought slaughter* haughty* thoughtless granddaughter thoughtful
	Check understanding of practice words.	*Students need to make sense of words that they segment and blend. If needed, help students with meanings. *Sought* means searched for. I *sought* out the best price. *Slaughter* means killing. The *slaughter* of baby seals is unlawful here. *Haughty* means too proud of yourself and unfriendly toward others. Kim seemed *haughty* after she won the race.
MORE PRACTICE	Distribute white boards. Model building and spelling words.	**Build Words** Write *ought.* Can you blend this word? (/ò/ /t/) Have students write words on white boards. Write *ought.* Now add a *b* to the beginning of the word. What is the new word? *(bought)* • Change the *b* in *bought* to *f.* What is the new word? *(fought)* • Change the *f* in *fought* to *th.* What is the new word? *(thought)* • Now add *-ful* to the end of *thought.* What is the new word? *(thoughtful)*

ACTIVITY 3 Read a Passage

Build Background "Coming to America," pp. 60–61

10 minutes

	To Do	To Say
Develop language and concepts.	See Routine Cards 3 and 7. Ask questions and elaborate on answers.	**Before Reading** Read the title aloud. Do a structured picture walk with students. p. 60 **What do you see?** (a group of people that looks like a family) **Yes, this looks like a family that might have come from somewhere in Asia. Immigrants to the United States are people from another country who come here to live. Immigrants might make their journey to America by plane or boat.**
Scaffold instruction.	Key concepts: *chopsticks, immigrants, journey, tradition*	p. 61 **What is happening in this picture?** (Two children are eating.) **The boy is eating a sandwich—a common American meal. The girl is eating rice with chopsticks. Many people in Asia eat with chopsticks. Using chopsticks is a tradition passed on from parents to their children. Have you ever tried eating with chopsticks?**
Guide compre-hension.	Read pp. 60–61 aloud.	**During Reading** Read the selection as students follow along. Then read it a second time, having students join in. If necessary, stop at the end of each paragraph to check comprehension. Ask questions to promote discussion and develop the concept. • **What country is this family from? Where have they moved to?** (They are from China and have moved to America.) • **What does the family do to learn about America?** (learn to speak English, eat American food, wear popular clothing styles, make new friends) • **What do many immigrants teach their sons and daughters?** (their traditions) • **What words on the concept web could help you describe the people pictured in this article?**
	Use vocabulary to develop the concept.	**After Reading** **What did you learn about *immigrants?* What are some countries people *journey* from to come to America? What country did you or your ancestors come from?**

Reread for Fluency "Coming to America," p. 60

5–10 minutes

	To Do	To Say
CORRECTIVE FEEDBACK	Monitor oral reading.	**Read p. 60 aloud. Read it three or four times so your reading gets better each time.** Give feedback on students' oral reading and use of the blending strategy. See Routine Cards 1 and 5.
MORE PRACTICE		Instead of rereading just p. 60, have students reread the entire selection three or four times. You may want to have students read along with the AudioText.

Homework Practice Book, p. 110, Phonics: Vowel Sound in *ball: augh, ough*

ACTIVITY 1 Reread for Fluency

Paired Reading "Coming to America," p. 61

	To Do	To Say
		5–10 minutes
CORRECTIVE FEEDBACK	Pair students. Monitor paired reading.	Students read aloud p. 61, switching readers for each sentence. Have partners reread; now the other partner begins. For optimal fluency, students should reread three or four times. Give feedback, using Routine Card 5.
MORE PRACTICE		Instead of rereading just p. 61, have students reread the entire selection three or four times. You may want to have students read along with the AudioText.

ACTIVITY 2 Word Work

Blending Strategy Prefixes *over-*, *under-*, *out-*

5–10 minutes

Routine

	To Do	To Say
Use the blending routine.	Write *reread* and *untie.*	**1 Connect** **You can already read words like these. What do you know about reading them?** (They begin with prefixes that are separate syllables from the base word.) **Today we will learn about adding prefixes** ***over-*, *under-*, and *out-* to the beginnings of words. Each prefix has a specific meaning:** **over- "above" or "too" under- "below" or "beneath"** **out- "outward"; "outside"; "longer or better than"**
Scaffold instruction.	Write *outran.*	**2 Model** Point to *outran.* **This is a two-syllable word formed from the base word *ran* and the prefix *out-*. You can cover the prefix, read the base word, and then blend the base word and the prefix to read the whole word. What is the word?** *(outran)* **What does it mean?** ("ran farther or longer") **Let's blend this word together:** ***out ran, outran.*** o u t r a n
	Write *outlive, overhead,* and *underage.*	Repeat with *outlive* ("live longer"), *overhead* ("above one's head"), and *underage* ("below a certain age").
	Distribute white boards.	**3 Listen and Write** Have students write on white boards. **Write the word *ran.* Write *out* in front of it. As you write, say the new word to yourself: *outran.* Now say the word aloud.** Do the same with *overhead* and *underage.*
CORRECTIVE FEEDBACK	Write each practice word. Monitor student practice.	**4 Group Practice** **Let's try the same thing with these words.** Support students as they blend progressively more difficult words. Give feedback, using the ***if . . . then*** statements on Routine Card 1. **outdo overall underfed undersea outgrow** **underground overthrown underwater outnumber underlining** **5 Individual Practice** Have each student blend several words from the row best matched to his or her ability. **outran overeat underpay overdo outside** **outdated overlooked underachieve outdistance overcoming**

For more practice, see next page.

MORE PRACTICE

Model spelling words with prefixes.	**Spell and Write** You can spell words with prefixes by thinking about the prefix and the base word. What prefix and base word make up *oversleep? (over-* and *sleep)* Start with the sounds in the base word: /slēp/. What letters spell *sleep?* Write *sleep.* Now add the prefix *over-.* Now spell *oversleep.* Repeat with *oversize, underdone, outbreak,* and *overhear.*

Vocabulary

5 minutes

	To Do	To Say
Review vocabulary.	Display the concept web from Day 1.	Review the concept web. See Routine Card 2 for the multisyllabic word routine. **The words *apartment, immigrant, journey,* and *museum* will be in the selection you are reading today.** Remind students that *immigrant* means "someone who comes into a country to live there."
	Deepen word understanding of *journey* and *museum.*	**A *journey* is a long trip you take to some place faraway. Think of a journey you have taken. Where did you leave from and where did you go?** (Encourage discussion of trips that students have taken with their families and friends. Emphasize the point of departure and the destination.) **A *museum* is a place where a collection of things is kept for people to see. Some museums show paintings by famous people. Other kinds of museums show things about the Earth. Still other kinds of museums have displays about science. What museums have you visited?** (Encourage discussion of museums students have visited either with family or on school field trips. Ask what they saw and some of the things they learned. Encourage students to suggest museums they might like to visit someday.)
Lead cumulative review.		Use the Tested Vocabulary Cards to review concept words from previous weeks.

ACTIVITY 3 Comprehension

Sequence

5 minutes

	To Do	To Say
Scaffold instruction.	Introduce sequence.	**Today you will read about a real place where immigrants to this country once lived. When you read about changing events, it is important to keep track of the *sequence,* or order, in which things happen, because it can help you better understand what you are reading. Pay attention to words and dates that tell you how old a place is and when things happened.**
	Model the skill.	**For example, if I read that the tenement was built in 1863, that immigrants lived there for many years, and that it became a museum in 1988, I need to pay attention to the sequence of events. The sequence helps me see how the building was used and how it has changed over time.**
	Distribute Graphic Organizer 5.	**As you read "New York's Tenement Museum," look for words and dates that help you trace the sequence of events in the building's past and the sequence of events in each family's life. Add the sequence words to your graphic organizer.** See Routine Card 8.

ACTIVITY 4 Read a Passage

Reading "New York's Tenement Museum," pp. 62–69

10–15 minutes

	To Do	To Say
Develop language and concepts.	See Routine Cards 3 and 7.	**Before Reading** Have students recall what they learned about coming to America. Read the title. Introduce proper nouns. Do a structured picture walk with students.
	Ask questions and elaborate on answers.	pp. 62–63 **This selection tells about people who immigrated to America many years ago. This is a building where some immigrant families once lived. It has been turned into a museum. How would you describe the building?** (It is old, large, and several stories high.) **This building is called a tenement. It had many small apartments.**
Scaffold instruction.	Key concepts: *apartment, immigrant, journey, museum, tenement*	pp. 64–69 **How would you describe the rooms on pp. 64, 65, and 67?** (They seem small and crowded but neat.) **This is what the inside of the tenement looked like. What do you think people had been doing in the room on p. 66?** (making a dress) **Judging from the furniture and other details, I'd guess that the people who lived here did not have much money. What does the picture on pp. 68–69 show?** (a view of a large city) **Yes, many immigrants came to large cities to live and find work. Imagine their journey to America. Think what it would be like to move to a large city in a new country.**
Guide compre-hension.	Use Routine Card 4.	**During Reading** **Read the pages in a whisper. Raise your hand if you need help with a word. As you read, ask yourself: What am I learning about the people who lived in this building? What is this mainly about?**
	Monitor independent reading.	pp. 62–63 **What did you learn about a tenement?** (A tenement was an apartment building with several floors. People had to share bathrooms.) **What happened to this tenement building?** (It was turned into a museum.)
	Model using context for word meaning.	Read aloud the paragraph with *tenement* on p. 63. Point out the phrases "building with several floors" and "three-room apartments," which provide clues to the meaning of *tenement.*
		pp. 64–67 **What families did you learn about?** (the Gumpertz, Levine, and Baldizzi families) **Tell me about one of the families you read about.** (Example: Harris and Jennie Levine were from Poland. Harris made women's clothing. Jennie took care of two children, cooked, and cleaned.)
		pp. 68–69 **Describe the lives of these immigrants.** (They had little. Many were very poor. They missed their old homes. They worked hard and wanted America to be their new home.)
Model summarizing.	Think aloud.	**After Reading** **What did you learn about immigrant families that came to America? What was the selection mainly about?** Model how to summarize. **The selection tells details about several immigrant families who lived in a tenement in New York City. It is mainly about where they lived and what their lives were like.**
MORE PRACTICE	Have students reread pp. 62–63.	**Reread** As they read, have students note the sequence in which things happen. Point out that the phrase *many years ago* tells us that the things in the story happened in the past. The dates in the article tell when the tenement was built and when it was turned into a museum.
	Homework	Practice Book, p. 111, Phonics: Prefixes *over-, under-, out-*

3

ACTIVITY 1 Reread for Fluency

Oral Reading "New York's Tenement Museum," pp. 62–63

5–10 minutes

	To Do	To Say
CORRECTIVE FEEDBACK	Monitor oral reading.	**Read pp. 62–63 aloud. Read them three or four times so your reading gets better each time.** Give feedback on students' oral reading and use of the blending strategy. Use Routine Cards 1 and 3.
MORE PRACTICE		Have students reread additional pages of the selection three or four times. You may want to have students read along with the AudioText.

ACTIVITY 2 Word Work

Fluent Word Reading Vowel Sound in *ball: augh, ough;* Prefixes *over-, under-, out-*

5–10 minutes

	To Do	To Say
Review phonics.	Review homework.	Ask students to share answers from Practice Book, pp. 110–111.
Use word-reading routine.	Write *underpay.*	Routine **1 Connect** **You can read this word because you know that a word beginning with *under-* is often a word formed from a base word and the prefix *under-*. What is the base word** *(pay)* **What is the word?** *(underpay).*
	Write *outlive, overeat, thought,* and *daughter.*	**2 Model** **When you come to a new word, look for meaningful parts. If you don't recognize any meaningful parts, then look for chunks you can read. Look at all the letters in the chunk and think about the vowel sound. Say the parts of the word to yourself, and then read the word.** Model reading *outlive, overeat, thought,* and *daughter* in this way. **When you come to a new word, what are you going to do?**
Scaffold instruction.	Write each practice word.	**3 Group Practice** **Let's read these words. Look for meaningful parts and chunks, think about the vowel sound in each chunk, and say the parts to yourself. We will read words with the vowel sound /ò/ and the prefixes *over-, under-,* and *out-*. When I point to the word, let's read it together.** Allow 2–3 seconds previewing time for each word. Support students as they blend progressively more difficult words. ought, caught, outlive, overcharge, underground slaughter, overwhelm, undergoing, naughty, overpower
CORRECTIVE FEEDBACK	**MONITOR PROGRESS**	***If . . .*** students have difficulty previewing and reading whole words, ***then . . .*** have them use sound-by-sound blending. ***If . . .*** students can't read words fluently at a rate of 1–2 seconds per word, ***then . . .*** continue practicing the list.
MORE PRACTICE	Model reading words in sentences.	**When I read a sentence, I read each word without stopping between the words. If I come to a word I don't know, I blend it. Then I read the sentence again.** Model reading this sentence, stopping to blend *bought: I bought my brother a baseball.*
	Write practice sentences.	Have each student read the sentence best matched to his or her ability. **My daughter outgrew her shoes.** **Ms. Jones taught us how roots grow underground.** **The clerk overcharged me for the book I bought.**

Vocabulary

	To Do	To Say — 5 minutes
Review vocabulary.	Display the concept web from Day 1.	Review the concept web. **The words *address, apartment, immigrant, journey,* and *photograph* are in today's selection.** Review meanings of the words.

ACTIVITY 3 Read a Passage

Reading "Kim Li's New Home," pp. 70–77

	To Do	To Say — 10–15 minutes
Scaffold instruction.	Review sequence.	Remind students that clue words and dates can help them follow the sequence. **Look for words and phrases like *today, first, after, when, last year,* and *used to live.* As you read "Kim Li's New Home," look for the sequence of events.**
Develop language and concepts.	See Routine Cards 3 and 7.	**Before Reading** Read the title. Introduce proper nouns. Do a picture walk.
	Ask questions and elaborate on answers.	pp. 70–73 **What do you think is happening on these pages?** (A family is moving or taking a journey.) **To whom might these postcards be going?** (maybe to a friend or a relative back home) **What do you think the writer is describing?** (the trip and school)
	Key concepts: *country, journey, postcard*	pp. 74–77 **How can you tell that the girl in these pictures is enjoying life in her new country?** (She looks happy playing with her friends and eating with her family.)
Guide compre-hension.	Use Routine Card 4.	**During Reading** **Read the pages in a whisper. Raise your hand if you need help with a word. As you read, ask yourself: Who are the characters? What happens first, next, and last?**
	Monitor independent reading.	pp. 70–75 **What is the first important thing that happens in the story?** (Kim Li has just come to America. She is playing with her new friend, Jessie.) **How does Kim Li feel?** (nervous about going to school) **What happens when Kim Li goes to school?** (The teacher introduces her to the class.) pp. 75–77 **What happens at the end?** (Kim Li makes friends at school. She goes to a party with her new friends.)
	Monitor comprehension.	**After Reading** Discuss the What Do You Think? question.
	Guide retelling.	Have one student retell the story while the others assist. Prompt students by asking: **Who are the main characters? What do they do in the story? How does the story end?** See Monitoring Retelling on p. 216.
MORE PRACTICE	Have students reread pp. 70–72.	**Reread** As they read, tell students to list some words and phrases they might use to describe Kim Li and Jessie.

ACTIVITY 4 Write

Response to Literature

	To Do	To Say — 5 minutes
Prompt journal writing.		**Take out your journals. How would you feel if you moved to a different country? Write about how you would think and feel.**

Homework Practice Book, p. 112, Sequence

4

ACTIVITY 1 Reread for Fluency

Paired Reading "Kim Li's New Home," pp. 76–77

	To Do	To Say	5–10 minutes
CORRECTIVE FEEDBACK	Pair students. Monitor paired reading.	Students read aloud pp. 76–77, switching readers for each paragraph. Have partners reread; now the other partner begins. For optimal fluency, students should reread three or four times. You may want to have students read along with the AudioText. Give feedback, using Routine Card 5.	
MORE PRACTICE	**READERS' THEATER**	Students can use the dialogue as a script for a Readers' Theater. Have them rehearse, with one student being the narrator and the others the story characters.	

ACTIVITY 2 Word Work

Spiral Review Vowel Sound in *ball: a, al, au, aw, augh, ough*

	To Do	To Say	5 minutes
Review blending: vowel sound in *ball*.	Write *haul* and *yawn.*	**You can read these words because you know that *au* and *aw* can stand for the vowel sound /ò/. What sound can *au* stand for?** (/ò/) **What is the word?** *(haul)* **What sound can *aw* stand for?** (/ò/) **What is the word?** *(yawn)* Remind students that the sound /ò/ can also be spelled *a, al, augh,* and *ough.*	
Scaffold instruction.	Write *caught* and *bought.*	**You can read these words because you know *augh* and *ough* stand for the sound /ò/. What sound can *augh* stand for?** (/ò/) **What is the word?** *(caught)* **What sound can *ou* stand for?** (/ò/) **What is the word?** *(bought).*	
CORRECTIVE FEEDBACK	Distribute white boards. Monitor student work.	**Build Words** Write *au, aw, augh,* and *ough* as headings on a four-column chart. Have students copy the chart on their white boards. Below each heading write several words with those letters omitted. For example, for *pause* write *p___se.* Have students add the missing letters to each word and copy the words on their white boards. Ask students to read the completed words. If students have difficulty reading words, have them blend words sound-by-sound.	

au	*aw*	*augh*	*ough*
p___se	str___	c___t	br___t
s___ce	sh___l	d___ter	th___t

Vocabulary

	To Do	To Say	5–10 minutes
Extend word knowledge.	Write on the board or a transparency: *The journey took twelve hours.*	Use the word *journey* to extend word knowledge. **We learned that this word means a long trip. Can you name some other words that mean about the same thing as *journey?*** *(trip, tour, voyage, expedition)* Write the words. Talk about the meanings of the words. Point out that a trip can be short (such as a trip to the grocery store). However, a tour, voyage, or expedition would take a much longer time.	
MORE PRACTICE	Deepen word understanding.	Have students use *journey* and *photograph* in the same sentence. (For example, *I took many photographs on my journey.*) Share sentences. Ask, **What are some photographs you have taken or enjoyed looking at?**	

ACTIVITY 3 Read a Passage

Read Together "Moving to America," pp. 78–81

10–15 minutes

	To Do	To Say
Scaffold instruction.	Review sequence (homework).	Ask volunteers to read the passage and share answers from Practice Book, p. 112. Remind students of the importance of following sequence. **When you read a selection, the sequence of events is important. Often there are dates or clue words that help you understand the order in which things happen. Look for these things as you read. Knowing the sequence of events may also help you to picture in your mind the events as they happen.**
Develop language and concepts.	See Routine Cards 3 and 4.	**Before Reading** **This selection is about some of the countries people have come from to America. What map do you see on these pages?** (a map of the world) **Look at the map carefully. Can you find North America on this map? We live in North America.**
Model fluent reading.	Read pp. 78–81 aloud. Model prosody.	**During Reading** **When I read a selection like this, first I read the paragraphs. Then I look at the map. I notice how the map and labels relate to the information in the paragraphs.** Read the pages as described. Point out on the map areas and continents mentioned in the text. **Read the selection with me. Try to make your voice sound like mine as we read.** Reread the selection several times with students.
Monitor compre-hension.	Monitor listening comprehension.	**After Reading** Prompt discussion to monitor comprehension. Listen as students answer questions. **How long have people been moving to the United States?** (hundreds of years) **How do the maps in the selection help you understand what you read?** (The maps show the continents of the world and Central America. Several continents are mentioned in the text.) **Do you know any people from other countries? If so, which ones? Which countries or continents would you be interested in visiting?** (Answers will vary.)
MORE PRACTICE	Have students reread pp. 78–81.	**Reread** As they read, tell students to think about the places mentioned in the selection. Afterward they can discuss relatives or other people they know who come from these areas of the world.

ACTIVITY 4 Write

Response to Literature

5 minutes

	To Do	To Say
Prompt personal narrative.	Writing elements: organization, conventions.	**Tell about a journey you have taken and some of the things you saw or did. Start with the word *first*. Use other sequence words. Be sure to begin sentences with capital letters and use correct end punctuation.**

Homework Practice Book, p. 113, Vocabulary

5

ACTIVITY 1 Assessment Options

Sentence Reading

	To Do	To Say 5 minutes
Assess sentence reading.	Use reproducible p. 219.	Have each student read the sentences. Record scores on the Sentence Reading Chart, p. 223. While you work with one student, others can complete the Write Sentences activity below. **Joe bought a heavy overcoat.** **I caught a cold outside.** **We thought the underwater photographs were good.**
CORRECTIVE FEEDBACK	**MONITOR PROGRESS**	***If . . .*** students have trouble reading words with *augh* and *ough* for the vowel sound in *ball* or the prefixes *over-, under-, and out-,* ***then . . .*** reteach the blending strategy lessons on pp. 103 and 105. ***If . . .*** students misread a word in the sentence, ***then . . .*** correct the error and have them reread the word and then the sentence.
Practice sentence writing.	Provide white boards.	**Write Sentences** Have students copy the sentences from reproducible p. 219 on white boards. Have them confirm spellings by comparing the words they wrote to the words in the sentences.

Mid-Unit Passage Reading

	To Do	To Say 5–10 minutes
Assess fluency and compre-hension.	Determine which students to assess. Use Assessment Book, p. 82.	Choose from these options: monitoring fluency (see pp. 214–215) and/or monitoring retelling (see p. 216). Have students read the Unit 5 Mid-Unit Fluency Passage in the Assessment Book. Be sure each student is assessed every other week.
		If you have time, assess every student.

ACTIVITY 2 Build Concepts

Vocabulary

	To Do	To Say 5–10 minutes
Review concept and vocabulary.	Review homework. Display the concept web you began on Day 1.	Ask students to go over answers and share their writing from Practice Book, p. 113. **This week's question is *What changes when people move from one culture to another?* How do this week's words relate to the question?** (Have students answer the question, using some of the vocabulary they learned this week.) Ask students to add more words to the concept web. Have students explain how each word relates to coming to America. Monitor students' understanding of vocabulary as they discuss the web. See Routine Card 6.
MORE PRACTICE		Have students see how many vocabulary words they can write in one sentence. Invite them to share their sentences with the class.

ACTIVITY 3 Read to Connect

Reread "Coming to America," pp. 60–61

10 minutes

	To Do	To Say
Monitor comprehension.	Have students reread "Coming to America" silently.	**As you read, think about what the selection says about what it is like to come to America.** After rereading, ask: • **Where is the family in the selection from?** (China) • **What happens when a family comes to America from another country?** (They learn about this country but keep many traditions from their other country.) **We also read "New York's Tenement Museum." Find that selection. What was life like for the people who came to America to live?** Record students' ideas. **We also read "Kim Li's New Home." What did Kim Li tell her grandmother about her new home in America?** Record students' ideas.
Make connections.	Have students make connections across texts.	**What can you say in general about the people who come to America and where they come from?** (Sample answers: People come to America for a better life. They come from all over the world.)

ACTIVITY 4 Write

Response to Literature "4 You 2 Do," p. 82

5–10 minutes

	To Do	To Say
Guide response activities.	Discuss the directions. Tell students to choose one activity to complete. Monitor handwriting. See pp. 227–229.	**Word Play** Have students suggest answers for the riddle. Then have them suggest riddles of their own. **Making Connections** Discuss the question in small groups. Responses will vary, but they should demonstrate an understanding of what immigrants face when they come to America. **On Paper** Before students write, brainstorm with the class challenges immigrants might face at school and ways to help them. Students can use Practice Book, p. 114, to structure their written responses, or you can send the Practice Book page home for them to complete later.
MORE PRACTICE		If you have more time, direct students to complete two or more of the activities.

Homework Practice Book, p. 114, Writing

Unit 5 Week 4 *Let's Eat!*

What is ethnic food?

Objectives *This week students will ...*

Vocabulary
- build concepts and vocabulary: *delicious, dinnertime, ethnic, mixture, recipe, restaurant*

Phonics
- read words with long *i: ind, ild;* long *o: ost, old;* and suffixes *-y, -ish*
- apply knowledge of letter-sounds and word structure to decode unknown words when reading

Text Comprehension
- read connected text
- draw conclusions to improve comprehension
- write in response to literature

Fluency
- practice fluency with oral rereading

Word Work *This week's phonics focus is ...*

Long *i: ind, ild* Long *o: ost, old* Suffixes *-y, -ish*

Concept Words *Tested Vocabulary*

The week's vocabulary is related to the concept of ethnic foods from around the world. The first appearance of each word in the Student Reader is noted below.

delicious	very good-tasting (p. 90)
dinnertime	when you eat the main meal of the day (p. 86)
ethnic	related to a group of people from the same race, nationality, or culture (p. 86)
mixture	a combination of different things (p. 91)
recipe	the steps to follow to make a kind of food (p. 92)
restaurant	a place to buy and eat a meal (p. 99)

Student Reader Unit 5 *This week students will read the following selections.*

86	**Ethnic Foods**	Expository Nonfiction
90	**The Food Sleuth**	Narrative Nonfiction
98	**The Sweet Surprise**	Realistic Fiction
106	**Menu, Please!**	Recipes
108	**4 You 2 Do**	Activity Page

Daily Lesson Plan

	ACTIVITIES	MATERIALS
Day 1	**Build Concepts** Weekly Concept: Let's Eat! Vocabulary: *delicious, dinnertime, ethnic, mixture, recipe, restaurant* **Word Work** Phonics: Long *i: ind, ild;* Long *o: ost, old* **Read a Passage** "Ethnic Foods," pp. 86–89 Comprehension: Use Strategies Reread for Fluency	Student Reader: Unit 5 Routine Cards 1, 3, 5, 6, 7 Tested Vocabulary Cards Sound-Spelling Card 16 Student White Boards AudioText Practice Book, p. 115, Long *i: ind, ild;* Long *o: ost, old*
Day 2	**Reread for Fluency** **Word Work** Phonics: Suffixes *-y, -ish* Vocabulary **Comprehension** Draw Conclusions **Read a Passage** "The Food Sleuth," pp. 90–97	Student Reader: Unit 5 AudioText Routine Cards 1, 2, 3, 4, 5, 7, 8 Tested Vocabulary Cards Student White Boards Graphic Organizer 2 Practice Book, p. 116, Suffixes *-y, -ish*
Day 3	**Reread for Fluency** **Word Work** Phonics: Long *i: ind, ild*; Long *o: ost, old* Suffixes *-y, -ish* Vocabulary **Read a Passage** "The Sweet Surprise," pp. 98–105 Comprehension: Draw Conclusions **Write** Response to Literature	Student Reader: Unit 5 AudioText Routine Cards 1, 3, 4, 5, 7 Student journals Practice Book, 115–117 Long *i: ind, ild;* Long *o: ost, old;* Suffixes *-y, -ish* Draw Conclusions
Day 4	**Reread for Fluency** **Word Work** Phonics: Spiral Review Vocabulary **Read a Passage** "Menu, Please!" pp. 106–107 Comprehension: Draw Conclusions; Listening **Write** Response to Literature	Student Reader: Unit 5 AudioText Routine Cards 3, 4, 5 Student White Boards Practice Book, pp. 117–118, Draw Conclusions; Vocabulary
Day 5	**Assessment Options** Fluency, Comprehension Sentence Reading Passage Reading **Build Concepts** Vocabulary **Read to Connect** **Write** Response to Literature: "4 You 2 Do," p. 108	Student Reader: Unit 5 Reproducible p. 219 Sentence Reading Chart, p. 223 Student White Boards Fluency Progress Chart, p. 215 Routine Card 6 Practice Book, pp. 118–119, Vocabulary; Writing

See pp. xvi–xvii for how *My Sidewalks* integrates instructional practices for ELL.
See pp. 251–254 for Phonemic Awareness Activities.

ACTIVITY 1 Build Concepts

Vocabulary

10–15 minutes

	To Do	To Say
Develop word meaning.	See Routine Card 6. Discuss pp. 85–89.	Read Words 2 the Wise on p. 85. Have students flip through pages 86–89. **Look at the pictures. What do you notice?** (a boy holding a plate of food, pictures of food from other lands) **Can you use the words *ethnic* and *dinnertime* to describe any of these pictures?** (Example: *Sometimes we have ethnic foods at dinnertime.*)
Scaffold instruction.	Create a concept web.	In the center of a web, write *Let's Eat.* **This week's concept is *let's eat. Let's eat* refers to the many different kinds of foods we eat that come from other lands.** Provide examples to demonstrate meaning. **People in different lands have their own unique kinds of foods. In this country, we enjoy food from many different cultures.** Add the other vocabulary words. Discuss the meaning of each word as it relates to the foods we eat, using the glossary as needed. (See p. 114 in this Teacher's Guide for definitions.)

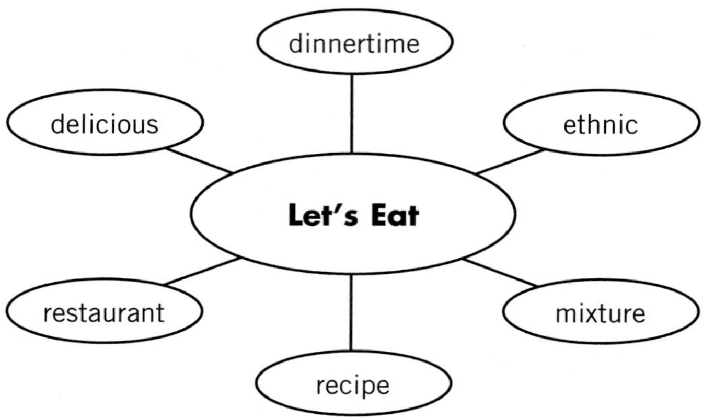

	To Do	To Say
Model the multisyllabic word strategy.	Display each word. Say it as you display it. Think aloud.	Use the Tested Vocabulary Cards. Follow this routine for each word: • **Look for Meaningful Parts** Remind students to look for meaningful parts. **As you say each word, ask yourself: Do I see any parts I know?** • **Model** **Do you recognize any parts of the word *dinnertime?*** (If students don't do so, point out that *dinnertime* is a compound word made up of *dinner* and *time.*) **I ask myself: What do the two parts mean? *Dinner* is the meal we eat at the end of the day. *Time* is when we do things. Use the word parts to read the word: *Dinnertime* is the time we eat dinner.** • **Chunk Words with No Recognizable Parts** Model how to chunk the word *restaurant* to read it. **I see a chunk at the beginning of the word: *res.* I see a chunk in the middle: *taur.* I see a part at the end of the word: *ant.* I say each chunk slowly: *res taur ant.* I say the chunks fast to make a whole word: *restaurant.* Is it a real word? Yes, I know the word *restaurant.*** • Have students practice reading each word.
Preview.	Read p. 84 with students.	**Do you see any of the words we just learned on this page?** Together with students, read the sentences on p. 84 describing each selection. Talk about how the concept words might be used in the selections.
MORE PRACTICE	Deepen understanding of *ethnic.*	Have students demonstrate understanding by answering questions. **Tacos are an *ethnic* food from Mexico. What is an *ethnic* food you have tried? What are some *ethnic* foods your family enjoys?**

ACTIVITY 2 Word Work

Blending Strategy Long *i: ind, ild;* Long *o: ost, old*

5–10 minutes

	To Do	To Say
Use the blending strategy.	Write *high* and *night.*	**1 Connect** You already can read words like these. What are the words? What is the vowel sound in *high?* (/ī/) in *night?* (/ī/) What three letters stand for this sound? *(igh)* Now you will learn another spelling for long *i.*
Scaffold instruction.	Display Sound-Spelling Card 16.	**2 Use Sound-Spelling Card** This is ice cream. What sound do you hear at the beginning of *ice?* (/ī/) Say it with me: /ī/.
	Distribute white boards.	**3 Listen and Write** Write the letter *i* for /ī/. As you write, say the sound to yourself: /ī/. Now say the sound aloud.
	Write *kind* and *wild.*	**4 Model** Sometimes *i* stands for long *i.* This is how I blend this word: /k/ /ī/ /n/ /d/, *kind.* Now you try: /k/ /ī/ /n/ /d/, *kind.* This is how I blend this word: /w/ /ī/ /l/ /d/, *wild.* Now you try: /w/ /ī/ /l/ /d/, *wild.* When *i* is followed by *nd* or *ld,* its sound is often long. k i n d → → → → w i l d → → → →
	Write *cold* and *most.*	Repeat with *cold* and *most.* Point out that when *o* is followed by *ld* or *st,* its sound is often long.
CORRECTIVE FEEDBACK	Write each practice word. Monitor student practice.	**5 Group Practice** Let's try the same thing with these words. Support students as they blend progressively more difficult words. Give feedback, using the *if . . . then* statements on Routine Card 1.

Routine

find	old	post*	mild	bind*	sold
grind*	scold	child	blind		
poster	behind	almost	mildest	older	blindfold

6 Individual Practice Have each student blend several words from the row that is best matched to his or her ability.

fold	host*	gold	told	mind	rind*
grind*	scold	child	blind	mostly	
billfold	unkind	remind	colder	almost	

Check understanding of practice words.

*Students need to make sense of words that they segment and blend. If needed, help students with meanings. A *post* is a long pole set up to support something. To *bind* is to tie up. To *grind* is to crush into very small pieces or a powder. A *host* is a person who invites and greets guests. If you invite friends to your house for a party, you are the *host.* A *rind* is the firm outer coating on melons or cheese.

MORE PRACTICE

Distribute white boards. Model building and spelling words.

Build Words Write *find.* Can you blend this word? (/f/ /ī/ /n/ /d/) Have students write words on white boards. Write *find.* Now change the *f* in *find* to *k.* What is the new word? *(kind)*

- Change the *k* in *kind* to *r.* What is the new word? *(rind)*
- Change the *r* in *rind* to *m.* What is the new word? *(mind)*
- Add *re* to the beginning of *mind.* What is the new word? *(remind)*

ACTIVITY 3

Read a Passage

Build Background "Ethnic Foods," pp. 86–89

10 minutes

	To Do	To Say
Develop language and concepts.	See Routine Cards 3 and 7.	**Before Reading** Read the title aloud. Introduce proper nouns, if necessary. Do a structured picture walk with students.
	Ask questions and elaborate on answers.	p. 86 **What do you see?** (a boy holding a plate of food) **Yes, it looks like the food was cooked outside. It is probably dinnertime. Maybe the boy's family is having a barbeque for dinner.**
Scaffold instruction.	Key concepts: *barbeque, country, crops, culture, dinnertime, dishes, ethnic, salad*	p. 87 **What do you see in this picture?** (things that have been grown to eat) **What kinds of crops have been grown?** (vegetables) **These vegetables are used in ethnic dishes from many cultures. Which vegetables do you like to eat cooked or raw?**
		p. 88 **What does this picture show?** (It looks like a salad.) **Let's look closely. What kinds of things are in the salad?** (lettuce, olives, cheese, onions) **Maybe this is a special kind of salad. Have you ever had a salad like this? Do you think this salad may be from another country? What kinds of salads do you like?**
		p. 89 **What does this picture show?** (different kinds of peppers hanging on wire or string) **Maybe the peppers are being hung to dry. Let's read to find out what ethnic dish comes from Mexico. As you read, ask yourself: What is this mainly about? What am I learning?**
Guide compre-hension.	Read pp. 86–89 aloud.	**During Reading** Read the article as students follow along. Then read it a second time, having students join in. If necessary, stop at the end of each paragraph to check comprehension. Ask questions to promote discussion and develop the concept. • **What are ethnic foods?** (foods from other lands, or nations) • **What is one ethnic food that Greece is famous for?** (Greek salad with olives) • **What is a kind of ethnic food from Mexico?** (salsa) • **What words on the concept web could help you describe the ethnic foods discussed in this article?**
	Use vocabulary to develop the concept.	**After Reading What did you learn about *ethnic* foods? What are some popular *ethnic* foods in this country? What special *ethnic* dishes have you tried and liked?**

Reread for Fluency "Ethnic Foods," p. 89

5–10 minutes

	To Do	To Say
CORRECTIVE FEEDBACK	Monitor oral reading.	**Read p. 89 aloud. Read it three or four times so your reading gets better each time.** Give feedback on students' oral reading and use of the blending strategy. See Routine Cards 1 and 5.
MORE PRACTICE		Instead of rereading just p. 89, have students reread the entire selection three or four times. You may want to have students read along with the AudioText.

Homework Practice Book, p. 115, Phonics: Long *i: ind, ild;* Long *o: old, ost*

ACTIVITY 1 Reread for Fluency

Paired Reading "Ethnic Foods," pp. 87–88

5–10 minutes

	To Do	To Say
CORRECTIVE FEEDBACK	Pair students Monitor paired reading.	Students read aloud pp. 87–88, switching readers for each paragraph. Have partners reread; now the other partner begins. For optimal fluency, students should reread three or four times. Give feedback, using Routine Card 5.
MORE PRACTICE		Instead of rereading just pp. 88–89, have students reread the entire selection three or four times. You may want to have students read along with the AudioText.

ACTIVITY 2 Word Work

Blending Strategy Suffixes *-y, -ish*

5–10 minutes

Routine

	To Do	To Say
Use the blending routine.	Write *slowly* and *careful.*	**1 Connect** **You can already read words like these. What do you know about reading them?** (They end with suffixes.) **Today we will learn about adding two other suffixes, *-y* and *-ish,* to the ends of words. Each suffix has a specific meaning:** ***-y*** **"having a certain quality"** ***-ish*** **"somewhat" or "a liking for"**
Scaffold instruction.	Write *rainy.*	**2 Model** **This is a two-syllable word formed from the base word *rain* and the suffix *-y.* You can cover the suffix, read the base word, and then blend the base word and the suffix to read the whole word. What is the word?** *(rainy)* **What does it mean?** ("having rain") **Let's blend this word together: *rain y, rainy.*** rain y
	Write *sandy, boyish,* and *coolish.*	Repeat with *sandy* ("having sand"), *boyish* ("somewhat like a boy"), and *coolish* ("somewhat cool").
	Distribute white boards.	**3 Listen and Write** **Write the word *rain*. Write *y* at the end of it. As you write, say the new word to yourself: *rainy.* Now say the word aloud.** Do the same with *boyish.*
CORRECTIVE FEEDBACK	Write each practice word. Monitor student practice.	**4 Group Practice** **Let's try the same thing with these words.** Support students as they blend progressively more difficult words. Give feedback, using the ***if . . . then*** statements on Routine Card 1. **windy foolish sunny dusty dirty cloudy** **sticky snowy thirsty frosty grouchy childish** **5 Individual Practice** Have each student blend several words from the row best matched to his or her ability. **soapy dressy tallish speedy bookish noisy** **youngish choppy crunchy greenish shiny pinkish**

For more practice, see next page.

MORE PRACTICE

Model spelling words with suffixes.	**Spell and Write You can spell words with suffixes by thinking about the suffix and the base word. What suffix and base word make up *stormy?*** *(storm* and *-y)* **Start with the sounds in the base word: /s/ /t/ /or/ /m/. What letters spell *storm?*** Write ***storm.* Now add the suffix *-y.* Now spell *stormy.*** Repeat with *gloomy, yellowish, dirty, coldish,* and *bumpy.*

Vocabulary

5 minutes

	To Do	To Say
Review vocabulary.	Display the concept web from Day 1.	Review the concept web. See Routine Card 2 for the multisyllabic word routine. **The words *delicious, dinnertime, ethnic, mixture,* and *recipe* will be in the selection you are reading today.** Remind students that *delicious* means "something that tastes really good."
	Deepen word understanding of *mixture* and *recipe.*	**A *mixture* is something that has two or more things mixed together. Name some things that are mixtures. Why are they mixtures?** (Answers may include any number of foods or beverages that contain more than one ingredient. For example, a salad is a mixture of different vegetables. Salad dressing can be a mixture of oil and vinegar.) **A *recipe* is a list of things that you mix together to make something to eat. What you end up with is a *mixture* of things put together to make something new. What are some *recipes* that you like? What are some of the things that you mix together to make the *recipe?*** (Encourage discussion of different examples, asking: *Can you think of some recipes that you've made or someone you know has made? What were some of the ingredients in the recipes? What was the mixture like?*)
Lead cumulative review.		Use the Tested Vocabulary Cards to review concept words from previous weeks.

ACTIVITY 3 Comprehension

Draw Conclusions

5 minutes

	To Do	To Say
Scaffold instruction.	Introduce draw conclusions.	**Today you will read about some places where delicious foods started. When you read a selection like this, it is important to draw conclusions to figure out what the author is trying to say. To draw a conclusion is to think about facts and details and decide something about them.**
	Model the skill.	**For example, if I read about different popular foods that started in different countries, I might draw the conclusion that many of the foods we eat actually came from different places and cultures.**
	Distribute Graphic Organizer 2.	**As you read "The Food Sleuth," look for facts and details that help you draw conclusions about the origins of foods. List in your graphic organizer some of the conclusions you draw. Also add facts and details to your graphic organizer that helped you draw your conclusions.** See Routine Card 8.

ACTIVITY 4 Read a Passage

Reading "The Food Sleuth," pp. 90–97

	To Do	To Say *10–15 minutes*
Develop language and concepts.	See Routine Cards 3 and 7.	**Before Reading** Have students recall what they learned about ethnic foods. Read the title. Introduce proper nouns, if necessary. Do a structured picture walk with students.
	Ask questions and elaborate on answers.	pp. 90–92 **The selection is about the places where some of our foods first came from. Judging from the pictures on p. 90, what do you think a sleuth is?** (a detective) **What foods do you see on these pages?** (hamburger, hot dog) **Look at the heads before the paragraphs. Where did these two popular foods come from?** (Germany) **Germany is a country in Europe. Many years ago, people came to this country from Germany. They brought their favorite foods and recipes with them.**
Scaffold instruction.	Key concepts: *mixture, noodles, pasta, recipe, sleuth, spicy, tacos*	pp. 93–95 **What foods do you see in these pictures?** (a potato, noodles, spaghetti) **Potatoes are often baked and served with toppings. Spaghetti and noodles are kinds of pasta. What countries did these foods come from?** (Peru and Italy) **Peru is a country in South America. Italy is in Europe.** pp. 96–97 **What food do you see on these pages?** (tacos, apple pie) **Where did these foods come from?** (Mexico, England) **Do you like tacos or apple pie? Do you prefer spicy foods or desserts?**
Guide comprehension.	Use Routine Card 4.	**During Reading** **Read the pages in a whisper. Raise your hand if you need help with a word. As you read, ask yourself: What am I learning about where and how some popular foods started? What is this mainly about?**
	Monitor independent reading.	pp. 90–93 **What did you learn about the origins of hamburgers, hot dogs, and potatoes? Tell me about one of the foods described on these pages. Can you come to any conclusions?** (Example: The hot dog, or frankfurter, probably came from the town of Frankfurt in Germany.) pp. 94–97 **What foods did you learn about on these pages? Tell me about one of the foods described on these pages. What conclusions can you draw?** (Example: The first noodles may have come from China. The Italians used them to make pasta dishes.)
Model summarizing.	Think aloud.	**After Reading** **What did you learn about where some of our popular foods started? What was the selection mainly about?** Model how to summarize. **The selection tells facts and details about the origins of several popular foods. It is mainly about how some of our favorite foods come from different countries and cultures.**
MORE PRACTICE	Have students reread pp. 94–95.	**Reread** As they read, have students note facts and details about pasta in Italy. Help them use these facts and details to draw the conclusion that pasta has been popular in Italy for a long time.

Homework Practice Book, p. 116, Phonics: Suffixes *-y, -ish*

3

ACTIVITY 1 Reread for Fluency

Oral Reading "The Food Sleuth," pp. 96–97

	To Do	To Say *5–10 minutes*
CORRECTIVE FEEDBACK	Monitor oral reading.	**Read pp. 96–97 aloud. Read them three or four times so your reading gets better each time.** Give feedback on students' oral reading and use of the blending strategy. Use Routine Cards 1 and 5.
MORE PRACTICE		Have students reread additional pages of the selection three or four times. You may want to have students read along with the AudioText.

ACTIVITY 2 Word Work

Fluent Word Reading Long *i: ind, ild;* Long *o: ost, old;* Suffixes *-y, -ish*

	To Do	To Say *5–10 minutes*
Review phonics.	Review the homework.	Ask students to share answers from Practice Book, pp. 115–116.
Use word-reading routine.	Write *foolish.*	Routine **1 Connect You can read this word because you know that a word that ends with *-ish* is often a two-syllable word with a base word and the suffix *-ish*. What is the base word?** *(fool)* **What is the word?** *(foolish)*
	Write *windy, mind, wild, most,* and *fold.*	**2 Model When you come to a new word, look for meaningful parts. If you don't recognize any meaningful parts, then look for chunks you can read. Look at all the letters in the chunk and think about the vowel sound. Say the parts of the word to yourself, and then read the word.** Model reading *windy, mind, wild, most,* and *fold* in this way. **When you come to a new word, what are you going to do?**
	Write each practice word.	**3 Group Practice Let's read these words. Look for meaningful parts and chunks, think about the vowel sound in each chunk, and say the parts to yourself. We will read words with the long vowel sounds /ī/ and /ō/ and the suffixes *-y* and *-ish*. When I point to the word, let's read it together.** Allow 2–3 seconds previewing time for each word. Support students as they blend progressively more difficult words. **find mild post hold rainy pinkish coldish** **rewind wilder poster golden thirsty childish noisy**
CORRECTIVE FEEDBACK	**MONITOR PROGRESS**	***If . . .*** students have difficulty previewing and reading whole words, ***then . . .*** have them use sound-by-sound blending. ***If . . .*** students can't read words fluently at a rate of 1–2 seconds per word, ***then . . .*** continue practicing the list.
MORE PRACTICE	Model reading words in sentences.	**When I read a sentence, I read each word without stopping between the words. If I come to a word I don't know, I blend it. Then I read the sentence again.** Model reading this sentence, stopping to blend *stylish: Ken's clothes are always stylish.*
	Write practice sentences.	Have each student read the sentence best matched to his or her ability. **The day is mild and sunny.** **Betty reminds us to be speedy.** **The weather got cloudy and colder.**

Vocabulary

5 minutes

	To Do	To Say
Review vocabulary.	Display the concept web from Day 1.	Review the concept web. **The words *dinnertime, restaurant,* and *delicious* will be in the selection you are reading today.** Review the meanings of the words.

ACTIVITY 3 Read a Passage

Reading "The Sweet Surprise," pp. 98–105

10–15 minutes

	To Do	To Say
Scaffold instruction.	Review draw conclusions.	Remind students that when they draw conclusions, they think about the facts and details and decide something more about them. **As you read "The Sweet Surprise," use details and facts to learn about events and characters in the story.**
Develop language and concepts.	See Routine Cards 3 and 7.	**Before Reading** Read the title. Introduce proper nouns, if necessary. Do a structured picture walk.
	Ask questions and elaborate on answers.	pp. 98–101 **Where are these children?** (in the cafeteria or lunchroom) **What are they doing?** (They are eating many kinds of food. One girl is using chopsticks.)
	Key concepts: *chopsticks, delicious, dinnertime, ethnic, restaurant, wok*	pp. 102–105 **Are the children in a restaurant or in a kitchen?** (They are helping to prepare food in a kitchen.) **Food is being cooked in a wok, and people are eating with chopsticks. How can you tell that everyone is helping to make an ethnic dinner?** (Everyone has a job. This looks like a Chinese meal.) **Does it appear that everyone likes this delicious dinner?** (Everyone seems to be enjoying dinnertime.)
Guide comprehension.	Use Routine Card 4.	**During Reading** **Read the pages in a whisper. Raise your hand if you need help with a word. As you read, ask yourself: Who are the characters? What conclusions can I draw about them?**
	Monitor independent reading.	pp. 98–103 **What conclusions can you draw about Gina, Bill, and Jon?** (They are friendly and curious. They enjoy cooking.)
		pp. 104–105 **What are the children and Ling's mother doing at the end of the story?** (They are making litchi rice balls to take to school.)
	Monitor comprehension.	**After Reading** Discuss the What Do You Think? question.
	Guide retelling.	Have one student retell the story while the others assist. Prompt students by asking: **Who are the main characters? What do they do in the story? How does the story end?** See Monitoring Retelling on p. 216.
MORE PRACTICE	Have students reread pp. 102–103.	**Reread** As they read, tell students to list words that describe Ling's mother.

ACTIVITY 4 Write

Response to Literature

5 minutes

	To Do	To Say
Prompt journal writing.		**Take out your journals. Write about how you have helped to cook something. Tell what you did.**

Homework Practice Book, p. 117, Draw Conclusions

4

ACTIVITY 1 Reread for Fluency

Paired Reading "The Sweet Surprise," pp. 98–99

5–10 minutes

	To Do	To Say
CORRECTIVE FEEDBACK	Pair students. Monitor paired reading.	Students read aloud pp. 98–99, switching readers for each paragraph. Have partners reread; now the other partner begins. You may want to have students read along with the AudioText. Give feedback, using Routine Card 5.
MORE PRACTICE	**READERS' THEATER**	Students can use the dialogue as a script for a Readers' Theater. Have them rehearse, with one student being the narrator and the others Ling, her mother, and the friends.

ACTIVITY 2 Word Work

Spiral Review Compound Words

5 minutes

	To Do	To Say
Review compounds.	Write *postcard.*	**Look at this word. You can read this word because you know it is a compound word made up of two shorter words. You also know the letter *o* followed by *st* often stands for the long *o* sound. What two shorter words do you see in this word?** *(post* and *card)* **Now read the shorter words from left to right: *post card, postcard.* What is the word?** *(postcard)*
Scaffold instruction. **CORRECTIVE FEEDBACK**	Distribute white boards. Monitor student work.	**Build Words** Write the three headings shown below. Distribute word cards or write these words on the board: *life, bill, blind, child, flowers, fire, water.* Have students take turns deciding where they can add the words to make compound words. If students have difficulty, have them read each possible two-word combination aloud. List the compounds as they name them. Have students read the completed lists.

wild____	***____proof***	***____fold***
wildlife	waterproof	billfold
wildfire	childproof	blindfold
wildflowers	fireproof	

Vocabulary

5–10 minutes

	To Do	To Say
Extend word knowledge.	Write on the board or a transparency: *The food we had was <u>delicious</u>.*	Use the word *delicious* to extend word knowledge. **We read this word earlier this week. We learned that it means very pleasing and satisfying especially to the taste or smell. Let's talk about other words that mean almost the same as *delicious.*** **Can you name some other words that mean almost the same thing as *delicious?*** *(tasty, pleasant, great, appetizing, good, yummy, flavorful)* Write words as students name them and add any they don't mention. Talk about the meanings of the words. Point out that *flavorful* is made up of the base word *flavor* and the suffix *-ful*, so *flavorful* means "full of flavor." *Appetizing* comes from the word *appetite* and means "seeming good to the appetite."
MORE PRACTICE	Deepen word understanding.	Have students use *ethnic* and *recipe* in the same sentence. (For example, *You can use recipes to make ethnic foods.*) Share sentences. Ask, **What are some ethnic foods?** (tacos, spaghetti, tamales, rice balls, dal, hummus)

ACTIVITY 3 Read a Passage

Read Together "Menu, Please!" pp. 106–107

	To Do	To Say *10–15 minutes*
Scaffold instruction.	Review draw conclusions (homework).	Ask volunteers to read the passage and share answers from Practice Book, p. 117. Remind students of the importance of drawing conclusions from the facts and details that they read. **When you read, drawing conclusions is important. As you read, think about the facts and details and decide something about them. Looking at the pictures and illustrations may also help you draw conclusions.**
Develop language and concepts.	See Routine Cards 3 and 4.	**Before Reading** **Here are two recipes that you can use to make a tasty meal. What foods do you see in the pictures?** (soup or chili, pudding) **Look at the headings on each of the recipes. What part of a meal is each recipe for?** (main course, dessert) **Let's read to find out how to make these dishes.**
Model fluent reading.	Read pp. 106–107 aloud.	**Reading** **Listen as I read this selection. Notice how I pause after each step in a recipe.** Read the introduction and recipes at an appropriate rate as students follow along. Read the selection a second time, having students point to each word. **Now read the selection aloud with me. Try to read at the same rate I do. Pause where I pause.** Reread the selection several times with students.
Monitor comprehension.	Monitor listening comprehension.	**After Reading** Prompt discussion to monitor comprehension. Listen as students answer questions. **What is each recipe for?** (chili and rice pudding) **What countries are these recipes from?** (Mexico and India) **What information is in each recipe?** (the name of the food and where it is from, a description, a list of the ingredients, and instructions for how to make each food) **Do you think the writer of "Menu, Please!" likes these recipes? Why or why not?** (Yes, because the descriptions make each food sound very good, and the writer calls the meal *tasty*.) **Which recipe do you think would be more difficult to make? Which one do you think you would like better?** (Answers will vary.) **Summarize** Have one student describe the ingredients and steps for one recipe while the others assist. Repeat the process with another student and the second recipe.
MORE PRACTICE	Have students reread pp. 106–107.	**Reread** As they read, tell students to think about which recipe they like better. Afterward they can describe their preferred recipe to a partner.

ACTIVITY 4 Write

Response to Literature

	To Do	To Say *5 minutes*
Prompt descriptive writing.	Writing elements: support, conventions	**Look at both recipes. Which dish do you think would taste better? Give a reason for your conclusion.** Use describing words. Check to see that your sentences begin with capital letters and have correct end punctuation.

Homework Practice Book, p. 118, Vocabulary

5

ACTIVITY 1

Assessment Options

Sentence Reading

	To Do	To Say 5 minutes
Assess sentence reading.	Use reproducible p. 219.	Have each student read the sentences. Record scores on the Sentence Reading Chart, p. 223. While you work with one student, others can complete the Write Sentences activity below. **The food is tasty and mild.** **It is foolish to go out in the cold.** **We can find most of the things to make this crunchy snack.**
CORRECTIVE FEEDBACK	**MONITOR PROGRESS**	***If . . .*** students have trouble reading words with long *i: ind, ild;* long *o: ost, old;* or suffixes *-y* and *-ish,* ***then . . .*** reteach the blending strategy lessons on pp. 117 and 119. ***If . . .*** students misread a word in the sentence, ***then . . .*** correct the error and have them reread the word and then the sentence.
Practice sentence writing.	Provide white boards.	**Write Sentences** Have students copy the sentences from reproducible p. 219 on white boards. Have them confirm spellings by comparing the words they wrote to the words in the sentences.

Passage Reading

	To Do	To Say 5–10 minutes
Assess fluency and compre-hension.	Determine which students to assess this week.	Choose from these options: monitoring fluency (see pp. 214–215) and/or monitoring retelling (see p. 216). Have students reread "The Sweet Surprise." Be sure each student is assessed every other week.
		If you have time, assess every student.

ACTIVITY 2

Build Concepts

Vocabulary

	To Do	To Say 5–10 minutes
Review concept and vocabulary.	Review homework. Display the concept web you began on Day 1.	Ask students to go over answers and share their writing from Practice Book, p. 118. **This week's question is *What is ethnic food?* How do this week's words relate to the question?** (Have students answer the question, using some of the vocabulary they learned this week.) Ask students to add more words to the concept web. Have students explain how each word relates to ethnic foods. Monitor students' understanding of vocabulary as they discuss the web. See Routine Card 6.
MORE PRACTICE		Have students see how many vocabulary words they can write in one sentence. Invite them to share their sentences with the class.

ACTIVITY 3 Read to Connect

Reread "Ethnic Foods," pp. 86–89

10 minutes

	To Do	To Say
Monitor comprehension.	Have students reread "Ethnic Foods" silently.	**As you read, think about what the article says about ethnic foods.** After rereading, ask: • **What is an ethnic food?** (An ethnic food is a food from the culture of people who share the same race or nationality.) • **What ethnic foods are mentioned in the article?** (Greek salad with black olives, salsa) **We also read "The Food Sleuth." Find that selection. Which foods did Stu the Food Sleuth explore?** Record students' ideas. **We also read "The Sweet Surprise." How did Ling and the rest of the children explore some ethnic foods?** Record students' ideas.
Make connections.	Have students make connections across texts.	**What can you say in general about the foods we eat and where they come from?** (Sample answers: We eat many different kinds of food that come from all around the world.)

ACTIVITY 4 Write

Response to Literature "4 You 2 Do," p.108

5–10 minutes

	To Do	To Say
Guide response activities.	Discuss the directions. Tell students to choose one activity to complete.	**Word Play** Have students complete the list on their own and then meet with a partner to share word lists. **Making Connections** Discuss the question in a group or in pairs. (Answers should acknowledge that these popular ethnic foods originated in a particular country or culture.)
	Monitor handwriting. See pp. 227–229.	**On Paper** Brainstorm a list of ethnic dishes with the group before students write. Have them write on their own. Students can use Practice Book, p. 119, to help prepare their written responses, or you can send the Practice Book page home for them to complete later.
MORE PRACTICE		If you have more time, direct students to complete two or more of the activities.

Homework Practice Book, p. 119, Writing

Unit 5 Week 5 *Other Times, Other Places*

How do we experience the past today?

Objectives *This week students will ...*

Vocabulary
- build concepts and oral vocabulary: *compare, hardship, improve, opposite, settle, surround*

Phonics
- blend and read words with syllable pattern VCCCV (as in *pilgrim, hundred, monster*)
- apply knowledge of letter-sounds and word structure to decode unknown words when reading

Text Comprehension
- read connected text
- use main idea to improve comprehension
- write in response to literature

Fluency
- practice fluency with oral rereading

Word Work *This week's phonics focus is ...*

Syllables VCCCV

Concept Words *Tested Vocabulary*

The week's vocabulary is related to the way we experience the past today. The first appearance of each word in the Student Reader is noted below.

compare to find things that are the same and different about two things (p. 113)

hardship a very difficult experience (p. 113)

improve to make or become better (p. 113)

opposite as different as can be (p. 124)

settle to go to live in a new place (p. 116)

surround to shut something in on all sides (p. 119)

Student Reader Unit 5 *This week students will read the following selections.*

Daily Lesson Plan

	ACTIVITIES	MATERIALS
Day 1	**Build Concepts** Weekly Concept: Other Times, Other Places Vocabulary: *compare, hardship, improve, opposite, settle, surround* **Word Work** Phonics: Syllables VCCCV **Read a Passage** "Changing Places," pp. 112–113 Comprehension: Use Strategies Reread for Fluency	Student Reader: Unit 5 Routine Cards 1, 3, 5, 6, 7 Tested Vocabulary Cards Student White Boards AudioText Practice Book, p. 120, Syllables VCCCV
Day 2	**Reread for Fluency** **Word Work** Phonics: Syllables VCCCV Vocabulary **Comprehension** Main Idea and Supporting Details **Read a Passage** "Home to Harlem," pp. 114–121	Student Reader: Unit 5 AudioText Routine Cards 1, 2, 3, 4, 5, 7, 8 Tested Vocabulary Cards Student White Boards Graphic Organizer 1 Practice Book, p. 120, Syllables VCCCV
Day 3	**Reread for Fluency** **Word Work** Phonics: Syllables VCCCV Vocabulary **Read a Passage** "A Trip Back in Time," pp. 122–129 Comprehension: Main Idea and Supporting Details **Write** Response to Literature	Student Reader: Unit 5 AudioText Routine Cards 1, 3, 4, 5, 7 Student journals Practice Book, pp. 120–121, Syllables VCCCV; Main Idea and Supporting Details
Day 4	**Reread for Fluency** **Word Work** Phonics: Spiral Review Vocabulary **Read a Passage** "Living as the Colonists Did," pp. 130–133 Comprehension: Main Idea and Supporting Details; Listening **Write** Response to Literature	Student Reader: Unit 5 AudioText Routine Cards 3, 4, 5 Student White Boards Practice Book, pp. 121–122, Main Idea and Supporting Details; Vocabulary
Day 5	**Assessment Options** Fluency, Comprehension Sentence Reading End-of-Unit Test **Build Concepts** Vocabulary **Read to Connect** **Write** Response to Literature: "4 You 2 Do," p. 134	Student Reader: Unit 5 Reproducible p. 220 Sentence Reading Chart, p. 223 Student White Boards Fluency Progress Chart, p. 215 Routine Card 6 Practice Book, pp. 122–123, Vocabulary; Writing Assessment Book, p. 60

See pp. xvi–xvii for how *My Sidewalks* integrates instructional practices for ELL.
See pp. 251–254 for Phonemic Awareness Activities.

ACTIVITY 1

Build Concepts

Vocabulary

To Do		To Say
		10–15 minutes
Develop word meaning.	See Routine Card 6. Discuss pp. 111–113.	Read Words 2 the Wise on p. 111. Have students turn to pp. 112–113. **What do you notice?** (boy pretending to be a knight, adults pretending to live in the past) **Can you use the words *surround* and *hardship* to describe any of these pictures?** (Example: *These people surround themselves with hardships from the past.*)
Scaffold instruction.	Create a concept web.	In the center of a web, write *Other Times, Other Places.* **This week's concept is *other times, other places. Other times* refers to times in the past. *Other places* refers to different locations, cities, or towns.** Provide examples to demonstrate meaning. **People lived differently in other times and other places. We can learn about the past by studying other times and other places.** Add the other vocabulary words. Discuss the meaning of each word as it relates to the foods we eat, using the glossary as needed. (See p. 128 in this Teacher's Guide for definitions.) 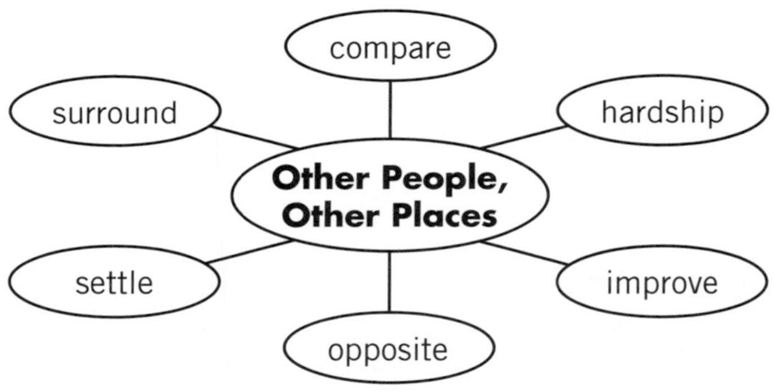
Model the multisyllabic word strategy.	Display each word. Say it as you display it. Think aloud.	Use the Tested Vocabulary Cards. Follow this routine for each word: • **Look for Meaningful Parts** Remind students to look for meaningful parts. **As you say each word, ask yourself: Do I see any parts I know?** • **Chunk Words with No Recognizable Parts** Model how to chunk the word *compare* to read it. • **Model I see a chunk at the beginning of the word: *com*. I see a part at the end of the word: *pare.* I say each chunk slowly: *com pare*. I say the chunks fast to make a whole word: *compare.* Is it a real word? Yes, I know the word *compare.*** • Have students practice reading each word.
Preview.	Read p. 110 with students.	**Do you see any of the words we just learned on this page?** Together with students, read the sentences on p. 110 describing each selection. Talk about how the concept words might be used in the selections.
MORE PRACTICE	Deepen understanding of *compare.*	Have students demonstrate understanding by answering questions. **We can *compare* the way people dress today with the way they dressed in the past. How would you *compare* the way you dress today with the way you dressed two years ago?**

ACTIVITY 2

Word Work

Blending Strategy Syllables VCCCV

5–10 minutes

Routine

	To Do	To Say
Use the blending routine.	Write *napkin* and *picnic.*	**1 Connect** **You can already read words like these. What do you know about how to divide these words?** (They have two consonants together in the middle between two vowels. The words divide between the two consonants.) **Today we will learn about dividing words that have three consonants together in the middle between two vowels.**
Scaffold instruction.	Write *hundred.*	**2 Model** Point to *hundred.* **Remember, a word has as many syllables as it has vowel sounds. So this word is a two-syllable word. What are the vowel sounds?** (/u/ and /ə/) **How many consonants are between the vowels?** (three) **When a word has three consonants together like this, the word often divides between a single consonant and a blend or digraph. The letters** ***dr*** **are a blend, so this word is divided between** ***n*** **and** ***dr.*** Draw a line between the *n* and *dr.* **What is the word?** *(hundred)* **Let's blend this word together:** ***hun dred, hundred.***
	Write *healthy.*	Repeat with the word *healthy.* Point out that *th* stands for /th/. 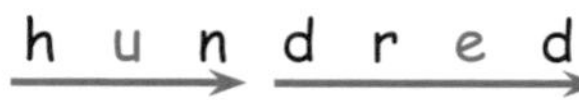
	Distribute white boards.	**3 Listen and Write** **Write the word** ***hundred.*** **Draw a line between the syllables. As you write, say the word to yourself:** ***hundred.*** **Now say the word aloud.**
CORRECTIVE FEEDBACK	Write each practice word. Monitor student practice.	**4 Group Practice** **Let's try reading these words.** Support students as they blend progressively more difficult words. Give feedback, using the ***if . . . then*** statements on Routine Card 1. **hungry entry instead complain upstairs** **distribute institute surprise complicated menthol***
	Check understanding of practice words.	**5 Individual Practice** Have each student blend several words from the row that best matches his or her ability. **actress mumbling wintry pilgrims employ* conflict*** **completed bobsledding* frustrated* wealthy hungrily merchant** *Students need to make sense of words that they segment and blend. If needed, help students with meanings. ***Menthol*** **is a substance used in medicine that comes from oil of peppermint. To** ***employ*** **someone is to hire them to do something. A** ***conflict*** **is a disagreement or struggle.** ***Bobsledding*** **is a sport that uses a special sled to race on ice. If you are** ***frustrated,*** **you feel angry about not being able to do something.**
MORE PRACTICE	Distribute white boards. Model building and spelling words.	**Build Words** Write *wintry.* **Can you blend this word?** (/w/ /i/ /n/ /t/ /r/ /ē/) Have children write words on white boards. **Write** ***wintry.*** **Now change the** ***win*** **in the beginning of** ***wintry*** **to** ***en.*** **What is the new word?** *(entry)* **An** ***entry*** **is a place where people come into a house or other building.** • **Add** ***s*** **to the beginning of** ***entry.*** **What is the new word?** *(sentry)* • **Change the** ***s*** **to** ***re*** **at the beginning of** ***entry.*** **What is the new word?** *(reentry)* Discuss the meanings of *sentry* (a guard) and *reentry* (returning to Earth after a space flight).

ACTIVITY 3 Read a Passage

Build Background "Changing Places," pp. 112–113

10 minutes

	To Do	To Say
Develop language and concepts.	See Routine Cards 3 and 7.	**Before Reading** Read the title aloud. Introduce proper nouns, if necessary. Do a structured picture walk with students.
	Ask questions and elaborate on answers.	p. 112 **What do you see?** (A boy is dressed in a costume and is standing on a rock. He is holding a make-believe sword.) **Yes, it looks like the boy is dressed like someone from the past. Maybe he is pretending to have an adventure as a warrior or knight from long ago. What do you see in the small picture next to the boy?** (A woman is placing a sword on a man's shoulder.) **Compare the two pictures. How are they alike?** (A sword is shown in both pictures.)
Scaffold instruction.	Key concepts: *adventure, compare, hardship, historic, improve*	p. 113 **What do you see at the top of the page?** (a row of covered wagons) **People traveled in covered wagons to settle the West. They faced many hardships. What do you think is happening in the other picture?** (A man is talking to a woman. They are dressed in unusual clothing.) **Yes, these people are dressed like people from colonial times. You can visit historic places like this and see how people lived in the past and how things have improved today. How does your life compare to those pictured here?**
Guide compre-hension	Read pp. 112–113 aloud.	**During Reading** Read the selection as students follow along. Then read it a second time, having students join in. If necessary, stop at the end of each paragraph to check comprehension. Ask questions to promote discussion and develop the concept. • **How does the author say you can learn about other times and other places?** • **How can you experience a different time and place?** • **What words on the concept web could help you describe the events pictured in this selection?**
	Use vocabulary to develop the concept.	**After Reading What did you learn about *comparing* the past to the present? How can you learn about the *hardships* of the past and how things have *improved* in the present?**

Reread for Fluency "Changing Places," p. 112

5–10 minutes

	To Do	To Say
CORRECTIVE FEEDBACK	Monitor oral reading.	**Read p. 112 aloud. Read it three or four times so your reading gets better each time.** Give feedback on students' oral reading and use of the blending strategy. See Routine Cards 1 and 5.
MORE PRACTICE		Instead of rereading just p. 112, have students reread the entire selection three or four times. You may want to have students read along with the AudioText.

Homework Practice Book, p. 120, Phonics: Syllables VCCCV

ACTIVITY 1 Reread for Fluency

Paired Reading "Changing Places," p. 113

	To Do	To Say *5–10 minutes*
CORRECTIVE FEEDBACK	Pair students. Monitor paired reading.	Students read aloud p. 113, switching readers for each paragraph. Have partners reread; now the other partner begins. For optimal fluency, students should reread three or four times. Give feedback, using Routine Card 5.
MORE PRACTICE		Instead of rereading just p. 113, have students reread the entire selection three or four times. You may want to have students read along with the AudioText.

ACTIVITY 2 Word Work

Blend and Build Words Syllables VCCCV

	To Do	To Say *5–10 minutes*
Review blending: syllable pattern VCCCV.	Write *hungry.*	**Remember, when a word has three consonants together like this, the word often divides between a single consonant and a blend or digraph.** Draw a line between the *n* and *g* in *hungry*. **This is how I read the word. First I read each syllable: *hun gry.* Then I blend the syllables together: *hun gry, hungry. Hungry* is a two-syllable word.**
Scaffold instruction. CORRECTIVE FEEDBACK	Write each practice word. Monitor student practice.	**Today we will read more words with this syllable pattern.** Support students as they blend progressively more difficult words. Give feedback, using the ***if . . . then*** statements on Routine Card 1. **control monster explain* children entrance constant*** **frustrated completely distrustful employer distraction***
	Check understanding of practice words.	*Students need to make sense of words that they segment and blend. If needed, help students with meanings. **To *explain* means to "tell about something." *Constant* means "without stopping." A *distraction* is something that takes your mind off what you are doing.**
MORE PRACTICE	Distribute white boards. Model building and spelling words.	**Build Words** Write *trust.* **Can you blend this word?** (/t/ /r/ /u/ /s/ /t/) Have students write words on their white boards. **Write *trust.*** • **Now add *dis* to the beginning of *trust.* What is the new word?** *(distrust)* • **Add *ful* to the end of *distrust.* What is the new word?** *(distrustful)*

2

Vocabulary

5 minutes

	To Do	To Say
Review vocabulary.	Display the concept web from Day 1.	Review the concept web. Use Routine Card 2 for the multisyllabic word routine. **The words *hardship, improve, settle,* and *surround* will be in the selection you read today.** Remind students that *improve* means "to make or become better."
	Deepen word understanding of *hardship* and *settle.*	**A *hardship* is a condition or situation that makes life difficult. Not having enough food to eat is certainly a *hardship.* When would having to walk someplace be a *hardship?*** (Answers may include when you have to walk a long distance, if it is difficult for you to walk, if you have to walk when you are not feeling well, and so on.) ***Settle* means "go to live in a new place." Immigrants from many different countries have *settled* in America. Do you know anyone who left to *settle* someplace else?** Encourage discussion of different examples, asking: **Where did they settle? Is there some place else you might like to settle someday?**
Lead cumulative review.		Use the Tested Vocabulary Cards to review concept words from previous weeks.

ACTIVITY 3 Comprehension

Main Idea and Supporting Details

5 minutes

	To Do	To Say
Scaffold instruction.	Introduce main idea and supporting details.	**Today you will read about a place that many African Americans dreamed of calling home. As you read selections like this, it is important to identify the main idea. Being able to recognize the main idea can help you remember the most important information. A main idea is the most important point an author makes about a topic. Pay attention to the details in the paragraphs you read. They will help explain the author's main idea.**
	Model the skill.	**For example, suppose I read that a particular place had great jobs, great schools, and great things to do. A lot of people dream of moving to this place. I would know that the author's main idea was that this place was a great place to live.**
	Distribute Graphic Organizer 1.	**As you read "Home to Harlem," look for details that help you identify the author's main idea about African Americans moving to Harlem. List in your graphic organizer some of the details you read about. Also add facts and details to your graphic organizer that help you identify the main idea.** See Routine Card 8.

ACTIVITY 4 Read a Passage

Reading "Home to Harlem," pp. 114–121

10–15 minutes

	To Do	To Say
Develop language and concepts.	See Routine Cards 3 and 7.	**Before Reading** Have students recall what they learned about changing places. Read the title. Introduce proper nouns, if necessary. Do a structured picture walk with students.
	Ask questions and elaborate on answers.	pp. 114–116 **This selection is about African Americans who settled in a neighborhood in New York City called Harlem. What are these people doing?** (A man is sitting in front of a building, people are in a restaurant, children are playing in water, and a child is walking with an adult.)
Scaffold instruction.	Key concepts: *culture, hardships, improve, neighborhood, settled*	pp. 117–118 **What businesses are shown in these pictures?** (newspaper office, produce market) **Yes, this shows reporters who worked for a newspaper called the *Amsterdam News.* It is a well-known African American newspaper. This man probably owns his own business selling produce.** pp. 119–121 **What do you think the man on p. 120 is doing?** (entertaining, singing, making records) **These two people are famous African Americans. The man on p. 119 is Langston Hughes. He was a famous writer. The man on p. 120 is Duke Ellington. He was a famous musician. Both men made great contributions to American culture, and both had to overcome many hardships during their lifetimes.**
Guide comprehension.	Use Routine Card 4.	**During Reading Read the pages in a whisper. Raise your hand if you need help with a word. As you read, ask yourself: What am I learning about these people and where they lived? What is this mainly about?**
	Monitor independent reading.	pp. 114–118 **What did you learn about why many African Americans moved to Harlem?** (It promised freedom, jobs, and culture. They wanted to improve their lives and leave the hardships of the South behind.) **What kinds of African American businesses were in Harlem?** (restaurants, newspapers, stores)
	Model using context for word meaning.	Read aloud the paragraph with *hardships* at the top of p. 115. Point out that the sentences that follow *hardships* are clues to the word's meaning. pp. 119–121 **Why did many black artists move to Harlem?** (Example: Harlem was becoming the center of black art and culture.) **Tell me about one of the people described on these pages.** (Example: Langston Hughes was a famous writer. He was born in Missouri and dreamed of moving to Harlem. He loved its spirit.)
Model summarizing.	Think aloud.	**After Reading What did you learn about African Americans who moved to Harlem? What was the selection mainly about?** Model how to summarize. **The selection told details about why many African Americans moved to Harlem and what their life was like after they settled there. It was mainly about why living in Harlem in the early 1900s was special for African Americans.**
MORE PRACTICE	Have students reread pp. 114–115.	**Reread** As they read, have students note some of the facts and details about why African Americans dreamed of moving to Harlem. Point out that after the Civil War many African Americans wanted to leave the hardships of the South. They looked to the North as a place of hope. Students can add these ideas to their graphic organizers.
	Homework	Practice Book, p. 120, Phonics: Syllables VCCCV

3

ACTIVITY 1 Reread for Fluency

Oral Reading "Home to Harlem," pp. 116–117

5–10 minutes

	To Do	To Say
CORRECTIVE FEEDBACK	Monitor oral reading.	**Read pp. 116–117 aloud. Read them three or four times so your reading gets better each time.** Give feedback on students' oral reading and use of the blending strategy. Use Routine Cards 1 and 5.
MORE PRACTICE		Instead of rereading just pp. 116–117, have students reread the entire selection three or four times. You may want to have students read along with the AudioText.

ACTIVITY 2 Word Work

Fluent Word Reading Syllables VCCCV

5–10 minutes

	To Do	To Say
Review phonics.	Review the homework.	Ask students to share answers from Practice Book, p. 120.
Use word-reading routine.	Write *pilgrims.*	Routine **1 Connect You can read this word because you know that when three consonants are together in the middle of a word, the word often divides between the consonant on its own and the blend or digraph. What are the two syllables in this word?** *(pil grims)* **What is the word?** *(pilgrims)*
Scaffold instruction.	Write *hundred, monsters,* and *hungry.*	**2 Model When you come to a new word, look for meaningful parts. If you don't recognize any meaningful parts, then look for chunks you can read. Look at all the letters in the chunk and think about the vowel sounds. Say the parts of the word to yourself, and then read the word.** Model reading *hundred, monsters,* and *hungry* in this way. **When you come to a new word, what are you going to do?**
	Write each practice word.	**3 Group Practice Let's read these words. Look for meaningful parts and chunks, think about the vowel sounds in each chunk, and say the parts to yourself. We will read words that have three consonants together in the middle of the words. When I point to the word, let's read it together.** Allow 2–3 seconds previewing time for each word. Support students as they blend progressively more difficult words. **monster hungry wintry hamster hundred panther** **healthy purchase umbrella distribute complicated mistreated**
CORRECTIVE FEEDBACK	**MONITOR PROGRESS**	***If . . .*** students have difficulty previewing and reading whole words, ***then . . .*** have them use sound-by-sound blending. ***If . . .*** students can't read words fluently at a rate of 1–2 seconds per word, ***then . . .*** continue practicing the list.
MORE PRACTICE	Model reading words in sentences.	**When I read a sentence, I read each word without stopping between the words. If I come to a word I don't know, I blend it. Then I read the sentence again.** Model reading this sentence, stopping to blend *hamster: Marta loves her pet hamster.*
	Write practice sentences.	Have each student read the sentence best matched to his or her ability. **I counted a hundred birds.** **The hungry children ate a big lunch.** **Joe used an umbrella in the wintry weather.**

Vocabulary

	To Do	To Say 5 minutes
Review vocabulary.	Display the concept web from Day 1.	Review the concept web. **The words *compare* and *opposite* will be in the selection you read today.** Review the meanings of the words.

ACTIVITY 3 Read a Passage

Reading "A Trip Back in Time," pp. 122–129

	To Do	To Say 10–15 minutes
Scaffold instruction.	Review main idea.	Remind students that details can help them identify the author's main idea. **As you read "A Trip Back in Time," pay attention to the details. Think about what they tell you about the author's main idea.**
Develop language and concepts.	See Routine Cards 3 and 7. Ask questions and elaborate on answers. Key concepts: *blacksmith, century, colonial, compare, opposite*	**Before Reading** Read the title. Do a structured picture walk. pp. 122–124 **How do these people compare to people today?** (They dress differently.) **These people dress like people from colonial times long ago.** pp. 125–129 **What kinds of jobs do you think these people have?** (printing, working as a blacksmith, making wigs) **What is the last picture?** (Someone is being punished.) **Yes, but this girl looks the opposite of someone being punished.**
	Use Routine Card 4.	**During Reading** **Read the pages in a whisper. Raise your hand if you need help with a word. As you read, ask yourself: What are the details? What do they tell me about the author's main idea?**
Guide comprehension.	Monitor independent reading.	pp. 122–124 **What is the main idea of these pages?** (People can visit Williamsburg to learn about life in colonial times.) **How are the streets today the opposite of how they were in colonial times?** (They are smooth. In colonial times they were bumpy.) pp. 125–127 **What main idea is supported by the details on these pages?** (You can see what kinds of jobs the people in colonial times had.) pp. 128–129 **What did you learn about African American colonists in Williamsburg?** (They often led lives of slavery and had to cook and clean for white colonists.)
	Monitor comprehension.	**After Reading** Discuss the What Do You Think? question.
	Guide retelling.	Have one student retell the story while the others assist. Prompt students by asking: **Who are the people in this selection? Where do the events take place? What is the author's main idea?** See Monitoring Retelling on p. 216.
MORE PRACTICE	Have students reread pp. 122–123.	**Reread** As they read, tell students to list some words and phrases they might use to compare Williamsburg of the present to Williamsburg of the past.

ACTIVITY 4 Write

Response to Literature

	To Do	To Say 5 minutes
Prompt journal writing.		**Take out your journals. If you were to visit Williamsburg, what would you find the most interesting? Write about what you saw and liked.**

Homework Practice Book, p. 121, Main Idea and Supporting Details

4

ACTIVITY 1 Reread for Fluency

Paired Reading "A Trip Back in Time," pp. 125–126

5–10 minutes

	To Do	To Say
CORRECTIVE FEEDBACK	Pair students. Monitor paired reading.	Students read aloud pp. 125–126, switching readers for each paragraph. Have partners reread; now the other partner begins. For optimal fluency, students should reread three or four times. You may want to have students read along with the AudioText. Give feedback, using Routine Card 5.
MORE PRACTICE	**READERS' THEATER**	Work with a group of three or four students to adapt pp. 125–126 for Readers' Theater. Have students write a script and read it as if it were a television broadcast. Each student can read a different section. Then have them perform for the class.

ACTIVITY 2 Word Work

Spiral Review Read Longer Words

5 minutes

	To Do	To Say
Review reading longer words, with syllable patterns VC/CV, VC/V, V/CV, C + le.	Write *happening.* Draw a line between *p* and *p.*	**You can read this word because you know how to divide the word into syllables and blend them together. This word has an ending.** Cover the *-ing* ending. **What is the base word?** *(happen)* **The base word has two consonants together in the middle. Where do you divide the base word?** (between the two *p's*) **Now read the word parts from left to right:** ***hap pen ing.*** **What is the word?** *(happening)*
	Write *famous.* Draw a line between *a* and *m.* Write *clever.* Draw a line between *v* and *e.*	**To read a word like** ***happening*****, I figure out its parts, read them from left to right, and blend the parts to read the whole word.** Repeat with *famous* and *clever.* Point out that the first syllable in *famous* ends with a long vowel sound. The first syllable in *clever* ends with a consonant and has a short vowel sound.
Scaffold instruction. **CORRECTIVE FEEDBACK**	Write practice words. Monitor student work.	**Decode Longer Words** Have individuals read the following words. If students make an error, have them blend syllables sound-by-sound and reread the word. To check meaning, call on individuals to use the words in sentences. **fossil, unfinished, hotel, reptile, connecting, never** **pilot, eagle, picnic, clutter, lilac, simple** **umpire, party, behind, maple, uncover, underpass**

Vocabulary

5–10 minutes

	To Do	To Say
Extend word knowledge.	Write on the board or a transparency: *Some people move to <u>improve</u> their way of life.*	Use the word *improve* to extend word knowledge. **We learned that** ***improve*** **means "to make or become better." We can use this word to read other words.** **What other words contain the word** ***improve?*** *(improves, improving, improved, improvement)* Write these words and discuss their meanings. Point out that *-ment* is a suffix that means "the result of," so *improvement* means "the result of making better."
MORE PRACTICE	Deepen word understanding.	Have students use *compared* and *improved* in the same sentence. (For example, *Compared to yesterday, the weather has improved.*) Share sentences.

ACTIVITY 3 Read a Passage

Read Together "Living as the Colonists Did," pp. 130–133

	To Do	To Say *10–15 minutes*
Scaffold instruction.	Review main idea and supporting details (homework).	Ask volunteers to read the passage and share answers from Practice Book, p. 121. Remind students of the importance of identifying the main idea from the facts and details that they read. **When you read, identifying main ideas is important. As you read, think about the main idea that the facts and details are describing. Looking at the pictures and illustrations may also help you identify main ideas.**
Develop language and concepts.	See Routine Cards 3 and 4.	**Before Reading** **This selection is about the way people lived in the past. What do the pictures show you about how they lived?** (They traveled in horse-drawn carriages, played games, and made things by hand.) **Look at the questions on each page. What do you think you will learn from this selection?** (how people got around, what they did for fun, where they went shopping) **Let's read to find out more about how these people lived.**
Model fluent reading.	Read pp. 130–133 aloud. Model prosody.	**During Reading** **Listen to how fast or slowly I read this selection. Notice how I raise my voice at the end of each question.** Read the selection with expression as students follow along. Read it a second time, having students point to each word. **Now read the selection aloud with me. Try to read at the same rate I do. Pause where I pause.** Reread the selection several times with students.
Monitor comprehension	Monitor listening comprehension.	**After Reading** Prompt discussion to monitor comprehension. Listen as students answer questions. **What is Colonial Williamsburg?** (It is a town where people live and work as the settlers did during the 1700s.) **How would you get around in Williamsburg?** (in horse-drawn carriages) **What were some of the things the colonists made?** (They made their own clothes, shoes, baskets, and barrels.) **Where did the settlers get their medicines from?** (plants, roots, and bark) **What do you think is the selection's main idea?** (The early colonists lived differently than we do today, but they needed many of the same things.) **Summarize** Have one student describe what life for the colonists was like in Williamsburg while the others assist.
MORE PRACTICE	Have students reread p. 132.	**Reread** As they read, tell students to look for information about the jobs the colonists had. After reading, they can tell a partner what they learned about jobs in colonial America.

ACTIVITY 4 Write

Response to Literature

	To Do	To Say *5 minutes*
Prompt personal narrative.	Writing elements: support, organization	**Pretend you are a colonist. Describe your activities throughout one day. Tell about some of the unique features of your home, job, town, or school. Use describing and sequence words.**

Homework Practice Book, p. 122, Vocabulary

5

ACTIVITY 1 Assessment Options

Sentence Reading

	To Do	To Say *5 minutes*
Assess sentence reading.	Use reproducible p. 220.	Have each student read the sentences. Record scores on the Sentence Reading Chart, p. 223. While you work with one student, others can complete the Write Sentences activity below. **I used to have a pet hamster.** **People lived differently two hundred years ago.** **I had a surprise party for my best friend.**
CORRECTIVE FEEDBACK	**MONITOR PROGRESS**	***If . . .*** students have trouble reading longer words with syllable pattern VCCCV, ***then . . .*** reteach the blending strategy lessons on pp. 131 and 133. ***If . . .*** students misread a word in the sentence, ***then . . .*** correct the error and have them reread the word and them the sentence.
Practice sentence writing.	Provide white boards.	**Write Sentences** Have students copy the sentences from reproducible p. 220 on white boards. Have them confirm spellings by comparing the words they wrote to the words in the sentences.

End-of-Unit Test

	To Do	To Say *10 minutes*
Assess fluency and compre-hension.	Use the Assessment Book, p. 60.	Options for end-of-unit assessment are available in the Assessment Book.

ACTIVITY 2 Build Concepts

Vocabulary

	To Do	To Say *5–10 minutes*
Review concept and vocabulary.	Review homework. Display the concept web you began on Day 1.	Ask students to go over answers and share their writing from Practice Book, p. 122. **This week's question is *How do we experience the past today?* How do this week's words relate to the question?** (Have students answer the question, using some of the vocabulary they learned this week.) Ask students to add more words to the concept web. Have students explain how each word relates to the question. Monitor students' understanding of vocabulary as they discuss the web. See Routine Card 6.
MORE PRACTICE		Have students see how many vocabulary words they can write in one sentence. Invite them to share their sentences with the class.

ACTIVITY 3 Read to Connect

Reread "Changing Places," p. 113

5 minutes

	To Do	To Say
Monitor comprehension	Have students reread p. 113 of "Changing Places" silently.	**Think about what this selection says about changing places with people in the past. How can you discover things about other places and other times?** (by reading books and visiting historic places) **We also read "Home to Harlem." Find that selection. What does the title of the selection refer to?** Record students' ideas. **We also read "A Trip Back in Time." What did the author describe in that selection?** Record students' ideas.
Make connections.	Have students make connections across texts.	**What can you say in general about how we learn about other times?** (Sample answers: We learn by reading and going places where we can learn about what it was like living in the past.)

ACTIVITY 4 Write

Response to Literature "4 You 2 Do," p. 134

5–10 minutes

	To Do	To Say
Guide response activities.	Discuss the directions. Tell students to choose one activity to complete. Monitor handwriting. See pp. 227–229.	**Word Play** Have children complete the activity on their own and then meet with a partner to share their new words. **Making Connections** Discuss the question in small groups or as a class. **On Paper** Brainstorm a list of feelings students might have about visiting other places before they write. Have students write on their own. Students can use Practice Book, p. 123, to help prepare their written responses, or you can send the Practice Book page home for them to complete later. (Descriptions should include the name of the place visited and the feelings experienced.)
MORE PRACTICE		If you have more time, direct students to complete two or more of the activities.

Homework Practice Book, p. 123, Writing

Unit 6 Week 1 *American Symbols*

What are some important American symbols or monuments?

Objectives *This week students will ...*

Vocabulary
- build concepts and vocabulary: *enormous, liberty, monument, president, sculptor, symbol*

Phonics
- blend and read words with suffixes *-hood, -ment* and prefixes *pre-, mid-, post-*
- apply knowledge of letter-sounds and word structure to decode unknown words when reading

Text Comprehension
- read connected text
- identify main idea to improve comprehension
- write in response to literature

Fluency
- practice fluency with oral rereading

Word Work *This week's phonics focus is ...*

Suffixes *-hood, -ment* Prefixes *pre-, mid-, post-*

Concept Words *Tested Vocabulary*

The week's vocabulary is related to the concept of American symbols. The first appearance of each word in the Student Reader is noted below.

enormous	very, very large; huge (p. 14)
liberty	freedom (p. 10)
monument	something set up to honor a person or event; a monument may be a building, pillar, statue, or stone (p. 13)
president	the leader of a country, business, or other group (p. 21)
sculptor	an artist who makes things by cutting or shaping them (p. 14)
symbol	something that stands for something else (p. 8)

Student Reader Unit 6 *This week students will read the following selections.*

Daily Lesson Plan

	ACTIVITIES	MATERIALS
Day 1	**Build Concepts** Weekly Concept: American Symbols Vocabulary: *enormous, liberty, monument, president, sculptor, symbol* **Word Work** Phonics: Suffixes *-hood, -ment* **Read a Passage** "Symbols of Freedom," pp. 8–11 Comprehension: Use Strategies Reread for Fluency	Student Reader: Unit 6 Routine Cards 1, 3, 5, 6, 7 Tested Vocabulary Words Student White Boards AudioText Practice Book, p. 124, Suffixes *-hood, -ment*
Day 2	**Reread for Fluency** **Word Work** Phonics: Prefixes *pre-, mid-, post-* Vocabulary **Comprehension** Main Idea **Read a Passage** "She Stands for Freedom," pp. 12–19	Student Reader: Unit 6 AudioText Routine Cards 1, 2, 3, 4, 5, 7, 8 Tested Vocabulary Cards Student White Boards Graphic Organizer 1 Practice Book, p. 125, Prefixes *pre-, mid-, post-*
Day 3	**Reread for Fluency** **Word Work** Phonics: Suffixes *-hood, -ment*; Prefixes *pre-, mid-, post-* Vocabulary **Read a Passage** "The Men on the Mountain," pp. 20–27 Comprehension: Main Idea **Write** Response to Literature	Student Reader: Unit 6 AudioText Routine Cards 1, 3, 4, 5, 7 Student journals Practice Book, pp. 124–126, Suffixes *-hood, -ment;* Prefixes *pre-, mid-, post-;* Main Idea
Day 4	**Reread for Fluency** **Word Work** Phonics: Spiral Review Vocabulary **Read a Passage** "Stars and Stripes," pp. 28–29 Comprehension: Main Idea; Listening **Write** Response to Literature	Student Reader: Unit 6 AudioText Routine Cards 3, 4, 5 Student White Boards Practice Book, pp. 126–127, Main Idea; Vocabulary
Day 5	**Assessment Options** Fluency, Comprehension Sentence Reading Passage Reading **Build Concepts** Vocabulary **Read to Connect** **Write** Response to Literature: "4 You 2 Do," p. 30	Student Reader: Unit 6 Reproducible p. 220 Sentence Reading Chart, p. 224 Student White Boards Fluency Progress Chart, p. 215 Routine Card 6 Practice Book, pp. 127–128, Vocabulary; Writing

See pp. xvi–xvii for how *My Sidewalks* integrates instructional practices for ELL.
See pp. 251–254 for Phonemic Awareness Activities.

ACTIVITY **1**

Build Concepts

Vocabulary

10–15 minutes

	To Do	To Say
Develop word meaning.	See Routine Card 6. Discuss pp. 7–11.	Read Words 2 the Wise on p. 7. Have students turn to pp. 8–11. **Look at the pictures. What do you see?** (a boy saluting the flag, an eagle, a bell, a picture of Uncle Sam) **Can you use the words *liberty* and *symbol* to tell about the picture?** (Example: *Uncle Sam is a symbol of liberty.*)
Scaffold instruction.	Create a concept web.	In the center of a web, write *American Symbols.* **This week's concept is *American symbols.* A *symbol* means "something that stands for something else."** Provide examples to demonstrate meaning. **You may see heart shapes used in designs in many places. We use this shape as a *symbol* of love. The heart shape stands for the idea of love.** Add the other vocabulary words. Discuss the meaning of each word as it relates to American symbols, using the glossary as needed. (See p. 142 in this Teacher's Guide for definitions.)

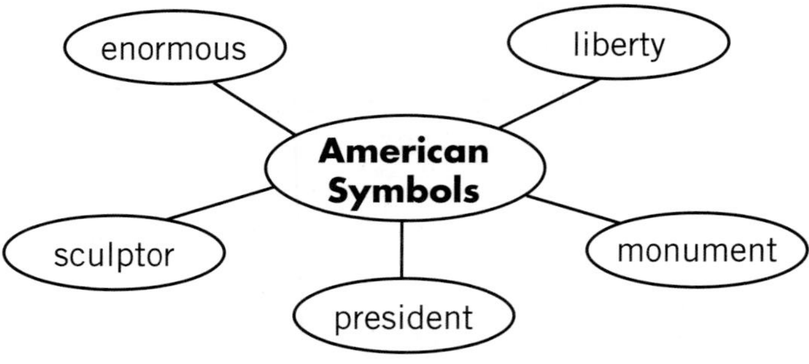

	To Do	To Say
Model the multisyllabic word strategy.	Display each word. Say it as you display it. Think aloud.	Use the Tested Vocabulary Cards. Follow this routine for each word: • **Look for Meaningful Parts** **Do you recognize any parts of a word? What do these parts mean? Use these parts to read the word.** • **Model** **I see the ending *-or* in the word *sculptor.* I know the ending *-or* can mean "one who does something." A *sculptor* is a person who *sculpts,* or makes statues.** Discuss other words with the suffix *-or. (actor, governor, collector)* • **Chunk Words with No Recognizable Parts** Model how to chunk the word *monument* to read it. **I see a chunk at the beginning of the word: *mon.* I see a syllable in the middle: *u.* I see a part at the end of the word: *ment.* I say each chunk slowly: *mon u ment.* I say the chunks fast to make a whole word: *monument.* Is it a real word? Yes, I know the word *monument.*** • Have students practice reading each word.
Preview.	Read p. 6 with students.	**Do you see any of the words we just learned on this page?** Together with students, read the sentences on p. 6 describing each selection. Talk about how the concept words might be used in the selections.
MORE PRACTICE	Deepen understanding of *symbol.*	Have students demonstrate understanding by answering questions. **Which bird is a *symbol,* an eagle that is shown on money or a chicken that you eat for dinner? What are some other *symbols* you know? What do they stand for?**

ACTIVITY 2 Word Work

Blending Strategy Suffixes *-hood, -ment*

	To Do	To Say 5–10 minutes
Use the blending routine.	Write *dusty* and *bookish.*	**1 Connect** You studied words like these already. What do you know about reading them? (They both contain suffixes.) What are the suffixes in *dusty* and *bookish? (-y* and *-ish)* Today we will learn about adding the suffixes *-hood* and *-ment* to the end of words. Each suffix has a special meaning: *-hood* "condition of being" *-ment* "act or process" (Routine)
Scaffold instruction.	Write *childhood.*	**2 Model** Point to *childhood.* This is a two-syllable word formed from the base word *child* and the suffix *-hood.* You can cover the suffix, read the base word, and then blend the base word and suffix to read the whole word. What is the word? *(childhood)* What does it mean? ("the condition or state of being a child")
	Write *government.*	Repeat with *government.* ("the act or process of governing or ruling") c h i l d h o o d g o v e r n m e n t
	Distribute white boards.	**3 Listen and Write** Have students write on white boards. Write the word *child.* Write *hood* after it. As you write, say the new word to yourself: *childhood.* Now say the word aloud. Do the same with *government.*
CORRECTIVE FEEDBACK	Write each practice word. Monitor student practice.	**4 Group Practice** Let's try the same thing with these words. Support students as they blend progressively more difficult words. Give feedback, using the *if . . . then* statements on Routine Card 1. boyhood payment pavement girlhood manhood enjoyment amazement brotherhood entertainment
		5 Individual Practice Have each student blend several words from the row best matched to his or her ability. childhood movement statehood adulthood amusement* parenthood astonishment* sisterhood measurement
	Check understanding of practice words.	*Students need to make sense of words that they segment and blend. If needed, help students with meanings. *Amusement* is the condition of being entertained. *Astonishment* is the condition of being very surprised.
MORE PRACTICE	Distribute white boards. Model building and spelling words with suffixes.	**Spell and Write** You can spell words with suffixes by thinking about the base word and suffix. What base word and suffix make up *boyhood? (boy* and *hood)* Start with the sounds in the base word *boy.* What letters spell *boy?* Now add the suffix *-hood.* Be sure you don't drop any letters in the base word when you add the suffix. How do you spell *boyhood? (boyhood)* Repeat with *statement, payment, childhood,* and *manhood.*

ACTIVITY 3 Read a Passage

Build Background "Symbols of Freedom," pp. 8–11

10 minutes

	To Do	To Say
Develop language and concepts. **Scaffold instruction.**	See Routine Cards 3 and 7. Ask questions and elaborate on answers. Key concepts: *bald eagle, country, government, flag, liberty, symbol*	**Before Reading** Read the title aloud. Introduce proper nouns, if necessary. Do a structured picture walk with students. p. 8 **What do you see?** (a boy saluting the United States flag) **Yes, the flag is a symbol of our country. It stands for our history and things that are important in our government.** p. 9 **What symbol is shown?** (bald eagle) **A bald eagle is a wild bird that lives in our country. It stands for strength and courage.** p. 10 **What do you see?** (a bell) **Yes, this is the Liberty Bell. *Liberty* means "freedom." The Liberty Bell is a symbol of freedom in the United States.** p. 11 **What symbol is pictured?** (Uncle Sam) **Where have you seen his picture before?** (Answers will vary.) **Let's read to find out about the history of these symbols and what they mean. As you read, ask yourself: What is this article mainly about? What am I learning?**
Guide compre-hension.	Read pp. 8–11 aloud.	**During Reading** Read the selection as students follow along. Then read it a second time, having students join in. If necessary, stop at the end of each paragraph to check comprehension. Ask questions to promote discussion and develop the concept. • **What symbols are described in the selection? What do these symbols represent?** • **What are some places where you might see symbols of our government?** • **Which words on the concept web could help you tell about the symbols described in this selection?**
	Use vocabulary to develop the concept.	**After Reading** **What did you learn about *symbols* of our country? Why do you think that a bird is a good *symbol* for freedom, or *liberty?***

Reread for Fluency "Symbols of Freedom," p. 8

5–10 minutes

	To Do	To Say
CORRECTIVE FEEDBACK	Monitor oral reading.	**Read p. 8 aloud. Read it three or four times so your reading gets better each time.** Give feedback on students' oral reading and use of the blending strategy. See Routine Cards 1 and 5.
MORE PRACTICE		Instead of rereading just p. 8, have students reread the entire selection three or four times. You may want to have students read along with the AudioText.

Homework Practice Book, p. 124, Phonics: Suffixes *-hood, -ment*

ACTIVITY 1 Reread for Fluency

Paired Reading "Symbols of Freedom," p. 9

	To Do	To Say *5–10 minutes*
CORRECTIVE FEEDBACK	Pair students. Monitor paired reading.	Students read aloud p. 9, alternating sentences. Have partners reread; now the other partner begins. For optimal fluency, students should reread three or four times. Give feedback, using Routine Card 5.
MORE PRACTICE		Instead of rereading just p. 9, have students reread the entire selection three or four times. You may want to have students read along with the AudioText.

ACTIVITY 2 Word Work

Blending Strategy Prefixes *pre-, mid-, post-*

5–10 minutes

Routine

	To Do	To Say
Use the blending strategy.	Write *outside* and *overjoyed.*	**1 Connect** **You already studied words such as these. What do you know about reading them?** (They both contain prefixes that are separate syllables from the base word.) **Today we will learn about adding prefixes *pre-, mid-,* and *post-* to the beginning of words. Each prefix has a special meaning:** **pre- "before" mid- "in the middle" post- "after"**
Scaffold instruction.	Write *midday.*	**2 Model** **This is a two-syllable word formed from the base word *day* and the prefix *mid-*. You can cover the prefix, read the base word, and then blend the prefix and base word to read the whole word. What is the word?** *(midday)* **What does it mean?** ("in the middle of the day") **Let's blend this word together:** *mid day, midday.* m i d d a y
	Write *preview, postwar,* and *midmorning.*	Repeat with *preview* ("to view beforehand"), *postwar* ("after war"), and *midmorning* ("in the middle of the morning").
	Distribute white boards.	**3 Listen and Write** Have students write on white boards. **Write the word *day.* Then write the prefix *mid-* before *day.* Say the new word to yourself: *midday.* Say the word aloud.** Do the same with *preview, postwar,* and *midmorning.*
CORRECTIVE FEEDBACK	Write each practice word. Monitor student practice.	**4 Group Practice** **Let's try the same thing with these words.** Support students as they blend progressively more difficult words. Give feedback, using the *if . . . then* statements on Routine Card 1. **midweek postpaid midnight postwar midterm prewrite** **midwinter preschooler postdated prerecord prepackage** **5 Individual Practice** Have each student blend several words from the row best matched to his or her ability. **preheat midair prepay postdate preheat** **midsummer Midwestern postscript precooking**

For more practice, see next page.

MORE PRACTICE	Model building and spelling words with prefixes.	**Spell and Write** **You can spell words with prefixes by thinking about the prefix and the base word. What prefix and base word make up *midday?*** (*mid-* and *day*) **Start with the sounds in the base word: /d/ /ā/. What letters spell *day?*** Write *day.* **Now add the prefix *mid-.* Now spell *midday.*** Repeat with *preschool, preheat, postdate.*

Vocabulary

5 minutes

	To Do	To Say
Review vocabulary.	Display the concept web from Day 1.	Review the concept web. See Routine Card 2 for the multisyllabic word routine. **The words *enormous, liberty, monument, president, sculptor,* and *symbol* will be in the selection you are reading today.** Remind students that *symbol* means "something that stands for something else."
	Deepen word understanding of *monument* and *enormous.*	**A *monument* is something set up to honor a person or an event. Can you think of any *monuments* in our community?** (Answers may include specific statues, plaques, buildings, and so on.) **A *monument* might be *enormous,* or really, really big. Can you think of some things that are *enormous?*** (Encourage discussion of different examples, focusing on objects that reflect other vocabulary words, such as enormous statues or monuments that honor someone or represent liberty.)
Lead cumulative review.		Use the Tested Vocabulary Cards to review concept words from previous weeks.

ACTIVITY 3 Comprehension

Main Idea

5 minutes

	To Do	To Say
Scaffold instruction.	Introduce main idea.	**Today you will read about a famous symbol of freedom. When you read a selection, try to find the main idea about the topic. This is the most important thing the writer wants you to know. Sometimes the main idea is given in a sentence near the beginning or end of the selection. Small bits of information, or supporting details, tell about the main idea.**
	Model the skill.	**For example, in the selection "Symbols of Freedom," we read about the bald eagle, the Liberty Bell, and Uncle Sam. The topic of the selection is symbols of freedom. If I wanted to tell the main idea, I would state the most important idea about the topic. I might say, "The bald eagle, the Liberty Bell, and Uncle Sam are all important symbols of freedom in the United States."**
	Distribute Graphic Organizer 1.	**As you read "She Stands for Freedom," look for the topic. Think about the most important thing the author wants you to know about the topic. Write this idea on your graphic organizer. Then we will look for details that tell more about this main idea.** See Routine Card 8.

ACTIVITY 4 Read a Passage

Reading "She Stands for Freedom," pp. 12–19

10–15 minutes

	To Do	To Say
Develop language and concepts.	Use Routine Cards 3 and 7.	**Before Reading** Have students recall what they learned about American symbols. Read the title. Introduce proper nouns, if necessary. Do a structured picture walk with students.
Scaffold instruction.	Ask questions and elaborate on answers.	pp. 12–13 **The selection is about building an important symbol of freedom. Describe what you see in the pictures.** (the Statue of Liberty) **The statue is enormous. People had to build the monument from many pieces.**
	Key concepts: *enormous, liberty, monument, president, sculptor, symbol*	pp. 14–17 **On pp. 14–15 you see a man from long ago, workers building a platform, and an enormous statue. Try to guess the man's connection to the statue.** (He may be a president, a sculptor, or a man who helped build the statue.) **What are some details you notice on pp. 16–17 about this monument?** (The statue is wearing a crown and holding a torch. Workers are cleaning or fixing the statue.)
		pp. 18–19 **These people are coming by ship to the United States. How do you think they feel when they see the Statue of Liberty?** (excited, hopeful)
Guide compre-hension.	Use Routine Card 4.	**During Reading** **Read the pages in a whisper. Raise your hand if you need help with a word. As you read, ask yourself: What is this article mainly about? What am I learning about this special symbol of freedom?**
	Monitor independent reading.	pp. 12–13 **What did you learn about an American symbol?** (Example: The Statue of Liberty was a gift from France. It stands for freedom.)
	Model using context for word meaning.	Point out the word *symbol* on p. 13. Explain that the phrase "stands for freedom" provides clues to the meaning of *symbol.*
		pp. 14–16 **What did you learn about the Statue of Liberty on pp. 14–15? Tell me the main idea in one sentence.** (Example: It took a great deal of time and planning to build this enormous statue and get it to America.) **What symbols did the sculptor include on the statue?** (torch, broken chains, book, and crown)
		pp. 17–19 **Tell me how immigrants probably felt when they saw the statue.** (They felt hopeful about the new lives they would find in America.)
Model summarizing.	Think aloud.	**After Reading** **What did you learn about the Statue of Liberty? What was the selection mainly about?** Model how to summarize. **The selection gave details about the Statue of Liberty. It was mainly about how a French sculptor designed and built this statue as a symbol of liberty. It also gave details about how people feel when they see the statue.**
MORE PRACTICE	Have students reread p. 16.	**Reread** As they read, have students look for a sentence that gives the main idea. Then ask them to find details on the page that support this main idea.
	Homework	Practice Book, p. 125, Phonics: Prefixes: *pre-, mid-, post-*

3

ACTIVITY 1 Reread for Fluency

Oral Reading "She Stands for Freedom," p. 16

5–10 minutes

	To Do	To Say
CORRECTIVE FEEDBACK	Monitor oral reading.	**Read p. 16 aloud three or four times so your reading gets better each time.** Give feedback on students' oral reading and use of the blending strategy. Use Routine Cards 1 and 5.
MORE PRACTICE		Instead of rereading just p. 16, have students read additional pages three or four times. You may want to have students read along with the AudioText.

ACTIVITY 2 Word Work

Fluent Word Reading Suffixes *-ment, -hood;* Prefixes *pre-, mid-, post-*

5–10 minutes

	To Do	To Say
Review phonics.	Review the homework.	Ask students to share answers from Practice Book, pp. 124–125.
Use word-reading routine.	Write *childhood.*	Routine **1 Connect** **You can read this word because you know that a word ending with *-hood* is often a two-syllable word formed from a base word and the suffix *-hood.* What is the base word?** *(child)* **What is the word?** *(childhood)*
	Write *commitment, presort,* and *midterm.*	**2 Model** **When you come to a new word, look for meaningful parts.** Model reading *commitment, presort,* and *midterm.* **If you don't recognize any meaningful parts, then look for chunks you can read. Look at all the letters in the chunk and think about the sounds. Say the parts of the word to yourself, and then read the word. When you come to a new word, what are you going to do?**
Scaffold instruction.	Write each practice word.	**3 Group Practice** **Let's read these words. Look for meaningful parts and chunks, think about the sounds in each chunk, and say the parts to yourself. We will read words with the suffixes *-hood* and *-ment* and with prefixes *pre-, mid-,* and *post-.* When I point to the word, let's read it together.** Allow 2–3 seconds previewing time for each word. Support students as they blend progressively more difficult words. **adulthood payment preview pavement childhood** **preschooler neighborhood prepayment midsection contentment**
CORRECTIVE FEEDBACK	**MONITOR PROGRESS**	***If . . .*** students have difficulty previewing and reading whole words, ***then . . .*** have them use sound-by-sound blending. ***If . . .*** students can't read words fluently at a rate of 1–2 seconds per word, ***then . . .*** continue practicing the list.
MORE PRACTICE	Model reading words in sentences.	**When I read a sentence, I read each word without stopping between the words. If I come to a word I don't know, I blend it. Then I read the sentence again.** Model reading this sentence, stopping to blend *childhood: Childhood is a time for fun.*
	Write practice sentences.	Have each student read the sentence best matched to his or her ability. **Preschool children nap at midday.** **Childhood is a time of enjoyment.** **Adulthood is a time for commitment.**

Vocabulary

	To Do	To Say	5 minutes
Review vocabulary.	Display the concept web from Day 1.	Review the concept web. **The words *liberty, monument, president, sculptor,* and *symbol* will be in the selection you read today.** Review meanings of the words.	

ACTIVITY 3 Read a Passage

Reading "The Men on the Mountain," pp. 20–27

	To Do	To Say	10–15 minutes
Scaffold instruction.	Review main idea.	Tell students that sometimes a selection title can give them a clue about the main idea. **As you read "The Men on the Mountain," ask yourself what the selection is about.**	
Develop language and concepts.	See Routine Cards 3 and 7.	**Before Reading** Read the title. Introduce proper nouns. Do a picture walk.	
	Ask questions and elaborate on answers.	pp. 20-21 **Now you will read about an enormous monument honoring U.S. Presidents. The man in the photo was a sculptor. What material did he carve?** (rock or granite)	
	Key concepts: *liberty, monument, presidents, sculptor, symbol*	pp. 22–25 **Who are the people on these pages?** (former U.S. Presidents) pp. 26–27 **What kinds of tools do you think the sculptors used?** (hammers, chisels, drills) **Do you think this monument is a good symbol for a great nation? Explain.** (It is large and important.)	
Guide compre-hension.	Use Routine Card 4.	**During Reading** **Read the pages in a whisper. Raise your hand if you need help with a word. As you read, ask yourself: What is the selection mainly about? What important details support this main idea?**	
	Monitor independent reading.	pp. 20–21 **Why did the sculptor choose these Presidents?** (He chose Presidents who would be good symbols of liberty.) pp. 22–25 **Which Presidents are pictured here?** (Washington, Jefferson, Lincoln, and Roosevelt) **Why are they good symbols of liberty?** (Answers will vary.) pp. 26–27 **How did the workers carve the monument?** (They used dynamite. Then they carved with drills, air hammers, and chisels.) **How big is it?** (Each head is 60 feet high.) **How long did it take to finish Mount Rushmore?** (14 years)	
	Monitor comprehension.	**After Reading** Discuss the What Do You Think? question.	
	Guide retelling.	Have one student retell the selection while the others assist. Prompt students by asking: **What are the most important ideas on each page? What do you think is the main thing the writer wants you to learn?** See Monitoring Retelling on p. 216.	
MORE PRACTICE	Have students reread pp. 22–25.	**Reread** As they read, tell students to decide which President they would choose to have carved on Mount Rushmore if there were room for just one more.	

ACTIVITY 4 Write

Response to Literature

	To Do	To Say	5 minutes
Prompt journal writing.		**Take out your journals. Choose a president from "The Men on the Mountain" and tell why you made that choice.**	

Homework Practice Book, p. 126, Main Idea

4

ACTIVITY 1 Reread for Fluency

Paired Reading "The Men on the Mountain," pp. 22–25

5–10 minutes

	To Do	To Say
CORRECTIVE FEEDBACK	Pair students. Monitor paired reading.	Students read aloud pp. 22–25, switching readers for each paragraph. Have partners reread; now the other partner begins. For optimal fluency, students should reread three or four times. You may want to have students read along with the AudioText. Give feedback, using Routine Card 5.
MORE PRACTICE	**READERS' THEATER**	Work with students to adapt these pages to a Readers' Theater. Assign a president to each student and have the student rehearse the part.

ACTIVITY 2 Word Work

Spiral Review Prefixes and Suffixes

5 minutes

	To Do	To Say
Review reading words with affixes and endings.	Write *unhealthy.*	**You can read this word because you know how to read words with prefixes and suffixes.** Cover the prefix and suffix. **What is the base word?** *(health)* Uncover the suffix. **What is the suffix?** *(-y)* Uncover the prefix. **What is the prefix?** *(un-)* **Read the word parts from left to right: *un health y, unhealthy.* What is the word?** *(unhealthy)* **To read a word such as *unhealthy,* I figure out its parts, read them from left to right, and blend the parts to read the whole word.**
Scaffold instruction. **CORRECTIVE FEEDBACK**	Write practice words. Monitor student work.	**Decode Longer Words** Have individuals read the following words. If students make an error, provide help blending the parts of the words. Model sound-by-sound blending and have students repeat after you. Have individuals use the words in sentences.

wonder	**wonderful**	**wonderfully**	**school**	**preschool**	**preschooler**
cook	**overcook**	**overcooked**	**pay**	**repay**	**repayment**
view	**preview**	**previewing**	**start**	**restart**	**restarting**
style	**stylish**	**unstylish**	**state**	**statement**	**restatement**

Vocabulary

5–10 minutes

	To Do	To Say
Extend word knowledge.	Write on the board or a transparency: *The sculptor made a beautiful statue.*	Use the word *sculptor* to extend word knowledge. **We learned that this word means "an artist who cuts or shapes things." We can use this word to read other related words.** **Can you think of other words related to the word *sculptor?*** *(sculpt, sculpted, sculpting, sculpture)* Write words as students name them and add any others. Discuss the meanings of the words. Remind students that *-or* is a suffix that means "one who" (the same as *-er*). Removing this ending forms an action word, *sculpt,* meaning "to carve or to make sculpture." A *sculpture* is a carved or modeled shape.
MORE PRACTICE	Deepen word understanding.	Have students use *sculptor* and *monument* in a sentence. (For example, *The sculptor carved a large monument.*) Share sentences. Ask, **What are some places where you might see a monument made by a sculptor?** (in a museum, at Liberty Island, at Mount Rushmore, and so on)

ACTIVITY 3 Read a Passage

Read Together "Stars and Stripes," pp. 28–29

	To Do	To Say *10–15 minutes*
Scaffold instruction.	Review main idea (homework).	Ask volunteers to read the passage and share answers from Practice Book, p. 126. Remind students of the importance of thinking about the main idea. **When you read a selection, look for the most important idea about the topic. Think about how the details you are reading connect to the main idea.**
Develop language and concepts.	See Routine Cards 3 and 4.	**Before Reading** **This selection is about an important symbol for our country and its liberty. What symbol do you see in the pictures?** (American flag) **What other symbols do you recall reading about that stand for liberty?** (the bald eagle, the Liberty Bell, Uncle Sam) **This selection includes a time line. The events in a time line are listed in sequence, or order. Time lines include important events and the dates these events occurred. The title of the time line on the right on p. 29 gives its main idea. What is this main idea?** (The American flag has changed.) **Now let's read to find out more about this symbol.**
Model fluent reading.	Read pp. 28–29 aloud. Model prosody.	**During Reading** **Listen to my voice as I read this selection and the time line that goes with it.** Read the selection with careful phrasing and expression as students follow along. Read it a second time, having students point to each word. **Now read the selection aloud with me. Use the punctuation marks to group words together as you read, as I do.** Reread the selection several times with students.
Monitor compre-hension.	Monitor listening comprehension.	**After Reading** Prompt discussion to monitor for comprehension. Listen as students answer questions. **What does the first paragraph on p. 28 tell mostly about?** (what the U.S. flag looks like and what each part represents) **Which sentence in this paragraph states the main idea?** (the first) **What do the flag's stripes stand for?** (They stand for the thirteen original colonies.) **How did the flag change from 1818 until today?** (One new star was added for each new state. The pattern of stars was rearranged.) **Summarize** Have volunteers tell how this selection is like others they have read this week.
 MORE PRACTICE	Have students reread p. 28.	**Reread** As they read, tell students to find details about how the flag looks. After reading, they can draw a picture of the flag based on these details.

ACTIVITY 4 Write

Response to Literature

	To Do	To Say *5 minutes*
Prompt expository writing	Writing elements: focus, support	**Of the symbols you have read about, which one do you think best represents the people of our country? Why? When you write, make sure all your sentences are about the symbol. Do your detail sentences explain why you think this symbol best represents the people of our country?**

Homework Practice Book, p. 127, Vocabulary

5

ACTIVITY 1 Assessment Options

Sentence Reading

	To Do	To Say 5 minutes
Assess sentence reading.	Use reproducible p. 220.	Have each student read the sentences. Record scores on the Sentence Reading Chart, p. 224. While you work with one student, others can complete the Write Sentences activity below. **Our neighborhood is quiet at midnight.** **We got a preview of the entertainment for tonight.** **He wrote about his postwar childhood.**
	MONITOR PROGRESS	***If . . .*** students have trouble reading words with suffixes or prefixes, ***then . . .*** reteach the blending strategy lessons on pp. 145–147. ***If . . .*** students misread a word in the sentence, ***then . . .*** correct the error and have them reread the word and then the sentence.
Practice sentence writing.	Provide white boards.	**Write Sentences** Have students copy the sentences from reproducible p. 220 on white boards. Have them confirm spellings by comparing the words they wrote to the words in the sentences.

Passage Reading

	To Do	To Say 5–10 minutes
Assess fluency and compre-hension.	Determine which students to assess this week.	Choose from these options: monitoring fluency (see pp. 214–215) and/or monitoring retelling (see p. 216). Have students reread "The Men on the Mountain." Be sure each student is assessed every other week.
		If you have time, assess every student.

ACTIVITY 2 Build Concepts

Vocabulary

	To Do	To Say 5–10 minutes
Review concept and vocabulary.	Review the homework.	Ask students to go over answers and share their writing from Practice Book, p. 127.
	Display the concept web you began on Day 1.	**This week's question is *What are some important American symbols or monuments?*** How do this week's words relate to the question? (Have students answer the question, using some of the vocabulary they learned this week.) Ask students to add more words to the concept web. Have students explain how each word relates to symbols. Monitor students' understanding of vocabulary as they discuss the web. See Routine Card 6.
MORE PRACTICE		Students can write an ad for visiting a national monument, using three of the vocabulary words.

ACTIVITY 3 Read to Connect

Reread "Symbols of Freedom," pp. 8–11

10 minutes

	To Do	To Say
Monitor compre-hension.	Have students reread "Symbols of Freedom" silently.	**As you read, think about the main idea of the selection.** After rereading, ask: • **What does the selection tell mostly about?** (symbols of our country) • **What do the bald eagle, the Liberty Bell, and Uncle Sam all represent?** (These symbols all stand for freedom in our country.) **We read "She Stands for Freedom." Find that selection. What symbol does this selection tell mostly about? How does it stand for freedom?** Record students' ideas. **We also read "The Men on the Mountain." Why are the faces carved on Mount Rushmore symbols of our country?** Record students' ideas.
Make connections.	Have students make connections across texts.	**What can you say in general about monuments and symbols of our country?** (Answers will vary. Sample answer: Monuments and symbols of our country remind us of our country's history and the fight for freedom.)

ACTIVITY 4 Write

Response to Literature "4 You 2 Do," p. 30

5–10 minutes

	To Do	To Say
Guide response activities.	Discuss the directions. Tell students to choose one activity to complete. Monitor handwriting. See pp. 227–229.	**Word Play** Have students unscramble the words on their own and then meet with a partner to share their answers. **Making Connections** Role play in a group. Discussions should show an understanding of monuments and symbols. **On Paper** Brainstorm with the group a list of meaningful symbols and colors to represent the school. Have students design individual flags. Students can complete Practice Book, p. 128, or you can send the Practice Book page home for them to complete later.
MORE PRACTICE		If you have more time, direct students to complete all the activities.

Homework Practice Book, p. 128, Writing

Unit 6 Week 2 *Animal Freedom*

What can we do to help animals?

Objectives *This week students will ...*

Vocabulary
- build concepts and vocabulary: *adopt, capture, comfort, exercise, provide, struggle*

Phonics
- read words with syllables V/V
- apply knowledge of letter-sounds and word structure to decode unknown words when reading

Text Comprehension
- read connected text
- use sequence to improve comprehension
- write in response to literature

Fluency
- practice fluency with oral rereading

Word Work *This week's phonics focus is ...*

Syllables V/V as in *piano*

Concept Words *Tested Vocabulary*

The week's vocabulary is related to the concept of helping animals.
The first appearance of each word in the Student Reader is noted below.

adopt	to accept something as your own or as your own choice (p. 37)
capture	to take by force; to make a prisoner (p. 46)
comfort	someone or something that makes life easier (p. 37)
exercise	using the body to improve it; working out (p. 37)
provide	to give something that is needed or wanted (p. 38)
struggle	to try hard; work hard against difficulties (p. 47)

Student Reader Unit 6 *This week students will read the following selections.*

34	**A Farm Sanctuary**	Expository Nonfiction
36	**Lost and Found**	Narrative Nonfiction
44	**Critters in the Corn Patch**	Realistic Fiction
52	**Running Free**	Expository Nonfiction
56	**4 You 2 Do**	Activity Page

Daily Lesson Plan

	ACTIVITIES	MATERIALS
Day 1	**Build Concepts** Weekly Concept: Animal Freedom Vocabulary: *adopt, capture, comfort, exercise, provide, struggle* **Word Work** Phonics: Syllables V/V **Read a Passage** "A Farm Sanctuary," pp. 34–35 Comprehension: Use Strategies Reread for Fluency	Student Reader: Unit 6 Routine Cards 1, 3, 5, 6, 7 Tested Vocabulary Cards Student White Boards AudioText Practice Book, p. 129, Syllables V/V
Day 2	**Reread for Fluency** **Word Work** Phonics: Syllables V/V Vocabulary **Comprehension** Sequence **Read a Passage** "Lost and Found," pp. 36–43	Student Reader: Unit 6 AudioText Routine Cards 1, 2, 3, 4, 5, 7, 8 Tested Vocabulary Cards Student White Boards Graphic Organizer 5 Practice Book, p. 129, Syllables V/V
Day 3	**Reread for Fluency** **Word Work** Phonics: Syllables V/V **Read a Passage** "Critters in the Corn Patch," pp. 44–51 Comprehension: Sequence **Write** Response to Literature	Student Reader: Unit 6 AudioText Routine Cards 1, 3, 4, 5, 7 Student journals Practice Book, pp. 129–130, Syllables V/V; Sequence
Day 4	**Reread for Fluency** **Word Work** Phonics: Spiral Review Vocabulary **Read a Passage** "Running Free," pp. 52–55 Comprehension: Sequence; Listening **Write** Response to Literature	Student Reader: Unit 6 AudioText Routine Cards 3, 4, 5 Student White Boards Practice Book, pp. 130–131, Sequence; Vocabulary
Day 5	**Assessment Options** Fluency, Comprehension Sentence Reading Passage Reading **Build Concepts** Vocabulary **Read to Connect** **Write** Response to Literature: "4 You 2 Do," p. 56	Student Reader: Unit 6 Reproducible p. 220 Sentence Reading Chart, p. 224 Student White Boards Fluency Progress Chart, p. 215 Routine Card 6 Practice Book, pp. 131–132, Vocabulary; Writing

See pp. xvi–xvii for how *My Sidewalks* integrates instructional practices for ELL.
See pp. 251–254 for Phonemic Awareness Activities.

ACTIVITY 1

Build Concepts

Vocabulary

To Do | To Say | *10–15 minutes*

Develop word meaning.

See Routine Card 6. Discuss pp. 33–35.

Read Words 2 the Wise on p. 33. Have students turn to pp. 34–35. **Look at the pictures. What do you notice?** (a person feeding milk to a calf, someone caring for a lamb) **Can you use *provide* and *comfort* to describe one of these pictures?** (Example: *The girl provides comfort to the lamb by holding it.*)

Scaffold instruction.

Create a concept web.

In the center of a web, write *Animal Freedom.* **This week's concept is *animal freedom.* What are some ways that people might help animals to be free?**

Add vocabulary words. Discuss the meaning of each word as it relates to animal freedom, using the glossary as needed. (See p. 156 in this Teacher's Guide for definitions.)

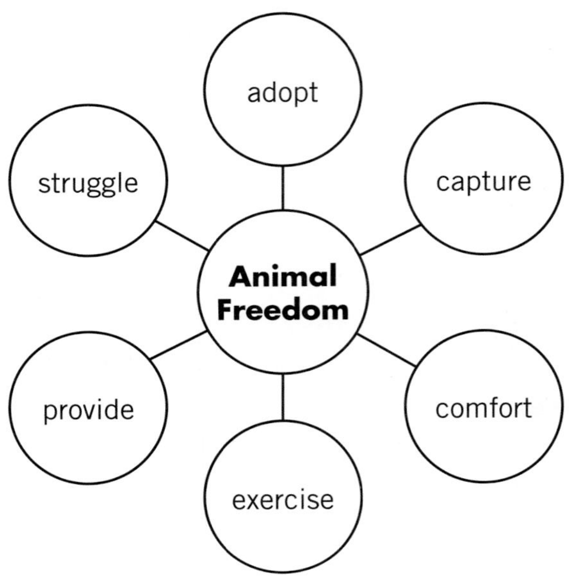

Model the multisyllabic word strategy.

Display each word. Say it as you display it.

Use the Tested Vocabulary Cards. Follow this routine for each word:

- **Look for Meaningful Parts** Remind students to look for meaningful parts. **As you say each word, ask yourself: Do I see any parts I know?**
- **Chunk Words with No Recognizable Parts** Model how to chunk the word *exercise* to read it.

Think aloud.

- **Model** **I see a chunk at the beginning of the word: *ex.* I see a part in the middle: *er.* I see a part at the end of the word: *cise.* I say each chunk slowly: *ex er cise.* I blend the chunks together to make a whole word: *exercise.* That's a word I've heard before.**
- Have students practice reading each word.

Preview.

Read p. 32 with students.

Do you see any of the words we just learned on this page? Together with students, read the sentences on p. 32 describing each selection. Talk about how the concept words might be used in the selections.

MORE PRACTICE

Deepen understanding of *exercise* and *comfort.*

Have students demonstrate understanding by answering questions. **What are some ways that you get *exercise?* How can animals *exercise?* What are some things that bring *comfort* to animals?**

ACTIVITY 2 Word Work

Blending Strategy Syllables V/V

5–10 minutes

Routine

	To Do	To Say
Use the blending routine.	Write *trail.*	**1 Connect** You already can read words like this. What is the word? *(trail)* What is the vowel sound in *trail?* (long *a*) What two letters stand for the long *a* sound in *trail?* *(ai)* Often, when you see two vowels together, they stand for one sound. Today we will learn about words that have two vowels together that stand for two sounds.
Scaffold instruction.	Write *diet.*	**2 Model** This word has two vowels in the middle. If a word has two vowels together that make two different sounds, divide between the two vowels. Draw a line between *i* and *e.* First, I read each syllable. Cover *et.* This is how I blend this syllable: /d/ /ī/, *di.* Cover *di.* This is how I blend this syllable: /ə/ /t/, *et.* Then I blend the syllables together: *di et, diet.* Point out that in most words like these, the first vowel in the pair of vowels has a long sound. d i e t
	Distribute white boards.	**3 Listen and Write** Write the word *diet.* Draw a line between *i* and *e.* As you write, say each syllable to yourself: *di et.* Now blend the two syllables and say the word aloud: *diet.*
CORRECTIVE FEEDBACK	Write each practice word. Monitor student practice.	**4 Group Practice** Let's try reading these words. Support students as they blend progressively more difficult words. Give feedback, using the *if . . . then* statements on Routine Card 1. dial lion riot duet* fluid giant annual cereal denial gradual media* piano **5 Individual Practice** Have each student blend several words from the row best matched to his or her ability. duo poet quiet neon trio meow idea Ohio museum patio polio create
	Check understanding of practice words.	*Students need to make sense of words that they segment and blend. If needed, help students with meanings. A *duet* is a musical performance by two people. *Media* refers to types of communication, such as radio, TV, newspapers, and the Internet.
MORE PRACTICE	Distribute white boards. Model building and spelling words.	**Build Words** Write *dial.* Can you blend this word? (/d/ /ī/ /ə/ /l/) Have students write words on white boards. Write *dial.* Now change the *d* in *dial* to *v.* What is the new word? *(vial)* A *vial* is a small bottle. • Change the *v* in *vial* to *den.* What is the new word? *(denial)* • Change the *den* in *denial* to *tr.* What is the new word? *(trial)* • Add *pre* to the beginning of *trial.* What is the new word? *(pretrial)* • Change *pre* to *mis.* What is the word? *(mistrial)* Discuss the meanings of *pretrial* (something that happens before a trial) and *mistrial* (a trial in which the jury fails to come to a decision).

ACTIVITY 3 Read a Passage

Build Background "A Farm Sanctuary," pp. 34–35

10 minutes

	To Do	To Say
Develop language and concepts.	See Routine Cards 3 and 7.	**Before Reading** Read the title aloud. Do a structured picture walk with students. Introduce proper nouns, if necessary.
	Ask questions and elaborate on answers.	pp. 34–35 **What are these people doing?** (feeding a bottle to a calf; holding a lamb) **These animals may have been rescued. They may have lost their mothers. They have been taken to an animal sanctuary—a place where they are safe from harm. The animals are getting kind treatment from workers in the sanctuary.**
Scaffold instruction.	Key concepts: *rescued, sanctuary, treatment*	**Let's read to find some ways that people help animals. As you read, ask yourself: What is this mainly about? What am I learning?**
Guide compre-hension.	Read pp. 34–35 aloud.	**During Reading** Read the selection as students follow along. Then read it a second time, having students join in. If necessary, stop at the end of each paragraph to check comprehension. Ask questions to promote discussion and develop the concept. • **What are some ways that Gene and Lorri Bauston help animals to be free and healthy?** (They help animals to be free from hunger or sickness. They let animals exercise outside in the fields.) • **Why do you think so many people are members of the Farm Sanctuary?** (They want to protect animals, and they feel good helping them.) • **What words on the concept web could help you describe the people, animals, and place in this article?**
	Use vocabulary to develop the concept.	**After Reading** **What help do workers *provide* to animals at the Farm Sanctuary? Why do the animals need the freedom to get *exercise?***

Reread for Fluency "A Farm Sanctuary," p. 35

5–10 minutes

	To Do	To Say
CORRECTIVE FEEDBACK	Monitor oral reading.	**Read p. 35 aloud. Read it three or four times so your reading gets better each time.** Give feedback on students' oral reading and use of the blending strategy. See Routine Cards 1 and 5.
MORE PRACTICE		Instead of rereading just p. 35, have students reread the entire selection three or four times. You may want to have students read along with the AudioText.

Homework Practice Book, p. 129, Phonics: Syllables V/V

ACTIVITY 1 Reread for Fluency

Paired Reading "A Farm Sanctuary," p. 35

	To Do	To Say 5–10 minutes
CORRECTIVE FEEDBACK	Pair students. Monitor paired reading.	Students read aloud p. 35, switching readers for each paragraph. Have partners reread; now the other partner begins. For optimal fluency, students should reread three or four times. Give feedback, using Routine Card 5.
MORE PRACTICE		Instead of rereading just p. 35, have students reread the entire selection three or four times. You may want to have students read along with the AudioText.

ACTIVITY 2 Word Work

Blend and Build Words Syllables V/V

	To Do	To Say 5–10 minutes
Review blending: syllable pattern V/V.	Write *fluid.*	**Remember, words with two vowels together that stand for two sounds are divided between the two vowels.** Draw a line between the *u* and *i* in *fluid.* **This is how I read the word. First I read each syllable: /f/ /l/ /ü/, /ə/ /d/. Then I blend the syllables together: *flu id, fluid.***
Scaffold instruction.	Write each practice word. Monitor student practice.	**Remember that in most words like these the first vowel in the pair has a long sound. Today we will read more words with this syllable pattern.** Support students as they blend progressively more difficult words. Give feedback, using the *if . . . then* statements on Routine Card 1. idea poet radio rodeo violin ruin dandelion medium oriole* stereo violent* terrarium*
CORRECTIVE FEEDBACK	Check understanding of practice words.	*Students need to make sense of words that they segment and blend. If needed, help students with meanings. **An *oriole* is a type of bird. *Violent* means "acting with great force." A *terrarium* is a glass enclosure in which to keep plants or small animals.**
MORE PRACTICE	Distribute white boards. Model building and spelling words.	**Build Words** Write *poem.* **Can you blend this word?** (/p/ /ō/ /ə/ /m/) Have students write words on their white boards. Write *poem.* **Now change the *m* in *poem* to *t.* What is the new word?** *(poet)* • **Add the letters *ry* to the end of *poet.* What is the new word?** *(poetry)* • **Add the letters *ic* to the end of *poet.* What is the new word?** *(poetic)* Explain that this word is accented on the second syllable. *Poetic* refers to a thing or person that seems or sounds like poetry.

Vocabulary

	To Do	To Say *5 minutes*
Review vocabulary.	Display the concept web from Day 1. Deepen word understanding of *exercise, adopt, comfort,* and *provide.*	Review the concept web. **The words *exercise, adopt, comfort,* and *provide* will be in the selection you are reading today.** See Routine Card 2 for the multisyllabic word routine. **When you *exercise,* you use your body to improve it. Can you name some ways to *exercise?*** (Answers may include jumping rope, lifting weights, and playing sports.) **What kinds of *exercise* do animals get? What are some ways you could *provide comfort* to an animal? Where could you go if you wanted to *adopt* a pet?** Encourage discussion, asking, **What are other ways you could help animals feel free?**
Lead cumulative review.		Use the Tested Vocabulary Cards to review concept words from previous weeks.

ACTIVITY 3 Comprehension

Sequence

	To Do	To Say *5 minutes*
Scaffold instruction.	Introduce main idea.	**Today you will read about people who help animals at an animal shelter. Pay attention to words that tell you the order in which events happen at the shelter. It is important to keep track of the order of events because it will help you understand how things are done at the shelter.**
	Model the skill.	**For example, if I want to know what a day at the shelter is like, it helps me to picture different tasks in the order they are done. I look for words that help me know what happens first, next, and last as I read.**
	Distribute Graphic Organizer 5.	**As you read "Lost and Found," note things that are done in a certain sequence, or order and write them on your graphic organizer. For example, before adopting a pet, you should talk to your family and find out about different shelters before visiting a place.** See Routine Card 8.

ACTIVITY 4 Read a Passage

Reading "Lost and Found," pp. 36–43

10–15 minutes

	To Do	To Say
Develop language and concepts.	Use Routine Cards 3 and 7. Ask questions and elaborate on answers.	**Before Reading** Have students recall what they learned about caring for animals. Read the title. Do a structured picture walk with students.
		pp. 36–39 **The selection tells how shelters care for animals that do not have real homes. What are people doing to help them?** (giving them medical care and exercise) **Would you like to adopt a pet from a shelter?**
Scaffold instruction.	Key concepts: *adopt, comfort, exercise, provide*	pp. 40–43 **How are the people caring for animals?** (A boy is washing a dog and feeding it; a volunteer is petting and playing with a dog.) **Which pet in these pictures would you want to adopt? Why? How would you provide comfort and exercise for your pet?**
Guide comprehension.	Use Routine Card 4.	**During Reading** **Read the pages in a whisper. Raise your hand if you need help with a word. As you read, ask yourself: What am I learning about ways people help animals? What is this mainly about?**
	Monitor independent reading.	pp. 36–39 **What different jobs do the workers do at the shelter each day? Use some sequence words.** (Each day people feed the animals and give them medicine, if needed. They check in new animals and write reports. Later, they take animals for walks and clean their cages. Sometimes vets come to give the animals check-ups.)
	Model using context for word meaning.	Read aloud the paragraph with *veterinarians* on p. 38. Explain how "Animal doctors" and "provide care to sick animals" provide clues to the meaning of *veterinarians.*
		pp. 40–43 **Why do shelters need volunteers and donations?** (Volunteers help by feeding, petting, and walking animals. Shelters use donations to pay for food and care.) **Why is a shelter a good place to go to adopt a pet?** (Millions of pets in shelters need homes.)
Model summarizing.	Think aloud.	**After Reading** **What did you learn about how people help animals at a shelter? What was the selection mainly about?** Model how to summarize. **The selection tells what people do each day at an animal shelter, such as feeding and caring for animals. It also tells how you can adopt a pet.**
MORE PRACTICE	Have students reread pp. 36–37.	**Reread** As they read, have students note the sequence in which people care for animals each day at a shelter. Point out the phrase *It starts,* which shows how a day begins. Draw attention to the phrase *Each day,* which indicates that these events happen over and over again. Students can add these phrases to their graphic organizers.
	Homework	Practice Book, p. 129, Phonics: Syllables V/V

3

ACTIVITY 1 Reread for Fluency

Oral Reading "Lost and Found," pp. 36–37

5–10 minutes

	To Do	To Say
CORRECTIVE FEEDBACK	Monitor oral reading.	**Read pp. 36–37 aloud. Read them three or four times so your reading gets better each time.** Give feedback on students' oral reading and use of the blending strategy. Use Routine Cards 1 and 5.
MORE PRACTICE		Have students reread additional pages of the selection three or four times. You may want to have students read along with the AudioText.

ACTIVITY 2 Word Work

Fluent Word Reading Syllables V/V

5–10 minutes

	To Do	To Say
Review phonics.	Review the homework.	Ask students to share answers from Practice Book, p. 129.
Use word-reading routine.	Write *lion.*	Routine **1 Connect** **You can read this word because you know that a word with two vowels together sometimes has two different vowel sounds. What vowels do you see?** *(i, o)* **What is the word?** *(lion)*
	Write *alias* and *trial.*	**2 Model** **When you come to a new word, look for two vowels together. If you don't recognize the word, try using separate vowel sounds for the vowels you see. If a word has two vowels together that make two different sounds, divide between the two vowels. Say the parts of the word to yourself, and then read the word.** Model reading *alias* and *trial* in this way. **When you come to a new word, what are you going to do?**
Scaffold instruction.	Write each practice word.	**3 Group Practice** **We will read words with two vowels together that make two different sounds. Think about the vowel sound in each syllable, and say the vowel to yourself. When I point to the word, let's read it together.** Allow 2–3 seconds previewing time for each word. Support students as they blend progressively more difficult words. **quiet diet idea area piano radio** **media stereo audience helium museum**
CORRECTIVE FEEDBACK	**MONITOR PROGRESS**	***If . . .*** students have difficulty previewing and reading whole words, ***then . . .*** have them use syllable-by-syllable blending. ***If . . .*** students can't read words fluently at a rate of 1–2 seconds per word, ***then . . .*** continue practicing the list.
MORE PRACTICE	Model reading words in sentences.	**When I read a sentence, I read each word without stopping between the words. If I come to a word I don't know, I blend it. Then I read the sentence again.** Model reading this sentence, stopping to blend *piano: The boy played the piano well.*
	Write practice sentences.	Have each student read the sentence best matched to his or her ability. **Let's eat in the patio area.** **We played a duet in the studio.** **The museum is quiet.**

Vocabulary

	To Do	To Say *5 minutes*
Review vocabulary.	Display the concept web from Day 1.	Review the concept web. **The words *capture, struggle,* and *provide* will be in the selection you are reading today.** Review the meanings of the words.

ACTIVITY 3 Read a Passage

Reading "Critters in the Corn Patch," pp. 44–51

	To Do	To Say *10–15 minutes*
Scaffold instruction.	Review sequence.	Remind students that clue words can help them follow the sequence. **Look for phrases such as *last summer, before dinner,* and *the next morning.* As you read "Critters in the Corn Patch," look for the sequence of events.**
Develop language and concepts.	Use Routine Cards 3 and 7. Ask questions and elaborate on answers. Key concepts: *cage, capture, problem, set (a trap), struggle, solution*	**Before Reading** Read the title. Do a structured picture walk. pp. 44–48 **Who are the main characters?** (a farm couple, a boy) **Where does this story take place?** (on a farm) **What do you think the farmer plans to capture in the cage?** (an animal) pp. 49–51 **Can you guess the problem the people are struggling with?** (Animals are stealing things from their garden.) **How do you think they will solve the problem?** (by setting a trap) **What clues does the picture on pp. 50–51 give about the ending of the story?** (They catch a skunk.)
Guide comprehension.	Use Routine Card 4.	**During Reading** **Read the pages in a whisper. Raise your hand if you need help with a word. As you read, ask yourself: Who are the important characters? What happens first, next, and last?**
	Monitor independent reading.	pp. 44–47 **What is the first important thing that happens in the story?** (Grandpa Joe builds a trap to keep the raccoons from stealing the corn.) pp. 48–51 **Does Grandpa's plan work?** (No, the raccoon chews through the bars of the cage.) **What does Grandpa try next?** (He covers the cage with steel.) **What happens at the end of the story?** (When Grandpa opens the trap, he finds a skunk.)
	Monitor comprehension. Guide retelling.	**After Reading** Discuss the What Do You Think? question. Have one student retell the story while the others assist. Prompt students by asking: **Who are the characters? What happens first? next? How does the story end?** See Monitoring Retelling on p. 216.
MORE PRACTICE	Have students reread p. 47.	**Reread** As they read, tell students to notice details about how the trap works. Then have them retell the steps in order.

ACTIVITY 4 Write

Response to Literature

	To Do	To Say *5 minutes*
Prompt journal writing.		**Take out your journals. How could you catch an animal without hurting it? Write the steps you would take.**

Homework Practice Book, p. 130, Sequence

4

ACTIVITY 1 Reread for Fluency

Paired Reading "Critters in the Corn Patch," p. 47

	To Do	To Say
		5–10 minutes
CORRECTIVE FEEDBACK	Pair students. Monitor paired reading.	Students read aloud p. 47, switching readers for each paragraph. Have partners reread; now the other partner begins. For optimal fluency, students should reread three or four times. You may want to have students read along with the AudioText. Give feedback, using Routine Card 5.
MORE PRACTICE	**READERS' THEATER**	Students can use pp. 47–48 as a script for a Readers' Theater. Have them rehearse, with one student being Grandpa and the other, the narrator.

ACTIVITY 2 Word Work

Spiral Review Read Longer Words

	To Do	To Say
		5 minutes
Review reading words with the syllable pattern VCCCV.	Write *control.* Draw a line between *n* and *t.*	**You can read this word because you know how to read two-syllable words with three or more consonants in the middle. Two of these consonants go together because they are a blend. What is the blend?** *(tr)* **Where do you divide the syllables?** (between the *n* and *t*) **Remember, divide the word, read each syllable, and then blend the syllables together. What is the word?** *(control)*
	Write *pilgrim.* Draw a line between *l* and *g.*	Repeat with *pilgrim.* Point out that the letters *gr* go together because they stand for a blend, /gr/.
Scaffold instruction. **CORRECTIVE FEEDBACK**	Distribute white boards. Monitor student work.	**Decode Longer Words** Have students copy the following words on their white boards. Ask them to draw a line between the syllables in each word. Then ask individuals to pronounce words. If students make an error, model syllable-by-syllable blending and have students repeat after you. To check meaning, call on individuals to use the words in sentences. **hungry hundred monster complain actress children** **entrance fortress parsley instruct surprise merchant**

Vocabulary

	To Do	To Say
		5–10 minutes
Extend word knowledge.	Write on the board or a transparency: *We tried to <u>capture</u> a raccoon.*	Use the word *capture* to extend word knowledge. **We learned earlier this week that *capture* means "to take by force." We can use *capture* to read other words.** **Can you think of other words related to the word *capture?*** *(captured, capturing, recapture, captive)* Write words as students name them and add any others. Talk about the meanings of the words. Point out that *re-* is a prefix that means "again," so *recapture* means "to catch again." A *captive* is "one who is captured."
MORE PRACTICE	Deepen word understanding.	Have students use *capture* and *struggle* in a sentence. (For example, *When we tried to capture the injured cat, it struggled and hissed.*) Share sentences.

ACTIVITY 3 Read a Passage

Read Together "Running Free," pp. 52–55

10–15 minutes

	To Do	To Say
Scaffold instruction.	Review sequence (homework).	Ask volunteers to read the passage and share answers from Practice Book, p. 130. Remind students of the importance of paying attention to the sequence. **The sequence of events is often important in a selection. Look for clue words that show the order in which things happen. Try to picture in your mind the events as they happen.**
Develop language and concepts.	See Routine Cards 3 and 4.	**Before Reading** **This article is about helping wild horses. Do these horses look like they can run free? Let's read to find out what people can *provide* to protect the freedom, *comfort,* and safety of these animals.**
Model fluent reading.	Read pp. 52–55 aloud. Model prosody.	**During Reading** **Listen to my voice as I read this article.** Read the article with attention to punctuation as students follow along. Read it a second time, having students point to each word. **Now read the article aloud with me. Try to make your voice sound like mine as we read. Remember to make your voice go up when you see a question mark and pause at commas and periods.** Reread the selection several times.
Monitor compre-hension.	Monitor listening comprehension.	**After Reading** Prompt discussion to monitor comprehension. Listen as students answer questions. **Why are there fewer wild horses now than in the past?** (Farmers want to use the land for raising cattle so the horses are rounded up.) **Where are most wild horses found?** (in western states) **How do people care for wild horses?** (Wild horse sanctuaries offer food and safe places to live. Groups work to change laws that will let horses run free once again.) **Summarize** Have students review ways that people help animals.
MORE PRACTICE	Have students reread p. 52.	**Reread** As they read, tell students to notice details about herds of wild horses. After reading, they can discuss the article with a partner, comparing wild horses with other animals they read about.

ACTIVITY 4 Write

Response to Literature

5 minutes

	To Do	To Say
Prompt narrative writing.	Writing elements: organization, conventions	**Write a story about someone who has a pet. Tell about a day in the life of the person and how the person keeps the animal healthy. Be sure to use words like *first* and *next* that help tell the order. Also check that you begin each sentence with a capital letter and end it with the correct punctuation.**

Homework Practice Book, p. 131, Vocabulary

5

ACTIVITY 1

Assessment Options

Sentence Reading

5 minutes

	To Do	To Say
Assess sentence reading.	Use reproducible p. 220.	Have each student read the sentences. Record scores on the Sentence Reading Chart, p. 224. While you work with one student, others can complete the Write Sentences activity below. **Let's eat in the patio area.** **Someone played piano music on the radio.** **Jon wrote a poem in his diary.**
	MONITOR PROGRESS	***If . . .*** students have trouble reading words with V/V syllables, ***then . . .*** reteach the blending strategy lessons on pp. 159 and 161. ***If . . .*** students misread a word in the sentence, ***then . . .*** correct the error and have them reread the word and then the sentence.
Practice sentence writing.	Provide white boards.	**Write Sentences** Have students copy the sentences from reproducible p. 220 on white boards. Have them confirm spellings by comparing the words they wrote to the words in the sentences.

Passage Reading

5–10 minutes

	To Do	To Say
Assess fluency and comprehension.	Determine which students to assess this week.	Choose from these options: monitoring fluency (see pp. 214–215) and/or monitoring retelling (see p. 216). Have students reread "Critters in the Corn Patch." Be sure each student is assessed every other week.
		If you have time, assess every student.

ACTIVITY 2

Build Concepts

Vocabulary

5–10 minutes

	To Do	To Say
Review concept and vocabulary.	Review the homework. Display the concept web you began on Day 1.	Ask students to go over answers and share their writing from Practice Book, p. 131. **This week's question is *What can we do to help animals?* How do this week's words relate to the question?** (Have students answer the question, using some of the vocabulary they learned this week.) Ask students to add more words to the concept web. Have students explain how each word relates to animal freedom. Monitor students' understanding of vocabulary as they discuss the web. See Routine Card 6.
MORE PRACTICE		Students can write sentences using three of the vocabulary words.

ACTIVITY 3 Read to Connect

Reread "A Farm Sanctuary," pp. 34–35

	To Do	To Say *10 minutes*
Monitor compre-hension.	Have students reread "A Farm Sanctuary" silently.	**As you read, think about what the selection says about animal freedom.** After rereading, ask: • **What are ways that people provide aid to animals at the farm sanctuary?** (They give animals clean, safe homes with healthy food, room to play, and plenty of attention from people.) • **Has the sanctuary grown?** (Yes. It started in 1986 when the Baustons rescued one sick sheep. Now it has more than 100,000 members.) **We also read "Lost and Found." Find that selection. How do people help animals that need homes?** Record students' ideas.
Make connections.	Have students make connections across texts.	**We also read "Critters in the Corn Patch." What did Grandpa Joe do to make sure wild animals could be free?** Record students' ideas. **In what ways can people help animals?** (Sample answers: People can help animals by giving them food, medicine, love, and homes.)

ACTIVITY 4 Write

Response to Literature "4 You 2 Do," p. 56

	To Do	To Say *5–10 minutes*
Guide response activities.	Discuss the directions. Tell students to choose one activity to complete. Monitor handwriting. See pp. 227–229.	**Word Play** Have students list synonyms on their own and then meet with a partner to share synonyms. **Making Connections** Discuss the question in a group or in pairs. **On Paper** Before students write, brainstorm with the group a list of animals in your community and how they might need help. Have students write on their own. Students can use Practice Book, p. 132, to help prepare their written response, or you can send the Practice Book page home for them to complete later.
MORE PRACTICE		If you have more time, direct students to complete all the activities.

Homework Practice Book, p. 132, Writing

Unit 6 Week 3 *Expressing Yourself*

How can we express ourselves?

Objectives *This week students will ...*

Vocabulary
- build concepts and vocabulary: *amuse, create, display, express, inspire, theater*

Phonics
- blend and read words with common syllables and practice multisyllabic words
- apply knowledge of letter-sounds and word structure to decode unknown words when reading

Text Comprehension
- read connected text
- compare and contrast to improve comprehension
- write in response to literature

Fluency
- practice fluency with oral rereading

Word Work *This week's phonics focus is ...*

Common Syllables   Multisyllabic Word Practice

Concept Words *Tested Vocabulary*

The week's vocabulary is related to the concept of how we express ourselves. The first appearance of each word in the Student Reader is noted below.

amuse	to cause to laugh or smile (p. 64)
create	to make something which has not been made before (p. 60)
display	a collection put where people can easily see it (p. 70)
express	to show something by your look, voice, or action (p. 60)
inspire	to cause a good thought or a good feeling in someone (p. 61)
theater	a place where people go to see movies or plays (p. 62)

Student Reader Unit 6 *This week students will read the following selections.*

60	**Expressing Yourself**	Narrative Nonfiction
62	**Not a Typical Theater**	Expository Nonfiction
70	**What Makes an Artist?**	Realistic Fiction
78	**Puppet Magic**	How-to Article
82	**4 You 2 Do**	Activity Page

Daily Lesson Plan

	ACTIVITIES	MATERIALS
Day 1	**Build Concepts** Weekly Concept: Expressing Yourself Vocabulary: *amuse, create, display, express, inspire, theater* **Word Work** Phonics: Common Syllables **Read a Passage** "Expressing Yourself," pp. 60–61 Comprehension: Use Strategies Reread for Fluency	Student Reader: Unit 6 Routine Cards 1, 3, 5, 6, 7 Tested Vocabulary Cards Student White Boards AudioText Practice Book, p. 133, Common Syllables
Day 2	**Reread for Fluency** **Word Work** Phonics: Multisyllabic Word Practice Vocabulary **Comprehension** Compare and Contrast **Read a Passage** "Not a Typical Theater," pp. 62–69	Student Reader: Unit 6 AudioText Routine Cards 1, 2, 3, 4, 5, 7, 8 Tested Vocabulary Cards Student White Boards Graphic Organizer 3 or 4 Practice Book, p. 134, Multisyllabic Word Practice
Day 3	**Reread for Fluency** **Word Work** Phonics: Common Syllables; Multisyllabic Word Practice Vocabulary **Read a Passage** "What Makes an Artist?" pp. 70–77 Comprehension: Compare and Contrast **Write** Response to Literature	Student Reader: Unit 6 AudioText Routine Cards 1, 3, 4, 5, 7 Student journals Practice Book, pp. 133–135, Common Syllables; Multisyllabic Word Practice; Compare and Contrast
Day 4	**Reread for Fluency** **Word Work** Phonics: Spiral Review Vocabulary **Read a Passage** "Puppet Magic," pp. 78–81 Comprehension: Compare and Contrast; Listening **Write** Response to Literature	Student Reader: Unit 6 AudioText Routine Cards 3, 4, 5 Student White Boards Practice Book, pp. 135–136, Compare and Contrast; Vocabulary
Day 5	**Assessment Options** Fluency, Comprehension Sentence Reading Mid-Unit Passage Reading **Build Concepts** Vocabulary **Read to Connect** **Write** Response to Literature: "4 You 2 Do," p. 82	Student Reader: Unit 6 Reproducible p. 221 Sentence Reading Chart, p. 224 Student White Boards Fluency Progress Chart, p. 215 Routine Card 6 Practice Book, pp. 136–137, Vocabulary; Writing Assessment Book, p. 83

See pp. xvi–xvii for how *My Sidewalks* integrates instructional practices for ELL.
See pp. 251–254 for Phonemic Awareness Activities.

ACTIVITY **1**

Build Concepts

Vocabulary

10–15 minutes

	To Do	To Say
Develop word meaning.	See Routine Card 6. Discuss pp. 59–61.	Read Words 2 the Wise on p. 59. Have students turn to pp. 60–61. **Look at the pictures. What do you notice?** (a child wearing a ballet costume, a girl writing in a notebook, a boy on a beach) **Can you use the words *amuse* and *express* to describe one or more of these pictures?** (Example: *The girl can amuse herself by writing stories. Writing and dancing are two ways to express yourself.*
Scaffold instruction.	Create a concept web.	In the center of a web, write *Expressing Yourself.* **This week's concept is *expressing yourself.* We'll be reading about ways that people express themselves.** Provide examples to demonstrate meaning. ***Express* means "to show something by your look, voice, or action."** Add the other vocabulary words. Discuss the meaning of each word as it relates to the concept of how we express ourselves, using the glossary as needed. (See p. 170 of this Teacher's Guide for definitions.)

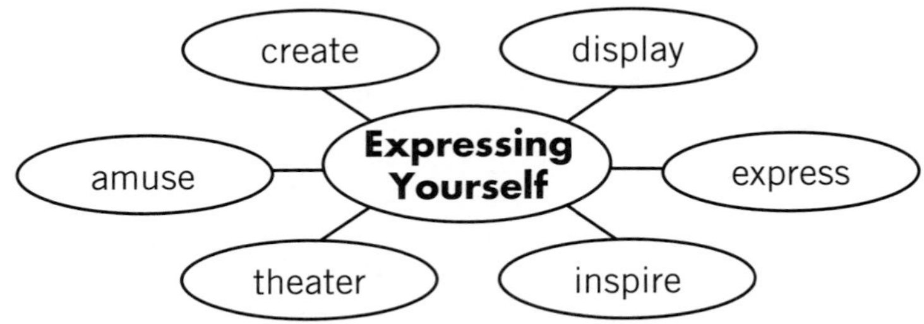

	To Do	To Say
Model the multisyllabic word strategy.	Display each word. Say it as you display it.	Use the Tested Vocabulary Cards. Follow this routine for each word: • **Look for Meaningful Parts** Remind students to look for meaningful parts. **As you say each word, ask yourself: Do I see any parts I know?** • **Chunk Words with No Recognizable Parts** Model how to chunk the word *inspire* to read it.
	Think aloud.	• **Model I see a chunk at the beginning of the word: *in.* I see a part at the end of the word: *spire.* I say each chunk slowly: *in spire.* I say the chunks fast to make a whole word: *inspire.* That's a real word I know.** • Have students practice reading each word.
Preview.	Read p. 58 with students.	**Do you see any of the words we just learned on this page?** Together with students, read the sentences on p. 58 describing each selection. Discuss ways the concept words might be used in the selections.
MORE PRACTICE	Deepen understanding of *create.*	Have students demonstrate understanding by answering questions. **What do artists *create?* What do composers and poets *create?* What are some things you *create?***

ACTIVITY 2

Word Work

Blending Strategy Common Syllables (such as *-tion, -sion, -ture*)

	To Do	To Say
		5–10 minutes
Use the blending routine.	Write *careful* and *childish.*	**1 Connect You already studied words like these. What syllables do you hear in *careful? (care ful)* in *childish? (child ish)* What do you know about reading these words?** (They each end with a common word part, *-ish* and *-ful.* You can blend the syllables to read the longer words.) **Now you will learn about words with other endings.**
Scaffold instruction.	Write *action.*	**2 Model** Point to *action.* **To read a word like *action,* I figure out its parts. How many syllables do you hear in *action?*** (two) **What is the first syllable?** *(ac)* **What is the second syllable?** *(tion)* **You have seen this syllable in many other words. Here's how you blend it: /shən/. Let's blend this word together: *ac tion, action.*** a c t i o n
	Write *nature* and *expression.*	Repeat with *nature* and *expression.* Point out that *-sion* in *expression* has the same sound as *-tion* in *action* and that *-ture* in *nature* is pronounced /chər/.
	Distribute white boards.	**3 Listen and Write Write the word *action.* Draw a line under *-tion.* As you write, say each syllable to yourself: *ac tion.* Now blend the syllables and say the word aloud.** Repeat with the words *nature* and *expression.*
CORRECTIVE FEEDBACK	Write each practice word. Monitor student practice.	**4 Group Practice Let's try the same thing with these words.** Support students as they blend progressively more difficult words. Give feedback, using the ***if . . . then*** statements on Routine Card 1. **picture question session* future mention section** **adventure invention permission vacation furniture** **5 Individual Practice** Have each student blend several words from the row best matched to his or her ability. **culture vision capture action tension* fraction** **vacation election manufacture comprehension possession***
	Check understanding of practice words.	*Students need to make sense of words that they segment and blend. If needed, help students with meanings. **A *session* is a meeting for a special purpose. *Tension* is a feeling of nervousness. A *possession* is a thing that is owned.**
MORE PRACTICE	Distribute white boards. Model building and spelling words with *-ture.*	**Spell and Write You can spell words with the syllable *-ture.* Think about the sound you hear in the first part of the word. Write the letters that form those sounds. Then add *-ture.*** Have students write *nature, picture, future,* and *adventure.*

Routine

ACTIVITY 3 Read a Passage

Build Background "Expressing Yourself," pp. 60–61

10 minutes

Routine

	To Do	To Say
Develop language and concepts.	See Routine Cards 3 and 7. Ask questions and elaborate on answers. Key concepts: *create, express, inspire*	**Before Reading** Read the title aloud. Do a structured picture walk with students. p. 60 **What do you see?** (a girl in a costume; a dancer) **How does she express herself?** (by dancing or pretending to be a dancer) **Does dancing appear to inspire her?** p. 61 **What are these children doing?** (writing, building a sand castle) **Let's read to find out things people create and ways they express themselves. As you read, ask yourself: What is this mainly about? What am I learning?**
Guide compre-hension.	Read pp. 60–61 aloud.	**During Reading** Read the selection as students follow along. Then read it a second time, having students join in. If necessary, stop at the end of each paragraph to check comprehension. Ask questions to promote discussion and develop the concept. • **What kinds of self-expression are described in the selection?** • **Which of these things would you enjoy doing?** • **What words on the concept web could help you describe the children pictured in this selection?**
	Use vocabulary to develop the concept.	**After Reading** **What did you learn about *expressing* yourself?**

Reread for Fluency "Expressing Yourself," p. 60

5–10 minutes

	To Do	To Say
CORRECTIVE FEEDBACK	Monitor oral reading.	**Read p. 60 aloud. Read it three or four times so your reading gets better each time.** Give feedback on students' oral reading and use of the blending strategy. See Routine Cards 1 and 5.
MORE PRACTICE		Instead of rereading just p. 60, have students reread the entire selection three or four times. You may want to have students read along with the AudioText.

Homework Practice Book, p. 133, Phonics: Common Syllables

ACTIVITY 1 Reread for Fluency

Paired Reading "Expressing Yourself," p. 60

	To Do	To Say 5–10 minutes
CORRECTIVE FEEDBACK	Pair students. Monitor paired reading.	Students read aloud p. 60, switching readers for each paragraph. Have partners reread; now the other partner begins. For optimal fluency, students should reread three or four times. Give feedback, using Routine Card 5.
MORE PRACTICE		Instead of rereading just p. 60, have students reread the entire selection three or four times. You may want to have students read along with the AudioText.

ACTIVITY 2 Word Work

Blending Strategy Multisyllabic Word Practice

	To Do	To Say 5–10 minutes
Use the blending routine.	Write *neighborhood* and *contentment.*	Routine **1 Connect** **You already studied words like these. What syllables do you hear in *neighborhood? (neigh bor hood)* in *contentment? (con tent ment)* What do you know about reading words with many syllables?** (Look for syllables you already know. Then blend the syllables to read these words.) **Today we will practice more words with many syllables.**
Scaffold instruction.	Write *connection.*	**2 Model** **This word has many syllables. It ends with the syllable *-tion.* To read words with many syllables like this, look for syllables you know. Then break the syllables apart, say each part, and blend the syllables together. Let's blend this word together: *con nec tion, connection.*** c o n n e c t i o n
	Write *adventure* and *decision.*	Repeat with *adventure* and *decision.*
	Distribute white boards.	**3 Listen and Write** Have students write on white boards. **Write the word *connection.* As you write, say the new word to yourself: *connection.* Now say the word aloud.** Do the same with *adventure* and *decision.*
CORRECTIVE FEEDBACK	Write each practice word. Monitor student practice.	**4 Group Practice** **Let's try the same thing with these words.** Support students as they blend progressively more difficult words. Give feedback, using the *if . . . then* statements on Routine Card 1. **payment mention childhood vision venture caption** **government convention neighborhood comprehension detection** **5 Individual Practice** Have each student blend several words from the row best matched to his or her ability. **boyhood creature pavement fracture version mention action** **tradition decision entertainment parenthood signature amazement**

For more practice, see next page.

MORE PRACTICE	Sort words.	**Sort Words** Have students sort the words from the list for Individual Practice by the common syllables.

Vocabulary

5 minutes

	To Do	To Say
Review vocabulary.	Display the concept web from Day 1.	Review the concept web. See Routine Card 2 for the multisyllabic word routine. **The words *amuse, express, inspire,* and *theater* will be in the selection you are reading today.** Remind students that *inspire* means "to cause a good thought or a good feeling in someone."
	Deepen word understanding of *amuse, inspire,* and *theater.*	**What are some things you might see at a *theater?* How would these *amuse* you? What things might *inspire* you?** (Answers will vary. Examples: You might see a play, a musical performance, or a movie. A person in a funny costume would amuse me. An important speech could inspire me to do something.)
Lead cumulative review.		Use the Tested Vocabulary Cards to review concept words from previous weeks.

ACTIVITY 3 Comprehension

Compare and Contrast

5 minutes

	To Do	To Say
Scaffold instruction.	Introduce compare and contrast.	**Today you will read about a theater that is unlike any other. To find how things are different, you contrast them. When you compare two things, you think about ways they are alike. Pay attention to words that show how this theater is different from others.**
	Model the skill.	**For example, the selection tells me the places where the Redmoon Theater group puts on plays. I thought that plays were held inside a theater building, so this is one way that Redmoon is different.**
	Distribute Graphic Organizer 3 or 4.	**As you read "Not a Typical Theater," look for words that help you compare and contrast this theater with others. Add these similarities and differences to your graphic organizer.** See Routine Card 8.

ACTIVITY 4 Read a Passage

Reading "Not a Typical Theater," pp. 62–69

10–15 minutes

	To Do	To Say
Develop language and concepts.	Use Routine Cards 3 and 7. Ask questions and elaborate on answers.	**Before Reading** Have students recall what they know about theaters. Read the title. Introduce proper nouns, if necessary. Do a structured picture walk with students.
Scaffold instruction.	Key concepts: *amuse, audience, express, inspire, performers, theater*	pp. 62–65 **The selection is about a theater that is unlike others. What happens in theaters?** (Performers express themselves before an audience.) **What do you see in this theater?** (People are outdoors.)
		pp. 66–69 **What do you see on the stage here?** (actors with masks; real people together with puppets) **Imagine how these performers could amuse or inspire an audience.**
Guide compre-hension.	Use Routine Card 4.	**During Reading** **Read the pages in a whisper. Raise your hand if you need help with a word. As you read, ask yourself: What am I learning about the Redmoon Theater? How is it different from other theaters?**
	Monitor independent reading.	pp. 62–64 **Where does the Redmoon Theater perform?** (in parks, on streets, even on museum steps) **What makes the puppets and masks unusual?** (They are so big that some puppets even have people inside of them. Some masks cover a person's whole head.)
		pp. 65–69 **How do the people from Redmoon Theater help others in their community?** (They teach students how to put on a show.)
	Model using context for word meaning.	Read aloud the paragraph with *props* on p. 68. Explain how the second, third, and fourth sentences provide clues to the meaning of *props*.
Model summarizing.	Think aloud.	**After Reading** **What did you learn about what makes the Redmoon Theater special? How is it different from other theaters?** Model how to summarize. **Performers for the Redmoon Theater put on plays and puppet shows in many places, not just in a theater. They use unusual props and costumes. They try to inspire their audiences.**
MORE PRACTICE	Have students reread pp. 63–64.	**Reread** As they read, have students compare the Redmoon Theater with any dramatic productions or traditional theaters they have experienced. Students can add these comparisons and contrasts to their graphic organizers.
	Homework	Practice Book, p. 134, Phonics: Multisyllabic Word Practice

3

ACTIVITY 1

Reread for Fluency

Oral Reading "Not a Typical Theater," pp. 63–64

5–10 minutes

	To Do	To Say
CORRECTIVE FEEDBACK	Monitor oral reading.	**Read pp. 63–64 aloud. Read them three or four times so your reading gets better each time.** Give feedback on students' oral reading and use of the blending strategy. Use Routine Cards 1 and 5.
MORE PRACTICE		Have students reread pp. 62–65 three or four times. You may want to have students read along with the AudioText.

ACTIVITY 2

Word Work

Fluent Word Reading Common Syllables; Multisyllabic Word Practice

5–10 minutes

	To Do	To Say
Review phonics.	Review the homework.	Ask students to share answers from Practice Book, pp. 133–134.
Use word-reading routine.	Write *picture.*	Routine **1 Connect** **You can read this word because you know that words with the end syllable *-ture* have the sound /chər/. What is the first syllable?** *(pic)* **What is the word?** *(picture)*
	Write *tradition, expression, girlhood,* and *commitment.*	**2 Model** **When you come to a new word, look for syllables you know, such as *-ture, -sion, -tion, -hood,* and *-ment.* Say the parts of the word to yourself, and then read the word.** Model reading *tradition, expression, girlhood,* and *commitment* in this way. **When you come to a new word, what are you going to do?**
Scaffold instruction.	Write each practice word.	**3 Group Practice** **Let's read these words. Look for meaningful parts and chunks, think about the vowel sound in each chunk, and say the parts to yourself. We will read words with common syllables. When I point to the word, let's read it together.** Allow 2–3 seconds previewing time for each word. Support students as they blend progressively more difficult words. **mission childhood vision creature nature fraction pavement** **furniture adventure permission imagination neighborhood**
CORRECTIVE FEEDBACK	**MONITOR PROGRESS**	***If . . .*** students have difficulty previewing and reading whole words, ***then . . .*** have them use syllable-by-syllable blending. ***If . . .*** students can't read words fluently at a rate of 1–2 seconds per word, ***then . . .*** continue practicing the list.
MORE PRACTICE	Model reading words in sentences.	**When I read a sentence, I read each word without stopping between the words. If I come to a word I don't know, I blend it. Then I read the sentence again.** Model reading this sentence, stopping to blend *imagination: Use your imagination to create something new.*
	Write practice sentences.	Have each student read the sentence best matched to his or her ability. **Draw a picture and answer the question.** **We had an adventure on our vacation.** **In the future, ask permission to move the furniture.**

Vocabulary

	To Do	To Say 5 minutes
Review vocabulary.	Display the concept web from Day 1.	Review the concept web. **The words *create, display,* and *express* will be in the selection you read today.** Review the meanings of the words.

ACTIVITY 3 Read a Passage

Reading "What Makes an Artist?" pp. 70–77

	To Do	To Say 10–15 minutes
Scaffold instruction.	Review compare and contrast.	Remind students that clue words can help them think about comparisons and contrasts. **Look for words and phrases such as *in a different way* on p. 75 and *both of us* on p. 77. As you read "What Makes an Artist?" look for ways that the characters and their art are alike and different.**
Develop language and concepts.	See Routine Cards 3 and 7.	**Before Reading** Read the title. Do a structured picture walk. Remind students that *Ms.* is a title placed before a woman's last name.
	Ask questions and elaborate on answers.	pp. 70–73 **What kind of display are the children talking about?** (a display of art and photos) **Do you think they like the same kinds of art?**
	Key concepts: *create, display, express*	pp. 74–77 **This art display has drawings and photos. Which do you like to create? Can artists express themselves with photos as well as with drawings?**
Guide compre-hension.	Use Routine Card 4.	**During Reading Read the pages in a whisper. Raise your hand if you need help with a word. As you read, ask yourself: Who are the characters? How are they alike? How are they different?**
	Monitor independent reading.	pp. 70–73 **Why is Frank disappointed?** (He hoped he would win a prize for his drawings.) **What kinds of artwork did Kim create to express herself?** (photos)
		pp. 74–77 **How do Frank's ideas change at the end of the story?** (He thinks it's good that Kim's photos won a prize.) **What does Kim say about how she and Frank are different, yet the same?** (They have different styles, but they are both artists.)
	Monitor comprehension.	**After Reading** Discuss the What Do You Think? question.
	Guide retelling.	Have one student retell the story while the others assist. Prompt students by asking: **Who are the characters? What happens first? next? In what ways are the characters the same? How are they different?** See Monitoring Retelling on p. 216.
MORE PRACTICE	Have students reread pp. 72–73.	**Reread** As they read, tell students to draw a picture of the artwork they liked best.

ACTIVITY 4 Write

Response to Literature

	To Do	To Say 5 minutes
Prompt journal writing.		**Take out your journals. What kind of art would you create to put in a display? Write about what you would show and why.**

Homework Practice Book, p. 135, Compare and Contrast

4

ACTIVITY 1

Reread for Fluency

Paired Reading "What Makes an Artist?" p. 72

5–10 minutes

	To Do	To Say
CORRECTIVE FEEDBACK	Pair students. Monitor paired reading.	Students read aloud p. 72, switching readers for each paragraph. Have partners reread; now the other partner begins. For optimal fluency, students should reread three or four times. You may want to have students read along with the AudioText. Give feedback, using Routine Card 5.
MORE PRACTICE	**READERS' THEATER**	Students can use the dialogue as a script for a Readers' Theater. Have them rehearse, with one student as the narrator and the others as different characters.

ACTIVITY 2

Word Work

Spiral Review Syllable Pattern V/V

5 minutes

	To Do	To Say
Review reading words with V/V syllables.	Write *create.*	**Look at this word. You can read this word because you know how to read words with vowel/vowel syllable patterns.**
	Write *creation.*	Point to *creation.* **When you try to read this word, you might forget that *ea* forms two separate syllables because you know that *ea* can also spell the vowel sound in *dream.* But you know that /krē/ /shən/ is not a word. The vowels *ea* in this word follow the V/V pattern and are pronounced as two syllables, just as they are in *create.*** **To read words with two vowels together, try pronouncing the vowels both ways. Then use context clues in the sentence to help you figure out the meaning.**
	Write practice sentences.	**Decode Words with Syllable Pattern V/V** Have individuals read the following sentences. If students make an error, remind them to try both vowel pronunciations and use the sentence context for clues to meaning if they are unsure how to read the underlined word.
CORRECTIVE FEEDBACK	Monitor student work.	**Did the <u>creature</u> in the movie scare you?** **That painting of green flying cats is very <u>creative</u>.** **I am too short to <u>reach</u> the top shelf.**

Vocabulary

5–10 minutes

	To Do	To Say
Extend word knowledge.	Write on the board or a transparency: *Do plays and paintings <u>inspire</u> you?*	Use the word *inspire* to extend word knowledge. **We learned that *inspire* means "to cause a good thought or a good feeling in someone." We can use this word to read other related words.** **What other words contain the word *inspire?*** *(inspired, inspiring, inspiration, inspirational)* Write words and discuss their meanings. Point out that an *inspiration* is someone or something that inspires others.
MORE PRACTICE	Deepen word understanding.	Have students use *express* and *amuse* in a sentence. (For example, *I amuse others when I express myself by telling jokes.)* Share sentences. Ask, **What are some ways you express yourself?** (writing, dancing, singing, and so on)

ACTIVITY 3 Read a Passage

Read Together "Puppet Magic," pp. 78–81

	To Do	To Say *10–15 minutes*
Scaffold instruction.	Review compare and contrast (homework).	Ask volunteers to read the passage and share answers from Practice Book, p. 135. Remind students of the importance of comparing and contrasting as they read. **Think of how creating a puppet is both like and different from drawing a picture or taking a photograph.**
Develop language and concepts.	See Routine Cards 3 and 4.	**Before Reading** **This selection is about making a puppet. Do puppet shows amuse you? Would you rather watch a puppet show or create a puppet of your own? Why? Let's read to find out more about another way to express yourself.**
Model fluent reading.	Read pp. 78–81 aloud. Model prosody.	**During Reading** **Listen to my voice as I read this selection.** Read the selection with attention to end punctuation as students follow along. Read it a second time, having students point to each word. **Now read the selection aloud with me. Try to make your voice sound like mine as we read.** Reread the selection several times with students.
Monitor comprehension.	Monitor listening comprehension.	**After Reading** Prompt discussion to monitor comprehension. Listen as students answer questions. **What are some materials you need to make a paper-plate puppet?** (paper plates, scissors, stapler, crayons or markers, and so on) **How is a paper-plate puppet different from a puppet at the Redmoon Theater?** (It is small; you put just your hand inside, not your whole head or body.) **What would amuse you about putting on a puppet show?** (Answers will vary.) **Summarize** Have one student describe the steps in making a paper-plate puppet while the others assist.
MORE PRACTICE	Have students reread p. 80.	**Reread** As they read, tell students to think about how a puppet show they might have at home would be different from the puppet shows of the Redmoon Theater. After reading, they can share ideas with a partner.

ACTIVITY 4 Write

Response to Literature

	To Do	To Say *5 minutes*
Prompt expository writing.	Writing elements: support, conventions	**Tell how a paper-plate puppet show is like or unlike a puppet show performed by the Redmoon Theater. Use compare and contrast words. Be sure to check that you spelled words correctly, began your sentences with capital letters, and used the correct end punctuation.**

Homework Practice Book, p. 136, Vocabulary

5

ACTIVITY 1 Assessment Options

Sentence Reading

5 minutes

	To Do	To Say
Assess sentence reading.	Use reproducible p. 221.	Have each student read the sentences. Record scores on the Sentence Reading Chart, p. 224. While you work with one student, others can complete the Write Sentences activity below. **I have a question about that picture.** **We had a real adventure on our vacation.** **We need to create ways to stop pollution.**
	MONITOR PROGRESS	***If . . .*** students have trouble reading words with common syllables or multisyllables, ***then . . .*** reteach the blending strategy lessons on pp. 173 and 175. ***If . . .*** students misread a word in the sentence, ***then . . .*** correct the error and have them reread the word and then the sentence.
Practice sentence writing.	Provide white boards.	**Write Sentences** Have students copy the sentences from reproducible p. 221 on white boards. Have them confirm spellings by comparing the words they wrote to the words in the sentences.

Mid-Unit Passage Reading

5–10 minutes

	To Do	To Say
Assess fluency and compre-hension.	Determine which students to assess this week. Use Assessment Book, p. 83.	Choose from these options: monitoring fluency (see pp. 214–215) and/or monitoring retelling (see p. 216). Have students read the Unit 6 Mid-Unit Fluency Passage in the Assessment Book. Be sure each student is assessed every other week.
		If you have time, assess every student.

ACTIVITY 2 Build Concepts

Vocabulary

5–10 minutes

	To Do	To Say
Review concept and vocabulary.	Review the homework. Display the concept web you began on Day 1.	Ask students to go over answers and share their writing from Practice Book, p. 136. **This week's question is *How can we express ourselves?* How do this week's words relate to the question?** (Have students answer the question, using some of the vocabulary they learned this week.) Ask students to add more words to the concept web. Have students explain how each word relates to the concept of how we express ourselves. Monitor students' understanding of vocabulary as they discuss the web. See Routine Card 6.
MORE PRACTICE		Students can write sentences using three of the vocabulary words.

ACTIVITY 3 Read to Connect

Reread "Expressing Yourself," pp. 60–61

10 minutes

	To Do	To Say
Monitor comprehension.	Have students reread "Expressing Yourself" silently.	**As you read, think about what the selection says about ways you can express yourself.** After rereading, ask: • **What ways of expressing yourself are described?** (dressing or wearing your hair a certain way; drawing, painting, building things; dancing, singing, acting; writing stories) • **Where can you find tools to express yourself?** (These tools are everywhere. Some are in nature; some you can buy; and some are just part of you, such as your face.) **We also read "Not a Typical Theater." Find that selection. How do people in the Redmoon Theater express themselves?** Record students' ideas.
Make connections.	Have students make connections across texts.	**We also read "What Makes an Artist?" What did Frank learn about creating art?** Record students' ideas. **What can you say in general about expressing yourself?** (Sample answer: There are unlimited ways to amuse yourself, be creative, and show what makes you special.)

ACTIVITY 4 Write

Response to Literature "4 You 2 Do," p. 82

5–10 minutes

	To Do	To Say
Guide response activities.	Discuss the directions. Tell students to choose one activity to complete. Monitor handwriting. See pp. 227–229.	**Word Play** Have students complete the puppet ad on their own and then meet with a partner to share ads. **Making Connections** Discuss the question in a group or in pairs. Lead students to recognize that sharing forms of art with others is a way of communicating. **On Paper** Tell students to think about details that relate to ways they express themselves, such as the materials or costumes they use and what inspires them. Students can use Practice Book, p. 137, to help prepare their written response, or you can send the Practice Book page home for them to complete later. (Answers should have details explaining why students express themselves in the ways they choose.)
MORE PRACTICE		If you have more time, direct students to complete all the activities.

Homework Practice Book, p. 137, Writing

Unit 6 Week 4 *It's the Law!*

Why do we have laws?

Objectives *This week students will ...*

Vocabulary
- build concepts and vocabulary: *annoy, cooperate, disturb, intention, pollution, require*

Phonics
- blend and read multisyllabic words
- apply knowledge of letter-sounds and word structure to decode unknown words when reading

Text Comprehension
- read connected text
- identify main idea to improve comprehension
- write in response to literature

Fluency
- practice fluency with oral rereading

Word Work *This week's phonics focus is ...*

Blending Multisyllabic Words

Concept Words *Tested Vocabulary*

The week's vocabulary is related to the concept of making laws.
The first appearance of each word in the Student Reader is noted below.

annoy	to make angry; disturb (p. 88)
cooperate	to work together (p. 96)
disturb	to bother a person by talking or by being noisy; to interrupt (p.88)
intention	a plan, goal, or purpose that you have (p. 98)
pollution	anything that affects the environment in a bad way (p. 88)
require	to say that you have to do something (p. 102)

Student Reader Unit 6 *This week students will read the following selections.*

86	**The Bill of Rights**	Expository Nonfiction
88	**Sound Off**	Expository Nonfiction
96	**Mr. Civil Rights**	Biography
104	**Silly State Laws**	Expository Nonfiction
108	**4 You 2 Do**	Activity Page

Daily Lesson Plan

	ACTIVITIES	MATERIALS
Day 1	**Build Concepts** Weekly Concept: It's the Law! Vocabulary: *annoy, cooperate, disturb, intention, pollution, require* **Word Work** Phonics: Multisyllabic Words **Read a Passage** "The Bill of Rights," pp. 86–87 Comprehension: Use Strategies Reread for Fluency	Student Reader: Unit 6 Routine Cards 1, 3, 5, 6, 7 Tested Vocabulary Cards Student White Boards AudioText Practice Book, p. 138, Blending Multisyllabic Words
Day 2	**Reread for Fluency** **Word Work** Phonics: Multisyllabic Words Vocabulary **Comprehension** Main Idea **Read a Passage** "Sound Off," pp. 88–95	Student Reader: Unit 6 AudioText Routine Cards 1, 2, 3, 4, 5, 7, 8 Tested Vocabulary Cards Student White Boards Graphic Organizer 1 Practice Book, p. 138, Blending Multisyllabic Words
Day 3	**Reread for Fluency** **Word Work** Phonics: Multisyllabic Words Vocabulary **Read a Passage** "Mr. Civil Rights," pp. 96–103 Comprehension: Main Idea **Write** Response to Literature	Student Reader: Unit 6 AudioText Routine Cards 1, 3, 4, 5, 7 Student journals Practice Book, pp. 138–139, Multisyllabic Words; Main Idea
Day 4	**Reread for Fluency** **Word Work** Phonics: Spiral Review Vocabulary **Read a Passage** "Silly State Laws," pp. 104–107 Comprehension: Main Idea; Listening **Write** Response to Literature	Student Reader: Unit 6 AudioText Routine Cards 3, 4, 5 Student White Boards Practice Book, pp. 139–140, Main Idea; Vocabulary
Day 5	**Assessment Options** Fluency, Comprehension Sentence Reading Passage Reading **Build Concepts** Vocabulary **Read to Connect** **Write** Response to Literature: "4 You 2 Do," p. 108	Student Reader: Unit 6 Reproducible p. 221 Sentence Reading Chart, p. 224 Student White Boards Fluency Progress Chart, p. 215 Routine Card 6 Practice Book, pp. 140–141, Vocabulary; Writing

See pp. xvi–xvii for how *My Sidewalks* integrates instructional practices for ELL.
See pp. 251–254 for Phonemic Awareness Activities.

ACTIVITY 1

Build Concepts

Vocabulary

10–15 minutes

	To Do	To Say
Develop word meaning.	See Routine Card 6. Discuss pp. 85–87.	Read Words 2 the Wise on p. 85. Have students turn to pp. 86–87. **Look at the pictures. What do you notice?** (a flag, the Bill of Rights, the Capitol) **Can you use the words *cooperate* and *require* to describe any of these pictures?** (Example: These symbols remind us that we *cooperate* to keep the freedoms that our laws *require.*)
Scaffold instruction.	Create a concept web.	In the center of a web, write *It's the Law.* **This week's concept is *it's the law.* Why do we have laws? What are some laws that you must obey?** Add vocabulary words. Discuss the meaning of each word as it relates to laws, using the glossary as needed. (See p. 184 in this Teacher's Guide for definitions.) 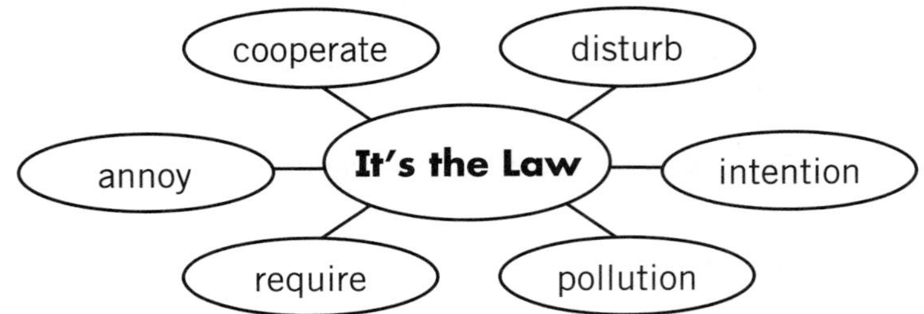
Model the multisyllabic word strategy.	Display each word. Say it as you display it. Think aloud.	Use the Tested Vocabulary Cards. Follow this routine for each word: • **Look for Meaningful Parts** Remind students to look for meaningful parts. **As you say each word, ask yourself: Do I see any parts I know?** • **Chunk Words with No Recognizable Parts** Model how to chunk the word *intention* to read it. • **Model I see a chunk at the beginning of the word: *in.* I see a part in the middle: *ten.* I see a part at the end of the word: *tion.* I say each chunk slowly: *in ten tion.* I blend the chunks together to make a whole word: *intention.* That's a word I've heard before.** • Have students practice reading each word.
Preview.	Read p. 84 with students.	**Do you see any of the words we just learned on this page?** Together with students, read the sentences on p. 84 describing each selection. Talk about how the concept words might be used in the selections.
MORE PRACTICE	Deepen understanding of *disturb* and *cooperate.*	Have students demonstrate understanding by answering questions. **What are some laws that keep people from *disturbing* others? Why is it a good idea to *cooperate* instead of breaking a law?**

ACTIVITY 2 Word Work

Blending Strategy Multisyllabic Words

5–10 minutes

Routine

	To Do	To Say
Use the blending routine. **Scaffold instruction.**	Write *easy.*	**1 Connect** You already can read words like this. What is the word? *(easy)* Today we will learn about reading words that have many syllables.
	Write *uneasy.*	**2 Model** This word has a prefix before the base word. If a word has a prefix, a suffix, or another ending, break the word into parts. Draw a line between *un* and *easy*. First I read each syllable. Cover *easy*. This is how I blend this syllable: /u/ /n/, *un.* Cover *un*. This is how I blend this syllable: /ē/, *ea.* Then I read the last syllable /z/ /ē/, *sy.* Then I blend the syllables together: *un ea sy, uneasy.* Notice that the syllable with the most stress is in the base word, not in another word part. u n e a s y
	Distribute white boards.	**3 Listen and Write** Write the word *uneasy.* Draw a line between *un* and *easy.* As you write, say each syllable to yourself: *un ea sy.* Now blend the three syllables and say the word aloud: *uneasy.*
CORRECTIVE FEEDBACK	Write each practice word. Monitor student practice.	**4 Group Practice** Let's try reading these words. Support students as they blend progressively more difficult words. Give feedback, using the *if . . . then* statements on Routine Card 1. unhappy uneasy unmade unfed unhurried disrespect disease disagree disagreement **5 Individual Practice** Have each student blend several words from the row best matched to his or her ability. untied unwise unhappily untested disturb unusual uncomfortable inhuman independent* incorporated*
	Check understanding of practice words.	*Students need to make sense of words that they segment and blend. If needed, help students with meanings. An *independent* person is not controlled by others. When something is *incorporated*, it is included as a part of something else.
MORE PRACTICE	Distribute white boards. Model building and spelling words.	**Build Words** Write *tend.* Can you blend this word? (/t/ /e/ /n/ /d/) Have students write words on white boards. Write *tend.* Now add *in* to the beginning of *tend.* What is the new word? *(intend)* When you *intend* to do something, you plan to do it or you do it on purpose. • Erase the *d* at the end. Add *tion.* What is the new word? *(intention)* • Change the first *t* to *v.* What is the new word? *(invention)* • Change the *in* to *pre.* What is the new word? *(prevention)* Discuss the meanings of *invention* (something made for the first time) and *prevention* (the act of keeping something from happening).

ACTIVITY 3

Read a Passage

Build Background "The Bill of Rights," pp. 86–87

10 minutes

	To Do	To Say
Develop language and concepts.	See Routine Cards 3 and 7. Ask questions and elaborate on answers.	**Before Reading** Read the title aloud. Introduce proper nouns, if necessary. Do a structured picture walk with students. p. 86 **Does this piece of paper look old or new?** (old) **This paper is the Bill of Rights. Rights are freedoms that we are given by our Constitution. This is an important document for all Americans.**
Scaffold instruction.	Key concepts: *rights, disagreements, Congress, assemble*	p. 87 **Have you ever seen a picture of this building? It is the United States Capitol building. This is where Congress meets to pass laws. Congress is made up of men and women who were elected to do our nation's business. When they do this, they sometimes have disagreements. Disagreements happen when people don't agree. This page has a list of some of our freedoms. One of our freedoms is the freedom to assemble. This means we have the right to come together peacefully and complain to our government.** **Let's read to find out about the Bill of Rights. As you read, ask yourself: What is this mainly about? What am I learning?**
Guide compre-hension.	Read pp. 86–87 aloud.	**During Reading** Read the selection as students follow along. Then read it a second time, having students join in. If necessary, stop at the end of each paragraph to check comprehension. Ask questions to promote discussion and develop the concept. • **Why did Congress add the Bill of Rights to the Constitution?** (Some basic rights and freedoms were not included in the Constitution.) • **Name some of the freedoms that are included in the Bill of Rights.** (freedom of religion, freedom of speech, freedom of the press, and so on) • **What words on the concept web could help you tell about the Bill of Rights?**
	Use vocabulary to develop the concept.	**After Reading Is it easy to make changes to the U.S. Constitution? What is *required* to make such changes?**

Reread for Fluency "The Bill of Rights," p. 86

5–10 minutes

	To Do	To Say
CORRECTIVE FEEDBACK	Monitor oral reading.	**Read p. 86 aloud. Read it three or four times so your reading gets better each time.** Give feedback on students' oral reading and use of the blending strategy. See Routine Cards 1 and 5.
MORE PRACTICE		Instead of rereading just p. 86, have students reread the entire selection three or four times. You may want to have students read along with the AudioText.

Homework Practice Book, p. 138, Phonics: Blending Multisyllabic Words

ACTIVITY 1 Reread for Fluency

Paired Reading "The Bill of Rights," p. 87

	To Do	To Say *5–10 minutes*
CORRECTIVE FEEDBACK	Pair students. Monitor paired reading.	Students read aloud p. 87, switching readers for each bulleted item. Have partners reread; now the other partner begins. For optimal fluency, students should reread three or four times. Give feedback, using Routine Card 5.
MORE PRACTICE		Instead of rereading just p. 87, have students reread the entire selection three or four times. You may want to have students read along with the AudioText.

ACTIVITY 2 Word Work

Blend and Build Words Multisyllabic Words

	To Do	To Say *5–10 minutes*
Review blending words with many syllables.	Write *unwanted.*	**Remember, words with many syllables can be divided between any prefixes, the base word, and any endings to make it easier to read the word.** Draw lines to separate the syllables un/want/ed. **This is how I read the word. First, I read the sounds in each syllable: /u/ /n/, /w/ /ä/ /n/ /t/, /i/ /d/. Then I read the syllables left to right: *un want ed.* Then I blend the syllables together: *unwanted.* The most important part of the word, the base word *want*, gets the most stress.**
Scaffold instruction. **CORRECTIVE FEEDBACK**	Write the practice words. Monitor student practice.	**Today we will blend more words with many syllables.** Support students as they blend progressively more difficult words. Give feedback, using the ***if . . . then*** statements on Routine Card 1. **unfair** **unwanted** **unpleasant** **untimely** **disturbance** **disagreement** **argument** **judgment** **uncontrollable*** **unbearable*** **unreasonable** **unthinkable**
	Check understanding of practice words.	*Students need to make sense of words that they segment and blend. If needed, help students with meanings. **Something that is *uncontrollable* cannot be controlled. Something that is *unbearable* is difficult to deal with.**
MORE PRACTICE	Distribute white boards. Model building and spelling words.	**Build Words** Write *distance.* **Can you blend this word?** *(dis tance)* Have students write words on their white boards. **Write *distance.* Now erase *ance* and write *urb.* What is the new word?** *(disturb)* • **Add the letters *ance* to the end of *disturb.* What is the new word?** *(disturbance)* • **Now erase *ance* and write *ed.* What is the new word?** *(disturbed)* **Add the prefix *un-* to the beginning of the word. What is the new word?** *(undisturbed)* **When people leave you alone, you are undisturbed.**

2

Vocabulary

	To Do	To Say 5 minutes
Review vocabulary.	Display the concept web from Day 1.	Review the concept web. See Routine Card 2 for the multisyllabic word routine. **The words *pollution, disturb,* and *annoy* will be in the selection you read today.** Remind students that *disturb* means "to bother a person by talking or by being noisy."
	Deepen word understanding of *pollution, disturb,* and *annoy.*	**When you drop litter on the ground, you are making *pollution*. When you make a lot of noise, you may *disturb* others. Too much noise pollution *annoys* people who like quiet. What are some noises that *disturb* people?** (Answers may include honking horns, playing loud music in the street, and yelling indoors.) Encourage discussion, asking, **What kinds of laws can keep people from annoying others?**
Lead cumulative review.		Use the Tested Vocabulary Cards to review concept words from previous weeks.

ACTIVITY 3 Comprehension

Main Idea

	To Do	To Say 5 minutes
Scaffold instruction.	Introduce main idea.	**Today you will read about the problem of noise pollution. Look for the main idea and important details as you read. It is important to keep track of the main idea to make sure you understand what the selection is all about.**
	Model the skill.	**If a friend asked about a TV show that I saw, I could tell what the show was about. I could tell the main idea in one sentence. I might give details that tell more about this main idea. I can do the same thing when I read—think about the main idea and look for details that tell more about it.**
	Distribute Graphic Organizer 1.	**Sometimes the main idea is given in a sentence near the beginning or end of a selection. Sometimes you may need to use your own words to state the main idea. As you read "Sound Off," think about what the selection is mainly about. Add the main idea to your graphic organizer.** See Routine Card 8.

ACTIVITY 4 Read a Passage

Reading "Sound Off," pp. 88–95

10–15 minutes

	To Do	To Say
Develop language and concepts.	See Routine Cards 3 and 7.	**Before Reading** Have students recall what they learned about why we have laws. Read the title. Introduce proper nouns, if necessary. Do a structured picture walk with students.
Scaffold instruction.	Ask questions and elaborate on answers.	pp. 88–91 **The selection tells how noise pollution can be a problem. This boy is holding his ears. What are some noises that make you want to hold your ears? This chart shows the level of noise different things make. The quietest things are on the left. The noisiest things are on the right. What things are shown?** (children whispering, a vacuum cleaner, a lawn mower, a motorcycle, a jet, a rocket)
	Key concepts: *pollution, disturb, annoy*	pp. 92–95 **What are some noisy things shown here that may disturb people?** (a plane over a home, a barking dog, a loud motorcycle, sirens) **Do these noises annoy you?**
Guide comprehension.	Use Routine Card 4.	**During Reading** **Read the pages in a whisper. Raise your hand if you need help with a word. As you read, ask yourself: What is the most important idea in this selection? What is this mainly about?**
	Monitor independent reading.	pp. 88–91 **Remember, supporting details in a passage tell more about the main idea. What do these pages tell mostly about?** (Too much noise can cause hearing loss and annoy people.)
	Model using context for word meaning.	Read aloud the paragraph with *unbearable* on p. 91. Explain how the phrase "can bother us" provides clues to the meaning of *unbearable*.
		pp. 92–95 **Why don't people agree about noise pollution laws?** (People are bothered by different types of noise.) **What would you do in each case?** (Answers will vary.)
Model summarizing.	Think aloud.	**After Reading** **What did you learn about noise pollution? What was the selection mainly about?** Model how to summarize. **The selection tells why noise pollution is a problem and explains how noise pollution laws should be fair to everyone.**
MORE PRACTICE	Have students reread pp. 90–93.	**Reread** As they read, have students note the main idea of each section. Point out the section headings, and explain that these help to show the main idea of each part of the selection. Explain that the different sections give details that support the main idea of the entire selection. Students can write a main idea statement and supporting details on their graphic organizers.
	Homework	Practice Book, p. 138, Phonics: Blending Multisyllabic Words

3

ACTIVITY 1 Reread for Fluency

Oral Reading "Sound Off," pp. 90–93

5–10 minutes

	To Do	To Say
CORRECTIVE FEEDBACK	Monitor oral reading.	**Read pp. 90–93 aloud. Read them three or four times so your reading gets better each time.** Give feedback on students' oral reading and use of the blending strategy. Use Routine Cards 1 and 5.
MORE PRACTICE		Have students reread additional pages of the selection three or four times. You may want to have students read along with the AudioText.

ACTIVITY 2 Word Work

Fluent Word Reading Multisyllabic Words

5–10 minutes

	To Do	To Say
Review phonics.	Review the homework.	Ask students to share answers from Practice Book, p. 138.
Use word-reading routine.	Write *unwanted.*	Routine **1 Connect You can read this word because you know how to chunk words with many syllables and blend them. What syllables do you see?** *(un want ed)* **What is the word?** *(unwanted)*
	Write *unfairly* and *unfairness.*	**2 Model When you come to a word with many syllables, look for word parts such as prefixes, base words, and endings. Divide the word into syllables and say each part to yourself. Then read the word.** Model reading *unfairly* and *unfairness* in this way. **When you come to a new word, what are you going to do?**
Scaffold instruction.	Write each practice word.	**3 Group Practice We will read words with many syllables. Think about the sounds in each syllable, say them to yourself, and blend the syllables together to say the word. When I point to the word, let's read it together.** Allow 2–3 seconds previewing time for each word. Support students as they blend progressively more difficult words. **agree agreement disagreement** **operate cooperate cooperation** **tend intend intention** **fair unfair unfairly unfairness** **law lawful unlawful unlawfulness** **respect respectful disrespect disrespectful**
CORRECTIVE FEEDBACK	**MONITOR PROGRESS**	***If . . .*** students have difficulty previewing and reading whole words, ***then . . .*** have them use syllable-by-syllable blending. ***If . . .*** students can't read words fluently at a rate of 1–2 seconds per word, ***then . . .*** continue practicing the list.
MORE PRACTICE	Model reading words in sentences.	**When I read a sentence, I read each word without stopping between the words. If I come to a word I don't know, I blend it. Then I read the sentence again.** Model reading this sentence, stopping to blend *respectful: Treat each other in a respectful way.*
	Write practice sentences.	Have each student read the sentence best matched to his or her ability. **Some people are treated unfairly.** **What was the reason for the disagreement?** **The baby was uncontrollable when his mother left.**

Vocabulary

	To Do	To Say — 5 minutes
Review vocabulary.	Display the concept web from Day 1.	Review the concept web. **The words *cooperate, intention,* and *required* will be in the selection you read today.** Review the meanings of the words.

ACTIVITY 3 Read a Passage

Reading "Mr. Civil Rights," pp. 96–103

	To Do	To Say — *10–15 minutes*
Scaffold instruction.	Review main idea.	Remind students that supporting details in a selection give more information about the main idea. **As you read "Mr. Civil Rights," look for the main idea as well as details that support the main idea.**
Develop language and concepts.	Use Routine Cards 3 and 7.	**Before Reading** Read the title. Do a structured picture walk. Introduce proper nouns, if necessary.
	Key concepts: *cooperate, intention, require*	pp. 96–99 **The pictures show Thurgood Marshall. Why do you think the Bill of Rights was important in his life?** (Answers will vary.) **The Constitution had good intentions, but Thurgood needed to cooperate with others to get African Americans equal rights. What is unfair in the picture on p. 98?** (Black people are in the back of the bus.)
		pp. 100–103 **What do you notice about the people in the picture on p. 102?** (They are all young people except the man in the middle.)
Guide compre-hension.	Use Routine Card 4.	**During Reading** **Read the pages in a whisper. Raise your hand if you need help with a word. As you read, ask yourself: What important ideas am I learning about?**
	Monitor independent reading.	pp. 96–98 **What unfair laws did African Americans have to live with?** (sitting at the back of a bus, separate entrances) **What did Thurgood think were the intentions of the Constitution?** (equal rights for all) Remind students that *Mr.* is a title.
		pp. 99–103 **Why did Thurgood Marshall become a lawyer?** (He saw unfairness and knew he could fight it in a courtroom.) **What laws did he help change?** (Examples: sitting at the back of a bus, voting rights, rights of soldiers, separate schools)
	Monitor comprehension.	**After Reading** Discuss the What Do You Think? question.
	Guide retelling.	Have one student retell the selection while others assist. Prompt students by asking: **What important details does this selection give? What is the most important idea?** See Monitoring Retelling on p. 216.
MORE PRACTICE	Have students reread pp. 99–100.	**Reread** As they read, tell students to look for details that show how Thurgood Marshall's parents helped him succeed.

ACTIVITY 4 Write

Response to Literature

	To Do	To Say — *5 minutes*
Prompt journal writing.		**Take out your journals. Write about how you think Thurgood Marshall helped change laws so that they carried out the intentions of the Constitution.**

Homework Practice Book, p. 139, Main Idea

4

ACTIVITY 1 Reread for Fluency

Paired Reading "Mr. Civil Rights," pp. 99–100

5–10 minutes

	To Do	To Say
CORRECTIVE FEEDBACK	Pair students. Monitor paired reading.	Students read aloud pp. 99–100 to develop accuracy, switching readers for each paragraph. Have partners reread; now the other partner begins. For optimal fluency, students should reread three or four times. You may want to have students read along with the AudioText. Give feedback, using Routine Card 5.
MORE PRACTICE	**READERS' THEATER**	Students can use the pages as a script for Readers' Theater. Have them rehearse, with one student as the narrator and the other reading the quotation by Thurgood Marshall's father. They can switch roles and reread.

ACTIVITY 2 Word Work

Spiral Review Read Longer Words: Suffixes and Prefixes

5 minutes

	To Do	To Say
Review prefixes and suffixes.	Write *unlawful.* Draw lines between *un, law,* and *ful.* Write *disagreement.* Write lines between *dis, agree,* and *ment.*	**Look at this word. You can read this word because you know how to blend a base word with prefixes or suffixes to read longer words. Blend the base word. What is the base word?** *(law)* **Blend the base word and the suffix. What is the word?** *(lawful)* **Now let's blend the prefix and the rest of the word:** ***un lawful; unlawful.*** Repeat with *disagreement.* Point out that *dis-* is a prefix and *-ment* is a suffix.
Scaffold instruction. **CORRECTIVE FEEDBACK**	Distribute white boards. Monitor student work.	**Build Words** Use a chart to make new words. Write *law, control, bear,* and *agree* under the heading *Base Words.* Have students copy the words and add affixes. Then have them record any new words they can form with the affixes. Remind them to chunk the words by syllable and then blend the syllables to read the words aloud. If students make an error, model blending each syllable and have students repeat after you. Call on individuals to use the new words in sentences.

Prefixes	Suffixes	Base Words	Words Formed
un-	-er	law	
re-	-ful	control	
dis-	-ment	bear	
	-able	agree	

Vocabulary

5–10 minutes

	To Do	To Say
Extend word knowledge.	Write on the board or a transparency: *Do not disturb a sleeping baby.*	Use the word *disturb* to extend word knowledge. **We learned that** ***disturb*** **means "to bother a person by being noisy." We can use** ***disturb*** **to read other words.** **Can you think of other words related to the word** ***disturb?*** *(disturbed, disturbing, disturbance, undisturbed)* Write these words and discuss their meanings. Point out that *-ance* is a suffix that means "the act of (doing something)," so *disturbance* means "the act of disturbing."
MORE PRACTICE	Deepen word understanding.	Have students use *disturb* in a sentence. (For example, *Cats do not like to be disturbed.*) Share sentences.

ACTIVITY 3 Read a Passage

Read Together "Silly State Laws," pp. 104–107

	To Do	To Say *10–15 minutes*
Scaffold instruction.	Review main idea (homework).	Ask volunteers to read the passage and share answers from Practice Book, p. 139. Remind students of the importance of thinking about the main idea. **The main idea of a selection is important. Look for a sentence that tells what the selection is all about, or try to state the main idea in your own words. Also read for details that give more information about the main idea.**
Develop language and concepts.	See Routine Cards 3 and 4.	**Before Reading** **This selection is about some laws in different states. These laws may surprise you. Let's read to find out ways you should not disturb certain animals and what some other silly laws are.**
Model fluent reading.	Read pp. 104–107 aloud. Model prosody.	**During Reading** **Listen to my voice as I read this selection.** Read the selection with attention to phrasing as students follow along. Read it a second time, having students point to each word. **Now read the selection aloud with me. Try to make your voice sound like mine as we read. Notice how I read a few words together as a group, so they make sense.** Reread the selection several times with students.
	Monitor listening comprehension.	**After Reading** Prompt discussion to monitor comprehension. Listen as students answer questions. **Why do you think you should not disturb a sleeping bear to take its picture?** (It might get angry.) **Which law do you think is the silliest?** (Answers will vary.) **How are the ideas grouped in this selection?** (Each page tells about silly laws in a different part of the United States.)
Monitor compre-hension.		**Summarize** Have students review some of the details in the selection. Ask what these details have in common.
 MORE PRACTICE	Have students reread p. 106.	**Reread** As they read, tell students to think about which laws help keep people or animals from being disturbed. After reading, they can talk about the selection with a partner, discussing why some laws they read about were probably passed.

ACTIVITY 4 Write

Response to Literature

	To Do	To Say *5 minutes*
Prompt narrative writing.	Writing elements: focus, support	**Write a story about someone who made up a new silly law. Be sure your story has a main idea and gives details that support the main idea.**

Homework Practice Book, p. 140, Vocabulary

5

ACTIVITY 1 Assessment Options

Sentence Reading

	To Do	To Say *5 minutes*
Assess sentence reading.	Use reproducible p. 221.	Have each student read the sentences. Record scores on the Sentence Reading Chart, p. 224. While you work with one student, others can complete the Write Sentences activity below. **It's unlawful to drive at your age.** **I try not to treat others unfairly.** **You can end a disagreement by saying you are sorry.**
CORRECTIVE FEEDBACK	**MONITOR PROGRESS**	***If . . .*** students have trouble reading multisyllabic words, ***then . . .*** reteach the blending strategy lessons on pp. 187 and 189. ***If . . .*** students misread a word in the sentence, ***then . . .*** correct the error and have them reread the word and then the sentence.
Practice sentence writing.	Provide white boards.	**Write Sentences** Have students copy the sentences from reproducible p. 221 on white boards. Have them confirm spellings by comparing the words they wrote to the words in the sentences.

Passage Reading

	To Do	To Say *5–10 minutes*
Assess fluency and comprehension.	Determine which students to assess this week.	Choose from these options: monitoring fluency (see pp. 214–215) and/or monitoring retelling (see p. 216). Have students reread "Silly State Laws." Be sure each student is assessed every other week.
		If you have time, assess every student.

ACTIVITY 2 Build Concepts

Vocabulary

	To Do	To Say *5–10 minutes*
Review concept and vocabulary.	Review the homework. Display the concept web you began on Day 1.	Ask students to go over answers and share their writing from Practice Book, p. 140. **This week's question is *Why do we have laws?* How do this week's words relate to the question?** (Have students answer the question, using some of the vocabulary they learned this week.) Ask students to add more words to the concept web. Have students explain how each word relates to laws. Monitor students' understanding of vocabulary as they discuss the web. See Routine Card 6.
MORE PRACTICE		Students can write sentences using three of the vocabulary words.

ACTIVITY 3 Read to Connect

Reread "The Bill of Rights," pp. 86–87

10 minutes

	To Do	To Say
Monitor comprehension.	Have students reread "The Bill of Rights" silently.	**As you read, think about what the selection says about laws.** After rereading, ask: • **What is the Bill of Rights?** (It is a list of the first ten additions to the United States Constitution.) • **Why is the Bill of Rights important?** (These rights are basic freedoms all people want.) **We also read "Sound Off." Find that selection. What are some noises that bother people? Why do people want laws to stop noise pollution?** Record students' ideas.
Make connections.	Have students make connections across texts.	**We also read "Mr. Civil Rights." How did Thurgood Marshall help change laws to require that everyone would be treated fairly?** Record students' ideas. **Why do we need laws?** (Sample answers: Laws help keep people safe, and they keep people from disturbing others.)

ACTIVITY 4 Write

Response to Literature "4 You 2 Do," p. 108

5–10 minutes

	To Do	To Say
Guide response activities.	Discuss the directions. Tell students to choose one activity to complete. Monitor handwriting. See pp. 227–229.	**Word Play** Have students match the synonyms on their own and then meet with a partner to share the synonym pairs. **Making Connections** Discuss the question in a group or in pairs. **On Paper** Before students write, brainstorm with the group a list of laws and the ways these laws would help people. Have students write on their own. Students can use Practice Book, p. 141, to help prepare their written response, or you can send the Practice Book page home for them to complete later. (Answers will vary.)
MORE PRACTICE		If you have more time, direct students to complete all the activities.

Homework Practice Book, p. 141, Writing

Unit 6 Week 5 *Poetry*

What is a poem?

Objectives *This week students will ...*

Vocabulary
- build concepts and vocabulary: *compose, delicate, emotion, poetry, recite, rhythm*

Phonics
- blend and read related words
- apply knowledge of letter-sounds and word structure to decode unknown words when reading

Text Comprehension
- read connected text
- draw conclusions to improve comprehension
- write in response to literature

Fluency
- practice fluency with oral rereading

Word Work *This week's phonics focus is ...*

Related Words

Concept Words *Tested Vocabulary*

The week's vocabulary is related to the concept of poetry.
The first appearance of each word in the Student Reader is noted below.

compose	to put together a work of art using words, sounds, or colors (p. 125)
delicate	thin or easily broken; not strong (p. 128)
emotion	a strong feeling (p. 112)
poetry	poems (p. 112)
recite	say something from memory, especially in front of an audience (p. 127)
rhythm	a strong beat that some music or poetry has (p. 114)

Student Reader Unit 6 *This week students will read the following selections.*

112	**Poetry**	Expository Nonfiction
116	**Bringing Words to Life**	Expository Nonfiction
124	**Amy the Shy**	Realistic Fiction
132	**Be a Poet**	How-to Article
134	**4 You 2 Do**	Activity Page

Daily Lesson Plan

	ACTIVITIES	MATERIALS
Day 1	**Build Concepts** Weekly Concept: Poetry Vocabulary: *compose, delicate, emotion, poetry, recite, rhythm* **Word Work** Phonics: Related Words **Read a Passage** "Poetry," pp. 112–115 Comprehension: Use Strategies Reread for Fluency	Student Reader: Unit 6 Routine Cards 1, 3, 5, 6, 7 Tested Vocabulary Cards Student White Boards AudioText Practice Book, p. 142, Related Words
Day 2	**Reread for Fluency** **Word Work** Phonics: Related Words Vocabulary **Comprehension** Draw Conclusions **Read a Passage** "Bringing Words to Life," pp. 116–123	Student Reader: Unit 6 AudioText Routine Cards 1, 2, 3, 4, 5, 7, 8 Tested Vocabulary Cards Student White Boards Graphic Organizer 2 Practice Book, p. 142, Related Words
Day 3	**Reread for Fluency** **Word Work** Phonics: Related Words Vocabulary **Read a Passage** "Amy the Shy," pp. 124–131 Comprehension: Draw Conclusions **Write** Response to Literature	Student Reader: Unit 6 AudioText Routine Cards 1, 3, 4, 5, 7 Student journals Practice Book, pp. 142–143, Related Words; Draw Conclusions
Day 4	**Reread for Fluency** **Word Work** Phonics: Spiral Review Vocabulary **Read a Passage** "Be a Poet," pp. 132–133 Comprehension: Draw Conclusions; Listening **Write** Response to Literature	Student Reader: Unit 6 AudioText Routine Cards 3, 4, 5 Student White Boards Practice Book, pp. 143–144, Draw Conclusions; Vocabulary
Day 5	**Assessment Options** Fluency, Comprehension Sentence Reading End-of-Unit Test **Build Concepts** Vocabulary **Read to Connect** **Write** Response to Literature: "4 You 2 Do," p. 134	Student Reader: Unit 6 Reproducible p. 221 Sentence Reading Chart, p. 224 Student White Boards Fluency Progress Chart, p. 215 Routine Card 6 Practice Book, pp. 144–145, Vocabulary; Writing Assessment Book , p. 69

See pp. xvi–xvii for how *My Sidewalks* integrates instructional practices for ELL.
See pp. 251–254 for Phonemic Awareness Activities.

ACTIVITY **1**

Build Concepts

Vocabulary

10–15 minutes

	To Do	To Say
Develop word meaning.	See Routine Card 6. Discuss pp. 111–113.	Read Words 2 the Wise on p. 111. Have students turn to pp. 112–113. **Look at the pictures. What do you notice?** (photographs of two men) **Can you use the words *compose* and *poetry* to describe any of these pictures?** (Example: *The men in these photos might compose poetry.*)
Scaffold instruction.	Create a concept web.	In the center of a web, write *Poetry.* **This week's concept is *poetry.* We will be reading about the power of poetry.** Provide examples to demonstrate meaning. **Poetry can be very powerful. The words in a poem can create a feeling or make you see things in a new way.** Add the other vocabulary words. Discuss the meaning of each word as it relates to poetry, using the glossary as needed. (See p. 198 in this Teacher's Guide for definitions.)

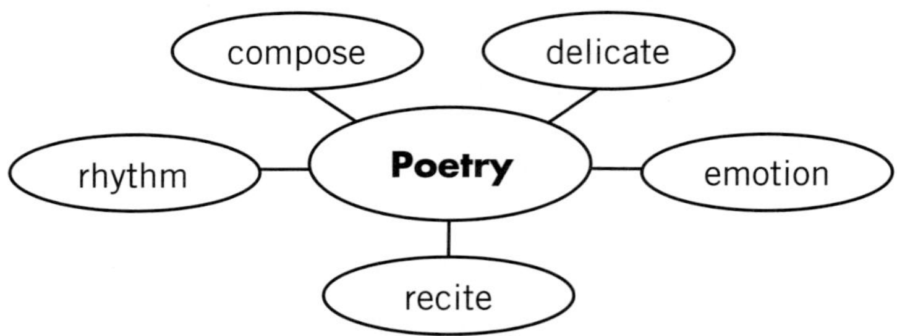

	To Do	To Say
Model the multisyllabic word strategy.	Display each word. Say it as you display it.	Use the Tested Vocabulary Cards. Follow this routine for each word: • **Look for Meaningful Parts** Remind students to look for meaningful parts. **As you say each word, ask yourself: Do I see any parts I know?** • **Chunk Words with No Recognizable Parts** Model how to chunk the word *emotion* to read it.
	Think aloud.	• **Model** **I see a chunk at the beginning of the word: *e.* I see a part in the middle: *mo.* I see a part at the end of the word: *tion.* I say each chunk slowly: *e mo tion.* I say the chunks fast to make a whole word: *emotion.* Is it a real word? Yes, I've heard the word *emotion.*** • Have students practice reading each word.
Preview.	Read p. 110 with students.	**Do you see any of the words we just learned on this page?** Together with students, read the sentences on p. 110 describing each selection. Talk about how the concept words might be used in the selections.
MORE PRACTICE	Deepen understanding of *delicate.*	Have students demonstrate understanding by answering questions. **Which one is *delicate*, a flower or a tree? Why? What might happen to a *delicate* plate if you are not careful? What are some other things that are *delicate?*** (an egg, glass, a baby)

ACTIVITY 2 Word Work

Blending Strategy Related Words

5–10 minutes

Routine

	To Do	To Say
Use the blending routine. **Scaffold instruction.**	Write *create.*	**1 Connect** You already can read this word. What is the word? Remember this word has a V/V syllable pattern. The letters *e* and *a* stand for two vowel sounds. Now you will learn more words that are related to this word.
	Write *creative.*	**2 Model** Some related words have a spelling change. Remove the *e* at the end of *create* before adding the ending. First I read each syllable. Cover *ative.* This is how I blend this syllable: /kr/ /ē/, *cre.* Cover *cre.* Read the next syllable /ā/. Then cover *crea* and blend the last syllable: /t/ /i/ /v/, tiv. Then I blend the syllables together: *cre a tive, creative.*
	Write *sign.*	Some related words have different syllable breaks. Let's read this word: *sign.* The *g* is silent in this word. Draw a slash after the *g* and then add *al* at the end of the word. This related word has a hard *g* sound. Now let's blend the syllables together: *sig nal, signal.*
	Distribute white boards.	**3 Listen and Write** Write the letters for each syllable in *signal.* As you write, say the sounds to yourself. Then blend the syllables and say the word aloud: *signal.*
CORRECTIVE FEEDBACK	Write each practice word. Monitor student practice.	**4 Group Practice** Let's try the same thing with these words. Support students as they blend progressively more difficult words. Point out that some related words have a spelling change and different syllable breaks. Give feedback, using the *if . . . then* statements on Routine Card 1.

sign	signal	signature
create	creation	creative*
spark	sparkle	sparkling
rhythm	rhythmic*	

5 Individual Practice Have each student blend several words from the row best matched to his or her ability.

poem	poet	poetry	poetic
produce	product	productive*	production
relate	relative	relation	

To Do	To Say
Check understanding of practice words.	*Students need to make sense of words that they segment and blend. If needed, help students with meanings. *Creative* means "having the power to create things or ideas." *Rhythmic* means "having rhythm." *Productive* means "able to make or produce much."

	To Do	To Say
MORE PRACTICE	Sort words.	**Sort Words** Have students sort the practice words into a group that has changes in the pronunciation of the same consonant in different related words *(sign/signal; create/creation)* and a group with no change.

ACTIVITY 3 Read a Passage

Build Background "Poetry," pp. 112–115

10 minutes

	To Do	To Say
Develop language and concepts.	See Routine Cards 3 and 7. Ask questions and elaborate on answers.	Routine **Before Reading** Read the title aloud. Introduce proper nouns, if necessary. Do a structured picture walk with students. pp. 112–113 **These men are famous poets. What do poets do?** (write poems) **Do you know the names of any famous poets? Have you ever heard a poem that made you feel a special emotion? Do you like listening to or reading poetry?**
Scaffold instruction.	Key concepts: *poetry, emotion, rhythm*	pp. 114–115 **The picture on p. 115 shows another famous poet. His poems are known for their rhythm. Do you recognize him?** (Dr. Seuss) Have students clap out the rhythm to a familiar song, such as Yankee Doodle.
Guide compre-hension.	Read pp. 112–115 aloud.	**During Reading** Read the selection as students follow along. Then read it a second time, having students join in. As needed, pause at the end of each paragraph to check comprehension. Ask questions to promote discussion and develop the concept. • **Where can we find poems?** • **Why is it helpful to hear a poem read aloud?** • **What words on the concept web could help you tell about how poets use words?**
	Use vocabulary to develop the concept.	**After Reading** **What did you learn about *poetry?* What does *rhythm* have to do with poetry?**

Reread for Fluency "Poetry," p. 114

5–10 minutes

	To Do	To Say
CORRECTIVE FEEDBACK	Monitor oral reading.	**Read p. 114 aloud. Read it three or four times, so your reading gets better each time.** Give feedback on students' oral reading and use of the blending strategy. See Routine Cards 1 and 5.
MORE PRACTICE		Instead of rereading just p. 114, have students reread the entire selection three or four times. You may want to have students read along with the AudioText.

Homework Practice Book, p. 142, Phonics: Related Words

ACTIVITY 1 Reread for Fluency

Paired Reading "Poetry," pp. 112–113

5–10 minutes

	To Do	To Say
CORRECTIVE FEEDBACK	Pair students. Monitor paired reading.	Students read aloud pp. 112–113. Have partners reread; now the other reads loudly while the second student whisper reads. For optimal fluency, students should reread three or four times. Give feedback, using Routine Card 5.
MORE PRACTICE		Instead of rereading just pp. 112–113, have students reread the entire selection three or four times. You may want to have students read along with the AudioText.

ACTIVITY 2 Word Work

Blend and Build Words Related Words

5–10 minutes

	To Do	To Say
Review blending of related words. **Scaffold instruction.**	Write *create* and *creation.*	**Remember, some words are related in meaning. When you add syllables to form related words, sometimes you pronounce certain letters differently. This is how I read this word. First, I read each syllable: /krē/ /ā/ /shun/. Then I blend the syllables together: *cre a tion*, *creation.* How many syllables does the word have?** (three) **How does the word change when you add *-tion?*** (The sound of *t* changes. The word has an extra syllable.) **Remember that some related words have spelling changes and different syllable breaks.**
CORRECTIVE FEEDBACK	Write each practice word. Monitor student practice.	**Today we will read more words that are related in meaning.** Support students as they blend progressively more difficult words. Give feedback, using the *if . . . then* statements on Routine Card 1. **sign signal signature** **create creation creative** **perform performance** **express expression expressive*** **nation national*** **rhyme rhythm**
	Check understanding of practice words.	Students need to make sense of words that they segment and blend. If needed, help students with meanings. ***Expressive* means "showing clearly what someone thinks or feels." *National* means "of or about a nation."**
MORE PRACTICE	Model building and spelling words.	**Spell and Write** **You can spell related words by thinking about the base word and the ending. What base word and ending make up *action?*** *(act* and *tion)* **Start with the letters in the base word: *a-c-t*. Now think about the sounds in the longer word: /ak/ /shun/. Remember the spelling change when you add the ending: first remove the ending letter in *act* before adding *-tion*. Now spell *action.*** Repeat with *perform/ performance.*

2

Vocabulary

	To Do	To Say *5 minutes*
Review vocabulary.	Display the concept web from Day 1.	Review the concept web. See Routine Card 2 for the multisyllabic word routine. **The words *poetry, rhythm,* and *emotion* will be in the selection you read today.** Remind students that *emotion* means "a strong feeling."
	Deepen word understanding of *rhythm* and *poetry.*	**A poem is sort of like a song without the music. Many poems have rhyme. Some words have the same ending sounds, such as *star* and *far*. What do you like about *poetry?*** (Answers will vary.) **Poetry often also has *rhythm. Rhythm* is a beat, or a sound pattern. Where else could you hear *rhythm*?** (Encourage discussion of different examples, asking, **Is this *rhythm?*** For example, windshield wipers in the rain have rhythm because they have a regular, repeated sound pattern.)
Lead cumulative review.		Use the Tested Vocabulary Cards to review concept words from previous weeks.

ACTIVITY 3 Comprehension

Draw Conclusions

	To Do	To Say *5 minutes*
Scaffold instruction.	Introduce draw conclusions.	**Today you will read about people who recite poems before an audience. It's helpful to draw conclusions when you read a story or a selection. You draw conclusions when you think about facts and details and then decide something about them.**
	Model the skill.	**For example, I read that people who recite poems in front of an audience have to work on how they use their voices. I use these details about reading poems to make a decision, or conclusion, about why these performers use their voices in a certain way. I have heard some very exciting poems. They are exciting to hear because people change their voices as they recite the poems. They say some parts loud or soft or fast or slow. I conclude that they do this to show the most important words and ideas.**
	Distribute Graphic Organizer 2.	**As you read "Bringing Words to Life," think about decisions you can make about the facts and details in the selection. Add these conclusions to your graphic organizer.** See Routine Card 8.

ACTIVITY 4 Read a Passage

Reading "Bringing Words to Life," pp. 116–123

10–15 minutes

	To Do	To Say
Develop language and concepts.	See Routine Cards 3 and 7. Ask questions and elaborate on answers.	**Before Reading** Have students recall what they learned about poetry. Read the title. Introduce proper nouns, if necessary. Do a structured picture walk with students.
		pp. 116–120 **The selection is about young people who recite poetry for an audience. What tools do they use to perform?** (microphone, chair, poem) **How would you feel about reciting poetry on a stage? What kinds of emotions do you think these performers are trying to share?** (Answers will vary.)
Scaffold instruction.	Key concepts: *rhythm, poetry, emotion*	pp. 121–123 **What are these children doing?** (performing, reciting poems for an audience) **Yes, they are reciting poetry for an audience. Poems have their own rhythm that makes reciting them enjoyable.**
Guide comprehension.	Use Routine Card 4.	**During Reading** **Read the pages in a whisper. Raise your hand if you need help with a word. As you read, ask yourself: What am I learning about people who perform at poetry slams and readings? What is this selection mainly about?**
	Monitor independent reading.	pp. 116–119 **What are some ways that poets work on how to say a poem?** (They practice how they use their bodies, faces, and voices to express themselves.) **Let's clap out the rhythm of these lines: "Stars are bright. They shine at night." What would be another good name for a poetry slam team?** (Answers will vary.)
	Model using context for word meaning.	Read aloud the paragraph with *rhyme* on p. 116. Explain how the lines "Stars are bright. They shine at night." provide clues to the meaning of *rhyme.*
		pp. 120–123 **Would you like to take part in a poetry slam? What emotion might you feel when you performed?**
Model summarizing.	Think aloud.	**After Reading** **What did you learn about performing poetry? What was the selection mainly about?** Model how to summarize. **The selection gave details about some of the things people do to prepare and perform in poetry slams and poetry readings.**
MORE PRACTICE	Have students reread pp. 122–123.	**Reread** As they read, have students draw conclusions or make decisions about facts and details in their reading. For example, students might use details about how WritersCorps prepares students to take part in a poetry slam to conclude that this is an exciting experience. Students can add these conclusions to their graphic organizers.
	Homework	Practice Book, p. 142, Phonics: Related Words

3

ACTIVITY 1 Reread for Fluency

Oral Reading "Bringing Words to Life," pp. 122–123

5–10 minutes

	To Do	To Say
CORRECTIVE FEEDBACK	Monitor oral reading.	**Read pp. 122–123 aloud. Read them three or four times so your reading gets better each time.** Give feedback on students' oral reading and use of the blending strategy. Use Routine Cards 1 and 5.
MORE PRACTICE		Instead of rereading just pp. 122–123, have students reread the entire selection three or four times. You may want to have students read along with the AudioText.

ACTIVITY 2 Word Work

Fluent Word Reading Related Words

5–10 minutes

	To Do	To Say
Review phonics.	Review the homework.	Ask students to share answers from Practice Book, p. 142.
Use word-reading routine.	Write *act* and *action.*	Routine **1 Connect You can read this word because you know that related words share the same base word. You read the base word and then look for other word parts. Think about how adding certain word parts might change a related word. How does adding -*tion* change the word *create?*** (You don't hear /t/.)
	Write *rhyme* and *rhythm.*	**2 Model When you come to a new word, look for familiar parts. Then look for chunks you can read. Say the parts of the word to yourself, and then read the word. Try to say the related word in a different way if it doesn't sound right.** Model reading in this way. **When you come to a new word, what are you going to do?**
Scaffold instruction.	Write each practice word.	**3 Group Practice Let's read these related words. Look for base words and other word parts that may or may not change the way you say the related parts. When I point to the word, let's read it together.** Allow 2–3 seconds previewing time for each word. Support students as they blend progressively more difficult words. **poem poet poetry perform performer performance** **act actor action express expression expressive**
CORRECTIVE FEEDBACK	**MONITOR PROGRESS**	***If . . .*** students have difficulty previewing and reading related words, ***then . . .*** have them use syllable-by-syllable blending. ***If . . .*** students can't read words fluently at a rate of 1–2 seconds per word, ***then . . .*** continue practicing the list.
MORE PRACTICE	Model reading words in sentences.	**When I read a sentence, I read each word without stopping between the words. If I come to a word I don't know, I blend it. Then I read the sentence again.** Model reading this sentence, stopping to blend *actors* and *performance: The actors put on a performance.*
	Write practice sentences.	Have each student read the sentence best matched to his or her ability. **The poet read her poem.** **You read poetry with great expression.** **What emotions does that poem express?**

Vocabulary

	To Do	To Say — 5 minutes
Review vocabulary.	Display the concept web from Day 1.	Review the concept web. **The words *recite, delicate,* and *compose* will be in the selection you read today.** Review the word meanings.

ACTIVITY 3 Read a Passage

Reading "Amy the Shy," pp. 124–131

	To Do	To Say — 10–15 minutes
Scaffold instruction.	Review draw conclusions.	Remind students to use details to make decisions, or draw conclusions, about their reading. **As you read "Amy the Shy," think about conclusions you can draw.**
	Use Routine Cards 3 and 7.	**Before Reading** Read the title. Do a structured picture walk.
Develop language and concepts.	Ask questions and elaborate on answers.	pp. 124–127 **Where are these children?** (in a classroom; in a lunchroom) **What can you tell about them?** (The girl with glasses seems shy; the other girl looks confident.) **What do you think is in the notebook the girl is reading?** (Answers will vary.)
	Key concepts: *recite, delicate, compose*	pp. 128–131 **Now what are the girls doing?** (performing) **What does the sign say that the girl is holding on p. 130?** (I am shy.) **Which girl would you think has a delicate voice?** (the girl with the sign)
Guide comprehension.	Use Routine Card 4.	**During Reading** **Read the pages in a whisper. Raise your hand if you need help with a word. As you read, ask yourself: What problem do the characters have? How do they solve the problem?**
	Monitor independent reading.	pp. 124–127 Remind students that *Mrs.* is a title put in front of a married woman's last name. **Why does Mrs. Key tell Amy and DeeDee to work together for the art show?** (Neither of them knows what piece to enter.) **What does the teacher suggest they do?** (DeeDee can compose music to go with Amy's poem.)
		pp. 128–131 **Why does DeeDee talk in a delicate way when she tells Amy that she has a plan?** (She doesn't want to hurt Amy's feelings.) **What kind of song does DeeDee compose?** (It retells Amy's poem.)
	Monitor comprehension.	**After Reading** Discuss the What Do You Think? question.
	Guide retelling.	Have one student retell the story while the others assist. Prompt students by asking: **How does the story end? What facts or details could help you answer the question?** See Monitoring Retelling on p. 216.
MORE PRACTICE	Have students reread pp. 126–127.	**Reread** As they read, tell students to use story details to picture how Amy looks and feels.

ACTIVITY 4 Write

Response to Literature

	To Do	To Say — 5 minutes
Prompt journal writing.		**Take out your journals. Suppose you were going to recite a poem to your class. Tell how you would feel and what you would do.**

Homework Practice Book, p. 143, Draw Conclusions

4

ACTIVITY 1 Reread for Fluency

Paired Reading "Amy the Shy," pp. 126–127

5–10 minutes

	To Do	To Say
CORRECTIVE FEEDBACK	Pair students. Monitor paired reading.	Students read aloud pp. 126–127, switching readers for each paragraph. Have partners reread; now the other partner begins. For optimal fluency, students should reread three or four times. You may want to have students read along with the AudioText. Give feedback, using Routine Card 5.
MORE PRACTICE	**READERS' THEATER**	Work with a group of three or four students to adapt pp. 126–127 for Readers' Theater. Have students rehearse reading the parts of Amy, DeeDee, and the narrator.

ACTIVITY 2 Word Work

Spiral Review Read Longer Words: Common Syllables *(-tion, -sion, -ture)*

5 minutes

	To Do	To Say
Review reading longer words. **Scaffold instruction.**	Write *pollution.*	**Look at this word. You can read this word because you know how to read longer words with common syllables such as *-tion.* What is the related base word?** *(pollute)* **What is the ending?** *(-tion)* **Now read the word parts from left to right: *pol lu tion.* What is the longer word?** *(pollution)* **To read a longer word such as *pollution,* I figure out its parts or syllables, read them from left to right, and blend the parts to read the whole word.**
CORRECTIVE FEEDBACK	Write practice words. Monitor student work.	**Decode Longer Words** Have individuals read the following words. If students make an error, provide help blending the parts of the words as needed. Point out that some longer words have common parts or syllables such as *-tion, -sion,* or *-ture.* Remind students that they have studied all of these common parts. To check meaning, call on individuals to use the words in sentences. **act actor action** — **create creator creation** — **furnish furniture** **sign signal signature** — **pollute pollution** **image imagine imagination** — **cooperate cooperation**

Vocabulary

5–10 minutes

	To Do	To Say
Extend word knowledge.	Write on the board or a transparency: *Let's <u>compose</u> a class song.*	Use the word *compose* to extend word knowledge. **We learned that *compose* means "put together a work of art." Today we'll talk about other words that are related to *compose.* We can use this word to read other words.** **Can you think of other words that contain the word *compose?*** *(composer, composed, composition, composure)* Write these words and discuss their meanings. Remind students that *-er* is a suffix that means "one who," so *composer* means "one who creates a work of art."
MORE PRACTICE	Deepen word understanding.	Have students use *recite* and *delicate* in a sentence. (For example, *She will recite the poem in a delicate voice.*) Share sentences. Ask, **What are some things you could recite?** (a poem, short story, a riddle, and so on)

ACTIVITY 3 Read a Passage

Read Together "Be a Poet," pp. 132–133

	To Do	To Say *10–15 minutes*
Scaffold instruction.	Review draw conclusions (homework).	Ask volunteers to read the passage and share answers from Practice Book, p. 143. Remind students of the importance of drawing conclusions. **When you read a story, drawing conclusions is often important. Think about how facts and details lead you to make a decision about your reading.**
Develop language and concepts.	See Routine Cards 3 and 4.	**Before Reading** **This selection is about planning a poetry slam. What do you see in the pictures?** (boy who is a poet) **Let's read to find out more about holding a slam.**
Model fluent reading.	Read pp. 132–133 aloud. Model prosody.	**Reading** **Listen to my voice as I read this selection.** Read the selection, varying your rate as students follow along. Read it a second time, having students point to each word. **Now read the selection aloud with me. Try to make your speed match mine as we read.** Reread the selection several times with students.
Monitor comprehension.	Monitor listening comprehension.	**After Reading** Prompt discussion to monitor comprehension. Listen as students answer questions. **Why does the author list steps for planning a poetry slam?** (to help readers see the work involved; to guide readers in planning their own poetry slam) **What does the writer suggest you should do if you cannot understand the poem using your own words?** (choose another poem) **Why do you think the writer says this?** (If you don't choose a poem you understand, you will not be able to present it well.) **What other conclusions can you draw about having a poetry slam from the facts and details you read?** (Answers will vary.) **Summarize** Have one student retell the steps involved in preparing to hold a poetry slam.
MORE PRACTICE	Have students reread p. 133.	**Reread** As they read, tell students to think about a poem they would choose to read at a poetry slam. After reading, they can tell a partner about their choice.

ACTIVITY 4 Write

Response to Literature

	To Do	To Say *5 minutes*
Prompt personal narrative.	Writing elements: focus, conventions	**Tell how you would feel if you were standing in front of an audience at a poetry slam. Be sure all your sentences are about this experience. Check that you begin each sentence with a capital letter and end it with the correct punctuation.**

Homework Practice Book, p. 144, Vocabulary

5

ACTIVITY 1

Assessment Options

Sentence Reading

5 minutes

	To Do	To Say
Assess sentence reading.	Use reproducible p. 221.	Have each student read the sentences. Record scores on the Sentence Reading Chart, p. 224. While you work with one student, others can complete the Write Sentences activity below. **You read that poem with great expression!** **We saw a performance with a poet and an artist.** **Let's perform poetry with strong rhythm and rhyme.**
CORRECTIVE FEEDBACK	**MONITOR PROGRESS**	***If . . .*** students have trouble reading related words, ***then . . .*** reteach the blending strategy lessons on pp. 201 and 203. ***If . . .*** students misread a word in the sentence, ***then . . .*** correct the error and have them reread the word and then the sentence.
Practice sentence writing.	Provide white boards.	**Write Sentences** Have students copy the sentences from reproducible p. 221 on white boards. Have them confirm spellings by comparing the words they wrote to the words in the sentences.

End-of-Unit Test

10 minutes

	To Do	To Say
Assess fluency and comprehen-sion.	Use the Assessment Book, p. 68.	Options for end-of-unit assessment are available in the Assessment Book.

ACTIVITY 2

Build Concepts

Vocabulary

5–10 minutes

	To Do	To Say
Review concept and vocabulary.	Review the homework. Display the concept web you began on Day 1.	Ask students to go over answers and share their writing from Practice Book, p. 144. **This week's question is *What is a poem?* How do this week's words relate to the question?** (Have students answer the question, using some of the vocabulary they learned this week.) Ask students to add more words to the concept web. Have students explain how each word relates to poetry. Monitor students' understanding of vocabulary as they discuss the web. See Routine Card 6.
MORE PRACTICE		Students can write sentences using three of the vocabulary words.

ACTIVITY 3 Read to Connect

Reread "Poetry," p. 112

	To Do	To Say *5 minutes*
Monitor compre-hension.	Have students reread p. 112 of "Poetry" silently.	**We read "Poetry." How are poems different from other kinds of writing?** (Poems teach new ways of looking at things and cause people to feel emotions.) **We also read "Bringing Words to Life." Find that selection. What would it be like to perform in a poetry slam?** Record students' ideas. **We also read "Amy the Shy." What problem did Amy and DeeDee have? How did they solve their problem?** Record students' ideas.
Make connections.	Have students make connections across texts.	**What can you say in general about the power of words?** (Sample answer: Words have the power to make people feel strong emotions and see things in a new way.)

ACTIVITY 4 Write

Response to Literature "4 You 2 Do," p. 134

	To Do	To Say *5–10 minutes*
Guide response activities.	Discuss the directions. Tell students to choose one activity to complete. Monitor handwriting. See pp. 227–229.	**Word Play** Have students write a sentence with the words listed on their own and then meet with a partner to share. Invite volunteers to share their sentences with the group. **Making Connections** Discuss the question in a group or in pairs. **On Paper** Before students write, brainstorm with the group a list of ways to perform poetry and discuss the pros and cons of each method. Have students write on their own. Students can use Practice Book, p. 145, to help prepare their written response, or you can send the Practice Book page home for them to complete later. (Answers will vary.)
MORE PRACTICE		If you have more time, direct students to complete all the activities.

Homework Practice Book, p. 145, Writing

Resources

Contents

Monitoring Fluency

Ongoing assessment of student reading fluency is one of the most valuable measures we have of students' reading skills. One of the most effective ways to assess fluency is taking timed samples of students' oral reading and measuring the number of words correct per minute (WCPM).

Fluency Goals

Level C End-of-Year Goal = 100–120 WCPM

Target Goals by Unit:

Unit 1 50 to 70 WCPM

Unit 2 60 to 80 WCPM

Unit 3 70 to 90 WCPM

Unit 4 80 to 100 WCPM

Unit 5 90 to 110 WCPM

Unit 6 100 to 120 WCPM

How to Measure Words Correct Per Minute—WCPM

Timed Reading of the Text

Make a copy of the text for yourself and have one for the student. Tell the student: **As you read this aloud, I want you to do your best reading. Read as quickly as you can without making mistakes. That doesn't mean it's a race. Just do your best reading. When I say *begin,* start reading.**

As the student reads, follow along in your copy. Mark words that are read incorrectly. Definitions and examples of these reading errors are given on p. 233.

Incorrect
- omissions
- substitutions
- mispronunciations
- insertions

Correct
- self-corrections within 3 seconds
- repeated words

After One Minute

At the end of one minute, draw a line after the last word that was read. Have the student finish reading but don't count any words beyond one minute. Arrive at the words correct per minute—WCPM—by counting the total number of words that the student read correctly in one minute.

Fluency Progress Chart

Copy the chart on the next page. Use it to record each student's progress across the year. Assist students in recording their scores on the chart and setting goals for the future.

Interpreting Results

Fluency goals are estimates, and students will vary considerably in their progress based on many factors. Also, student progress will depend greatly on where they start with respect to WCPM. Level C End-of-Year goals are the same as for students without reading difficulties at the end of Grade 3.

Student's Name ______________________

Fluency Progress Chart, Level C

130																														
125																														
120																														
115																														
110																														
105																														
100																														
95																														
90																														
85																														
80																														
75																														
70																														
65																														
60																														
55																														
50																														
45																														
40																														
35																														
	1	2	3*	4	5*	1	2	3*	4	5*	1	2	3*	4	5*	1	2	3*	4	5*	1	2	3*	4	5*	1	2	3*	4	5*
	Unit 1					Unit 2					Unit 3					Unit 4					Unit 5					Unit 6				

*= Fluency Assessment Using Unfamiliar Text

Monitoring Retelling

Retelling is a way to monitor and assess comprehension. Through retelling, students show whether they understand story grammar and can follow sequence, grasp main ideas, and draw conclusions about what they read. Help students learn how to retell by giving them many opportunities to retell stories and nonfiction selections. Scaffold their retellings by prompting them to tell more.

How to Do a Retelling

Have the student read quietly. If the student has difficulty with the passage, you may read it aloud.

Tell the student: **Read the story quietly to yourself. When you finish reading, I will ask you to tell me about what you read.**

When the student has finished, or when you have finished reading aloud, ask:

- (For fiction) **What happened in the story?**
- (For nonfiction) **What was the selection mostly about?**

Prompts for Retelling

If a retelling is incomplete, use prompts to encourage the student to tell more.

Narrative Prompts

- **Who is in the story?**
- **Where and when does the story take place?**
- **What happens first?**
- **Then what happens?**
- **What happens at the end?**

Expository Prompts

- **What did you learn about ________?**
- **What are the most important ideas?**

Looking Back

Encourage students to look back in the text to find answers or to confirm their answers.

- **Let's check the book to make sure.**
- **Show me where the book tells you that.**
- **Where can we look in the book to find the answer?**

See Assessment Book, pp. 12–13, for scoring rubrics for retelling. Use the rubrics to help students move toward a fluent retelling.

Unit 4, Week 1

Joy was unhappy when she lost the coins.
We enjoyed watching the rerun on TV.
The boy spoke with an unfriendly voice.

Unit 4, Week 2

Did you know a lamb came to school today?
The tiny gnome sat on a tree limb in the moonlight.
The knight's pet owl, Hoot, likes to sit on his knee.

Unit 4, Week 3

Both the bluebird and the wren flew away.
I knew the book about castles was overdue.
Andrew will fasten a red bow to the wreath.

Unit 4, Week 4

Our walk in the woods seemed endless.
The happy bulldog jumped up with eagerness.
Don't be careless when you put away my tools!

Unit 4, Week 5

Do you dislike this leather bag?
I already fixed that mistake on the test.
The baker discounts bread that is a day old.

Unit 5, Week 1

My brother is too small to reach the ledge.
We walked along the ridge of the hill.
The photos of the bridge were beautiful.

Unit 5, Week 2

The inventor saw his mistake.
I can draw a picture of the teacher.
Several visitors paused outside the house.

Unit 5, Week 3

Joe bought a heavy overcoat.
I caught a cold outside.
We thought the underwater photographs were good.

Unit 5, Week 4

The food is tasty and mild.
It is foolish to go out in the cold.
We can find most of the things to make this crunchy snack.

Unit 5, Week 5

I used to have a pet hamster.
People lived differently two hundred years ago.
I had a surprise party for my best friend.

Unit 6, Week 1

Our neighborhood is quiet at midnight.
We got a preview of the entertainment for tonight.
He wrote about his postwar childhood.

Unit 6, Week 2

Let's eat in the patio area.
Someone played piano music on the radio.
Jon wrote a poem in his diary.

Unit 6, Week 3

I have a question about that picture.
We had a real adventure on our vacation.
We need to create ways to stop pollution.

Unit 6, Week 4

It's unlawful to drive at your age.
I try not to treat others unfairly.
You can end a disagreement by saying you are sorry.

Unit 6, Week 5

You read that poem with great expression!
We saw a performance with a poet and an artist.
Let's perform poetry with strong rhythm and rhyme.

Student's Name ________________________________

Unit 4 Sentence Reading Chart

	Phonics			Reassess
	Total Words	Words Correct	Reteach ✓	Words Correct
Week 1 *Being Unique*				
Diphthongs *oi, oy*	5			
Prefixes *un-, re-*	3			
Week 2 *From Top to Bottom*				
Sound *oo* in *moon*	3			
Silent Consonants *mb, kn, gn*	6			
Week 3 *Hobbies*				
Vowel Patterns *ew, ue*	5			
Silent Consonants *st, wr*	4			
Week 4 *Being the First*				
Sound *oo* in *foot, u* in *put*	3			
Suffixes *-ness, -less*	3			
Week 5 *People and Animals*				
Short *e: ea*	3			
Prefixes *mis-, dis-*	3			
Unit Scores	38			

- **RECORD SCORES** Use this chart to record scores for the Day 5 Sentence Reading Assessment.
- **RETEACH PHONICS SKILLS** If the student is unable to read all the target phonics words, then reteach the phonics skills using the Blending Strategy lessons.
- **REASSESS** Use the same set of sentences or an easier set for reassessment.

Student's Name ______________________________

Unit 5 Sentence Reading Chart

	Phonics			Reassess
	Total Words	Words Correct	Reteach ✓	Words Correct
Week 1 *Dressing Up*				
Vowel Sound in *ball: a, al*	2			
Consonant Digraphs *ph*/f/, *dge*/j/	4			
Week 2 *Our World*				
Vowel sound in *ball*: *au, aw*	3			
Suffixes *-er, -or*	3			
Week 3 *Coming to America*				
Vowel Sound in *ball: augh, ough*	3			
Prefixes *over-*, *under-*, *out-*	3			
Week 4 *Let's Eat!*				
Long *i: ind, ild;* long *o: ost, old*	4			
Suffixes *-y, -ish*	3			
Week 5 *Other Times, Other Places*				
Syllables VCCCV	3			
Unit Scores	28			

- **RECORD SCORES** Use this chart to record scores for the Day 5 Sentence Reading Assessment.
- **RETEACH PHONICS SKILLS** If the student is unable to read all the target phonics words, then reteach the phonics skills using the Blending Strategy lessons.
- **REASSESS** Use the same set of sentences or an easier set for reassessment.

Student's Name ______________________________

Unit 6 Sentence Reading Chart

	Phonics			Reassess
	Total Words	Words Correct	Reteach ✓	Words Correct
Week 1 *American Symbols*				
Suffixes *-hood, -ment*	3			
Prefixes *pre-, mid-, post-*	3			
Week 2 *Animal Freedom*				
Syllables V/V	6			
Week 3 *Expressing Yourself*				
Common Syllables	5			
Multisyllabic Word Practice	3			
Week 4 *It's the Law!*				
Blending Multisyllabic Words	3			
Week 5 *Poetry*				
Related Words	7			
Unit Scores	30			

- **RECORD SCORES** Use this chart to record scores for the Day 5 Sentence Reading Assessment.
- **RETEACH PHONICS SKILLS** If the student is unable to read all the target phonics words, then reteach the phonics skills using the Blending Strategy lessons.
- **REASSESS** Use the same set of sentences or an easier set for reassessment.

Using End-of-Unit Assessment Results

To make instructional decisions at the end of each unit, consider scores for

- Unit Sentence Reading (Day 5 Assessments)
- Unit Test
- Benchmark Reader reading

Record Scores

Several forms are provided for recording students' progress across the year.

- Sentence Reading Charts: Record results of the weekly Day 5 assessments. See pp. 222–224.
- Record Chart for Unit Tests: Record scores for each Unit Test. See the Assessment Book, p. 16.
- Fluency Progress Chart: Record each student's WCPM across the year. See p. 215.
- Retelling Charts: Record the student's retelling scores for each unit. See the Assessment Book, pp. 12–14.

Questions to Consider

- Has the student's performance met expectations for daily lessons?
- What can the student read alone? What can the student read with supervision?
- Is the student progressing toward grade-level goals?

Evaluate Student Progress

To move into the next unit of *My Sidewalks,* the student should

- score 80% or better on cumulative Unit scores for Sentence Reading for phonics skills
- score 80% or better on the Unit Test
- be able to read and retell the end-of-unit Benchmark Reader accurately
- be capable of working in the Level C group based on teacher judgment

If . . . the student scores below 80% on the tested phonics words,
then . . . reteach the phonics skills and reassess following the reteaching.

If . . . the student's scores indicate a specific weakness in one area of literacy, such as fluency or comprehension,
then . . . focus the student's instruction and practice on that area.

If . . . the student has not met the fluency benchmarks for the unit,
then . . . consider that the benchmark WCPM at the high end of a range is more typical of on-level students, and students in intensive intervention may be progressing well even if they are not meeting fluency benchmarks.

The student may be more appropriately placed in *My Sidewalks,* Level B if the student

- scores 60% or lower on Unit Tests
- is struggling to keep up with the Level C group
- is unable to decode the simplest word types

Exiting the MY SIDEWALKS Intervention Program

In Level C of *My Sidewalks,* there are two opportunities for students to exit the program—at midyear and at the end of the year. Many factors govern decisions concerning instruction for individual students. Understandably, guidelines in your school or district regarding adequate yearly progress, in addition to processes such as Individualized Education Plans, will influence each student's placement in or exit from any intervention program.

Midyear Exit Criteria

Has the student scored 80% or above on Unit Tests?

YES ↓ **NO** → continue in *My Sidewalks*

Is the student able to profit from instruction in the regular classroom?

YES ↓ **NO** → continue in *My Sidewalks*

Is the student performing successfully in a classroom reading program with or without extra support?

YES ↓ **NO** → continue in *My Sidewalks*

Check Reading of On-Level Material

- Select the next unread fictional passage from the classroom reading text.
- Briefly discuss the passage and preteach words identified in the program teacher's guide.
- Read aloud the title and the first paragraph.
- Ask the student to reread the first paragraph and to continue reading for three minutes.
- As the student reads, record errors.
- After reading, ask the student to retell what was read.

Determine Accuracy At the end of the reading, count the number of words read and the number of errors. Did the student read with 85% accuracy?

YES **NO** → continue in *My Sidewalks*

Determine Comprehension Was the student able to retell effectively?

YES ↓ **NO** → continue in *My Sidewalks*

Students who can read the classroom text accurately and with comprehension may exit *My Sidewalks*. If you are hesitant to exit the student, follow the Check Reading procedure on more than one occasion. If all data confirm that the student is ready to exit *My Sidewalks,* then exit the student with confidence. If results are mixed, then continue the student in the program.

End-of-Year Exit Criteria

Has the student scored 80% or above on Unit Tests?

YES ↓ **NO** → continue in *My Sidewalks*

Is the student able to profit from instruction in the regular classroom?

YES ↓ **NO** → continue in *My Sidewalks*

Is the student performing successfully in a classroom reading program with or without extra support?

YES ↓ **NO** → continue in *My Sidewalks*

Based on your school or district end-of-year assessment, is the student making adequate yearly progress?

YES ↓ **NO** → continue in *My Sidewalks*

Students who are making adequate yearly progress on school or district end-of-year assessments may be prepared to exit *My Sidewalks.*

D'Nealian™ Alphabet

a b c d e f g h i
j k l m n o p q r s t
u v w x y z

A B C D E F G
H I J K L M N O
P Q R S T U V
W X Y Z . , ' ?

1 2 3 4 5 6
7 8 9 10

Manuscript Alphabet

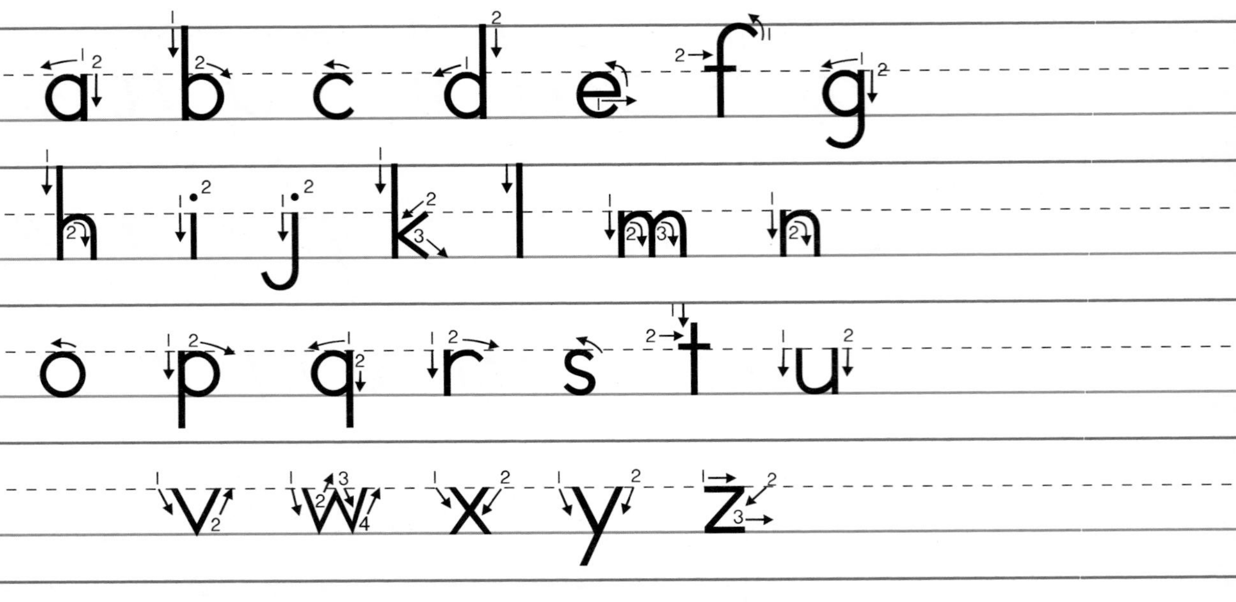

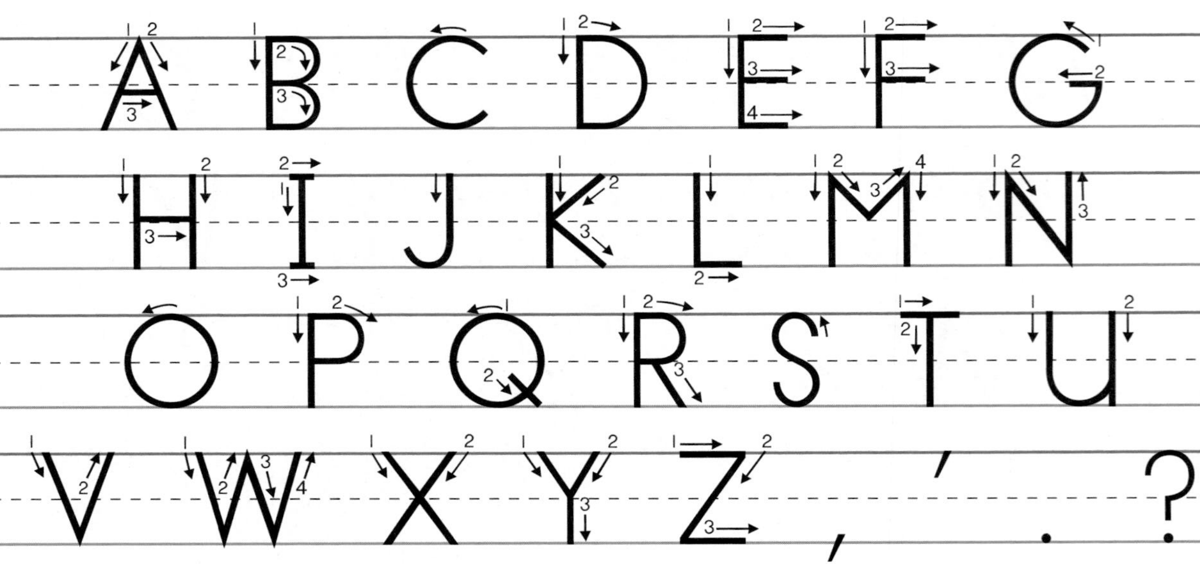

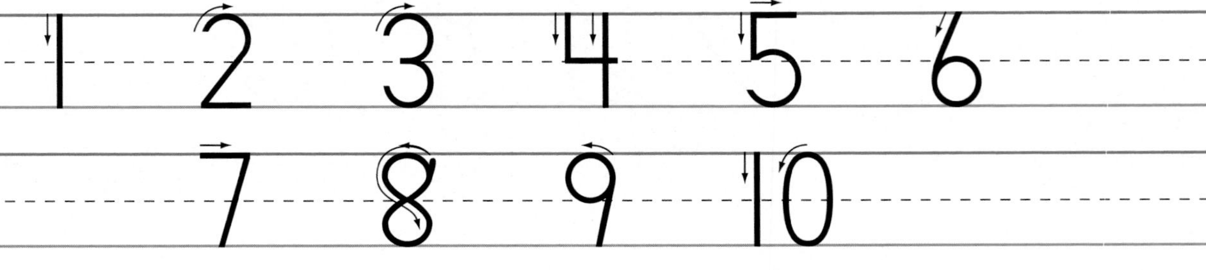

D'Nealian™ Cursive Alphabet

a b c d e f g
h i j k l m n
o p q r s t u
v w x y z

A B C D E F G
H I J K L M N
O P Q R S T U
V W X Y Z . , ' ?

1 2 3 4 5 6
7 8 9 10

Matching Students to Text

Providing students with reading materials they can and want to read is an important step toward developing fluent readers. A fluency test allows you to determine each student's instructional and independent reading level. Information on how to take a fluency test is provided on pp. 232–233.

Instructional Reading Level

Only approximately 1 in 10 words will be difficult when reading a selection from the Student Reader for students in the *My Sidewalks* intervention program. Students reading at their instructional level need teacher support and will benefit from guided instruction.

Independent Reading Level

Students should read regularly in independent-level texts in which no more than approximately 1 in 20 words is difficult for the reader. Other factors that make a book easy to read include the student's interest in the topic, the amount of text on a page, how well illustrations support meaning, and the complexity and familiarity of the concepts.

Guide students in learning how to self-select books at their independent reading level. As you talk about a book with students, discuss the challenging concepts in it, list new words students find in sampling the book, and ask students about their familiarity with the topic. A blackline master to help students evaluate books for independent reading is provided on p. 231.

Self-Selected/Independent Reading

While oral reading allows you to assess students' reading level and fluency, independent reading is of crucial importance to students' futures as readers and learners. Students need to develop their ability to read independently for increasing amounts of time.

- Specify the amount of time you wish students to read independently each week. During the year, gradually increase the amount of time devoted to independent reading.
- Encourage students to read to a partner or a family member.
- Help students track the amount of time they read independently. Tracking will help motivate them to gradually increase their duration and speed. A blackline master for tracking independent reading is provided on p. 231. Check it on a regular basis to monitor progress.

Name ______________________ Date ____________

Choosing a Book to Read by Yourself

These questions can help you pick a book to read.

_____ 1. Is this book about something that I like?

_____ 2. This book may be about a real person, about facts, or a made-up story. Do I like reading this kind of book?

_____ 3. Have I read other things by this author? Do I like the author?

If you say "yes" to question 1, 2, or 3, go on.

_____ 4. Were there fewer than 5 hard words on the first page?

_____ 5. Does the number of words on a page look about right to me?

If you say "yes" to questions 4 and 5, the book is right for you.

Independent Reading

Write the date, the title of the book, and the number of minutes you read.

Date	Title	Minutes

Matching Students to Text

Taking a Fluency Test

A fluency test is an assessment of a student's oral reading accuracy and oral reading fluency. Reading accuracy is based on the number of words read correctly. Reading fluency is based on the reading rate (the number of words correct per minute) and the degree to which a student reads with a "natural flow."

How to Measure Reading Accuracy

1. Choose a text of about 80 to 120 words that is unfamiliar to the student.
2. Make a copy of the text for yourself. Make a copy for the student or have the student read aloud from a book.
3. Give the student the text and have the student read aloud. (You may wish to record the student's reading for later evaluation.)
4. On your copy of the text, mark any miscues or errors the student makes while reading. See the fluency test sample on p. 233, which shows how to identify and mark miscues.
5. Count the total number of words in the text and the total number of errors made by the student. Note: If a student makes the same error more than once, such as mispronouncing the same word multiple times, count it as one error. Self-corrections do not count as actual errors. Use the following formula to calculate the percentage score, or accuracy rate:

$$\frac{\text{Total Number of Words} - \text{Total Number of Errors}}{\text{Total Number of Words}} \times 100 = \text{percentage score}$$

Interpreting the Results

- A student who reads 95–100% of the words correctly is reading at an independent level and may need more challenging text.
- A student who reads 90–94% of the words correctly is reading at an instructional level and will likely benefit from guided instruction.
- A student who reads 89% or fewer of the words correctly is reading at a frustrational level and may benefit most from targeted instruction with lower-level texts and further intervention.

How to Measure Reading Rate (WCPM)

1. Follow Steps 1–3 above.
2. Note the exact times when the student begins and finishes reading.
3. Use the following formula to calculate the number of words correct per minute (WCPM):

$$\frac{\text{Total Number of Words Read Correctly}}{\text{Total Number of Seconds}} \times 60 = \text{words correct per minute}$$

Interpreting the Results

An appropriate reading rate for an on-level third-grader is 110–120 WCPM.

Matching Students to Text

Fluency Test Sample

Fluency Test Sample

"In that case, can you help me make my lunch?" Curtis asked.

Yelp clapped her hands twice. Then she handed Curtis a card filled with notes.

"Crackers with butter and jam," Curtis read. "Yum. Let's try it." But when Curtis turned, he didn't ~~spot~~ stop Yelp.

After class, both tires on Curtis's (H) bike were flat. "Yelp! Help!" Curtis cried.

Along came Yelp. She clapped her hands twice (/tī/), and a pump landed next to Curtis.

Then Curtis pumped (SC) up his tires.

Curtis had to admit that Yelp's pump helped.

—From *Yelp! Help!*
My Sidewalks Student Reader, Level B

Miscues

Insertion
The student inserts words or parts of words that are not in the text.

Omission
The student omits words or word parts.

Substitution
The student substitutes words or parts of words for the words in the text.

Hesitation
The student hesitates over a word, and the teacher provides the word. Wait several seconds before telling the student what the word is.

Mispronunciation/Misreading
The student pronounces or reads a word incorrectly.

Self-Correction
The student reads a word incorrectly but then corrects the error. Do not count self-corrections as actual errors. However, noting self-corrections will help you identify words the student finds difficult.

Fluency Test Results ▶
Total Number of Words: **86**
Number of Errors: **5**

Reading Time: **64 seconds**

Reading Accuracy ▶

$\frac{86 - 5}{86} = \frac{81}{86} = .9418 = 94\%$

Accuracy Percentage Score: **94%**

Reading Rate—WCPM

$\frac{81}{64} \times 60 = 75.9 = 76$ words correct per minute

Reading Rate: **76 WCPM**

Scope and Sequence

Concepts of Print and Print Awareness	Level A	Level B	Level C	Level D	Level E
Develop awareness that print represents spoken language and conveys and preserves meaning	•				
Identify parts of a book and their functions (front cover, title, page numbers)	•				
Understand the concept of letter and word (including constancy of words and word boundaries)	•				
Track print (front to back of book, top to bottom of page, left to right on line, sweep back left for next line)	•				
Match spoken to printed words	•				
Know capital and lowercase letter names and match them	•				
Write capital and lowercase letters	•				

Phonemic Awareness	Level A	Level B	Level C	Level D	Level E
Identify sounds that are the same or different	•				
Identify and isolate initial, final, and medial sounds	•				
Blend sounds orally	•	•			
Segment a word into sounds	•	•			
Add or delete phonemes	•	•			

Phonics	Level A	Level B	Level C	Level D	Level E
Understand and apply the *alphabetic principle* that spoken words are composed of sounds that are represented by letters	•				
Know letter-sound relationships	•	•	•		
Blend sounds of letters to decode					
Consonants	•	•			
Consonant blends	•	•	•		

Consonant digraphs	•	•	•		
Vowels					
Short	•	•	•	•	•
Long	•	•	•	•	•
r-Controlled	•	•	•	•	•
Digraphs	•	•	•	•	•
Diphthongs		•	•	•	•
Other vowel patterns	•	•	•	•	•
Phonograms/word families	•	•	•		
Decode words with common word parts					
Base words and inflected endings	•	•	•	•	•
Contractions	•	•	•	•	•
Possessives	•	•			
Compounds	•	•	•	•	•
Suffixes and prefixes		•	•	•	•
Blend syllables to decode words					
VC/CV	•	•	•	•	•
Consonant + *le*	•	•	•	•	•
VC/V and V/CV	•	•	•	•	•
VCCCV			•	•	•
V/V			•	•	•

Spelling					
Use sound-letter knowledge to spell	•	•	•	•	•
Use knowledge of word structure to spell	•	•	•	•	•
Blend multisyllabic words	•	•	•	•	•
Reading Fluency	**Level A**	**Level B**	**Level C**	**Level D**	**Level E**
Read aloud fluently with accuracy, comprehension, and appropriate pace/rate	•	•	•	•	•
Practice fluency in a variety of ways, including choral reading, partner/paired reading, repeated oral reading, tape-assisted reading, and Readers' Theater	•	•	•	•	•
Work toward appropriate fluency goals	40–60 WCPM	70–90 WCPM	100–120 WCPM	110–130 WCPM	120–140 WCPM
Vocabulary (Oral and Written)	**Level A**	**Level B**	**Level C**	**Level D**	**Level E**
Recognize regular and irregular high-frequency words automatically	•	•			
Recognize and understand lesson vocabulary	•	•	•	•	•
Develop vocabulary through direct instruction, concrete experiences, reading, and listening to text read aloud	•	•	•	•	•
Use concept vocabulary	•	•	•	•	•
Use speaking vocabulary	•	•			
Use knowledge of word structure to figure out word meaning		•	•	•	•
Use context clues					
to confirm word identification	•	•	•		
to determine word meaning of multiple-meaning words, homonyms, homographs			•	•	•
to determine word meaning of unfamiliar words			•	•	•
Understand synonyms and antonyms			•	•	•

Text Comprehension	Level A	Level B	Level C	Level D	Level E
Comprehension Strategies					
Preview the text	•	•	•	•	•
Set and monitor purpose for reading	•	•	•	•	•
Activate and use prior knowledge	•	•	•	•	•
Make predictions	•	•	•	•	•
Ask and answer questions	•	•	•	•	•
Look back in text for answers			•	•	•
Recognize story structure: characters, plot, setting	•	•	•	•	•
Summarize text by retelling stories or identifying main ideas	•	•	•	•	•
Use graphic and semantic organizers			•	•	•
Comprehension Skills					
Compare and contrast	•	•	•	•	•
Draw conclusions		•	•	•	•
Main idea and supporting details	•	•	•	•	•
Sequence of events	•	•	•	•	•
Write in response to text	•	•	•	•	•

Unit 1 Word List

The words listed below are read and practiced each week in the *My Sidewalks* Student Readers and/or in practice activities.

Unit 1 Week 1 Building a Community

Short *a, i, o*

act, and, Ann, black, Brad, cabs, camp, can, cap, cat, clam, clamp, clap, class, classes, craft, dads, damp, dash, facts, flap, Fran, grand, hand, has, hat, last, pal, pals, pang, passes, past, path, plans, sad, sand, slant, slap, stand, swam, tank, that, track, trap

big, blimp, bring, did, dig, drip, fish, fished, fit, flip, him, his, kick, kids, Kim, link, lint, list, lists, pick, pink, sing, singing, sip, sit, sits, skimp, skip, slip, spill, swim, swims, things, think, thinks, this, trick, tricks, which, will, with

blond, Bob, box, dog, drop, honk, hop, hops, jobs, jog, lot, lots, moms, mop, not, plot, pond, pop, rock, shop, shops, spot, spots, stop, Tom

Short *e, u*

Ben, bench, best, bet, check, chess, chest, deck, end, ends, fresh, get, help, Jen, left, let, met, neck, next, pet, rest, shelf, shell, spend, steps, tell, ten, theft, them, then, web, well, when, yes

brush, bug, bugs, bus, but, Chuck, chum, club, clump, crush, crust, duck, dust, fun, fuss, Gus, hut, jump, just, luck, lunch, much, Mugs, pump, pup, run, rush, rust, spun, stunk, stump, stung, stunt, thump, truck, up, us

Sounds Reviewed

b/b/*, *c*/k/*, *ck*/k/*, *d*/d/*, *f*/f/*, *g*/g/*, *h*/h/*, *j*/j/*, *k*/k/*, *l*/l/*, *m*/m/*, *n*/n/*, *p*/p/*, *r*/r/*, *s*/s/*, *s*/z/*, *t*/t/*, *w*/w/*, *x*/ks/*, *y*/y/*

ch/ch/*, *ng*/ng/*, *nk*/ngk/*, *sh*/sh/*, *th*/th/*, *wh*/hw/*

bl/bl/*, *br*/br/*, *cl*/kl/*, *cr*/kr/*, *dr*/dr/*, *fl*/fl/*, *fr*/fr/*, *gr*/gr/*, *mp*/mp/*, *nd*/nd/*, *nt*/nt/*, *pl*/pl/*, *sk*/sk/*, *sl*/sl/*, *sp*/sp/*, *st*/st/*, *sw*/sw/*, *tr*/tr/*

*-ed**, *-es**, *-ing**, plural *-s**, *-s**

Concept Vocabulary

build, center, city, community

Unit 1 Week 2 Let's Make a Trade

Long Vowels CVC*e*

bike, bone, bones, brave, cage, cane, cape, choke, close, code, cute, date, Dave, delete, drove, eve, face, file, fire, five, flute, froze, game, gate, gave, globe, Grace, grade, grape, home, hope, ice, Kate, kite, lake, lane, life, like, likes, line, lone, Luke, made, Mike, nice, nine, pile, pine, place, plate, prune, rake, ride, rides, rode, rose, rule, shade, shine, shines, slide, smile, spade, stage, Steve, stone, take, takes, tales, tame, these, time, times, tone, trade, tribe, tribes, tube, tune, vase, wave, waves, while, white, wide, woke

Consonants *c*/s/, *g*/j/, *s*/z/

ace, brace, cell, dice, Grace, ice, lace, mice, nice, pace, place, race, rice, slice, space, spice, trace, twice

age, cage, gem, Gen, huge, magic, page, rage, stage

as, chose, has, his, hose, is, nose, pose, rise, rose, Rose, these, those, use

Sounds Reviewed

a/a/, *b*/b/*, *c*/k/*, *ck*/k/*, *d*/d/*, *e*/e/, *f*/f/*, *g*/g/*, *h*/h/*, *i*/i/, *j*/j/, *k*/k/*, *l*/l/*, *m*/m/*, *n*/n/*, *p*/p/*, *r*/r/*, *s*/s/*, *t*/t/*, *v*/v/*, *w*/w/*, *z*/z/*

ch/ch/*, *ng*/ng/*, *sh*/sh/*, *tch*/ch/*, *th*/th/*, *wh*/hw/*

br/br/*, *cl*/kl/*, *dr*/dr/*, *fl*/fl/*, *fr*/fr/*, *gl*/gl/*, *gr*/gr/*, *pl*/pl/*, *pr*/pr/*, *sl*/sl/*, *sm*/sm/*, *sp*/sp/*, *st*/st/*, *tr*/tr/*, *tw*/tw/*

plural *-s**, *-s**

Concept Vocabulary

goods, money, swap, trade, worth

*** = letter-sounds reviewed from Level B**

Unit 1 Word List

Unit 1 Week 3 Smart Saving

Plurals and Inflected Endings -s, -es

adds
ashes
bakes
banks
beds
benches
bikes
bills
bosses
boxes
boys
brushes
bumps
bunches
catches
cats
cents
chimps
classes
clocks
codes
crunches
cubes
dashes
days
digs
dimes
dishes
drops
fixes
flips
foxes
games
gets
gifts
grasses
gulls
hands
helps
hints
hisses
homes
hugs
jobs
kids
kisses
likes
limes
lines
lists
lots
misses
others
pals
papers
passes
pets
piles
pitches
plans
plants
prizes
punches
ranches
rashes
ropes
rots
rushes
saves
savings
sends
shakes
shines
ships
slants
socks
spends
spills
steps
takes
taxes
thanks
things
tracks
trees
tunes
uses
waxes
wheels
whines
wishes

Endings *-ed, -ing*

asked
blasted
blinked
brushed
bumped
chanted
checked
clinked
dressed
dumped
dusted
filled
handed
helped
hinted
jumped
landed
limped
listened
looked
packed
passed
pressed
printed
rested
rusted
shocked
spilled
thumped
tracked
tricked
walked
wanted
washed
watched
wished
worked
yelled

asking
blinking
brushing
building
bumping
chanting
checking
clinking
cracking
dumping
dusting
going
handing
helping
hinting
hissing
holding
jumping
limping
looking
packing
planting
pressing
printing
resting
rusting
stacking
testing
thanking
ticking
tracking
tricking
twisting
wanting
watering
wishing

Sounds Reviewed

a/a/
a/ā/
al/ȯl/*
ay/ā/*
b/b/*
c/k/*
c/s/
ck/k/*
d/d/*
e/e/
ee/ē/*
f/f/*
g/g/*
h/h/*
i/i/
i/ī/
j/j/*
k/k/*
l/l/*
m/m/*
n/n/*
o/o/
o/ō/
oo/u̇/*
p/p/*
r/r/*
s/s/*
t/t/*
u/u/
u/ū/
v/v/*
w/w/*
x/ks/*
z/z/*

ch/ch/*
ng/ng/*
nk/ngk/*
sh/sh/*
tch/ch/*
th/th/*
wh/hw/*

oy/oi/*

bl/bl/*
br/br/*
cl/kl/*
cr/kr/*
dr/dr/*
fl/fl/*
mp/mp/*
nd/nd/*
nt/nt/*
pl/pl/*
pr/pr/*
sl/sl/*
sp/sp/*
st/st/*
tr/tr/*
tw/tw/*

Concept Vocabulary

allowance
amount
deposit
expensive
savings

Unit 1 Week 4 Money! Money!

Endings *-ed, -ing,* Double Final Consonant

begged
blabbed
bopped
bragged
chopped
clipped
dragged
dripped
dropped
flipped
grabbed
grinned
hugged
kidded
robbed
rubbed
scrubbed
shipped
shopped
sipped
skimmed
slammed
stepped
stopped
swapped
tagged
tanned
trimmed
tripped

begging
chatting
chopping
clipping
dragging
dropping
flipping
getting
grabbing
grinning
hugging
planning
rubbing
running
scrubbing
shipping
shopping
skimming
skipping
sledding
slipping
spinning
stepping
stopping
tagging
tanning
tipping
tripping
trotting
wagging
winning

Endings *-ed, -ing,* Dropped *e*

blamed
braked
changed
chimed
framed
hiked
hoped
joked
piled
placed
poked
raced
raked
saved
shaved
shined
skated
sloped
taped
traded
waved

blaming
braking
changing
chiming
framing
hiking
hoping
joking
piling
placing
poking
riding
saving
shining
sliding
sloping
smiling
striking
taking
taping
trading

Sounds Reviewed

a/a/
a/ā/
b/b/*
c/k/*
c/s/
d/d/*
e/e/
f/f/*
g/g/*
g/j/
h/h/*
i/i/
i/ī/
j/j/*
k/k/*
l/l/*
m/m/*
n/n/*
o/o/
o/ō/
p/p/*
r/r/*
s/s/*
t/t/*
u/u/
v/v/*
w/w/*

ch/ch/*
sh/sh/*

bl/bl/*
br/br/*
cl/kl/*
dr/dr/*
fl/fl/*
fr/fr/*
gr/gr/*
pl/pl/*
scr/skr/*
sk/sk/*
sl/sl/*
sm/sm/*
sp/sp/*
st/st/*
str/str/*
sw/sw/*
tr/tr/*

Concept Vocabulary

coin
dollar
nickel
penny
quarter

*** = letter-sounds reviewed from Level B**

Unit 1 Word List

Unit 1 Week 5 Kid Business

Syllables VC/CV

admit
admitted
admitting
Anton
attic
basket
baskets
blanket
blossomed
blossoming
Brendan
cabbage
cactus
canyon
catnip
collect
collected
connected
connecting
contest
dentist
discussing
Emma
fabric
fossil
fossils
gossiping
happen
happened
happening
helmet
infect
insect
insects
intend
intended
intending
invent
invented
inventing
kitten
kittens
lesson
lessons
mammal
mitten
napkin
object
objects
pencil
picnic
plastic
problem
problems
publish
rabbit
rabbits
rubbish
Shannon
success
summer
tennis
traffic
tunneling
unless
until
velvet
zigzag

Syllables VC/CV with Long Vowel CVC*e*

admire
advice
cascade
costume
empire
engage
engrave
entire
escape
estate
excite
excuse
exhale
expose
immune
inhale
inline
insane
inside
invade
invite
mistake
Primrose
reptile
stampede
sunrise
suppose
tadpole
trombone
umpire
unlike
unmade
unripe

Sounds Reviewed

a/a/
a/ā/
b/b/*
c/k/*
c/s/
d/d/*
e/e/
e/ē/
f/f/*
g/g/*
g/j/
h/h/*
i/i/*
i/ī/
j/j/*
k/k/*
l/l/*
m/m/*
n/n/*
o/o/
o/ō/
p/p/*
r/r/*
s/s/*
s/z/
t/t/*
u/u/
u/ū/
v/v/*
x/ks/*
y/y/*
z/z/*

ng/ng/*
nk/ngk/*
sh/sh/*

bl/bl/*
br/br/*
gl/gl/*
gr/gr/*
nd/nd/*
nt/nt/*
pl/pl/*
pr/pr/*
st/st/*
tr/tr/*

plural *-s**
*-ing**
*-ed**

mis-
un-

Concept Vocabulary

business
customer
earn
idea
product

*** = letter-sounds reviewed from Level B**

Unit 2 Word List

Unit 2 Week 1 Animal Answers

r-Controlled *ar*

arch
Arctic
arm
art
bark
barn
car
carpet
carton
charge
charm
chart
dark
darken
darkened
dart
darts
far
farm
garden
garlic
harbor
hard
harm
harsh
harvest
jar
large
lark
mar
margin
Mark
market
marsh
parcel
part
party
shark
sharp
sharpen
smart
smarter
snarl
spark
star
starch
stars
start

r-Controlled *or, ore*

acorn
born
chore
cork
corn
explore
exploring
for
force
forest
forests
forgave
forgot
fork
form
fort
horn
horse
ignore
more
nor
North
or
orb
ore
popcorn
porch
pore
restore
scorch
score
shore
short
snort
sore
sort
sport
store
storm
story
support
thorn
torn
worn

Sounds Reviewed

a/ā/
b/b/*
c/k/*
c/s/
d/d/*
e/e/
e/ē/
f/f/*
g/g/*
g/j/
h/h/*
i/i/
j/j/*
k/k/*
l/l/*
m/m/*
n/n/*
o/o/
p/p/*
r/r/*
s/s/*
s/z/
t/t/*
u/u/
v/v/*
w/w/*
x/ks/*
y/ē/
ch/ch/*
sh/sh/*
th/th/*
gl/gl*/
pl/pl/*
rl/rl/*
sc/sk/*
sm/sm/*
sn/sn/*
sp/sp/*
st/st/*
re-
-ed
-er
*-hood**
-ing
plural *-s*

Concept Vocabulary

adapt
environment
protect
survive
wildlife

Unit 2 Week 2 Good Choices

Possessives (singular and plural)

artists'
barn's
bikes'
cat's
charm's
circus's
class's
crab's
Curt's
dogs'
firm's
fort's
Fred's
garden's
gerbils'
Gertrude's
gifts'
girl's
Grace's
harbor's
horses'
June's
kids'
Kirk's
lanterns'
Mike's
mittens'
Mom's
pals'
people's
person's
reptiles'
Rosa's
shirt's
sister's
snake's
stores'
sun's
tadpoles'
trucks'
trumpets'

r-Controlled Vowels *er, ir, ur*

after
batter
better
clerk
corner
enter
fern
ferns
gerbil's
Gertrude
her
herself
lantern's
letter
lumber
Luther
manner
manners
member
mister
other
others
perch
perfect
permit
person
person's
pester
serve
sister's
summer
term
termite
twister
verb
verse
whisper
wonder
bird
birds
birth
chirp
chirped
circus's
dirt
firm's
first
girl
girl's
Kirk's
shirts'
sir
stir
stirred
stirrup
stirrups
thirst
twirl
blurt
blurted
burn
burner
burst
curb
curl
Curt
fur
hurt
purr
purring
purse
surprise
turban
turn
turned
turnip
urgent

Sounds Reviewed

a/a/
a/ā/
ar/är/
b/b/*
c/k/*
c/s/
d/d/*
e/e/
f/f/*
g/g/*
g/j/
h/h/*
i/i/
i/ī/
k/k/*
l/l/*
m/m/*
n/n/*
o/o/
or/ôr/
ore/ôr/
p/p/*
r/r/*
s/s/*
s/z/
t/t/*
u/u/
u/ū/
v/v/*
w/w/*
ch/ch/*
sh/sh/*
th/th/*
wh/hw/
bl/bl/*
cl/kl/*
cr/kr/*
fr/fr/*
gr/gr/*
nt/nt/*
pr/pr/*
sn/sn/*
st/st/*
tr/tr/*
tw/tw/*
-ed
-s

Concept Vocabulary

advice
choice
decide
decision
problem

Unit 2 Week 3 Brainstorms

Endings *-er, -est*

bigger
brisker
crisper
darker
dimmer
duller
faster
fresher
grander
harder
hotter
later
madder
newer
nicer
sadder
shorter
sicker
slimmer
smarter
softer
thicker
thinner
wetter
biggest
blackest
briskest
darkest
dullest
fastest
fattest
flattest
freshest
grandest
greatest
hardest
hottest
maddest
pinkest
saddest
shortest
sickest
slimmest
smartest
snuggest
softest
thickest
wettest
wildest

Vowel Sounds in *y*: long *i*, long *e*

by
cry
dry
fly
fry
my
pry
shy
sky
spy
Sy
try
trying
why
candy
choppy
Cindy
daddy
dirty
dizzy
dusty
easy
Fluffy
funny
handy
happy
hilly
Lindy
lucky
Mandy
Mary
Mindy
nanny
nutty
pretty
Sandy
shiny
silly
Spilsbury
sticky
story
sunny
Tammy
tummy
twenty
very
Wendy

Sounds Reviewed

a/a/
ar/är/
b/b/
c/k/
c/s/
ck/k/*
d/d/
e/e/
ea/ē/*
f/f/
g/g/
h/h/
i/i/
i/ī/
ir/ėr/
k/k/
l/l/
m/m/
n/n/
o/o/
or/ôr/
p/p/
r/r/
s/s/
s/z/
t/t/
u/u/
w/w/
z/z/
ch/ch/
nk/ngk/
sh/sh/
th/th/
wh/hw/
bl/bl/
br/br/
cr/kr/
dr/dr/
fl/fl/
fr/fr/
gr/gr/
nd/nd/
pr/pr/
sl/sl/
sm/sm/*
sn/sn/*
st/st/*
tr/tr/*
tw/tw/*
-ed
-es
-ing
plural *-s*
-s

Concept Vocabulary

fail
invention
puzzle
solution
solve

* = letter-sounds reviewed from Level B

Unit 2 Word List

Unit 2 Week 4 Your Fair Share

Endings *-es, -ed, -er, -est:* Spelling Change *y* to *i*

berries
bodies
buddies
bunnies
carries
cries
daddies
dries
flies
fries
guppies
hobbies
kitties
parties
patties
pennies

poppies
puppies
spies
stories
tries

cried
dried
fried
hurried
married
tried

curlier
dirtier
drier

funnier
happier
muddier
prettier
sunnier
windier

driest
fanciest
funniest
happiest
muddiest
prettiest
sunniest

3-letter Consonant Blends

describe
inscribe
scrap
scrape
scraping
scratches
scratchy
scribe
script
scrub
scrubbed
scrubbing
splash
splashing
splashy
splatter
splendid

splint
splinter
split
sprang
spring
sprint
sprinted
sprung
strand
strap
stretch
stretched
strict
strike
string
strong

Sounds Reviewed

a/a/
a/ā/
*ar/âr/**
ar/är/
*b/b/**
*c/k/**
c/s/
*d/d/**
e/e/
*f/f/**
*g/g/**
*h/h/**
i/i/
i/ī/
ir/ėr/
*k/k/**
*l/l/**
*m/m/**

*n/n/**
o/o/
or/ôr/
*p/p/**
*r/r/**
*s/s/**
*t/t/**
u/u/
ur/ėr/
*w/w/**
y/ē/
y/ī/

*ch/ch/**
*ng/ng/**
*sh/sh/**
*tch/ch/**
*th/th/**

*cr/kr/**
*dr/dr/**
*fl/fl/**
*fr/fr/**
*nd/nd/**
*nt/nt/**
*pr/pr/**
*sp/sp/**
*st/st/**
*tr/tr/**

-ing
-y

Concept Vocabulary

proud
responsibility
responsible
right
wrong

Unit 2 Week 5 Home Sweet Home

Read Syllables V/CV (open) and VC/V (closed)

bacon
began
climate
crazy
David
delayed
even
event
evil
female
flavor
Friday
Gomez
hotel
label
lazy
lilac
major
motel
motors
open
opening
over
paper

pilot
piloted
prefer
prefix
silent
spider
spiders
tiger
tiny

body
city
clever
cleverest
closet
comet
copy
desert
finish
finished
Janet
level
liver
modern

never
panic
planet
river
shiver
shivered
sliver
Spanish
study
travel
Trevor

Long *a: ai, ay*

afraid
bait
braid
braided
brain
brains
chain
contain
detail
drain
exclaim
exclaimed
explain
gain
grain
main
nail
nailing
nails
obtain
pail
pain
paint
plainer
rail

railway
rain
rains
raisin
remain
sailing
snail
snail's
snails
sprain
sprains
strain
trails
train
waist
wait
waited

bay
birthday
clay
day
delay
delayed
Friday

gray
hay
jay
lay
may
maybe
Monday
okay
pathway
pay
play
playtime
ray
say
spray
sprayed
stay
staying
stays
stray
subway
sway
today
tray
way

Sounds Reviewed

a/a/
a/ā/
*b/b/**
*c/k/**
*d/d/**
e/e/
e/ē/
er/ėr/
*f/f/**
*g/g/**
*h/h/**
i/i/
i/ī/
ir/ėr/
*j/j/**
*k/k/**
*l/l/**
*m/m/**
*n/n/**
o/o/
o/ō/
*p/p/**
*r/r/**
*s/s/**
s/z/

*t/t/**
u/u/
*v/v/**
*w/w/**
*x/ks/**
y/ē/
*z/z/**

*ch/ch/**
*sh/sh/**
*th/th/**

*br/br/**
*cl/kl/**
*cr/kr/**
*fl/fl/**
*fr/fr/**
*gr/gr/**
*nt/nt/**
*pl/pl/**
*pr/pr/**
*sn/sn/**
*sp/sp/**
spr/spr/
*st/st/**
str/str/
*sw/sw/**

*tr/tr/**

pre-

-ed
-er
-est
-ing
plural *-s*
's
-s

Concept Vocabulary

climate
extreme
protection
shelter
weather

***= letter-sounds reviewed from Level B**

Unit 3 Word List

Unit 3 Week 1 Green Thumbs in Action

Long *e: e, ee, ea*

be
he
me
she
we

bee
Bree
cheese
deep
feed
feel
fifteen
green
greet
indeed
keep
meet

see
seeds
seen
sleep
street
succeed
succeeded
thirteen
trees
weeding
weeds
wheel
wheels

beach
beans
beat
clean

easy
eat
feast
feasting
heat
leaf
meals
Neal
pea
peach
peaches
peanut
peas
repeat
tea

Contractions *'ll, 's, n't, 'm*

he'll
I'll
she'll
they'll
we'll
who'll
you'll

he's
here's
it's
let's
she's
that's
what's
where's

aren't
can't
couldn't
didn't
doesn't
don't
hadn't
haven't
isn't
shouldn't
wasn't
weren't
won't
wouldn't

I'm

Sounds Reviewed

a/a/
a/ā/
ay/ā/
*b/b/**
*c/k/**
c/s/
ck/k/
*d/d/**
e/e/
*f/f/**
*g/g/**
*h/h/**
i/ī/
*ir/ėr/**
*k/k/**
*l/l/**
*m/m/**
*n/n/**

o/o/
*p/p/**
*r/r/**
s/s/
s/z/
*t/t/**
u/u/
*w/w/**
*y/y/**

ch/ch/
sh/sh/
th/th/
wh/hw/

br/br/
cl/kl/
gr/gr/
ng/ng/

nt/nt/
scr/scr/
sl/sl/
sn/sn/
str/str/

-ed
-es
-ing
plural *-s*

Concept Vocabulary

flower
grow
scatter
soil
vegetable

Unit 3 Week 2 Nature: The True Story

Long *o: oa, ow*

boast
coach
coaster
coating
cocoa
float
goal
goat
goats
loading
loan
oak
oat
oatmeal
road

soap
soapy
toaster
truckload

below
bowl
bowling
flow
follow
grow
growing
grown
growth
know

known
knows
low
lowly
rainbow
rowboat
shadow
show
showing
slowly
snow
snowy
yellow
rainbows

Contractions *'ve, 're, 'd*

I've
we've
you've

they're
we're
you're

he'd
I'd
she'd
they'd
we'd
you'd

Sounds Reviewed

a/a/
*b/b/**
*c/k/**
*d/d/**
e/e/
ea/ē/
*f/f/**
*g/g/**
*h/h/**
i/ī/
*ir/ėr/**
*k/k/**
*l/l/**
*m/m/**
*n/n/**

o/o/
*p/p/**
*r/r/**
s/s/
s/z/
*t/t/**
u/u/
*w/w/**
*y/y/**

ch/ch/
sh/sh/
th/th/
wh/hw/

cl/kl/

fl/fl/
gr/gr/
ng/ng/
nt/nt/
scr/scr/
sn/sn/
st/st/
tr/tr/
ts/ts/

-er
-ing
-ly
-s
-y

Concept Vocabulary

discover
explain
myth
nature
scientist

Unit 3 Week 3 A Closer Look

Compound Words

afternoon
airplane
airplanes
anthill
backyard
bedtime
birdseed
bluebird
butterfly
catfish
classmate
daylight
daytime
dragonfly

eggshell
fireplace
flashlight
haircut
homework
inside
nearby
nighttime
outside
overnight
playtime
pinecone
seashell
something

sometimes
spaceship
sunflowers
sunglasses
sunset
sunshine
teapot
weekend
wildflowers

Long *i: igh, ie*

bright
daylight
delight
fight
flashlight
flight
fright
high
highway
light
midnight
might
moonlight
night

nightfall
nights
nighttime
overnight
right
sigh
slight
tight
tonight

cried
denied
denies
died

dried
flies
lie
spied
tie
tied
tried
untied

Sounds Reviewed

a/a/
a/ā/
ay/ā/
*b/b/**
*c/k/**
c/s/
*d/d/**
e/e/
e/ē/
ea/ē/
ee/ē/
*f/f/**
*g/g/**
*h/h/**
i/i/
i/ī/
*ir/ėr/**
*k/k/**
*l/l/**

*m/m/**
*n/n/**
o/o/
o/ō/
*p/p/**
*r/r/**
*s/s/**
*s/z/**
*t/t/**
u/u/
v/v/
*w/w/**
*y/y/**
*y/ī/**

sh/sh/
th/th/

bl/bl/
br/br/
cl/kl/

cr/kr/
dr/dr/
fl/fl/
fr/fr/
ft/ft/
gl/gl/
ld/ld/
ng/ng/
nt/nt/
pl/pl/
sl/sl/
sp/sp/
st/st/
tr/tr/

-ed
-es
-s

Concept Vocabulary

observe
senses
sight
taste
touch

***= letter-sounds reviewed from Level B**

Unit 3 Word List

Unit 3 Week 4 To the Rescue!

Syllables: Consonant + *le*

able
beagle
beetle
bridle
bubble
bugle
bundle
cable
candle
cattle
cradle
crumble
cuddle
eagle
fable
giggle
grumble
grumbled
handle
idle
jungle
little
maple
marble
middle
people
poodle
puddle
purple
puzzle
rifle
rifles
rumble
scramble
settle
settled
shuttle
simple
smuggle
sparkle
stable
startle
startled
table
tackle
tackled
thimble
tickle
title
topple
toppled
trample
trampled

Sounds Reviewed

a/a/
a/ā/
b/b/*
c/k/*
d/d/*
e/e/
e/ē/
ea/ē/
f/f/*
g/g/*
i/i/
i/ī/
k/k/*
m/m/*
n/n/*
o/o/
o/ō/
p/p/*
r/r/*
s/s/*
t/t/*
u/u/

sh/sh/
th/th/

br/br/
cr/kr/
gr/gr/
nd/nd/
sm/sm/
sp/sp/
st/st/
tr/tr/

-s
-ed

Concept Vocabulary

elephant
endangered
extinct
rescue
vanish

Unit 3 Week 5 Dodging Disasters

Diphthongs *ou, ow* /ou/

about
around
bounce
bounced
cloud
clouds
ground
house
loud
loudly
mounds
mouse
ouch
our
out
pound
pounded
shouted
sound
surround
surrounded
without

allow
brown
cows
crowd
down
flower
growled
how
Howard
howling
now
powder
powerful
town

Suffixes *-ly, -ful*

badly
barely
brightly
completely
heavily
lightly
loudly
luckily
nicely
quickly
really
sadly
safely
slowly
suddenly
tightly
usually

careful
cheerful
forceful
grateful
harmful
powerful
thankful
wonderful

Sounds Reviewed

a/a/
a/ā/
b/b/*
c/k/*
c/s/
d/d/*
e/e/
ea/ē/
f/f/*
g/g/*
h/h/*
i/i/
i/ī/
k/k/*
l/l/*
m/m/*
n/n/*
o/o/
p/p/*
q/kw/
r/r/*
s/s/*
t/t/*
u/u/
w/w/*

ch/ch/
th/th/

br/br/
cl/kl/
fl/fl/
gr/gr/
nd/nd/
nk/ng/
sl/sl/

-ed
-s

Concept Vocabulary

emergency
flood
hurricane
natural
warning

* = letter-sounds reviewed from Level B

Unit 4 Word List

Unit 4 Week 1 Being Unique

Diphthongs *oi, oy*

- boil
- boiling
- broil
- broiler
- choice
- coin
- coins
- foil
- join
- joined
- moist
- noise
- noisily
- point
- pointed
- pointing
- poison
- rejoice
- soil
- spoil
- spoiling
- voice
- voices

- annoy
- boy
- cowboy
- cowboys
- destroy
- employ
- enjoy
- enjoyed
- enjoying
- Joy
- joy
- joyful
- joyfully
- loyal
- oyster
- Roy
- royal
- soy
- toy
- toys

Prefixes *un-, re-*

- unafraid
- unclear
- uncover
- uncovered
- uneasy
- uneven
- unexpected
- unfair
- unfed
- unfold
- unfriendly
- unhappy
- unhealthy
- unjust
- unkind
- unlike
- unlikely
- unlock
- unlucky
- unmade
- unneeded
- unpack
- unplug
- unseen
- untie
- untruthful
- unusual
- unwanted

- reappear
- rebuilding
- rediscover
- redo
- reelect
- refill
- refinish
- refreeze
- reinvent
- relocate
- rematch
- rename
- reopen
- repay
- replay
- replayed
- reprint
- reread
- rerun
- restart
- restarted
- retell
- retelling
- rethink

Sounds Reviewed

- *a/a/*
- *a/ā/*
- *ay/ā/*
- *b/b/**
- *c/k/**
- *c/s/*
- *d/d/**
- *e/e/*
- *f/f/**
- *g/g/**
- *h/h/**
- *i/i/*
- *i/ī/*
- *j/j/**
- *k/k/**
- *l/l/**
- *m/m/**
- *n/n/**
- *o/o/*
- *o/ō/*
- *p/p/**
- *r/r/**
- *s/s/**
- *s/z/*
- *t/t/**
- *u/u/*
- *v/v/**
- *w/w/**

- *ch/ch/*
- *tch/ch/*
- *th/th/*

- *br/br/*
- *fr/fr/*
- *nt/nt/*
- *pl/pl/*
- *pr/pr/*
- *sp/sp/*
- *st/st/*
- *tr/tr/*

- *-ed*
- *-er*
- *-es*
- *-ful*
- *-ing*
- *-ly*
- plural *-s*

Concept Vocabulary

- audience
- famous
- instrument
- perform
- talent
- unique

Unit 4 Week 2 From Top to Bottom

Sound *oo* in *moon*

- blooming
- boohoo
- boost
- boot
- booth
- choose
- choosing
- cool
- coolest
- droop
- food
- fool
- Hoot
- hoot
- igloo
- kangaroo
- loop
- loosely
- moo
- mood
- moonbeam
- moonlight
- noon
- pooch
- pool
- proof
- room
- roosting
- school
- schools
- scoop
- scooter
- shampoo
- shoot
- smooth
- smoother
- soon
- spoon
- spoonful
- stool
- too
- tool
- toot
- toothbrush
- tooting
- zoo
- zoom

Silent Consonants *mb, kn, gn*

- climb
- climbed
- climbers
- climbing
- crumb
- dumb
- dumber
- dumbest
- jamb
- lamb
- limb
- numb
- plumb
- plumber
- thumb
- thumbtack
- knapsack
- knee
- kneel
- kneepad
- knees
- knife
- knight
- knights
- knit
- knitted
- knob
- knock
- knocked
- knocking
- knot
- knothole
- knotted
- know
- knowing
- knuckle

- gnarl
- gnash
- gnat
- gnome
- sign
- signed

Sounds Reviewed

- *a/a/*
- *b/b/**
- *c/k/**
- *d/d/**
- *e/e/*
- *f/f/**
- *g/g/**
- *h/h/**
- *i/i/*
- *i/ī/*
- *j/j/**
- *k/k/**
- *l/l/**
- *m/m/**
- *n/n/**
- *o/o/*
- *ow/ō/*
- *p/p/**
- *r/r/**
- *s/s/**
- *s/z/**
- *t/t/**
- *u/u/*
- *w/w/**
- *z/z/**

- *ch/ch/*
- *ck/k/*
- *sh/sh/*
- *th/th/*
- *bl/bl/*
- *br/br/*
- *cl/kl/*
- *cr/kr/*
- *dr/dr/*
- *ng/ng/*
- *pl/pl/*
- *pr/pr/*
- *sc/sk/*
- *sm/sm/*
- *sp/sp/*
- *st/st/*
- *tr/tr/*

- *-ed*
- *-er*
- *-est*
- *-ful*
- *-ing*
- *-ly*
- plural *-s*

Concept Vocabulary

- depth
- height
- peak
- position
- scale
- summit

Unit 4 Week 3 Hobbies

Vowel Patterns *ew, ue*

- Andrew
- brew
- chew
- chewing
- chews
- crew
- dew
- dewdrop
- dewdrops
- drew
- few
- flew
- grew
- jewel
- jewelry
- knew
- new
- news
- newspaper
- pews
- renewal
- shrewd
- stew
- threw

- avenue
- blue
- blueberry
- bluebird
- clue
- clues
- continue
- cue
- due
- glue
- overdue
- pursue
- rescue
- statue
- Sue
- true
- unglued
- untrue

Silent Consonants *st, wr*

- bristles
- bustle
- castle
- castles
- fasten
- glisten
- glistened
- hasten
- listen
- nestle
- rustling
- thistle
- whistle
- unwrap
- unwritten
- wrap
- wrapped
- wrapping
- wraps
- wreath
- wreck
- wren
- wrench
- wrestle
- wring
- wrinkle
- wrinkled
- wrist
- write
- writing
- wrong
- wrote

Sounds Reviewed

- *a/a/*
- *a/ā/*
- *b/b/**
- *c/k/**
- *d/d/**
- *e/e/*
- *ea/ē/*
- *f/f/**
- *g/g/**
- *i/i/*
- *i/ī/*
- *j/j/**
- *k/k/**
- *l/l/**
- *m/m/**
- *n/n/**
- *o/o/*
- *o/ō/*
- *p/p/**
- *r/r/**
- *s/s/**
- *t/t/**
- *u/u/*
- *v/v/**
- *w/w/**

- *ch/ch/*
- *kn/n/*
- *nk/ngk/*
- *sh/sh/*
- *th/th/*

- *bl/bl/*
- *br/br/*
- *cl/kl/*
- *cr/kr/*
- *dr/dr/*
- *gl/gl/*
- *gr/gr/*
- *ng/ng/*
- *nt/nt/*
- *st/st/*
- *tr/tr/*

- *-ed*
- *-ing*
- *-s*

Concept Vocabulary

- collection
- delight
- interest
- rare
- special
- unusual

***= letter-sounds reviewed from Level B**

Unit 4 Word List

Unit 4 Week 4 Being the First

Sound *oo* in *foot*, *u* in *put*

book
bookcase
bookmark
bookstore
bookworm
brook
cookies
cooking
crook
crooked
foot
football
footprint
footstep
footstool
good
hardwood
hood
look
looking
notebook
overlook
redwood
shook
stood
took
understood
wood
wooden
woods
wool

bull
bulldog
bush
full
pudding
pull
pulled
pullover
pushes
put
puts

Suffixes *-ness*, *-less*

careless
carelessness
coldness
dryness
eagerness
fondness
forgiveness
gladness
happiness
heaviness
newness
playfulness
prettiness
sadness
shyness
silliness
softness
tiredness
togetherness
wetness

careless
countless
effortless
endless
fearless
friendless
homeless
hopeless
leafless
painless
pointless
sightless
soundless

Sounds Reviewed

a/a/
b/b/*
c/k/*
d/d/*
e/e/
ea/ē/
f/f/*
g/g/*
h/h/*
i/i/
i/ī/
j/j/*
k/k/*
l/l/*
n/n/*
o/o/
p/p/*
r/r/*
s/s/*
t/t/*
u/u/
v/v/*
w/w/*

sh/sh/
th/th/

br/br/
cr/cr/
dr/dr/
ft/ft/
fr/fr/
nd/nd/
ng/ng/
nt/nt/
pl/pl/
pr/pr/
st/st/

un-

-ed
-ies
-ing
-less
-ness
-s

Concept Vocabulary

adventure
attempt
distance
impossible
remarkable
waterfall

Unit 4 Week 5 People and Animals

Short *e*: *ea*

already
bread
breath
dead
deaf
death
dread
gingerbread
feather
head
health
healthy
heavy
instead
leather
meadow
meant
pleasant
pleasure
read
ready
spread
steady
sweater
thread
treasure
weapon
weather

Prefixes *mis-*, *dis-*

misbehave
misfile
misfit
mislead
mismatch
misplace
misprint
mispronounce
misspell
mistreated
mistrust
misunderstand

disappear
disappoint
disarm
disband
disconnect
dishonest
dislike
dismount
disobey
disorder
disown
displease
displeased
disrespect
distrust

Sounds Reviewed

a/a/
a/ā/
d/d/*
e/e/
f/f/*
h/h/*
i/i/
k/k/*
l/l/*
m/m/*
n/n/*
o/o/
p/p/*
r/r/*
s/s/*
t/t/*
u/u/
v/v/*
w/w/*

ch/ch/
th/th/

br/br/
ct/kt/
dr/dr/
nd/nd/
nt/nt/
pl/pl/
pr/pr/
st/st/
sw/sw/
tr/tr/

-ed
-s

Concept Vocabulary

adjust
adult
communicate
mimic
opportunity
realize

*** = letter-sounds reviewed from Level B**

Unit 5 Word List

Unit 5 Week 1 Dressing Up

Vowel sound in *ball: a, al*

all-star
almost
already
also
although
always
bald
ball
ballpoint
basketball
call
called
chalk
false
hall
halt
install
installing
mall
salt
small
smaller
smallest
stalk
stall
stalling
talk
talked
tall
tallest
walk
walked
wall

Consonant Digraphs *ph*/f/, *dge*/j/

gopher
graph
graphic
nephew
phase
phone
phonics
phoning
phony
photo
photograph
photos
phrase
telephone
triumph
trophies
trophy

badge
bridge
bridges
dodge
dodging
edge
fudge
grudge
hedge
hodgepodge
judge
judged
judges
ledge
lodge
pledges
ridge
ridges
wedge

Sounds Reviewed

a/a/
a/ā/
b/b/*
c/k/*
c/s/
d/d/*
e/e/
ea/e/
ew/ü/
f/f/*
g/g/*
h/h/*
i/i/
i/ī/
ie/ē/*
j/j/*
k/k/*
l/l/*
m/m/*
n/n/*
o/o/
o/ō/
p/p/*
r/r/*
s/s/*
s/z/
t/t/*
u/u/
w/w/*
y/ē/

br/br/
gr/gr/
sm/sm/
st/st/
tr/tr/

ch/ch/
th/th/

-ed
-er
-est
-ing
plural *-es*
-s

Concept Vocabulary

clothing
custom
decade
ordinary
style
tradition

Unit 5 Week 2 Our World

Vowel sound in *ball: au, aw*

auto
because
cause
fault
haul
hauled
launch
laundry
maul
pause
paused
sauce
vault
drawn
fawn
law
lawful
lawn
paw
raw
saw
sawdust
seesaw
straw
unlawful
Warsaw

awe
awful
awkward
claw
dawn
draw
drawing

Suffixes *-er, -or*

dreamer
employer
farmer
farmers
founder
learner
painter
performer
player
printer
reporter
singer
skater
speaker
talker
teacher
toaster
trainer
traveler
washer
worker

actor
conductor
director
inspector
projector
sailor
translator
visitor
visitors

Sounds Reviewed

a/a/
a/ā/
ai/ā/
al/ȯ/
ar/är/
ay/ā/
b/b/*
c/k/*
c/s/
d/d/*
e/e/
e/ē/
ea/ē/
f/f/*
h/h/*
i/i/
i/ī/
j/j/*
k/k/*
l/l/*
m/m/*
n/n/*
o/ō/
oa/ō/
or/ôr/
p/p/*
r/r/*
s/s/*
s/z/
t/t/*
u/u/
v/v/*
w/w/*
y/ē/

ch/ch/*
sh/sh/*

oy/oi/
ou/ou/

cl/kl/
dr/dr/
lk/lk
lt/lt/
nd/nd/
ng/ng/*
nt/nt/
pl/pl/
pr/pr/
sk/sk/
sl/sl/
sp/sp/
st/st/
str/str/
tr/tr/

-un

-ed
-ful
-ing
plural *-s*

Concept Vocabulary

country
culture
language
popular
similar
transfer

Unit 5 Week 3 Coming to America

Vowel sound in *ball: augh, ough*

caught
daughter
granddaughter
haughty
naughty
retaught
slaughter
taught
bought
brought
fought
ought
sought
thought
thoughtful
thoughtless

Prefixes *out-, over-, under-*

outbreak
outdated
outdistance
outdo
outgrew
outgrow
outlive
outnumber
outran
overeat
overhead
overhear
overlooked
overpower
oversize
oversleep
overthrown
overwhelm
underpaid
underpay
undersea
underwater

overall
overcharge
overcharged
overcoat
overcoming
overcooked
overdo
underachieve
underage
underdone
underfed
undergoing
underground
underlining

Sounds Reviewed

a/a/
a/ā/
al/ȯ/
ar/är/
ay/ā/
au/ȯ/
aw/ȯ/
b/b/*
c/k/*
c/s/
d/d/*
e/e/
e/ē/
ea/ē/
ea/e/
ee/ē/
ew/ü/
f/f/*
g/g/*
h/h/*
i/i/
i/ī/
k/k/*
l/l/*
m/m/*
n/n/*
o/ō/
oa/ō/
oo/u̇/
ow/ō/
p/p/*
r/r/*
s/s/*
t/t/*
u/u/
u/u̇/
v/v/*
w/w/*
y/ē/
z/z/*

th/th/*
ch/ch/*

ou/ou/
ow/ou/

br/br/
gr/gr/
nd/nd/
sl/sl/
st/st/
thr/thr/

re-
un-

-ed
-ful
-ing
-less

Concept Vocabulary

address
apartment
immigrant
journey
museum
photograph

*= letter-sounds reviewed from Level B

Unit 5 Word List

Unit 5 Week 4 Let's Eat!

Long *i: ild, ind*

child
childproof
mild
mildest
wild
wilder
wildfire
wildflowers
wildlife

bind
blind
blindfold
find
grind
kind
mind
remind
reminds
rewind
rind
unkind

Long *o: old, ost*

billfold
blindfold
cold
colder
fold
gold
golden
hold
old
older
scold
sold
told

almost
host
most
mostly
post
poster

Suffixes *-y, -ish*

bumpy
cheesy
choppy
cloudy
crunchy
dirty
dressy
dusty
frosty
gloomy
grouchy
noisy
rainy
sandy
shiny
snowy
soapy
speedy
spicy
sticky
stormy
sunny
tasty
thirsty
windy

bookish
boyish
childish
coldish
coolish
foolish
greenish
pinkish
stylish
tallish
yellowish
youngish

Sounds Reviewed

a/a/
a/ā/
al/ȯ/
ai/ā/
*b/b/**
*c/k/**
*ck/k/**
*d/d/**
e/e/
e/ē/
ee/ē/
*f/f/**
*g/g/**
*h/h/**
i/i/
i/ī/
ir/ėr/
*k/k/**
*l/l/**
*m/m/**
*n/n/**
o/o/
oa/ō/
oo/u̇/
oo/ü/
or/ôr/
ow/ō/
*p/p/**
*r/r/**
*s/s/**
s/z/
*t/t/**
u/u/
*w/w/**
y/ē/
y/ī/
*y/y/**

*ch/ch/**
*sh/sh/**
*th/th/**

oi/oi/
ou/ou/
ow/ou/
oy/oi/

bl/bl/
cl/kl/
cr/kr/
dr/dr/
fl/fl/
fr/fr/
gr/gr/
ld/ld/
mp/mp/
nd/nd/
*ng/ng/**
*nk/ngk/**
sc/sk/
sn/sn/
sp/sp/
st/st/

re-
un-

-er
-ing
-ly
plural *-s*
-s

Concept Vocabulary

delicious
dinnertime
ethnic
mixture
recipe
restaurant

Unit 5 Week 5 Other Times, Other Places

Syllables VCCCV

actress
bobsledding
children
complain
completed
completely
complicated
conflict
constant
control
distraction
distribute
employ
employer
entrance
entry
explain
frustrated
hamster
healthy
hundred
hungrily
hungry
instant
instead
institute
menthol
monster
monsters
panther
pilgrims
reentry
sentry
transport
umbrella
upstairs
wealthy
wintry

Sounds Reviewed

a/a/
a/ā/
ai/ā/
*b/b/**
*c/k/**
c/s/
*d/d/**
e/e/
e/ē/
ea/e/
ea/ē/
er/ėr/
*f/f/**
*h/h/**
i/i/
i/ī/
*l/l/**
*m/m/**
*n/n/**
o/o/
ol/ôl/
*p/p/**
*r/r/**
*s/s/**
s/z/
*t/t/**
u/u/
u/u̇/
u/ü/
ur/ėr/
*w/w/**
*x/ks/**
y/ē/

*ch/ch/**
*th/th/**

oy/oi/

sl/sl/
br/br/
dr/dr/
fl/fl/
fr/fr/
gr/gr/
*ng/ng/**
pl/pl/
pr/pr/
st/st/
str/str/
tr/tr/

dis-
re-

-ed
-er
-ing
-ly
plural *-s*
-tion
-y

Concept Vocabulary

compare
hardship
improve
opposite
settle
surround

***= letter-sounds reviewed from Level B**

Unit 6 Word List

Unit 6 Week 1 American Symbols

Suffixes *-hood, -ment*

adulthood
boyhood
brotherhood
childhood
girlhood
manhood
neighborhood
parenthood
sisterhood
statehood

amazement
amusement
astonishment
commitment
contentment

enjoyment
entertainment
government
measurement
movement
pavement
payment
prepayment
repayment
restatement
statement

Prefixes *pre-, mid-, post-*

precooking
preheat
prepackage
prepaid
prepay
prepayment
prerecord
preschool
preschooler
presort
prewrite

midair
midday
midmorning
midnight

midsection
midsummer
midterm
midway
midweek
Midwestern
midwinter

postdate
postdated
postpaid
postscript
postwar

Sounds Reviewed

a/a/
*a/ā/**
*ar/är/**
*ay/ā/**
*b/b/**
*c/k/**
ck/k/
*d/d/**
e/e/
*g/g/**
*h/h/**
i/i/
i/ī/
*l/l/**
*m/m/**
*n/n/**

o/o/
*p/p/**
*r/r/**
*s/s/**
s/z/
*t/t/**
u/u/
*v/v/**
*w/w/**
*y/y/**
*z/z/**

ch/ch/
th/th/

br/br/
fl/fl/
ld/ld/

lt/lt/
nt/nt/
scr/skr/
st/st/

oy/oi/

-ed
-er
-ing

Concept Vocabulary

enormous
liberty
monument
president
sculptor
symbol

Unit 6 Week 2 Animal Freedom

Syllables V/V

alias
annual
area
areas
audience
cereal
create
dandelion
denial
dial
diary
diet
duet
duo
fluid
giant
gradual

helium
idea
lion
media
medium
meow
mistrial
museum
neon
Ohio
oriole
patio
piano
poem
poet
poetic
poetry

polio
pretrial
quiet
radio
riot
rodeo
ruin
sanctuary
stereo
studio
terrarium
trial
trio
violent
violin

Sounds Reviewed

a/a/
*ar/är/**
*c/k/**
*d/d/**
e/e/
e/ē/
ea/ē/
*f/f/**
*g/g/**
g/j/
*h/h/**
i/i/
i/ī/
*l/l/**
*m/m/**
*n/n/**

o/o/
*p/p/**
*q/kw/**
*r/r/**
*s/s/**
s/z/
*t/t/**
u/u/
*v/v/**
*y/y/**

al/ô/
cr/kr/
fl/fl/
gr/gr/
nt/nt/
pr/pr/

st/st/
tr/tr/

pre-

Concept Vocabulary

adopt
capture
comfort
exercise
provide
struggle

Unit 6 Week 3 Expressing Yourself

Common Syllables (such as *-tion, -sion, -ture*)

action
caption
connection
convention
election
fraction
imagination
invention
mention
pollution
question
section
tradition
vacation

comprehension
decision
expression
mission

permission
possession
session
tension
version
vision

adventure
capture
creature
culture
fracture
furniture
future
manufacture
nature
picture
signature
venture

Multisyllabic Word Practice

connection
convention
imagination
tradition

amazement
commitment
entertainment
government

neighborhood
parenthood

comprehension
decision
expression
permission

adventure
furniture
signature

Sounds Reviewed

a/a/
a/ā/
ai/ā/
ar/är/
ay/ā/
*c/k/**
*d/d/**
e/e/
ea/ē/
*f/f/**
*g/g/**
*g/j/**
*h/h/**
i/i/
*l/l/**
*m/m/**

*n/n/**
o/o/
*p/p/**
*q/kw/**
*r/r/**
*s/s/**
*t/t/**
u/u/
*v/v/**
*x/ks/**
*y/y/**

ch/ch/

cr/kr/
ct/kt/
fr/fr/

gr/gr/
lt/lt/
mp/mp/
nt/nt/
pr/pr/
pt/pt/
st/st/
tr/tr/

-sion
-tion
-ture

Concept Vocabulary

amuse
create
display
express
inspire
theater

*** = letter-sounds reviewed from Level B**

Unit 6 Word List

Unit 6 Week 4 It's the Law!

Blending Multisyllabic Words

unbearable
uncomfortable
uncontrollable
undisturbed
uneasy
unfairly
unfairness
unhappily
unhappy
unhurried
unlawful
unlawfulness
unpleasant
unreasonable
untested
unthinkable
untimely
unusual
unwanted

disagree
disagreement
disagreements
disrespect
disrespectful
disturbance
disturbing
incorporated
independent
inhuman
intention
intentions
invention

agreement
amendment
amendments
argument

Sounds Reviewed

a/a/
a/ā/
ai/ā/
*ar/ar/**
ay/ā/
*c/k/**
*d/d/**
e/e/
ea/ē/
*f/f/**
*g/g/**
g/j/
*h/h/**
i/i/
*l/l/**

*m/m/**
*n/n/**
o/o/
*p/p/**
*q/kw/**
*r/r/**
*s/s/**
*t/t/**
u/u/
*v/v/**
*x/ks/**
*y/y/**

---

ch/ch/

---

fr/fr/
gr/gr/

lt/lt/
mp/mp/
nt/nt/
pr/pr/
pt/pt/
st/st/
tr/tr/

---

ct/ct/

---

dis-
un-

-ed
-ing
-ly
plural *-s*

Concept Vocabulary

annoy
cooperate
disturb
intention
pollution
require

Unit 6 Week 5 Poetry

Related Words

act
action
actor

compose
composed
composer
composition
composure

cooperate
cooperation

create
creation
creative
creator

express
expression
expressive

furnish
furniture

image
imagine
imagination

nation
national

perform
performance
performer

poem
poet
poetic
poetry

produce
product
productive

pollute
pollution

relate
relative
relation

rhyme
rhythm
rhythmic

sign
signal
signature

spark
sparkle
sparkling

Sounds Reviewed

a/a/
a/ā/
*ar/är/**
*c/k/**
*c/s/**
*d/d/**
e/e/
ea/ē/
*f/f/**
*g/g/**
g/j/

*h/h/**
i/i/
*l/l/**
*m/m/**
*n/n/**
o/o/
*p/p/**
*r/r/**
*s/s/**
*t/t/**
*v/v/**

*x/ks/**
*y/i/**
y/ē/

---

cr/kr/
ng/ng/
pr/pr/
sp/sp/

---

pro-

-ion

Concept Vocabulary

compose
delicate
emotion
poetry
recite
rhythm

*** = letter-sounds reviewed from Level B**

Phonemic Awareness

Many of the following activities can be used at any grade level by adapting the phonic element being practiced and the degree of difficulty.

Activity Bank

Blending and Segmenting Sounds

This Is the Way

Teach students the song below, substituting different words at the end. You may wish to use words such as *can, cap, tan, tap, rat,* and *ran.*

This is the way we sound out a word,

Sound out a word, sound out a word.

This is the way we sound out a word,

Like cat, /k/ /a/ /t/.

Searching for Sounds

Tell students they are going to search for a sound in the words you say. Use questions such as the following:

- What is the ending sound in *bag?* /g/
- What is the middle sound in *right?* /ī/
- What is the beginning sound in *cat?* /k/

Continue with other three-phoneme words. You may want to use the Word Lists on pp. 238–250 of this book.

Bubble Gum Words

Tell students you are going to slowly pull words out of your mouth, as you would pull out bubble gum. Have them identify each word as you "pull it out." Model sounding out the word *him,* /hhh/ /iii/ /mmm/, as you slowly say its sounds. Have students repeat after you as you pull other words out.

What Am I?

Play a riddle game with sounds.
Use items such as these:

/g/ /ā/ /t/ You open me. (gate)

/k/ /ā/ /v/ Bears sleep in me. (cave)

I Spy Some Phonemes

Choose an object in the classroom. Ask students to guess the name of your object by the clues you give them. Use clues such as these: *I spy an object with four sounds. The first sound is /t/. The last sound is /l/. The second sound is /ā/. The third sound is /b/.* Continue to provide clues until students can name the object. Repeat with other objects around the room. You may wish to have students take turns providing clues for the class.

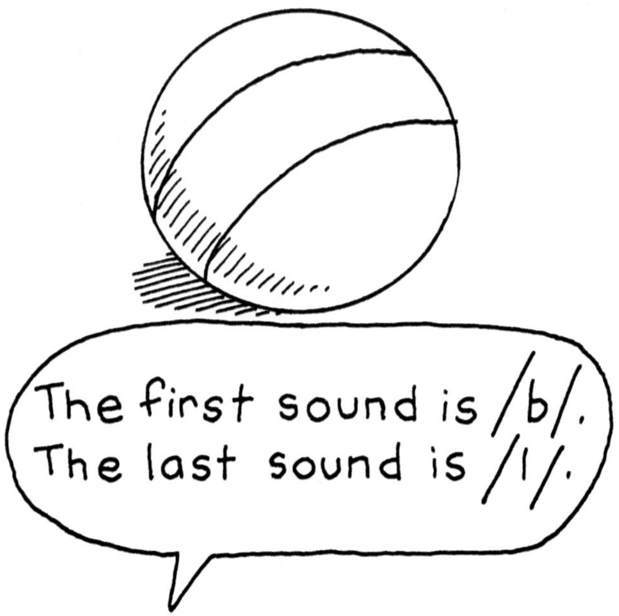

Listen and Draw

Have students divide a paper into six sections. Say a word by its phonemes. Ask students to blend the sounds and draw the picture (for example, /h/ /a/ /t/).

You may wish to use the following words: *bat, bag, rug, mug, bug, van, fan, man, can, boat, cake, bone.*

Sound Count

Make a copy of the five-sound boxes pattern on p. 254 for each student. Supply markers, such as erasers, buttons, or checkers. Slowly say a word that has up to five sounds in it. Have each student put a marker in a box for each sound in the word.

Say the Sounds

Have a student show a picture card to another student. Ask the student to name the picture and then segment the sounds in the name of the picture (for example, *tent,* /t/ /e/ /n/ /t/).

For students who need more support with this activity, provide the appropriate number of sound boxes for the word and have students move a marker into a box for each sound.

Working with Vowels

Say a one-syllable word with a short vowel. Have students change the vowel sound to another short vowel to make a new word. Work with words such as *cab, bet, sit, log,* and *bug.* Use the Word Lists on pp. 238–250 of this book for more words.

Substituting Sounds

Switcheroo

Give each student letter cards for *c, m, p, n, t,* and *a* in an envelope. Guide students in making new words by changing the letters. You may wish to begin with directions such as these:

Find the letters that make these sounds, /k/ /a/ /t/.

Blend the sounds together. What word did you spell? *(cat)*

Change the /k/ sound to /m/.

Blend the sounds together. What word did you spell? *(mat)*

Change the /t/ to /p/.

Blend the sounds together. What word did you spell? *(map)*

Continue substituting different sounds until you have made all of the following words: *nap, tap, cap, can, tan, man, pan,* and *pat.*

Make New Words

Have students make words that end with /t/ by changing the initial sound of *sit*. Model how to change the beginning sound and blend it with the middle and end sounds: /s/ *it* becomes /h/ *it*. Ask students to join you as you make other words, such as *pit, bit, wit, kit, lit, fit.*

This activity can be adapted for other consonant sounds by referring to the Word Lists on pp. 238–250 of this book.

Sound Switching

Tell students you will say a word. Ask them to listen carefully because you are going to switch one of the sounds and make a new word. Ask them to tell you which sound, beginning, middle, or end, was switched. For example, say *bat* and *bag,* and ask students which sound was switched. Continue the activity with these word pairs: *tab, tag; hot, hat; rake, wake; dad, sad; mad, made; red, read; page, cage; cap, cape; miss, mess; fan, fat; met, men; bug, rug.*

Name ______________________________

Sound Boxes

Student's Name ______________________ Date ____________

Level C *My Sidewalks*

Observation Checklist

Use this checklist to record your observations of students' reading skills and behaviors.

	Always (Proficient)	Sometimes (Developing)	Rarely (Novice)
Applies knowledge of letter-sounds to decode words			
Uses word structure and syllabication to decode longer words			
Reads at an appropriate reading rate			
Reads with appropriate intonation and stress			
Uses concept vocabulary in discussion			
Previews and uses prior knowledge to understand text			
Asks questions while reading			
Recognizes main ideas			
Recognizes sequence			
Makes comparisons and contrasts			
Draws conclusions to understand text			
Understands story structure (character, setting, plot)			
Summarizes plot or main ideas accurately			
Responds thoughtfully to the text			

General Comments

Word Parts

Students need to become familiar with meaningful parts of words so they can recognize them instantly as they read. This will improve both their reading fluency and the size of their vocabulary. Teach the meaning and pronunciation of these common word parts whenever students encounter them in words they are reading.

Common Prefixes	Meaning	Examples
dis-	not, opposite	disagree, disarm, disobey, disrespect
in-, im-, il-, ir-	not	injustice, insane, impolite, impossible, illegal, illiterate, irregular, irresponsible
mid-	during, middle	midnight, midsummer, midyear
mis-	bad, not, wrongly	misbehave, misfile, misspell, misunderstand
non-	not	nonfiction, nonsense, nonstop, nonviolent
out-	surpassing	outbid, outdo, outlive
over-	over, too much	overdo, overlook, overpriced
post-	after	postgame, postwar
pre-	before	preheat, preview
re-	again	redo, retake, retell, rewrite
un-	not	undo, unkind, uncut, unhappy, unsafe, unlucky
under-	below, less than	underpriced, underground, undercover
Common Suffixes	**Meaning**	**Examples**
-er, -or	doer, one who	teacher, painter, writer, actor, sailor, visitor, inventor
-ful	full of	careful, hopeful, helpful, wonderful
-hood	state or quality of	childhood, falsehood, adulthood
-ish	relating to	foolish, childish, selfish
-less	without	fearless, careless, hopeless, harmless
-ly	like, characteristic of	quickly, happily, briefly, gently, sadly
-ment	action or process	enjoyment, government, experiment
-ness	state of, quality of	kindness, laziness, happiness, goodness
-ous	full of	dangerous, joyous, nervous

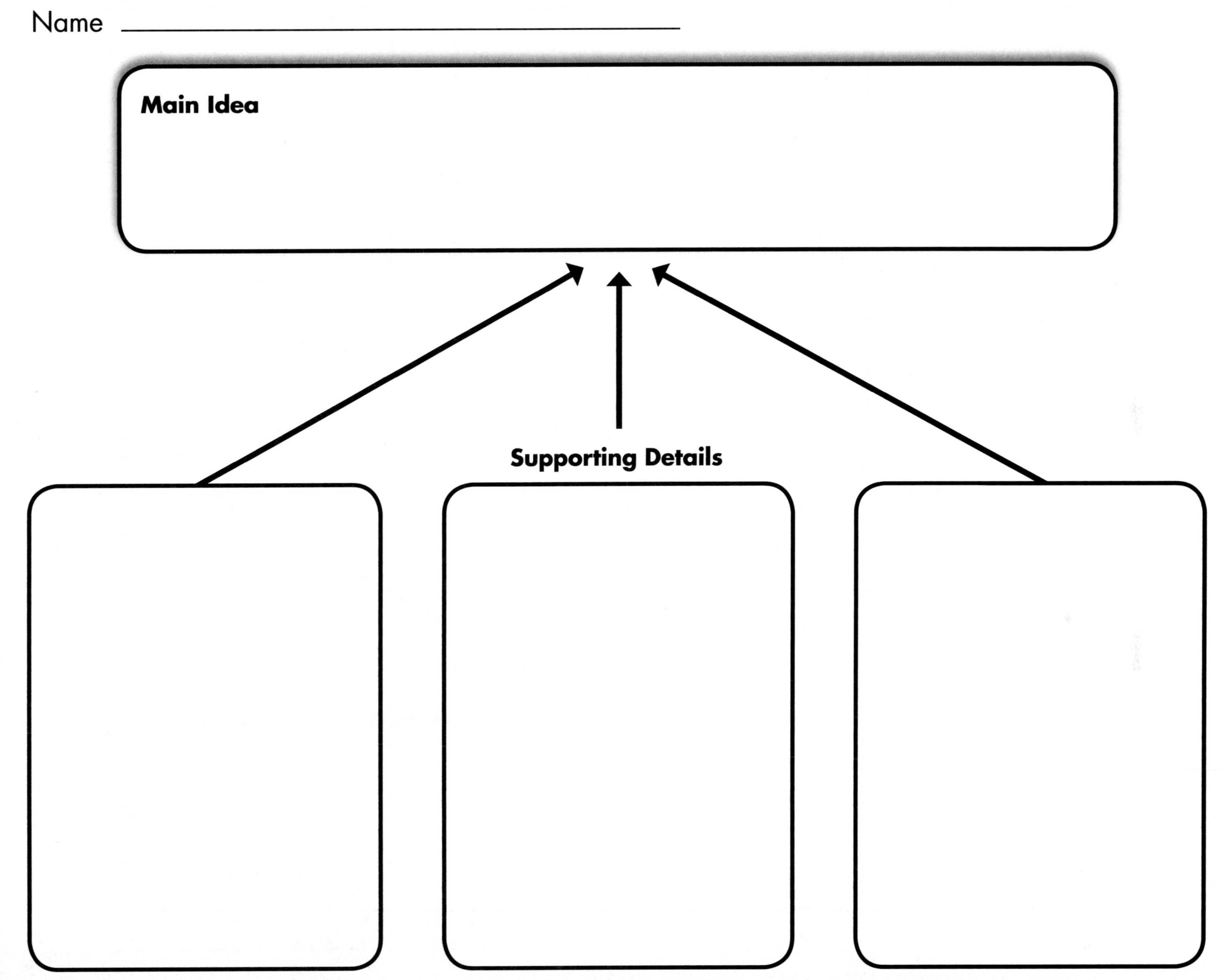
Name
Main Idea
Supporting Details

Draw Conclusions

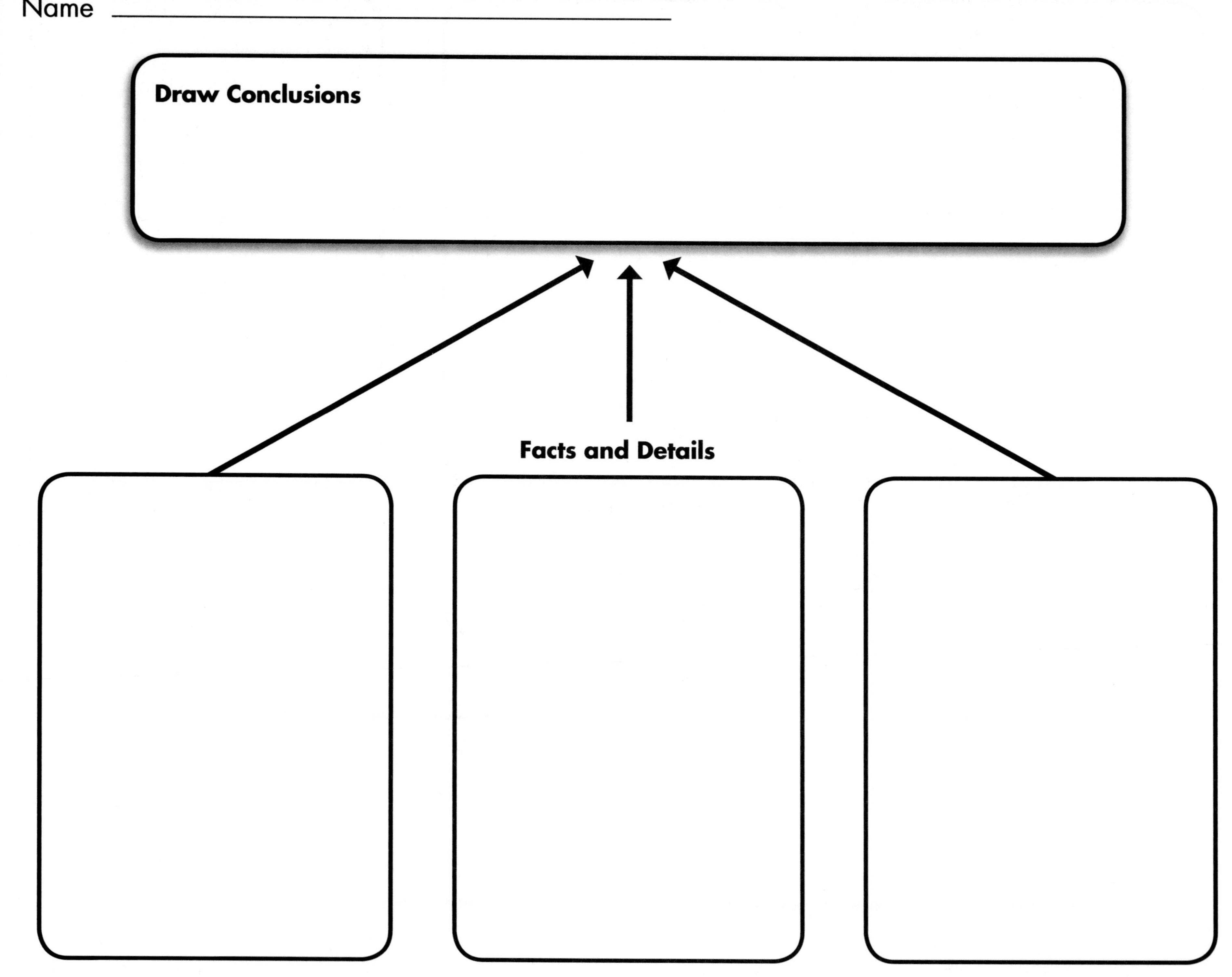

Name ______________________________

Compare and Contrast Words

________ ________ ________ ________

________ ________ ________ ________

Compare and Contrast

Name ______________________________

Compare and Contrast Words

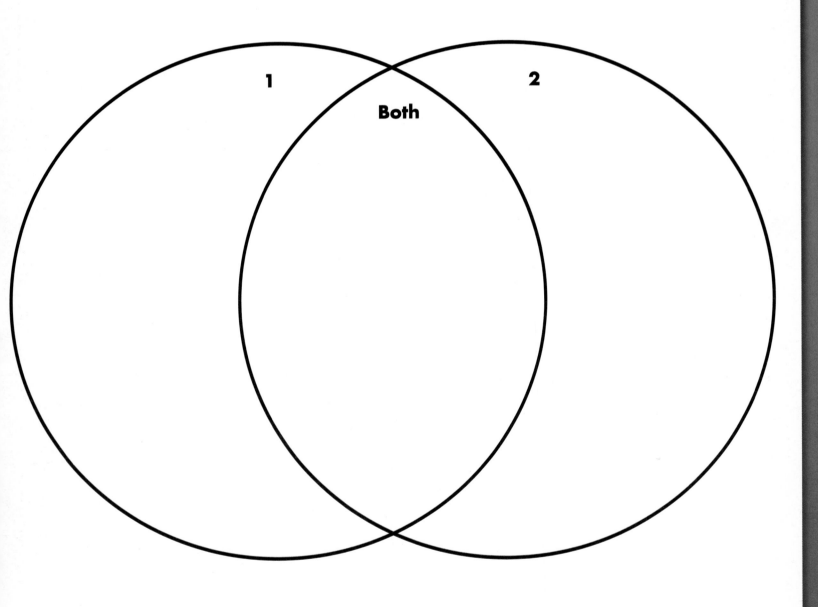

__________ __________ __________ __________

__________ __________ __________ __________

1

Both

2

Name ______________________________

Sequence Words

__________ __________ __________ __________

__________ __________ __________ __________

Beginning

Middle

End

Sequence—Steps in a Process

Name ______________________________

Sequence Words

______ ______ ______ ______

______ ______ ______ ______

Steps:

1

2

3

4

5

Bookmarks

Fiction

- Who are the characters?
- Where does the story take place?
- When does the story take place?
- What happens . . .
  in the beginning?
  in the middle?
  at the end?

Nonfiction

- What did I learn?
- What is this mainly about?

Connections Between *My Sidewalks* and Scott Foresman *Reading Street*

My Sidewalks is designed to parallel essential elements in *Scott Foresman Reading Street.* Connections between the two programs are reflected in the indexes of the Teacher's Guides.

- Corresponding **priority skills** ensure that students receive instruction in the critical elements of reading—phonemic awareness, phonics, fluency, vocabulary, and comprehension.
- Parallel **concepts and themes** enable smooth transitions between *My Sidewalks* and *Reading Street.*
- Consistency of **scaffolded instruction** promotes familiarity with routines and terminology.
- Alignment of **before, during, and after reading strategies** reinforces successful reading habits.
- **Comprehension** skill links provide Tier III readers with additional instruction and practice with main idea, compare/contrast, sequence, and drawing conclusions.
- **Vocabulary** links provide Tier III readers with additional instruction and practice with oral vocabulary.
- Consistent procedures for **corrective feedback** promptly reveal and address student needs, providing guidance for error correction.
- Connected **writing** modes offer student opportunities to respond to literature.
- **Cross-curricular** links lay out the same science and social studies foundations for Tier III readers as for students in the core program.

Index

Concept development

Corrective feedback

ELL

Fluency

Graphic and semantic organizers

Listening comprehension

Oral language

Oral vocabulary

Phonics

Phonological and phonemic awareness

Research

Spelling

Vocabulary

Development

Strategies

Word structure

Writing

Teacher Notes

Routine Card 1

Blending Strategy

Teach students to blend words using this Routine.

1 Connect Relate the new sound-spelling to previously learned sound-spellings.

2 Use Sound-Spelling Card Display the card for the sound-spelling. Say the sound. Have students say it.

3 Listen and Write Have students write the letter(s) as they say the sound.

4 Model Model how to blend words with the sound-spelling. Have students blend a word with you.

5 Group and Individual Practice Have students work together and then individually to blend words. Monitor student ability as they read the progressively more difficult words provided in the Word Work activities.

Routine Card 2

Multisyllabic Word Routine

Teach students this Routine for reading long words.

1 Look for Meaningful Parts Think about the meaning of each part. Use the parts to read the word. Help students analyze long words for base words, endings *(-ing, -ed, -s)*, prefixes *(un-, re-, dis-, mis-, non-)*, and suffixes *(-ly, -ness, -less, -ful, and so on)*.

2 Chunk Words with No Recognizable Parts Say each chunk slowly. Then say the chunks fast to make a word.

Routine Card 3

Comprehension Strategies

Teach students these comprehension strategies.

1 Preview Before reading, look at text features to determine the genre and get an idea of the topic.

2 Ask Questions During reading, ask questions:

- Nonfiction **What did I learn? What is this mainly about?**
- Fiction **Who is in the story? Where/When does it take place? What happens in the beginning/the middle/the end?**

3 Look Back to Answer Questions After reading, look back in the text to find answers to questions.

4 Summarize or Retell Summarize the main ideas of a nonfiction selection or retell the main events of a story.

Routine Card 4

Reading Engagement

***If** . . . students do not appear to be engaged with the text,*

***then** . . . use one of these strategies.*

- Read chorally.
- Have students read in a whisper.
- Ask questions.
- Assign reading partners.
- Sit next to a student and alternate reading paragraphs aloud.
- Stop at designated points to check understanding.
- Read aloud while students echo-read.

Routine Card 1

Use immediate corrective feedback to help students blend words.

If . . . students pause between sounds,

then . . . model blending the word without pauses. Then have students say the sounds again slowly and then quickly to make it sound like a real word.

If . . . students say the wrong sound,

then . . . keep your finger on the missed sound, model it correctly, and have students repeat the sound. Then have them blend the word again.

If . . . students cannot read the easier words in the first practice row,

then . . . continue practicing words at that level of difficulty before going on to more difficult words.

Routine Card 2

Routine Card 3

Before, During, and After Reading strategies should be reinforced daily. Use this Routine to teach comprehension strategies.

1 **Teach** Describe each strategy explicitly, explaining when, why, and how to use it.

2 **Model** Think aloud to model applying the strategy with different selections.

3 **Practice** Have students practice using the strategy, with support and prompting.

4 **Apply Independently** Expect students to begin using these strategies independently.

Routine Card 4

To become engaged with the text, students need to understand what they read. How do we know when we understand what we've read and when we are only reading words without understanding? Model monitoring your reading.

- Think out loud frequently as you read, so students can hear how good readers make meaning as they read.
- Model fix-up strategies, such as rereading and summarizing, to use when understanding breaks down.
- Teach strategies readers use to hold their attention as they read, such as taking notes, stopping frequently to retell, or using a graphic organizer.
- Have students practice these strategies in small groups or with a partner.

Routine Card 5

Fluency Practice

Use one of these Routines for fluency practice. Provide corrective feedback as you listen to each student read.

- **Oral Reading** Students read a passage orally. To achieve optimal fluency, they should reread three or four times.
- **Paired Reading** Partners read, switching readers at the end of each page. For optimal fluency, students should reread three or four times.
- **Audio-Assisted Reading** A student reads aloud while listening to the recording.
- **Readers' Theater** Groups of students rehearse reading the parts of each character and the narrator until they can read fluently and with expression. Then they read aloud as a performance or radio play.

Routine Card 6

Concept Vocabulary

Use this Routine to teach concept vocabulary.

1 **Introduce the Word** Relate the word to the week's concept. Supply a student-friendly definition.

2 **Demonstrate** Provide several familiar examples to demonstrate meaning.

3 **Apply** Have students demonstrate understanding with a simple activity.

4 **Display the Word** Relate the word to the concept by displaying it on a concept web. Have students identify word parts and practice reading the word.

5 **Use the Word Often** Encourage students to use the word often in their writing and speaking. Ask questions that require students to use the word.

Routine Card 7

Picture Walk Routine

To build concepts and vocabulary, conduct a structured picture walk before reading.

1 **Prepare** Preview the selection and list key concepts and vocabulary you wish to develop.

2 **Discuss** As students look at the pages, discuss illustrations, have students point to pictured items, and/or ask questions that target key concepts and vocabulary.

3 **Elaborate** Elaborate on students' responses to reinforce correct use of the vocabulary and to provide additional exposure to key concepts.

4 **Practice** For more practice with key concepts, have each student turn to a partner and do the picture walk using the key concept vocabulary.

Routine Card 8

Using Graphic Organizers

Use the graphic organizers on pp. 257–262 to provide a visual framework for students to organize, comprehend, and synthesize information.

- Students can use the organizers both to record what they read and to plan their own written work.
- Model how to fill out each organizer and how to select only relevant information.
- Use a paragraph or the beginning of a selection to help students begin filling out an organizer.
- Have additional copies of organizers available for different selections in a lesson.

Routine Card 5

Use these strategies to help children develop fluency.

- **Model Fluency** Model reading "as if you were speaking," attending to punctuation and phrasing and reading with expression (prosody).
- **Provide Corrective Feedback** Provide feedback on oral reading.

  If... *students misread a word,*
  then... *help them decode it and have them reread the sentence.*

  If... *students read at an inappropriate or unsteady pace,*
  then... *model an appropriate pace, having children echo.*

  If... *students lack oral expression,*
  then... *model how to read based on the meaning of the passage. Tell students that their expression should show their understanding.*
- **Monitor Fluency** See pp. 214–215 for assessment options.

Routine Card 6

If . . . students are unable to use vocabulary words to answer questions or to add words to the concept web,

then . . . use one of these strategies.

- Model using the words to discuss the lesson concept.
- Provide word pairs, one of which fits on the web. Have students choose the word and explain why it fits.
- Provide cloze sentences for students to complete with vocabulary words.
- Brainstorm additional words for the web. Keep the web on display and add words throughout the week.
- Reteach words using the Vocabulary Routine.

Routine Card 7

Routine Card 8